ASIAN STUDIES ASSOCIATION OF AUSTRALIA
Southeast Asia Publications Series

THE ORIGINS OF ISLAMIC REFORMISM IN SOUTHEAST ASIA

ASIAN STUDIES ASSOCIATION OF AUSTRALIA
Southeast Asia Publications Series

The Southeast Asia Publications Series (SEAPS) supports the dissemination of quality research on all aspects of Southeast Asia by scholars who have, or have had, close links with Australia.

Sponsored by the Asian Studies Association of Australia (ASAA), in conjunction with Allen & Unwin and the University of Hawai'i Press, SEAPS aims to promote the work of first-time as well as established authors and to bring their research to the widest possible audience.

Further details on how to order SEAPS books are posted on both the ASAA and the Allen & Unwin websites.

Titles in print

The Challenge of Sustainable Forests, F.M. Cooke
The Emergence of a National Economy: An Economic History of Indonesia, 1800–2000, Howard Dick, Vincent J.H. Houben, J. Thomas Lindblad and Thee Kian Wie
Indonesian Islam: Social Change Through Contemporary Fatāwā, M.B. Hooker
Fragments of the Present, Philip Taylor
Power and Prowess: The Origins of Brooke Kingship in Sarawak, J.H. Walker
The Riddle of Malaysian Capitalism, Peter Searle
The Seen and Unseen Worlds in Java, 1726–1749, M.C. Ricklefs
War, Nationalism and Peasants: The Situation in Java, 1942–1945, Shigeru Sato
Writing a New Society: Social Change through the Novel in Malay, Virginia Matheson Hooker

THE ORIGINS OF ISLAMIC REFORMISM IN SOUTHEAST ASIA

Networks of Malay-Indonesian and Middle Eastern *'Ulamā'* in the seventeenth and eighteenth centuries

Azyumardi Azra

Asian Studies Association of Australia
in association with

ALLEN & UNWIN
and
UNIVERSITY OF HAWAI'I PRESS
HONOLULU

First published in 2004

Published in Australia by
Allen & Unwin
83 Alexander Street
Crows Nest NSW 2065
Australia

www.allenandunwin.com
http://coombs.anu.edu/ASAA/

Published in North America by
University of Hawai'i Press
2840 Kolowalu Street
Honolulu, Hawai'i 96822

National Library of Australia Cataloguing-in-Publication entry:

Azra, Azyumardi.
The Origins of Islamic reformism in Southeast Asia: networks of Malay-Indonesian and Middle Eastern 'Ulamā' in the seventeenth and eighteenth centuries.

Bibliography.
Includes index.
ISBN 1 74114 261 X.

1. Islam - Asia, Southeastern - History. 2. Ulamā - Indonesia - History. 3. Ulamā - Middle East - History. I. Title. (series: Southeast Asia publications series).

297.60959

Library of Congress Cataloging-in-Publication Data:

A catalog record of this book is available from the Library of Congress

ISBN 0-8248-2848-8

Set in 10/11 pt Times by Midland Typesetters, Maryborough, Victoria
Printed by SRM Production Services Sdn Bhd, Malaysia

10 9 8 7 6 5 4 3 2 1

Contents

Maps and Charts

Transliteration

Excepting the common terms such as Islam or Muhammad (the Prophet), the transliteration of Arabic words, terms and names in this book basically follows the rules employed by the *International Journal of Middle Eastern Studies*. I apply this rule also to Malay-Indonesian persons, whose names are of Arabic origin, rather than using their popular Malay-Indonesian spelling. Thus I will use 'Abd al-Ra'ūf al-Sinkīlī' rather than 'Abdurrauf Singkel' or other Malay-Indonesian variations of it. Non-Arabic Malay-Indonesian names will be retained in their original spelling.

All foreign words (or non-English words) are italicised through the text. Names of places that have been anglicised are used in their familiar form: thus I employ 'Mecca' instead of 'Makkah', or 'Medina' instead of 'Madinah'.

Diacritic marks for Arabic words are used throughout the text, except for words used in their common English form, such as Islam, the Prophet Muhammad.

The plural of all Arabic and Malay-Indonesian words is formed simply by adding 's' to their more familiar singular form: thus, '*ḥadīth*s' instead of '*aḥādīth*', or '*ṭarīqah*s' instead of '*ṭuruq*' (or '*ṭarā'iq*' or *ṭarīqat*—other Arabic plural forms).

All dates cited will include both the Muslim date or Anno Hijrah (AH), which is given first, followed by the Gregorian date or Christian/Common Era (CE) after an oblique stroke: thus 1068/1658, 1115/1693. This will allow readers unfamiliar or confused with the Hijrah calendar dates to readily know the equivalent Common Era dates. For the conversion of both dates, this book employs the table printed in J.L. Bacharach, *A Middle East Studies Handbook* (Seattle: University of Washington Press, 1984).

Preface

For many of my friends, publication of this book is long overdue. While the Indonesian edition of the *Jaringan Ulama* (*'ulamā'* networks) has been published in several editions by Mizan (Bandung) since 1994, followed by Arabic translation in 1997, the English version has been delayed for several years. Increased interest in the subject of 'the transmission of Islamic learning' from the Middle East to Indonesia or elsewhere in the Muslim world in the past several years has further enhanced the need for publication of this work.

Based mostly on my PhD dissertation at Columbia University in New York City, defended in 1992, most of the research draws on primary sources that have not been considered in detail by other scholars. Although completed 10 years ago, my dissertation has not been available to a non-Indonesian audience and I have been encouraged to present it to a wider readership. An epilogue has been added to take account of some of the more recent research in this field and to add a broader context. The bibliography has been updated with references kindly supplied by Dr Michael Feener (Reed College).

The revisions would not have been possible without the concrete support of a number of friends. Barry Hooker was instrumental not only in providing substantive advice for the improvement of the contents in the light of new scholarly developments on the subject but also in the editing of the manuscript. His wife, Mbak Nia (Virginia Hooker), was also very supportive, and gave me continued encouragement to publish the work in the midst of my almost overwhelming administrative duties as rector of the State Institute for Islamic Studies (IAIN), which on 20 May 2002 was converted into a fully fledged university, the Syarif Hidayatullah State Islamic University (UIN), Jakarta.

My younger colleagues at the Pusat Pengkajian Islam dan Masyarakat (PPIM) of UIN Jakarta, particularly Jamhari Makruf, Oman Fathurahman and Burhanuddin, have helped to edit and retype the manuscript. I owe them all a great debt.

I should mention a number of long-time friends who have always encouraged me to continue with the work: among these are William Roff, Richard Bulliet, John Voll, Barbara Metcalf, Barbara Andaya, Anthony Johns, Merle Ricklefs, James Fox, Martin van Bruinessen, Peter Riddell, Karel Steenbrink, Johan H. Meuleman, Nurcholish Madjid, Taufik Abdullah, Abdurrahman Wahid, Sumit Mandal and Mohammad Redzuan Othman.

My greatest debt is of course to my family—my wife Ipah Farihah and our sons and daughter, Raushanfikr Usada Azra, Firman el-Amny Azra, M. Subhan Azra and Emily Sakina Azra who over the years have sustained my scholarly spirit with their love and understanding, especially when I have had to travel across the continents in the search for knowledge. May God bless all of them.

Azyumardi Azra
UIN Campus, Ciputat
July 2003

Introduction

The transmission of Islamic renewal and reformism is a neglected area of Islamic studies. In contrast to the abundance of studies of the transmission of learning and ideas, for instance, from the Greeks to the Arabs and further to the Western world,[1] there has not yet been any comprehensive study devoted to examining the transmission of religious ideas from centres of Islamic learning to other parts of the Muslim world. There are, of course, several studies on the transmission of *ḥadīth*s (Prophetic tradition) from one generation of early Muslims to another by way of unbroken *isnād*s (chains of transmission).[2]

The study of the transmission of Islamic renewalism and reformism, particularly on the eve of European expansion in the seventeenth and eighteenth centuries, is important for several reasons. The Islamic socio-intellectual history of this period has been little studied; most attention has been given to Islamic political history. Given the decline of Muslim polities, this period has often been considered a dark age in Islamic history. In contrast to this widely held belief, it will be shown that the seventeenth and eighteenth centuries constituted one of the most dynamic periods in the socio-intellectual history of Islam.[3]

The origins of Islamic dynamic impulses in the seventeenth and eighteenth centuries were networks of Muslim scholars (*'ulamā'*), centred in Mecca and Medina. The central position of these two Holy Cities in Islam, especially in conjunction with the annual *ḥajj* pilgrimage, attracted a large number of scholars and students who produced a unique scholarly discourse there. These scholarly networks consisted of a significant number of leading *'ulamā'* who came from different parts of the Muslim world; they thus brought together various traditions of Islamic learning to Mecca and Medina. There were conscious, if not concerted, efforts among these scholars to reform and revitalise the prevailing teachings of Islam; their central theme was the intellectual and socio-moral reconstruction of

Muslim societies. Because of the extensive connections of the networks, the spirit of reform and renewal soon found its expression in many parts of the Muslim world.

The transmission of Islamic renewalism and reformism in the scholarly networks involved very complex processes. There were highly intricate crisscrossings of scholars within the networks, by way of both their studies of Islamic sciences, particularly *ḥadīth*, and their adherence to Islamic mystical brotherhood (*ṭarīqah*s). An examination of this crisscrossing of the networks, and of works produced by scholars in the networks, throws much light on how Islamic renewalism and reformism were transmitted from centres of the networks to many parts of the Muslim world.

Understanding the processes of transmission becomes more important in connection with the course of Islam in the Malay-Indonesian world. As it is situated on the periphery of the Muslim world, there is a tendency among scholars to exclude the Malay-Indonesian world from any discussion of Islam. It is assumed that the region has no single stable core of Islamic tradition. Islam in the archipelago has long been regarded as not 'real Islam'. It is considered distinct from Islam in the centres in the Middle East. We will not, of course, ignore local influences on Islam in the archipelago, but one should not assume that Malay-Indonesian Islamic tradition has little to do with Islam in the Middle East.[4]

Similarly, it is incorrect to assume that the links between Malay-Indonesian Islam and Middle Eastern Islam have more political overtones than religious. The links, at least from the seventeenth century onwards, though marked by intense political relations between several Malay-Muslim kingdoms and the Ottoman Empire, were mostly religious in their nature. If these religious relationships later stimulated some kind of political 'consciousness' especially vis-à-vis European imperialism, it was simply a logical consequence of the impact of the rising 'Islamic identity' that resulted from such links.

Links between Muslims in the Malay-Indonesian world and the Middle East have existed since the earliest times of Islam in the archipelago, around the eleventh and twelfth centuries. Muslim merchants from Arabia, Persia and the Indian subcontinent frequented the harbour cities of the archipelago, where they engaged not only in trade but also in the transmission of Islam to the native population. Later penetration of Islam in the archipelago, however, was carried out less by Muslim traders than by wandering *ṣūfī*s and scholars who came in increasingly large numbers to the area from the thirteenth century onwards.

The prosperity of Malay-Indonesian Muslim states provided an opportunity for a certain segment of Malay-Indonesian Muslims to travel to the centres of Islamic learning in the Middle East. The Ottoman efforts to improve the security along *ḥajj* routes also encouraged Malay-Indonesian Muslims to make their pilgrimages to Mecca. As economic, diplomatic and religio-social relations between Malay-Indonesian and Middle Eastern states developed in the fourteenth and fifteenth centuries, it is probable that Malay-Indonesian pilgrims and students were able to pursue Islamic learning in a variety of places along the trade and *ḥajj* routes. This led to the rise of a non-Arab community in the Ḥaramayn (Mecca and Medina), which was called *'aṣḥāb al-Jāwiyyīn'* (fellow Malay-Indonesians) by Meccans and Medinese. The term *'Jāwī'* (or Jāwah), though derived from the name Java, came to signify anyone from the Malay-Indonesian world.

The *Jāwī* students in the Ḥaramayn represented major lines of intellectual tradition among Malay-Indonesian Muslims. Examination of their history and the textual materials they produced and taught from will help to illuminate not only the nature of religious and intellectual relationships between Malay-Indonesian and Middle Eastern Muslims but also the contemporary development of Islam in the archipelago. Their lives and experience presented a vivid picture of the various networks that existed among them and Middle Eastern *'ulamā'*.

These scholarly networks involved a number of prominent Middle Eastern *'ulamā'* teaching in Mecca and Medina. They constituted a cosmopolitan scholarly community linked together in a relatively solid fashion by way of their studies, particularly of *ḥadīth*, and their involvement in the *ṣūfī ṭarīqah*s. Contacts and interactions between these scholars and students from distant places of the Muslim world resulted in further expansion of the international networks of the *'ulamā'*. There were several Malay-Indonesian students involved in such networks in the seventeenth and eighteenth centuries. Having studied in the Ḥaramayn with its leading scholars, most of them returned to the archipelago, and thus became essential transmitters of the Islamic tradition in the centres of Islamic learning in the Middle East to the Malay-Indonesian world.

The most salient feature of the intellectual tendencies that emerged from the scholarly networks was the harmony between *sharī'ah* (Islamic legal doctrine) and *taṣawwuf* (Islamic mysticism). This has been called by many modern scholars 'neo-Sufism'. Even though the reconciliation between *sharī'ah* and *taṣawwuf* had been emphasised earlier by such scholars as al-Qushayrī and al-Ghazālī, it apparently gained its strongest momentum through these scholarly networks. Scholars in the networks were actively taught, and ardently believed that only by way of total commitment to the *sharī'ah* could the extravagant features of earlier Sufism be controlled. The renewed commitment to *sharī'ah* and *taṣawwuf*, in turn, led to a socio-moral reconstruction of Muslim societies.

Although all scholars in the networks shared a commitment to Islamic renewal and reform, there was no uniformity among them as to their method of achieving this aim. Most of them chose a peaceful and evolutionary approach, but some of them, prominent among these Ibn 'Abd al-Wahhāb in Arabia, and 'Uthmān Ibn Fūdī in West Africa, preferred a more radical and far-reaching reform, which in turn was adopted by some of the scholars in the archipelago.

Despite their differences, the networks of scholars in the Ḥaramayn provided a basis for the renewalist drive within Muslim communities in the archipelago in the seventeenth and eighteenth centuries. The exchange of ideas and the maintenance of lines of intellectual discourse during the period are crucial to the history of Islamic religious thought and to understanding the influence foreign Muslim ideas exerted on the outlook and daily lives of many Malay-Indonesians. The ferment of ideas arising from these intense relations and contacts through scholarly networks had a revitalising effect on the communal and personal lives of most Malay-Indonesian Muslims.

SIGNIFICANCE OF THE STUDY

As far as I am aware, no comprehensive work, historical or otherwise, has been done of networks of Middle Eastern and Malay-Indonesian *'ulamā'*. Little attempt has been made to provide a critical analysis of the origins of Islamic reformism in the Malay-Indonesian world before the nineteenth and twentieth centuries through networks of the *'ulamā'*; and of how Islamic teachings were transmitted and how the transmission affected the course of Islam in the archipelago.

The works of Voll[5] have discussed the existence of the international networks of the *'ulamā'* centred in Mecca and Medina and their connections in other parts of the Muslim world. He deals mostly with the emergence of such networks among Middle Eastern and South Asian *'ulamā'*, and simply mentions in passing the involvement of such Malay-Indonesian *'ulamā'* as 'Abd al-Ra'ūf al-Sinkīlī and Muḥammad Yūsuf al-Maqassārī in the international scholarly networks in the seventeenth century.

Johns, on the other hand, in several studies[6] discusses at length these relationships, particularly between al-Sinkīlī and Ibrāhīm al-Kūrānī. However, he has made no attempt to examine further networks of al-Sinkīlī with other leading Ḥaramayn scholars. The lack of studies dealing with networks of other Malay-Indonesian scholars is even more striking. Studies dealing with leading Malay-Indonesian *'ulamā'* other than al-Sinkīlī in the seventeenth and eighteenth centuries fail to trace their linkages with Middle Eastern scholars in the period.

Furthermore, where the scholarly networks are actually mentioned, discussion centres on the 'organisational' aspect of the networks, namely, the nature of the relationships that existed between scholars in centres of Islamic learning in the Middle East and those coming from other parts of the Muslim world. No study has yet been done to examine the 'intellectual content' of the networks. This examination is crucial to determining the kinds of ideas and teachings transmitted through such scholarly networks.

This book will seek to answer the following questions: (i) How did the networks of Middle Eastern and Malay-Indonesian *'ulamā'* come into being? What were the nature and characteristics of the networks? What were the teachings or intellectual tendencies developed in the networks?

(ii) What was the role of Malay-Indonesian *'ulamā'* in the transmission of the intellectual contents of the networks to the archipelago? What were the modes of transmission? (iii) What was the larger impact of the networks on the course of Islam in the Malay-Indonesian world?

In sum, this study attempts to elucidate a number of important subjects. It is the first comprehensive study of the global scholarly networks, with particular reference to Malay-Indonesian *'ulamā'* and their intellectual tendencies in the seventeenth and eighteenth centuries; the first treatment of the role of such networks in the transmission of Islamic renewal and reform to the archipelago; and a pioneering study of the origins of early Islamic renewal and reform in the Malay-Indonesian world.

SCOPE OF DISCUSSION

To present an accurate and comprehensive account of the scholarly networks and their role in the transmission of Islamic renewal and reform to the archipelago, this study is divided into seven chapters which, in turn, consist of several sections. Within each chapter, several topics will be explored and a conclusion drawn at the close of each section.

Chapter 1 examines the rise of the international scholarly networks in the Ḥaramayn. The discussion centres first on how the political and economic situation affected pilgrimage and the world of learning in Mecca and Medina. Then follows an examination of a number of *'ulamā'* who constituted the core of scholarly networks in the seventeenth century; particular attention is given to the nature of their relationships in the networks.

Chapter 2 deals with a discussion of 'neo-Sufism' and of how its characteristics represented the intellectual contents and tendencies of the networks in the seventeenth century.

Chapters 3 to 5 are devoted to examining the careers and teachings of the leading precursors of Malay-Indonesian *'ulamā'* in seventeenth century scholarly networks, namely al-Rānīrī, al-Sinkīlī and al-Maqassārī. Special attention is given to their connections with leading scholars in the networks in the Middle East, and to how teachings spread in the archipelago related to Islamic renewalism and reformism in the centres.

Chapter 6 constitutes a final discussion of a number of Malay-Indonesian *'ulamā'* who were involved in the scholarly networks in the eighteenth century. The chapter begins with a discussion of the origins and date of Islamic renewalism in the archipelago. Discussion is then focused on the biographies of Malay-Indonesian *'ulamā'* and some of their teachers in the Ḥaramayn and Cairo. The chapter continues with a discussion of their teachings and of how they translated Islamic reformism in the Malay-Indonesian world.

Finally, in chapter 7, we look forward to the nineteenth century and the networks in the face of the European challenge.

NOTES ON SOURCES

This study is the first to use Arabic sources extensively in any discussion relating to the history of Islam in the Malay-Indonesian world. The Arabic biographical dictionaries of the seventeenth and eighteenth centuries, most of which have by now been printed,[7] are goldmines of information on teachers of the Malay-Indonesion students involved in the networks, and on scholarly discourse in the Middle East, particularly in the Ḥaramayn and Cairo.

It is striking that most of these biographical dictionaries have not been utilised earlier for examining, for instance, the world of learning in the Ḥaramayn. It is not surprising therefore that, unlike other centres of Islamic learning in the Middle East such as Baghdad, Cairo or even Nishapur, which have been studied a great deal, those of the Ḥaramayn have only received scanty treatment. These biographical dictionaries have proven essential to an accurate account of the institutions of Islamic learning, such as the Holy Mosques, *madrasah*s and *ribāṭ*s in the Ḥaramayn.

Malay-Indonesian texts, either written by *'ulamā'* discussed in this study or by modern scholars, in many cases do provide the names of the teachers of Malay-Indonesian students in the Ḥaramayn. Contemporaneous Arabic biographical dictionaries are used to trace not only the scholarly careers of these teachers but more importantly their connections with one another. By using these Arabic biographical dictionaries we are now on firm ground in speaking about the existence of the scholarly networks between Malay-Indonesian and Middle Eastern *'ulamā'*.

Furthermore, these biographical dictionaries in some instances show evidence of intense contacts between Malay-Indonesian students and their Middle Eastern teachers. The *Fawā'id al-Irtiḥāl* of al-Hamawī, for instance, provides vivid accounts of intellectual and religious confusion among Malay-Indonesian Muslims because of their misunderstanding of Islamic mysticism and of the reactions of such outstanding scholars as al-Kūrānī to this. Al-Muḥibbī's *Khulāṣat al-Athar* and al-Murādī's *Silk al-Durar* inform us of several leading Ḥaramayn scholars who wrote special works to fulfil the requests of their Malay-Indonesian students.

Beginning in the eighteenth century, scholarly accounts of Malay-Indonesian scholars began to make their appearance in Arabic biographical dictionaries. The first, who was given a respected place in this genre of Arabic literature, is 'Abd al-Ṣamad al-Palimbānī, discussed in chapter 6. His Yemeni student, Wajīh al-Dīn al-Ahdal, includes the biography of al-Palimbānī in his *al-Nafs al-Yamanī wa al-Rūḥ al-Rayḥānī*. Later, al-Palimbānī's biography is reproduced by al-Bayṭār in his *Ḥilyat al-Bashar fī Tārīkh al-Qarn al-Thālith 'Ashar*.

Arabic biographical dictionaries are thus an indispensable source for the study of Malay-Indonesian *'ulamā'* who studied or established their careers in the Ḥaramayn. A cursory observation of Arabic biographical dictionaries in the nineteenth and twentieth centuries gives even more striking evidence of the involvement of Malay-Indonesian scholars in the scholarly networks of this period. A substantial number of Malay-Indonesian *'ulamā'* also make their appearance.[8]

1

Networks of the *'Ulamā'* in the Seventeenth Century Ḥaramayn

Mecca and Medina (the Ḥaramayn, the two *Ḥarams*, forbidden sanctuaries) occupy a special position in Islam and the life of Muslims. The twin *Ḥarams* are the places where Islam was revealed to the Prophet Muhammad and initially developed. Mecca is the *qiblah* towards which the believers turn their faces in their *ṣalāhs* (prayers) and the holy city where they make the *ḥajj* pilgrimage. With all their religious importance, it is not surprising that some special qualities and merits (*faḍā'il*) have been attributed to both Mecca and Medina.

The combination between the *faḍā'il* of Mecca and Medina, and the injunction of the Qur'ān and the *ḥadīth* to the Muslims to search for knowledge (*ṭalab al-'ilm*), undoubtedly raised the value of the knowledge acquired in the two cities in the eyes of many believers. As a consequence, the scholars who taught and studied in the Ḥaramayn enjoyed a more esteemed position in Muslim societies, particularly those of the Malay-Indonesian world, than their counterparts who underwent a similar experience in the other centres of Islamic learning.

Furthermore, with the coming and going of countless pilgrims every year, Mecca and Medina became the largest gathering point of Muslims from all over the globe, the intellectual hub of the Muslim world, where *'ulamā'*, *ṣūfīs*, rulers, philosophers, poets and historians met and exchanged information. This is why scholars and students who taught and studied in Mecca and Medina were generally more cosmopolitan in their religious outlook than their counterparts in other Muslim cities. Such an experience for the seeker of *'ilm* (knowledge) in the Ḥaramayn not only emphasised universal traits common to all Muslims but moulded them into a formulation for their self-definition vis-à-vis both the larger scholarly community of the Muslim world and their much smaller ones.

The emergence of networks of the *'ulamā'*, which included a substantial number of non-Middle Eastern scholars in Mecca and Medina, was not independent of other developments in the Ḥaramayn and the Muslim societies as a whole. Their rise can be attributed to several important factors which were not only religious but also economic, social and political, working at the regional level in a given Muslim society and at the level of the larger Muslim world.

For instance, contacts and relations between Malay-Indonesian Muslims and the Middle East began to gain momentum with the flowering of Muslim kingdoms in the archipelago in the late sixteenth century. The intensification of their participation in the trade of the Indian Ocean brought them into closer contact not only with Muslim traders but also with political authorities in the Middle East. The increasing presence of Europeans, particularly the Portuguese, was also an important factor that pushed their relations much further into the politico-diplomatic realm. The intensification of these relations contributed significantly to the growth of the Malay-Indonesian pilgrimage to the Ḥaramayn, which in turn spurred the pilgrims' involvement in the scholarly networks.

The growth of the international networks of the *'ulamā'* in the Ḥaramayn, particularly in the sixteenth and seventeenth centuries, should therefore be viewed not only from a wider perspective but through the longer span of historical discourse between Muslim societies of both the Middle East and the Indian Ocean region.

SCHOLARLY DISCOURSES IN THE ḤARAMAYN: EARLY NETWORKS OF THE *'ULAMĀ'*

The tradition of learning among the *'ulamā'* throughout Islamic history has been closely associated with religious and educational institutions such as mosques, madrasahs, *ribāṭ*s, and even the houses of the teachers. This is particularly evident in the Ḥaramayn, where the tradition of learning created a vast network of scholars, transcending geographical boundaries as well as differences in religious outlook. In this chapter we discuss how networks of the *'ulamā'* developed surrounding these institutions, and how leading scholars in the Ḥaramayn, through their traditions of learning, created links that connected them with each other as well as with earlier and later scholars.

There is no doubt that the two great mosques in Mecca and Medina were the most important loci of scholars involved in the networks from the last decades of the fifteenth century onwards. Despite the fact that the number of madrasahs and *ribāṭ*s continually increased after the the first and second madrasahs in Mecca were built in 571/1175 and 579/1183 respectively, the Ḥarām Mosques continued to be the most important centres for the process of learning. The madrasahs and *ribāṭ*s by no means replaced the two great mosques so far as the process of learning was concerned. However, they became vital complements to the scholarly world in the Holy Land.

Before we go any further, it seems important to note that the madrasahs were organised in a more formal way. They had their officially appointed heads of madrasahs, teachers, *qāḍī*s (judges) and other functionaries. Furthermore, they each had their own curriculum, and even a certain quota of students, as well as an exact allocation of the time of study according to their *madhhab*. This is particularly true in the case of madrasahs, which consisted of four divisions of Sunnī legal *madhhab*s. The Madrasah al-Ghiyāthiyyah, for instance, had a quota of 20 students for each *madhhab*. The Shāfi'ī and Ḥanafī students had their classes in the morning, while the Mālikī and Ḥanbalī students had theirs in the afternoon.[1] Similar arrangements applied at the Sulaymāniyyah madrasahs.[2] It is also clear from our sources that these madrasahs were mainly devoted to teaching basic and intermediate levels of various Islamic disciplines. With all their formality, the madrasahs had few opportunities to bring their students to higher levels of Islamic learning.

However, such a disadvantage, which resulted from the nature of the Ḥaramayn madrasahs, was soon filled by the *ribāṭ*s, and more importantly by the two great mosques. Those who aspired to seek advanced learning, as a rule, joined the *ḥalqah*s in the Ḥarām Mosques, or the *ribāṭ*s, and in many cases they also studied privately in teachers' houses. As can be expected, there was little formality in such halqahs. Personal relationships were formed and became the ties that connected them to each other. Teachers were well acquainted personally with each of their students; they thus recognised the special needs and talents of each student, and they attempted to meet these special needs. The significance of this should not be underestimated; it is through these processes that the teachers issued ijazah (authority) to their students or appointed them the *khalīfah* (successor or deputy) of their *ṭarīqah*s.

Al-Fāsī relates many examples of teachers in the Ḥarām Mosque in Mecca who were authorised to teach privately not only advanced students but also rulers and traders intending to pursue special Islamic disciplines. Among them was 'Ali b. Aḥmad al-Fuwwiyī (d. 781/1389), who was authorised to teach a ruler of Shirāz, Shāh Shujā' b. Muḥammad al-Yazdī, about the *ḥadīth* of the Prophet. So satisfied was he with the way al-Fuwwiyī taught him that the ruler granted 200 *mithqāl* of gold, a portion of which was spent on building a *ribāṭ*.[3] Similarly, when Bashīr al-Jumdar al-Nāṣirī, a Mamlūk ruler in Egypt, wished to study various Islamic disciplines in Mecca, several *qāḍī*s were assigned to teach him. The most important among them was *Qāḍī al-Quḍāh* Muḥammad Jamāl al-Dīn Ẓahīrah (d. 817/1414).[4] Another scholar, Muḥammad Ḍiyā' al-Dīn al-Hindī (d. 780/1378), and his son, Muḥammad b. Ḍiyā' al-Dīn al-Ṣāghānī (d. 825/1422), were also appointed to teach Ḥanbalī *fiqh* to several members of the Egyptian Mamlūk ruling dynasty.[5]

Furthermore, scholars who taught in the Ḥarām Mosques were often asked to answer questions coming from many parts of the Muslim world.

As a rule, they held special *majlis* (sessions), discussing these matters. In many instances they issued written *fatwā*s, but it was also not unusual for them to write special books, which attempted to answer the questions in detail. Al-Fāsī again relates the story of Jamāl al-Dīn al-Ẓahīrah, one of his teachers, who received hundreds of questions from various parts of the Middle East.[6] Such an important role played by the scholars in the Ḥarām-Mosques vis-à-vis many believers becomes a distinctive feature in the later periods, when the scholarly networks increasingly gained momentum. As we shall see, several leading scholars in seventeenth century Ḥaramayn wrote about, and discussed, certain religious issues that arose among Indian and Malay-Indonesian Muslims. For example, at the end of the seventeenth century the Chief *Qāḍī* of Mecca issued a *fatwā* on the deposition of Sulṭānah Kamālat Shāh (of the Acehnese Sultanate) stating that, in his opinion, an Islamic kingdom could not be ruled by a woman.[7]

One essential question to ask is how scholars who came from many different places in the Muslim world were able to get teaching positions in the Ḥaramayn madrasahs and at the Ḥarām Mosque of Mecca and the Prophet Mosque in Medina. In order to be allowed to teach, a teacher, either in the madrasah or at the Holy Mosques, was required to have *ijāzah* (authority), which established the academic credentials of the holder. The most important credential was the *isnād*, namely, the chain of authority that indicated the unbroken teacher-student link in the transmission of certain books or teachings. The *ijāzah* was issued by a recognised teacher to his students, generally after they studied with him.[8] However, there were a few cases, as we see later, showing that the *ijāzah* might also be issued through relatively short meetings and even through correspondence with teachers.[9]

The appointment of scholars to teaching positions at the Holy Mosques in Mecca and Medina was decided by a religious bureaucracy, which was responsible not only for administration of the Holy Mosques but also for religious life in the Ḥaramayn as a whole. The highest official in the bureaucracy was the *Qāḍī* (judge), often called *Qāḍī al-Quḍāh* (Chief *Qāḍī*), who was in charge of religious laws and of leadership of the four *qāḍī*s—each of them representing a Sunnī legal school. It appears that prior to the Ottoman period, the *Qāḍī al-Quḍāh* also held the office of *Muftī*. Next came the Shaykh al-Ḥaramayn, the two directors of the Ḥarām Mosque in Mecca and Medina. In each city there was a *Shaykh al-'Ulamā'* (chief of scholars), who oversaw all scholars.[10]

We have no information as to when such a religious bureaucracy was instituted, but it is clear that it was already well established from at least the fifteenth century onwards. When the Ottomans rose to power in the Ḥijāz that structure was largely maintained. Although the holders of most of the posts needed to be confirmed by the Ottoman authorities, the Ḥaramayn scholars were relatively free to choose those who would fill these positions. There was a tendency, however, for those positions to be dominated by scholars belonging to certain families.

This is demonstrated in the careers of many *'ulamā'* in the Ḥaramayn. For instance, Jamāl al-Dīn al-Ẓahīrah, the *Qāḍī* of *Quḍāh*, mentioned above, was succeeded to the position by his son Aḥmad b. Muḥammad al-Ẓahīrah in the early fifteenth century.[11] Similarly, the historian al-Fāsī—whose father, Aḥmad (d. 819/1416), happened to be related by marriage to the Chief *Qāḍī* of Mecca, Muḥammad b. Aḥmad b. 'Abd al-'Azīz al-Nuwayrī—was appointed the Mālikī *Qāḍī* of Mecca in 807/1405 with a letter of investiture from al-Malik al-Nāṣir Faraj b. Barqūq, a Mamlūk ruler in Cairo.[12] An important scholar in the networks, Muḥammad b. 'Abd al-Rasūl al-Barzanjī, who migrated to the Ḥaramayn in the second half of the seventeenth century, led scholars of the Barzanjī family to prominence in Mecca; three members of this family dominated the office of the Shāfi'ī Mufti after 1269/1852.[13] 'Abd al-Ḥafīẓ al-'Ajamī (or Ujaymī) became a mufti of Mecca after Ḥasan b. 'Alī al-'Ajamī, a prominent scholar in the networks, established the fame of the 'Ajamī family towards the end of the seventeenth century.[14]

It was the Shaykh al-'Ulamā', the *Qāḍī al-Quḍāh*, Shaykh al-Ḥaramayn and four *qāḍī*s of the four *madhhab*s who collectively made decisions on the appointment of scholars to teaching positions in the Ḥarām Mosques. Once or twice a year they sat together to examine candidates for future teachers. The candidates, as a rule, were longtime students of the mosques and were well acquainted with senior teachers. The examiners, in addition to checking the *ijāzah* of the candidates, posed a number of questions concerning various branches of Islamic discipline. If the candidates were able to answer all questions satisfactorily, they were issued *ijāzah*, or permission to teach in the Holy Mosques. The names of these new teachers were made public, and students were able to begin their studies with them.[15]

Our sources make no mention of the number of teachers in the Ḥarām Mosques in the period under discussion. An Ottoman report for the year 1303/1884-5, however, mentioned that there were 270 teachers in that year. Snouck Hurgronje considers this number unreliable, 'for many of those men are named professors because the Governor [Ottoman] wished to favor them with a salary from a fund destined for the advancement of science'.[16] Thus, Snouck believes that the total number of actual teachers was only between 50 and 60.[17] There is no way we can substantiate this number. However, I would suggest that the average number of teachers at any given time during the seventeenth and eighteenth centuries was between 100 and 200. If this number is added to teachers who taught only in the madrasahs and visiting teachers, then the total number of teachers in the Ḥaramayn was clearly quite large.

PERSONAGE AND LINKAGES IN THE NETWORKS

There is little doubt that some of the scholars mentioned above, in one way or another, had connections with each other. What is important is that several leading scholars of that period had links to the core of scholarly networks in the seventeenth century. We have noted that al-Fāsī, for instance, was a student and good friend of Ibn Ḥajar al-'Asqalānī and Shihāb al-Dīn al-Ramlī, two great *muḥaddith*s who lived in Egypt. Similarly, al-Nahrawālī, a leading scholar in the sixteenth century Ḥaramayn, had extensive connections not only with earlier scholars, such as Ibn Ḥajar al-'Asqalānī, but also with those of the seventeenth century, such as Ibrāhīm al-Kūrānī. Almost all scholars who constitute the core of seventeenth century networks of the *'ulamā'* could trace their *ḥadīth isnād* and *ṭarīqah silsilah* to these scholars. The nature of their connections will become clearer as we proceed with this discussion.

The scholarly networks in the seventeenth century had cosmopolitan origins. There were at least two non-Ḥijāzī scholars who appear to have contributed largely to the growth of the networks in this century: the first was Indian by birth and Persian (Isfahan) by origin, Sayyid Ṣibghat Allāh b. Rūḥ Allāh Jamāl al-Barwajī (some spell it al-Barūjī or the modern Barauch in Gujarat), and the second was an Egyptian named Aḥmad b. 'Alī b. 'Abd al-Quddūs al-Shinnāwī al-Miṣrī al-Madanī. Their relationship represents a good example of how scholarly interactions resulted both in exchanges of knowledge and in the transmission of the 'little' traditions of Islam from India and Egypt to the Ḥaramayn (see Chart 1).

Sayyid Ṣibghat Allāh (d. in Medina 1015/1606) was undoubtedly a typical wandering scholar who ended up being a 'grand immigrant' in the Ḥaramayn. Hailing from a Persian immigrant family in India, one of his famous Indian teachers was Wajīh al-Dīn al-Gujarātī (d. 997/1589), a leading Shaṭṭāriyyah master, who lived in Ahmadabad. For several years Ṣibghat Allāh, under the patronage of the local ruler, taught the Shaṭṭāriyyah doctrines in the town of his birth. In 999/1591 he travelled to Mecca in order to make the *ḥajj* pilgrimage. After returning to India, he travelled to various places before staying in Ahmadnagar for one year. Later he moved to Bijapur, a strong *ṣūfī* centre in India, where he won the favour of Sulṭān Ibrāhīm 'Ādil Shāh, who then made a special arrangement for him to travel back to the Ḥaramayn in the royal ship during the *ḥajj* season of 1005/1596.[18]

After performing the pilgrimage Ṣibghat Allāh decided to settle in Medina, where he built a house and a *ribāṭ* from the *waqf* and gifts he received from the Sulṭāns of Ahmadnagar, Bijapur, and Ottoman officials in Medina. Ṣibghat Allāh was generally known as a leading Shaṭṭāriyyah Shaykh; he was regarded as being responsible for introducing the *Jawāhir-i Khamsah* of the famous Shaṭṭāriyyah shaykh, Muḥammad Ghauth al-Hindī (d. 970/1563), and other Shaṭṭāriyyah treatises to Ḥaramayn scholars. However, he also initiated disciples into the Chishtiyyah, Suhrāwardiyyah, Madāriyyah, Khalwātiyyah, Hamadāniyyah, Naqshbandiyyah and Firdausiyyah orders. This is not surprising, as his teacher, Wajīh al-Dīn, had also been initiated into all

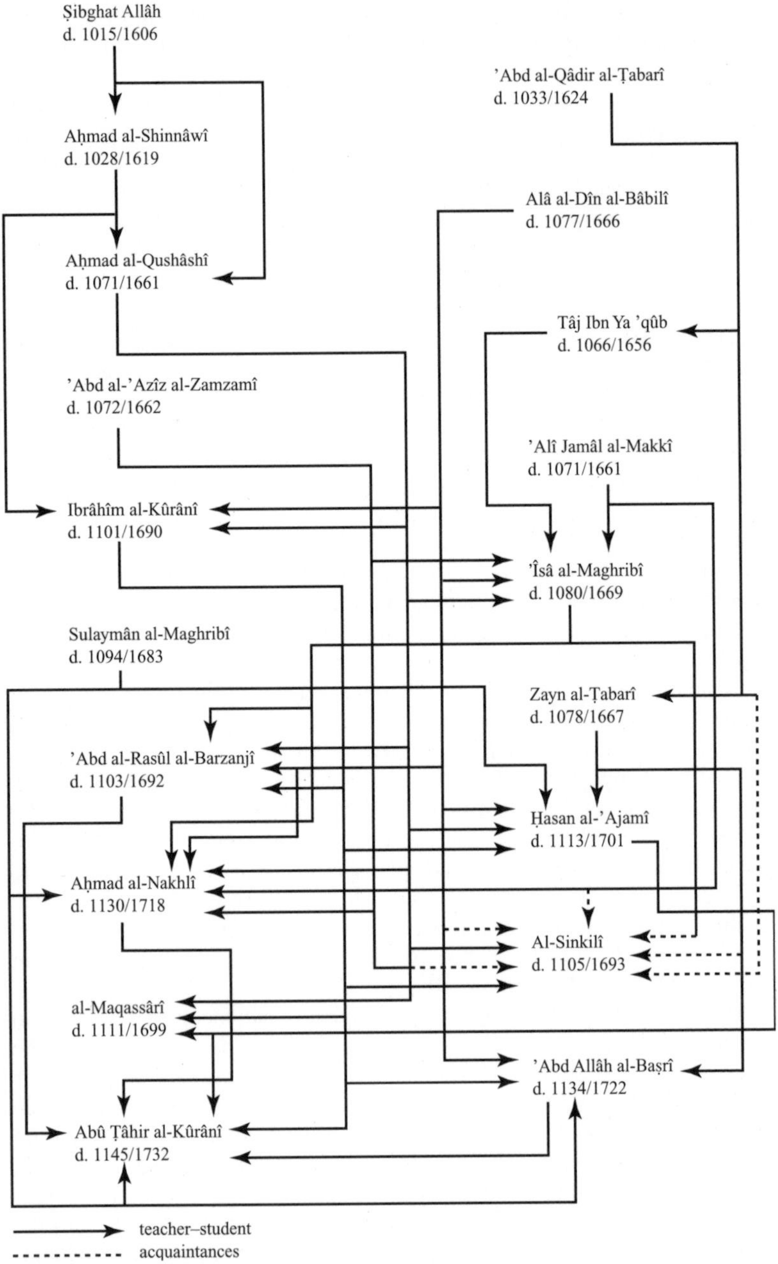

Chart 1 The core of the seventeenth century networks

eight orders.[19] In Medina, Ṣibghat Allāh was active in teaching at the Nabawī Mosque; he also wrote several works on Sufism, theology, and a commentary on the Bayḍāwī Qur'ānic exegesis.[20]

The diversity of Ṣibghat Allāh's most prominent disciples clearly reflects the cosmopolitan nature of the scholarly discourse in the Ḥaramayn. Among his disciples were Aḥmad al-Shinnāwī, Aḥmad al-Qushāshī, Sayyid Amjad Mīrzā, Sayyid As'ad al-Balkhī, Abū Bakr b. Aḥmad al-Nasfī al-Miṣrī, Ibn 'Abd Allāh b. Walī al-Ḥaḍramī, Muḥammad b. 'Umar al- Ḥaḍramī, Ibrāhīm al-Hindī, Muḥy al-Dīn al-Miṣrī, al-Mulā Shaykh b. Ilyās al-Kurdī, Mulā Niẓām al-Dīn al-Sindī, 'Abd al-Aẓīm al-Makkī and Ḥabīb Allāh al-Hindī.[21] His *ḥalqah*s were also attended by some students and pilgrims from the Sultanate of Aceh, who in turn provided information about Islam in the archipelago.[22] It is worth mentioning that Ṣibghat Allāh was also a friend of Faḍl Allāh al-Burhānpūrī al-Hindī (d. 1029/1620),[23] whose work, entitled *al-Tuḥfat al-Mursalah ilā Ruḥ al-Nabī*,[24] had provoked intense discussion at the time.

Two prominent scholars responsible for the spread of Ṣibghat Allāh's teachings in the Ḥaramayn were Aḥmad al-Shinnāwī and Aḥmad al-Qushāshī. Born in 975/1567 to a noted scholarly family in Egypt, Aḥmad b. 'Alī b. 'Abd al-Quddūs Abū al-Mawāhib al-Shinnāwī acquired his early education in his own land.[25] His grandfather, Muḥammad al-Shinnāwī, a prominent *ṣūfī* shaykh, was a master of the famous Egyptian *ṣūfī* 'Abd al-Wahhāb al-Sha'rānī. The latter, in turn, initiated Aḥmad al-Shinnāwī's father, 'Alī al-Shinnāwī, into the Aḥmadiyyah *ṭarīqah*.[26] Even though Aḥmad al-Shinnāwī was from an early age exposed extensively to Sufism, he had an interest in studying *ḥadīth*. Among his teachers in *ḥadīth* were two leading Egyptian *muḥaddith*s: the Shāfi'ī *muftī*, Shams al-Dīn al-Ramlī (d. 1004/1596),[27] and Muḥammad b. Abī al-Ḥasan al-Bakrī, who was also known as a *ṣūfī*.[28] Aḥmad al-Shinnāwī travelled to the Ḥaramayn and took up residence in Medina, where he died in 1028/1619.

There can be no doubt that Aḥmad al-Shinnāwī attained fame in the City of the Prophet. He established a friendship and studied with Ṣibghat Allāh, who initiated him into the Shaṭṭāriyyah order. His erudition in the Shaṭṭāriyyah and other orders earned him the title of the *al-Bāhir al-Ṭarīqah* ('the dazzling light of the *ṣūfī* order'). With his expertise in *ḥadīth* and Sufism, he attracted numerous students to his *ḥalqah*s. Among his leading students were Sayyid Sālim b. Aḥmad Shaykhānī, Aḥmad al-Qushāshī and Sayyid al-Jalīl Muḥammad al-Ghurābī.

Aḥmad al-Shinnāwī's scholarly connections through *ḥadīth* studies and *ṭarīqah* were extensive. For instance, he had *isnād*s with earlier scholars and *ṣūfī*s such as Muḥammad Ẓahīrah al-Makkī, Quṭb al-Dīn al-Nahrawālī, Ibn Ḥajar al-'Asqalānī, al-Suyūṭī and Ibn al-'Arabī.[29] He wrote several works dealing with theology and Sufism; al-Baghdādī and Brockelmann respectively list 16 and five of them.[30] One of his works,

Tajalliyah al-Baṣā'ir Ḥāshiyat 'alā Kitāb al-Jawāhir li al-Ghauth al-Hindī, is a commentary on the *Kitāb al-Jawāhir* [*al-Khamsah*] of Muḥammad Ghauth al-Hindī.

THE EXPANSION OF NETWORKS

How the scholarly networks in the Ḥaramayn developed further can be seen in the experience of Aḥmad al-Qushāshī. His career demonstrates how the web of scholars was becoming wider and more pregnant with intellectual exchange. Undoubtedly he was the most influential among the disciples of Ṣibghat Allāh and Aḥmad al-Shinnāwī. In the colophon of one of al-Qushāshī's works, *al-Simṭ al-Majīd*,[31] we are told about the career of this great scholar. The most complete biography of al-Qushāshī, however, is provided by Musṭafā b. Fatḥ, Allāh al-Ḥamawī al-Makkī (d. 1124/1712), a leading *muḥaddith* and historian in Mecca. Al-Ḥamawī himself was a student of Ibrāhīm al-Kūrānī, the most prominent and influential disciple of al-Qushāshī.[32] In his yet unpublished three-volume biographical dictionary entitled *Fawā'id al-Irtiḥāl wa Natā'ij al-Safar fī Akhbār Ahl al-Qarn al-Ḥādī 'Ashar*,[33] al-Ḥamawī devotes a long account (no fewer than 13 folios—26 pages) to the biography of al-Qushāshī, which is based mostly on the recollection of al-Kūrānī.[34] Al-Kūrānī himself includes biographical notes of his great shaykh towards the end of his *al-Umam li Īqāẓ al-Himam*.[35] Al-Ḥamawī's accounts were later condensed by al-Muḥibbī in his *Khulāṣat al-Athar fī A'yān al-Qarn al-Ḥādī 'Ashar*.[36]

Ṣafī al-Dīn Aḥmad b. Muḥammad Yūnus al-Qushāshī al-Dajānī al-Madanī was born in Medina in 991/1538 of a Palestinian family, whose genealogy traced his ancestors back to Tamīm al-Dārī, a prominent Medinese companion of the Prophet. His grandfather, Yūnus al-Qushāshī, a *ṣūfī*, decided to take his family back to Medina from Dijana, a village near Jerusalem. In the City of the Prophet, Shaykh Yūnus, who had also been known as 'Abd al-Nabī, earned his living by selling *qushāsh*, second-hand goods, from which Aḥmad got his first *laqab* (surname or nickname). Our sources suggest that he took this lowly position in order to retain his anonymity as a great *ṣūfī*.[37]

Aḥmad al-Qushāshī acquired his rudimentary religious knowledge according to the Mālikī school of law from his father and Muḥammad b. 'Isā al-Tilmisānī, a renowned *'ālim* in Medina. In 1011/1602 his father took him on a trip to Yemen, where he studied with most of the *'ulamā'* with whom his father had studied, such as al-Amīn b. Ṣiddīqī al-Marwāḥī, Sayyid Muḥammad Gharb, Aḥmad al-Saṭḥah al-Zaila'ī, Sayyid 'Alī al-Qab'ī and 'Alī b. Muṭayr. They stayed in Yemen for some years before returning to Mecca, where he made the acquaintance of many of its leading scholars, such as Sayyid Abī al-Ghayth Shajr and Sulṭān al-Majzūb. Although he spent the rest of his life in Medina, al-Qushāshī often visited Mecca, particularly during the pilgrimage seasons.[38] It was in Medina that

Aḥmad al-Qushāshī established his scholarly career. As al-Ḥamawī tells us, he associated himself with the city's leading *'ulamā'*, exchanging knowledge and information. Among them were Aḥmad b. al-Faḍl b. 'Abd al-Nāfi', Walī 'Umar b. al-Quṭb Badr al-Dīn al-'Ādalī, Shihāb al-Dīn al-Malkā'ī, Sayyid As'ad al-Balkhī and, of particular importance, Aḥmad al-Shinnāwī. Al-Shinnāwī not only taught him *ḥadīth*, *fiqh*, *kalām* and other sciences related to Islamic law and theology, but also initiated him into and appointed him his *khalīfah* of the Shaṭṭāriyyah *ṭarīqah*. The relationship between these two scholars went beyond the scholarly realm: al-Qushāshī married al-Shinnāwī's daughter.

Despite their very close relationship, al-Qushāshī differed from al-Shinnāwī in that he maintained his adherence to the Mālikī school of law; only after al-Shinnāwī's death did he adopt the Shāfi'ī *madhhab*, the legal school his father-in-law adhered to. In long accounts of al-Qushāshī's change of *madhhab*, al-Ḥamawī reports that al-Qushāshī adopted the Shāfi'ī *madhhab* after he got guidance from the Prophet Muhammad himself through his reading of the whole Qur'ān in one single night. Al-Qushāshī also gives several other valid reasons to change one's *madhhab*,[39] as we see later. It is evident that Aḥmad al-Qushāshī was a scholar of extraordinary erudition and humility. This is confirmed, for instance, by Ayyūb al-Dimashqī al-Khalwatī (994-1071/1586-1661), a great *ṣūfī* (who was, it is worth mentioning, a teacher of al-Maqassārī). Ayyūb al-Dimashqī points out that he had never met a scholar as learned as al-Qushāshī.[40] Al-Qushāshī was also a prolific author. The number of his works is listed as 16 by al-Baghdādī,[41] as 19 by Brockelmann[42] and more than 50 by other sources.[43] These works deal with *taṣawwuf*, *ḥadīth*, *fiqh*, *uṣūl fiqh*, and *tafsīr*. Only *al-Simṭ al-Majīd* has been published thus far.

Although al-Qushāshī is generally known as a shaykh of the Shaṭṭāriyyah *ṭarīqah*, he was actually affiliated with almost a dozen other *ṣūfī* orders. It must be admitted, however, that he was particularly instrumental in the transmission of the Shaṭṭāriyyah *ṭarīqah*, through his students, to many different parts of the Muslim world. According to al-Ḥamawī, his principal disciples were no fewer than 100; they came from many regions (*aqṭār*) of the world,[44] and they constituted crucial links among scholars in the networks.[45] The best known among his disciples were Ibrāhīm al-Kūrānī (1023-1101/1614-1690); 'Abd Allāh b. Shaykh al-'Aydarūs (1027-1073/1618-1662), a teacher of Bā Shaybān, who was a teacher of al-Rānīrī;[46] Ḥasan b. 'Alī al-'Ajamī (1049-1113/1639-1701);[47] Sayyid al-'Allāmah al-Walī Barakāt al-Tūnisī; Sayyid 'Abd al-Khāliq al-Hindī al-Lāhūrī (d.1059/1649);[48] Sayyid 'Abd al-Raḥmān [al-Maḥjūb] al-Maghribī al-Idrīsī (1023-1085/1614-1674);[49] 'Isā b. Muḥammad al-Maghribī al-Ja'farī al-Makkī (1020-1080/1611-1669);[50] Miḥnān b. 'Awd Bā Mazrū'; Sayyid 'Abd Allāh Bā Faqīh, Sayyid 'Alī al-Shaybānī al-Zabīdī (d. 1072/1662) and a number of other leading Yemeni scholars, especially those of the 'Alawī and Ja'mān families;[51] Muḥammad b. 'Abd al-Rasūl al-Barzanjī al-Kurdī (1040-1103/1630-1692);[52] and al-Sinkīlī and al-Maqassārī. Al-Qushāshī died in Medina in 1071/1661.

Our scholarly networks gained strong impetus when Ibrāhīm al-Kūrānī, the most celebrated student of Aḥmad al-Qushāshī, established his career in Medina after travelling in quest of Islamic sciences in various places in the Middle East. The fact that Ibrāhīm al-Kūrānī occupied a position of extraordinary importance in the further development of the scholarly networks is shown by the large number of his students and his vast connections, but more importantly by his numerous works. He was the common starting point for the lines of linkage of many scholars in the seventeenth and eighteenth centuries. Being a scholar of intellectual distinction, al-Kūrānī made a substantial contribution to the further growth of the intellectual currents developed by al-Shinnāwī and al-Qushāshī.

By all accounts, Ibrāhīm al-Kūrānī was a great scholar. Al-Murādī calls him 'a mountain among mountains of *'ilm* and a sea among seas of *'irfān* (spiritual knowledge)'.[53] A prominent nineteenth century scholar, Abī Ṭayyib Muḥammad Shams al-Ḥaq al-'Aẓīmābādī (born 1273/1857), a noted Indian *muḥaddith*, has singled out al-Kūrānī as the reformer (*mujaddid*) of the eleventh century AH/seventeenth century CE.[54] Discussing extensively the *ḥadīth* which states that 'God sends to this community (*ummah*) at the "head" [*ra's*] of each century one who regenerates its religion for it', al-'Aẓīmābādī gives a list of Muslim scholars who have been considered as the *mujaddid*s of Islamic beliefs and practices at the end of each hundred years of the Hijrah. It is important to note that for the ninth century AH/fifteenth century CE *mujaddid*, al-'Aẓīmābādī states a preference for Jalāl al-Dīn al-Suyūṭī (d. 911/1505) over Zakariyyā al-Anṣārī (d. 926/1520), who had been chosen by other scholars.[55] Despite this difference in preferences, the two great *muḥaddith*s were recognised by the leading exponents of the networks as their intellectual and spiritual precursors.

As for the *mujaddid* of the tenth century AH/sixteenth century CE, al-'Aẓīmābādī follows al-Muḥibbī,[56] who chose Shams al-Dīn al-Ramlī, the great Egyptian *muḥaddith*, who was a teacher of Aḥmad al-Shinnāwī. In the twelfth century AH/eighteenth century CE, according to al-'Aẓīmābādī, there were two *mujaddid*s: the first was the great lexicographer, theologian and historian Murtaḍā al-Zabīdī (d. 1205/1791), and the second was the West African *muḥaddith* who settled in Medina, Ṣāliḥ b. Muḥammad al-Fullānī (d. 1218/1803-1804). These two scholars were among the most prominent personages in the international networks of *'ulamā'* in the eighteenth century.

Why is Ibrāhīm al-Kūrānī chosen as the *mujaddid* of the eleventh century of the Islamic calendar? According to al-Kattānī, al-Kūrānī was a Shaykh al-Islam and a teacher of the scholarly world, who was a 'proof of Sufism' (*ḥujjat al-ṣūfiyyah*) and a reviver of the Sunnī mystical tradition. Furthermore, he was one of the scholars most responsible in Islamic history for spreading the science of *ḥadīth* studies, *ḥadīth* narration and its *isnād*s in the Muslim world.[57] Al-Zarkalī credits al-Kūrānī with being a leading *mujtahid* among the Shāfi'ī *fuqahā'* and *muḥaddith*s.[58]

Burhān al-Dīn Ibrāhīm b. Ḥasan b. Shihāb al-Dīn al-Kūrānī al-Shahrazūrī al-Shahrānī al-Kurdī, later also al-Madanī, was born in Shahrīn, a village in the mountainous region of Kurdistan close to the borders of Persia.[59] Our sources provide no account of his background. Al-Kūrānī initially studied Arabic, *kalām* ('theology'), *manṭiq* (logic) and philosophy and, curiously enough, also *handasah* ('engineering') in his own region (*quṭr*). Thus, in his early studies, he had already explored various sophisticated subjects, but he seems to have had a special interest in languages. He pursued rather detailed studies of Arabic, such as *ma'āni* and *bayān* and at the same time studied Persian and Turkish. He later concentrated on *uṣūl fiqh*, *fiqh*, *ḥadīth* and *taṣawwuf*, mainly under the guidance of al-Mulā Muḥammad Sharīf al-Kūrānī al-Ṣiddīqī (d. 1078/1667).[60]

After the death of his father, Ibrāhīm al-Kūrānī left for Mecca to perform the *ḥajj* pilgrimage. The younger brother who travelled with him became gravely ill, which instead caused him to go to Baghdad. He remained there for a year and a half and took this opportunity to advance his knowledge of Arabic and Persian as well as to observe more closely the practice of the Qādiriyyah *ṭarīqah*. Al-Kūrānī met 'Abd al-Qādir al-Jaylānī in one of his dreams. He was going westward, and al-Kūrānī followed him to Damascus, where he lived for the next four years. During this period he became increasingly interested in mystical doctrines, particularly in that of Ibn 'Arabī (562-638/1165-1240). His main teacher in Sufism was Muḥammad b. Muḥammad al-'Amirī al-Ghazī. But, as he told al-Ḥamawī, it was al-Qushāshī, whom he met later in Medina, who was mostly responsible for instilling understanding in him of the intricate mystico-philosophical doctrine of Ibn 'Arabī.[61]

Despite his growing fascination with Sufism, Ibrāhīm al-Kūrānī did not put aside his genuine interest in *ḥadīth*. For that reason, he travelled to Egypt in 1061/1650, where he studied *ḥadīth* with its great *muḥaddith*s, such as Muḥammad 'Alā' al-Dīn Shams al-Dīn al-Bābilī al-Qāhirī al-Azharī (1000-1077/1592-1666),[62] Aḥmad Shihāb al-Dīn al-Khafājī al-Ḥanafī al-Maṣrī (d. 1069/1659)[63] and Shaykh Sulṭān b. Aḥmad b. Salāmah b. Ismā'il al-Mazzāḥī al-Qāhirī al-Azharī (987-1075/1577-1644).[64] As al-Kūrānī tells us in his *al-Umam li Īqāẓ al-Himam*, these scholars issued him *ijāzah*s to teach *ḥadīth*, after he had studied with them not only the standard books on the subject, such as the *Kutub al-Sittah* (six canonical books of the Tradition of the Prophet), but also a great number of lesser-known *ḥadīth* books. They connected him with many leading Egyptian *isnād*s, including Shams al-Dīn al-Ramlī and Zakariyyā al-Anṣārī.[65] It is important to note that al-Kūrānī was also linked to the Egyptian *isnād*s by way of al-Qushāshī, who received them from al-Shinnāwī, who in turn got them from his teacher, Shams al-Dīn al-Ramlī. In addition to *ḥadīth*, he studied *tafsīr* (until 1087/1677) with the Azhar Imām, Nūr al-Dīn 'Alī al-Shabrāmalisī, and 'Abd al-Raḥmān Shihādha al-Yamanī.[66]

In 1062/1651 Ibrāhīm al-Kūrānī returned to Mecca and then proceeded to Medina, where he attended the *ḥalqah*s of al-Qushāshī and 'Abd al-Karīm b. Abī Bakr al-Kūrānī, among others. He was also appointed by al-Qushāshī as his *khalīfah* in the Shaṭṭāriyyah order. Despite this, al-Kūrānī was better known as a shaykh of the Naqshbandiyyah order. Later he taught in the Nabawī Mosque at the site where Ṣibghat Allāh, Aḥmad al-Shinnāwī and Aḥmad al-Balkhī had taught. Al-Kūrānī, as al-Ḥamawī tells us, devoted his *ḥalqah*s to teaching *ḥadīth*, *fiqh*, *tafsīr*, and *taṣawwuf*. The books he used in his *ḥalqah*s were, among others, the *Kutub al-Sittah*, and standard works by such scholars as al-Suyūṭī, al-Ghazālī and Ibn 'Arabī.[67]

Because of his intellectual distinction and personality, al-Kūrānī attracted scholars and students from distant parts of the Muslim world to attend his *ḥalqah*s or *majlis* to study and learn from him. As a friend and a teacher he was extraordinarily humble. He loved to intermingle with his students. Furthermore, instead of simply swamping them with all the necessary sciences, he preferred to discuss them. To be present in his *majlis* was like, as al-Ḥamawī puts it, being in 'one of the gardens of paradise' (*rawḍah min riyāḍ al-jannah*).[68]

Our sources do not tell us the exact number of al-Kūrānī's students. But al-Kattānī points out that practically all seekers after *'ilm* during his time in the Ḥaramayn were his students. Therefore, his networks were enormously extensive.[69] The best known among his disciples were Ibn 'Abd al-Rasūl al-Barzanjī, Aḥmad al-Nakhlī (1044-1130/1639-1701),[70] Muḥammad 'Abd al-Hādī al-Sindī or Abū al-Ḥasan al-Sindī al-Kabīr (d. 1138/1726),[71] 'Abd Allāh b. Sa'd Allāh al-Lāhūrī (d. in Medina in 1083/1673),[72] 'Abd Allāh al-Baṣrī (1048-1134/1638-1722),[73] Abū Ṭāhir b. Ibrāhīm al-Kūrānī (1081–1145/1670–1732),[74] 'Alī al-Shaybānī al-Zabīdī (d. 1072/1662),[75] Isḥāq b. Muḥammad b. Ja'mān al-Yamānī (d. 1096/1685),[76] al-Sinkīlī 1024–1105/1615–93) and al-Maqassārī (1037–1111/1627–99).

Al-Kūrānī wrote prolifically which added to his intellectual importance in the networks. He is said to have written at least 100 works;[77] al-Baghdādī provides 49 titles,[78] while Brockelmann lists 42 of them.[79] Most of his texts deal with *ḥadīth*, *fiqh*, *tawḥīd* (and *kalām*), *tafsīr* and *taṣawwuf*. In addition, he wrote a number of works that were intended to be his reply or explanation of certain problems either directly posed to him or contained in particular writings of other scholars. Although many of his works are available in manuscript form, so far only two have been published.[80]

So far our discussion has centred on the networks in Medina. This does not mean that those of Mecca were not important. Before discussing the networks in Mecca, it should be remembered that even though all the great scholars mentioned earlier had settled and taught in Medina, they regularly visited Mecca. During these visits they made contact with other scholars and taught students as well. We should not underestimate the significance of such contacts in the scholarly networks: they were an important means of exchanging information on various issues and, more importantly, of linking scholars. And for students like al-Sinkīlī, contacts with a number of great *'ulamā'* in the networks significantly contributed to their learning. A great scholar of enormous importance in connecting scholars both in Mecca and Medina with Egyptian *ḥadīth* scholarship was Muḥammad b. 'Alā' al-Dīn al-Bābilī al-Qāhirī al-Azharī (d. 1077/1666). He was a disciple of Shams al-Dīn al-Ramlī, Abū Bakr al-Shinnāwī, and a number of other leading Egyptian scholars.[81] Both Shams al-Dīn al-Ramlī and al-Bābilī have been mentioned as teachers of Aḥmad al-Shinnāwī and al-Kūrānī respectively. He was acclaimed as a superior *isnād* and as one of the most reliable memorisers of the *ḥadīth*s (*al-ḥāfiẓ*). He was even compared to the ḥāfiẓ Ibn ḥajar al-'Asqalānī. Murtaḍā al-Zabīdī, another ḥāfiẓ of *ḥadīth*s, maintains that there were no other great ḥāfiẓs except al-Bābilī after the death of the ḥāfiẓ and historian al-Sakhāwī in 902/1497. As a testimony to al-Bābilī's eminent position in *ḥadīth* studies, Murtaḍā al-Zabīdī wrote two works, entitled *al-Murabbī al-Kamilī fī man rawā 'an al-Bābilī* and *al-Fajr al-Bābilī fī Tarjamat al-Bābilī*.[82]

Hailed as a major *muḥaddith* in the seventeenth century, 'Alā' al-Dīn al-Bābilī travelled to various cities in Arabia and thus had extensive networks of colleagues and disciples.[83] Later, he mostly lived in his home town, Bābil, and held a teaching post in the Ṣalāhiyyah Madrasah until his death. But he regularly visited the Ḥaramayn, where he performed the *ḥajj* and stayed for a while to establish contact with prominent scholars there as well as to teach. The best known among his students were in Mecca, Aḥmad al-Nakhlī and Ḥasan al-'Ajamī and, in Medina, al-Kūrānī. Al-Sinkīlī tells us that he also came into contact with this eminent scholar. Al-Bābilī was a very dedicated teacher, who preferred to meet students in person rather than by way of writing. Although he actually discouraged writing, he wrote a work entitled *al-Jiḥād wa Faḍā'ilih*.[84]

Another great scholar who played a remarkable role in connecting the scholarly networks in Mecca, this time with the Indian tradition of Sufism, was Tāj al-Dīn b. Zakariyyā b. Sulṭān al-'Uthmānī al-Naqshbandī al-Hindī (d. in Mecca in 1052/1642). He hailed from Sambhal, India, and immigrated to Mecca when he was unable to secure the position of highest-ranking master in the Indian Naqshbandiyyah order after the death of Muḥammad Bāqī bi Allāh (971-1012/1563-1603).[85]

In Mecca, Tāj al-Dīn al-Hindī succeeded in initiating a number of prominent Ḥaramayn scholars into the Naqshbandiyyah *ṭarīqah*, the most prominent being Aḥmad b. Ibrāhīm b. 'Alān (d. 1033/1624), a noted Meccan *ṣūfī* and *muḥaddith*, and Aḥmad al-Nakhlī. These two disciples largely helped the Naqshbandiyyah become more commendable to the Arabs. Thanks to Ibn 'Alan's prestige and influence in the Ḥaramayn, Tāj al-Dīn al-Hindī's translation of Persian Naqshbandiyyah texts into Arabic could win a much wider audience.[86] As for al-Nakhlī, who was also known as a *muḥaddith*, such a connection helped not only to bring about the Naqshbandiyyah reorientation but to link the community of *ḥadīth* scholars to the *ṣūfī*s. He had also *silsilah*s of the Naqshbandiyyah and Shaṭṭāriyyah from Sayyid Mīr Kalāl b. Maḥmūd al-Balkhī, connecting him to Ṣibghat Allāh.[87]

Scholars from the Maghrib region played a substantial role in the networks. Like the Egyptian scholars mentioned earlier, they were responsible for introducing the North African tradition of *ḥadīth* studies and thus for strengthening the intellectual trends of returning to a more *sharī'ah*-oriented Islam. There were two prominent Maghribī scholars whose names have been mentioned in passing: 'Isā b. Muḥammad al-Maghribī al-Ja'farī al-Tha'ālibī al-Maghribī (1020-80/1611-69), and Muḥammad b. Sulaymān al-Raddānī al-Maghribī al-Makkī (1037-94/1626-83). By settling down in Mecca, they not only brought the North African tradition of *ḥadīth* scholarship to the Ḥaramayn but also helped create more linkages among scholars from many regions of the Muslim world. Considering their important roles in the scholarly networks, we will now examine them briefly.

'Isā al-Maghribī, later also al-Makkī, traced his ancestors to Ja'far b. Abī Ṭālib, a cousin of the Prophet Muhammad. He spent most of his early years studying with local *'ulamā'* in his home town in the al-Jazāirī region.[88] Of all branches of Islamic science, he was particularly interested in *fiqh* and *ḥadīth*. For this reason he first travelled to Algiers, where he studied *ḥadīth* and other Islamic religious sciences, mostly with its *Muftī*, Sa'īd b. Ibrāhīm Qaddūrah. After continuing his studies in Tunis and other places in this region, he went for a pilgrimage to Mecca in 1062/1652. After the pilgrimage he extended his sojourn for one year at the Dāwūdiyyah *ribāṭ*, where he taught *ḥadīth* and *fiqh*. Again he went travelling, this time to Cairo, where he attended *ḥalqah*s of great Egyptian *'ulamā'* such as *Qāḍī* Aḥmad al-Shihāb al-Khafājī, Sulṭān al-Mazzāḥī and Nūr 'Alī al-Shabrāmalisī—all of whom were also teachers of al-Kūrānī.

Having gained from these *ijāzah* to teach and to relate *ḥadīth*, 'Isā al-Maghribī returned to Mecca. In the Holy City he exchanged knowledge and studied with prominent Ḥaramayn scholars, such as Tāj al-Dīn b. Ya'qūb al-Mālikī al-Makkī (d. 1066/1656),[89] Zayn al-'Ābidīn al-Ṭabarī (1002– 78/1594–1667),[90] 'Abd al-Azīz al-Zamzamī (997–1072/1589–1662)[91] and 'Alī al-Jamāl al-Makkī (1002-72/1594-1661).[92] All of these scholars also authorised him to *ḥadīth*s through their *isnād*s, which mostly began with 'Alā' al-Dīn al-Bābilī.

The significance of 'Isā al-Maghribī in the scholarly communities of the Ḥaramayn cannot be overestimated. He was acclaimed as one of the most prominent Mālikī legal scholars in his time. In the Holy Cities he was known by the honorary title '*Imām al-Ḥaramayn*'. He taught at the Holy Mosques in Mecca and Medina. As al-Qannūjī tells us, he attracted many Ḥaramayn students to attend his *ḥalqah*s. Ibrāhīm al-Kūrānī, Ḥasan al-'Ajamī and Aḥmad al-Nakhlī were among his best-known students. Al-Sinkīlī, as we will see later, also established contact with 'Isā al-Maghribī while he was studying in Mecca. At a certain period every year, 'Isā al-Maghribī taught in Medina, where he had a warm friendship with Aḥmad al-Qushāshī.[93]

All biographers of 'Isā al-Maghribī are in accord that he was of great importance in connecting the tradition of *ḥadīth* studies in the Maghrib region and Egypt with that of the Ḥaramayn. The scope of his narration (*riwāyah*) was wide; as al-Kattānī puts it, 'nobody was more learned than he in these matters during his time'. Because of his extensive travels, Murtaḍā al-Zabīdī believes that al-Maghribī was a '*musnad al-dunyā*' (*ḥadīth* narrator for the world).[94] These claims find their support in one of al-Maghribī's own works, entitled *Kanz al-Riwāyat al-Majmū' fī Durar al-Majāz wa Yawāqit al-Masmū'*. This work consists of two volumes and, as its title indicates, is indeed of the *ḥadīth* narration. In it, al-Maghribī lists his *ḥadīth* teachers, and more importantly draws a picture of their complex connections with one another. In addition, he provides the titles of the books that were produced by scholars involved in these *ḥadīth* networks.[95] The *Kanz al-Riwāyat*, therefore, is an important work which sheds more light on the role of *ḥadīth* narration in the growth of the scholarly networks.

In terms of his educational background our next scholar, Muḥammad b. Sulaymān al-Raddānī al-Maghribī, was not so very different from his countryman, 'Isā al-Maghribī. But in contrast to 'Isā al-Maghribī, who preferred to lead a quiet life, Sulaymān al-Maghribī was an outspoken scholar; he had a strong tendency to exercise his religious influence in the political realm. As al-Sibā'ī points out, he was the only scholar in Mecca who dared to speak out against the abuse of power among the ruling Sharīfian family, with their continuous struggles among themselves. He also attempted to bring about radical changes in the religious life of the Holy City. His close relations with the Ottoman ruling elite gave him additional weight in launching his reforms in Mecca.[96]

After studying in his home region, Sulaymān al-Maghribī travelled to al-Jazair and Egypt, where he learned from leading *'ulamā'*, such as Shaykh al-Islām Sa'īd b. Ibrāhīm Qaddūrah, Aḥmad al-Khafājī, 'Alā' al-Dīn al-Bābilī and Shaykh Sulṭān al-Mazzāḥī. These same men, as mentioned earlier, were also the teachers of Ibrāhīm al-Kūrānī and 'Isā al-Maghribī. In 1079/1668 Sulaymān al-Maghribī travelled to the Ḥaramayn, where he remained for two years. After long travels to Istanbul and other cities in Turkey, Syria, Palestine and Lebanon, he finally returned to Mecca. There he built what was known as the Ibn Sulaymān *ribāṭ*. However, he did not confine his activities to scholarly and religious matters: he was also occupied with public affairs, which led to open conflicts with the Sharīfs of Mecca.[97] As a result, he was expelled from

Mecca and died in Damascus. We return to Sulaymān al-Maghribī's activism in the next section.

In addition to his activism, Sulaymān al-Maghribī was known as a distinguished *muḥaddith* with strong links to superior *isnāds* in *ḥadīth* narration. Among his works, two were devoted to *ḥadīth* studies: *Jam' al-Fawā'id fī al-Ḥadīth*, and *Ṣilat al-Khalaf bi Mawṣūl al-Salaf*. In these works the author described, among other things, his connections with a number of earlier prominent muḥaddīths, such as Ibn Ḥajar, and the *ḥadīth* books he studied.[98] The biographical accounts of Sulaymān al-Maghribī do not explicitly mention the names of his students in the Ḥaramayn. However, according to al-Muhibbī (1061-1111/1651-99), the author of *Khulāṣat al-Athar*, who was himself a student of Sulaymān al-Maghribī, the latter had numerous students in the Ḥaramayn, including Aḥmad al-Nakhlī and Ḥasan al-'Ajamī.[99] And, as al-Kattānī shows us, Sulaymān al-Maghribī had vast connections by way of *ḥadīth* studies with his contemporaries and later scholars in the networks.[100]

So far, we have seen that many leading scholars in the seventeenth century networks were 'grand immigrants'. This does not mean that native scholars from the Ḥaramayn did not play an important role in this cosmopolitan scholarly community. There were in fact a number of native scholars of Mecca and Medina who took part actively in the networks in the seventeenth and eighteenth centuries.

One of the leading scholars of Meccan origin was Tāj al-Dīn b. Aḥmad, better known as Ibn Ya'qūb. He was born in Mecca, where he died in 1066/1656. He studied primarily in Mecca with its leading scholars, such as 'Abd al-Qādir al-Ṭabarī, 'Abd al-Mulūk al-'Asāmī and Khālid al-Mālikī, who issued *ijāzah* for him to teach in the Ḥarām Mosque. Ibn Ya'qūb had close relationships with scholars involved in the networks, particularly with 'Isā al-Maghribī. Similarly, his connections through *ḥadīth* studies were extensive. Known as an expert on the *sharī'ah*, *kalām* and *taṣawwuf*, Ibn Ya'qūb was later appointed to the office of the *Qāḍī al-Quḍāh* of Mecca. In addition to this position, he taught in several madrasahs in Mecca. He was a prolific writer on various topics from Arabic to Sufism. As we shall see, one of his works was devoted to answering religious questions from Malay-Indonesian Muslims.[101]

Another important scholar of Meccan origin was Zayn al-'Ābidīn al-Ṭabarī (1002-78/1594-1667), a leading scholar of the Ṭabarī family in Mecca. This family traced their ancestors to 'Alī b. Abī Ṭālib. Zayn al-'Ābidīn's principal teacher was his own father, 'Abd al-Qādir b. Muḥammad b. Yahyā al-Ṭabarī (976-1033/1568-1624). But it is clear that Zayn al-'Ābidīn was also involved in scholarly discourses with other prominent scholars in the Ḥaramayn. By virtue of the scholarly reputation of his family, he was able not only to gain a great deal of benefit from many prominent scholars in the Ḥaramayn but also to assert his own role and that of the Ṭabarī family in the networks. Being a *muḥaddith* of distinction in Mecca, Zayn al-'Ābidīn was a teacher of the next generation of scholars, including Ḥasan al-'Ajamī, Aḥmad al-Nakhlī, 'Abd Allāh al-Baṣrī and Abū Ṭāhir al-Kūrānī.[102]

It is worth noting that Zayn al-'Ābidīn's father, 'Abd al-Qādir al-Ṭabarī (976-1033/1568-1624), was also a major scholar: he was a *muḥaddith*, whose *isnāds* included great traditionists like Shams al-Dīn al-Ramlī, Zakariyyā al-Anṣārī and Jalāl al-Dīn al-Suyūṭī. He also inherited the Meccan scholarly tradition from the Ẓahīrah family, mentioned earlier. Thus, 'Abd al-Qādir was a scholar of special importance in connecting the scholarly networks of an earlier period with those under discussion here. 'Abd al-Qādir was also a historian of Mecca: several of his numerous works were devoted to exploring the history of Mecca.[103]

Another son of 'Abd al-Qādir, 'Alī (d. 1070/1660), was also a noted scholar, especially in *fiqh*. With an expertise in this field he was often asked to give religious opinions (*fatwās*) on various matters. Like his brother, Zayn al-'Ābidīn, in addition to studying with his father he gained a great deal of benefit from scholars in the Ḥaramayn. If Zayn al-'Ābidīn inherited his father's expertise in *ḥadīth*, 'Alī took over his father's talent as an historian. Thus, 'Alī wrote several works on the history of Mecca and its notables.[104] As we shall see later, 'Alī al-Ṭabarī was also one of al-Sinkīlī's teachers.

It is obvious that the Ṭabarī family played a significant role in scholarly discourse in the Ḥaramayn. Al-Sibā'ī points out that the three Ṭabarī scholars mentioned above revived the reputation of the Ṭabarī family as an old scholarly family in Mecca. A daughter of 'Abd al-Qādir al-Ṭabarī, named Sayyidah Mubārakah, was also a noted scholar.[105] The Ṭabarī family continued to maintain its eminence in subsequent periods. One such well-known later Ṭabarī scholar was Muḥammad b. al-Muḥibb al-Ṭabarī (1100–73/1689– 1760), a faqīh and an historian.[106]

The list of scholars involved in the networks in the second half of the seventeenth century is a very long one. For the purpose of our discussion, it suffices to say that all the scholars discussed above played major roles in the networks during the period. We will, however, mention other scholars of this generation whenever necessary throughout this discussion.

SCHOLARS AT THE TURN OF THE EIGHTEENTH CENTURY

Most scholars of Ibrāhīm al-Kūrānī's generation died in the second half of the seventeenth century. But the chain of the networks continued with their students who, in turn, became crucial links to scholars into the eighteenth century. These students were generally at the peak of their scholarly careers at the turn of the seventeenth century or in the early decades of the eighteenth century. We now deal briefly with some of the most prominent among these scholars (see Chart 2).

There is no doubt that Ḥasan b. 'Alī b. Muḥammad b. 'Umar al-'Ajamī (العجمي) some spell his name al-'Ujaymī (العجيمي) al-Makkī, was one of these prominent scholars at the turn of the seventeenth century. He was also

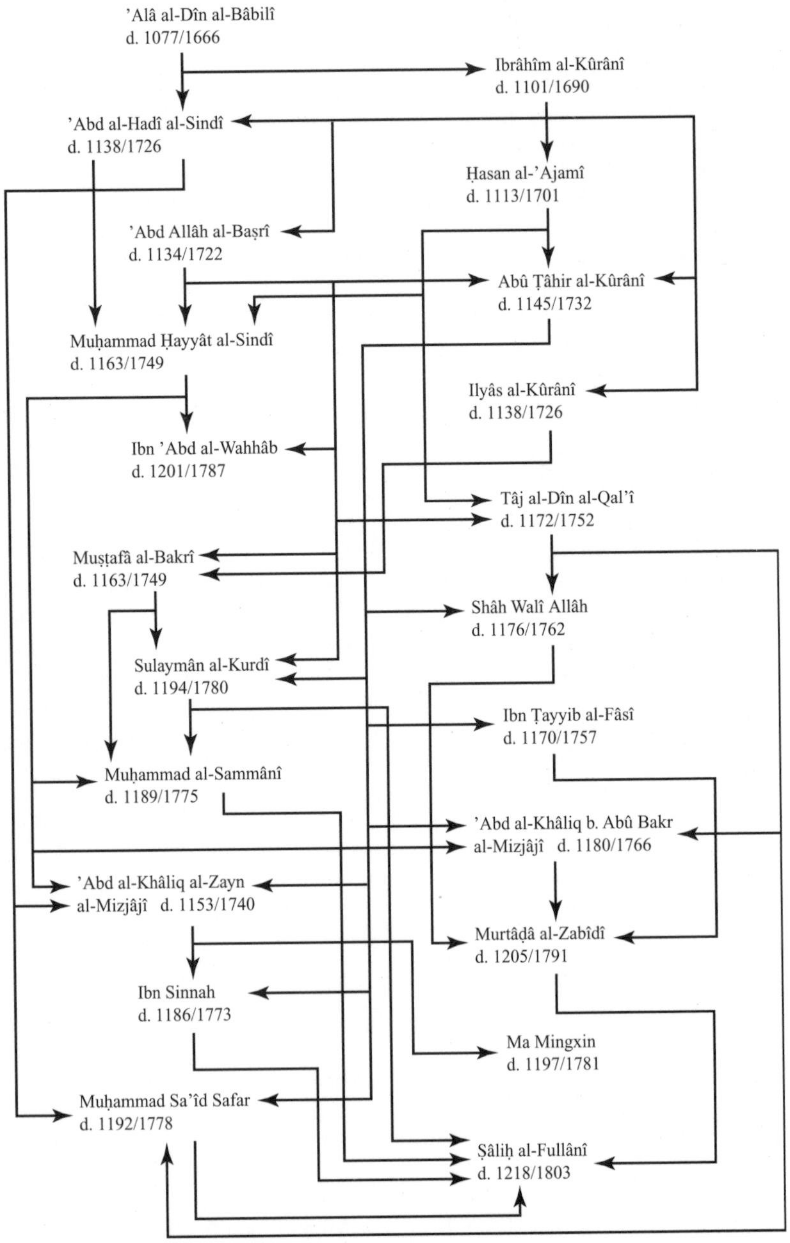

Chart 2 The core of the eighteenth century networks

known as *'Abū al-Asrār'* ('father of spiritual mysteries'). Born in Mecca, Ḥasan al-'Ajamī hailed from a noted scholarly family in Egypt. His great grandfather, Muḥammad b. 'Abd al-Majīd al-'Ajamī (d. 822/1419), was a well-known scholar in Cairo. Ḥasan al-'Ajamī studied with virtually every leading scholar in the Ḥaramayn. In addition to al-Qushāshī and al-Kūrānī, he studied with prominent scholars such as 'Alā' al-Dīn al-Bābilī, 'Abd al-Qādir and Zayn al-'Ābidīn al-Ṭabarī, 'Isā al-Maghribī, 'Alī al-Shabrāmalisī, Sa'īd al-Lāhūrī, 'Abd al-Raḥīm al-Khāṣṣ and Ibrāhīm b. 'Abd Allāh Ja'mān. The last two, as we will see later, were also teachers of al-Sinkīlī. It is certain that Ḥasan al-'Ajamī possessed a thorough knowledge of various branches of Islamic discipline. He was renowned as an outstanding faqīh, *muḥaddith*, *ṣūfī* and historian. In *ḥadīth* studies, al-Kattānī regards him as one of the few scholars in his time blessed by God to be a 'lighthouse of the *ḥadīth*'. He died in Ṭā'if in 1113/1701-2.[107]

Ḥasan al-'Ajamī played an important role in connecting the scholarly networks in the seventeenth century with those of the eighteenth century, particularly by way of *ḥadīth* studies and *ṭarīqah silsilah*s. He was a meeting point of various traditions of *ḥadīth* studies: Syria, Egypt, the Maghrib, the Ḥijāz, Yemen and the Indian subcontinent. It is not surprising, as al-Kattānī points out, that students in the Ḥaramayn did not feel satisfied in their *ḥadīth* studies until they had met and received *ḥadīth*s from him. They flocked to his *ḥalqah*s in proximity to the Gate of al-Wadā' and the Gate of Umm Hānī' at the Ḥarām Mosque in Mecca.[108] As a result, al-'Ajamī's *isnād*s and narrations of *ḥadīth* were extensive.[109]

To demonstrate the importance of the connections in the *ṭarīqah*s, Ḥasan al-'Ajamī wrote a special work, entitled *Risālat al-'Ajamī fī al-Ṭuruq*, which deals with the *silsilah*s of 40 *ṭarīqah*s that existed in the Muslim world up until his time.[110] In this work, in addition to discussing special distinctions of the teachings of each *ṭarīqah* the author provides the *silsilah*s to shaykhs of the *ṭarīqah*s and the benefits of affiliating with them. This is one of the main reasons why al-'Ajamī was also known as 'Abū al-Asrār'. By virtue of his works, the *Risālat al-'Ajamī fī al-Ṭuruq* together with the *Ihdā' al-Laṭā'if min Akhbār al-Ṭā'if*, al-'Ajamī established himself as a historian in his own right.

Ḥasan al-'Ajamī's best known disciples were, among others, Muḥammad Ḥayyāt al-Sindī (d. 1163/1653), Abū Ṭāhir b. Ibrāhīm al-Kūrānī (1081-1145/1670-1732), Tāj al-Dīn al-Qal'ī, *Qāḍī* of Mecca,[111] al-Maqassārī and the historian Fatḥ Allāh al-Ḥamāwī. Ḥasan al-'Ajamī built the reputation of the 'Ajamīs as a noted scholarly family in Mecca. Among the most prominent members of the 'Ajamī family in later periods were 'Abd al-Ḥafīẓ al-'Ajamī, Muftī of Mecca; Muḥammad b. Ḥusayn al-'Ajamī; and Abū al-Fatḥ al-'Ajamī.[112]

The next scholar worth mentioning was Muḥammad b. 'Abd al-Rasūl al-Barzanjī. Tracing his ancestors to 'Alī b. Abī Ṭālib, he was born in

Shahrazūr, Kurdistan. He acquired his early education in his own region and later travelled to Iraq, Syria, the Ḥaramayn and Egypt. His teachers in the Ḥaramayn included al-Mulā Muḥammad Sharīf al-Kūrānī, Ibrāhim al-Kūrānī, Isḥāq b. Ja'mān al-Zabīdī, 'Isā al-Maghribī and several other scholars. While he was in Egypt, al-Barzanjī studied with, among others, 'Alā' al-Dīn al-Bābilī, Nūr al-Dīn al-Shabrāmalisī and Sulṭān al-Mazzāḥī.[113]

After studying in Egypt, al-Barzanjī returned to the Ḥaramayn, and later settled in Medina, where he died. He was a noted *muḥaddith*, *faqīh* and shaykh of the Qādiriyyah order. He devoted his life to teaching and writing. He was a prolific writer: al-Baghdādī lists 52 of his works, two of which were devoted to refuting Aḥmad Sirhindī's claim to be the 'renewer of the Second Millennium of Islam'. Al-Barzanjī's connections in the networks were far-reaching.[114] Al-Barzanjī was the earliest scholar of the Barzanjī family to settle down and become famous in the Ḥaramayn. One of the most prominent scholars of the Barzanjī family in Medina after 'Abd al-Rasūl al-Barzanjī was Ja'far b. Ḥasan b. 'Abd al-Karīm al-Barzanjī (1103-80/1690-1766), the Shāfi'ī *Muftī* in Medina and author of the *'Iqd al-Jawāhir*, a famous text relating to the celebration of the birthday of the Prophet.[115]

Aḥmad b. Muḥammad b. Aḥmad 'Alī al-Nakhlī al-Makkī was also evidently one of the most prominent scholars in the networks after the generation of Ibrāhīm al-Kūrānī. He was born and studied mostly in Mecca and became known as a *muḥaddith-ṣūfī*.[116] In his work entitled *Bughyat al-Ṭālibīn li Bayān al-Mashā'ikh al-Muḥaqqiqīn al-Mu'tamidīn*, al-Nakhlī provides a complete list of his teachers, his *isnād*s in various branches of Islamic discipline, and his *silsilah* in a number of *ṭarīqah*s.

It is of particular importance that, in the *Bughyat al-Ṭālibīn*, al-Nakhlī also gives an account of the learning at the Ḥarām Mosque of Mecca. For instance, he tells us that he attended lectures held in the *halqah*s in proximity to the Gate of Peace (*Bāb al-Salām*). Lectures were given by his teachers every day after the *Ṣubḥ* (dawn), *'Aṣr* (afternoon), *Maghrib* (sunset) and *'Ishā'* (night) prayers. It was in the *ḥalqah*s that he received some of his *ijāzah*s in the exterior sciences—such as *sharī'ah* or *fiqh*—and was initiated into several *ṭarīqah*s: the Shādhiliyyah, Nawawiyyah, Qādiriyyah, Naqshbandiyyah, Shaṭṭāriyyah and Khalwatiyyah. And it was also in the Ḥarām Mosques that he most of the time practised the *dhikr* of these *ṭarīqah*s.[117]

Like al-'Ajamī and al-Barzanjī, al-Nakhlī studied with most of the leading Ḥaramayn scholars of his time. The list of his masters includes 'Alā' al-Dīn al-Bābilī, al-Qushāshī, al-Kūrānī, Tāj al-Dīn al-Hindī, 'Isā al-Maghribī, Muḥammad 'Alī b. 'Alān al-Ṣiddīqī, Zayn al-'Ābidīn al-Ṭabarī, 'Abd al-'Azīz al-Zamzamī and 'Alī al-Jamāl al-Makkī. Al-Nakhlī also had numerous teachers from Egypt, the Maghribī region, Syria and Iraq. Thus, as Murtaḍā al-Zabīdī correctly puts it, al-Nakhlī linked numerous scholars by way of his *ḥadīth* studies.[118] Likewise, his students came from various parts of the Muslim world and carried the networks even further.[119]

Another important scholar who belonged to the group discussed under this heading was 'Abd Allāh b. Sālim b. Muḥammad b. Sālim b. 'Isā al-Baṣrī al-Makkī. He was born and died in Mecca. As one can see in al-Baṣrī's own work, *Kitāb al-Imdād bi Ma'rifah 'Uluw al-Isnād*, his education was thorough; he studied many sciences, including *ḥadīth*, *tafsīr*, *fiqh*, the history of the Prophet (*sirah*), Arabic and *taṣawwuf*. In the *Kitāb al-Imdād*, he devotes long pages to providing the titles of *ḥadīth* books he has studied, along with the *isnād*s to each of them. He goes on to mention books in other fields. As for *taṣawwuf*, he studied books written by such scholars as al-Ghazālī, al-Qushayrī, Ibn 'Atā' Allāh and Ibn 'Arabī.[120]

Though al-Baṣrī was an expert in various branches of Islamic science, he was mainly known as a great *muḥaddith*; he was called an *Amīr al-Mu'minīn fī al-Ḥadīth* ('commander of the believers in the *ḥadīth*'). Al-Sibā'ī points out that al-Baṣrī was one of the greatest *ḥadīth* teachers in the Ḥarām Mosque in the early eighteenth century.[121] Through the *Kitāb al-Imdād* he contributed significantly to *ḥadīth* studies by providing the names of scholars who were included among the superior *isnād*s. But like other scholars in the networks, al-Baṣrī was an eminent *ṣūfī*. He was a master of several *ṭarīqah*s, such as the Naqshbandiyyah, Shādhiliyyah and Nawawiyyah. Furthermore, he established the reputation of the Baṣrī family in the scholarly discourses in the Ḥaramayn.[122]

Al-Baṣrī played an important role in connecting the earlier generation of seventeenth century scholars and later networks. This can be seen in the composition of his teachers and disciples. Besides Ibrāhīm al-Kūrānī, his principal teachers included such familiar names as 'Alā' al-Dīn al-Bābilī, 'Isā al-Ja'farī al-Maghribī, Sulaymān al-Maghribī and 'Alī al-Ṭabarī. Among his disciples were 'Alā' al-Dīn b. 'Abd al-Bāqī al-Mizjājī al-Zabīdī, Abū Ṭāhir al-Kūrānī, Muḥammad Ḥayyāt al-Sindī and Muḥammad b. 'Abd al-Wahhāb, all of whom, as we will see shortly, were leading exponents of the networks in the eighteenth century.[123]

The last scholar to be dealt with here is Abū Ṭāhir b. Ibrāhīm al-Kūrānī (1081-1145/1670-1733). Abū Ṭāhir was born and died in Medina. It appears that he studied mostly in the Ḥaramayn. His principal teachers were his father, Ibrāhīm al-Kūrānī, Sulaymān al-Maghribī, Ḥasan al-'Ajamī, Ibn 'Abd al-Rasūl al-Barzanjī, 'Abd Allāh al-Baṣrī and Aḥmad al-Nakhlī. We have no detailed information on his studies with them, but there is no doubt that his religious learning was thorough.[124]

Abū Ṭāhir was primarily known as a *muḥaddith*, but he was also a *faqīh* and a *ṣūfī*. He was heir to much of his father's expertise in *ḥadīth* studies. As a faqīh, he occupied the post of Shāfi'ī *Muftī* of Medina for some time. He was a prolific writer as well. According to al-Kattānī, he wrote about a hundred treatises, the most important among them being *Kanz al-'Amal fī Sunan al-Aqwāl* and *Shurūḥ al-Fuṣūṣ lī al-Shaykh al-Akbar*. This last work was apparently intended to explicate the doctrine of Ibn 'Arabī. It also reflects Abū Ṭāhir's learning in the realm of philosophical mysticism. Abū

Ṭāhir had wide connections in the networks, by way of both *ḥadīth isnād*s and *ṭarīqah silsilah*s. Among his best-known students were Muḥammad Ḥayyāt al-Sindī, Shāh Walī Allāh and Sulaymān al-Kurdī, all of whom are examined in greater detail in chapter 2.[125]

THE NETWORKS: BASIC CHARACTERISTICS

After discussing a number of the most important *'ulamā'* involved in the networks, it is useful to make some generalisations about the basic characteristics of the networks. The scholarly networks became increasingly extensive in the seventeenth century. It is clear that there had been some connections between earlier scholars and the ones who were involved in seventeenth century scholarly networks. However, networks that developed during the seventeenth century appear to have been much more complicated; the crisscrossing of linkages by way of both *ḥadīth* studies and *ṭarīqah* affiliations was enormously complex. Despite the historiographical problems one finds in sources of information on these scholars and their networks, their connections to one another can be traced down to our time.

The crisscrossing of scholars who were involved in the networks produced intertwined, international intellectual communities. Relations among them generally existed in conjunction with the quest for learning through religious educational institutions such as the mosques, madrasahs and *ribāṭ*s. The very basic linkages among them, therefore, were 'academic' in their nature. Their connections to each other, as a rule, took the form of teacher–student (or 'vertical') relationships. This academic linkage included other forms: teacher–teacher, which may also be termed 'horizontal links'; and student–student relations, all of which could also crisscross each other. Such forms of linkages were not strictly or formally organised in any kind of hierarchical structure. The relatively high mobility of both teachers and students allowed the growth of vast networks of scholars transcending geographical boundaries, ethnic origins and religious leanings.

Even though the relationships among scholars probably seem quite informal, especially from the point of view of the modern academic world, their common interest in regenerating the *ummah* (Muslim 'nation') stimulated cooperation, which in turn resulted in closer interpersonal relationships. These close personal relationships were maintained in various ways after scholars or students in the networks returned to their own countries or travelled elsewhere after their sojourn in the Ḥaramayn. The need to establish stronger ties with scholars in the centres was increasingly felt when the returning teachers and students faced problems in their homelands, thus needing the guidance of their former teachers and colleagues in the Ḥaramayn. All this helps to explain the continuing scholarly connections in the networks.

Furthermore, as we have seen, two important vehicles in solidifying the linkages of the networks were the *ḥadīth isnād* and *ṭarīqah silsilah*. Voll has pointed out that both played crucial roles in linking scholars involved in the networks centred in the Ḥaramayn in the eighteenth century.[126] My own research for the same period supports this conclusion.

The same was true of the seventeenth century scholarly networks. In this period, scholars of the networks brought together Egyptian and North African traditions of *ḥadīth* studies, thus connecting them with those of the Ḥaramayn, which had been known in the early period of Islam as the strongest centre of *ḥadīth* scholarship. The scholars in the networks played a crucial role in reviving the position of Mecca and Medina as centres of *ḥadīth* scholarship.

As for the *ṭarīqah silsilah*s, traditionally they had been an important means of creating close linkages between scholars. Disciples of the mystical way, by definition, must succumb to their master's will. This created a very strong bond between those who followed the *ṭarīqah*s. Voll[127] emphasises that this type of relationship 'provided a more personal tie and a common set of affiliations that helped to give the informal groupings of scholars a greater sense of cohesion'.

The increasing importance of the esoteric way (*ḥaqīqah*) in the Ḥaramayn, introduced for instance by South Asian scholars, resulted in bringing together scholars, who had mainly been associated with the exoteric way (*sharī'ah*), in an even more personal way. The involvement of South Asian scholars in the networks certainly helped widen the reach of the networks. But, not less importantly, they expanded the realm of influence of *ṭarīqah*s, in particular the Shaṭṭāriyyah and Naqshbandiyyah orders, previously mostly associated with the Indian subcontinent version of Sufism, which had been almost unknown in the Ḥaramayn in earlier periods. But it must be kept in mind that by entering the realm of Mecca and Medina which now, once again, had become important centres of *ḥadīth* scholarship, these *ṭarīqah*s, as we elaborate in chapter 2, underwent a sort of reorientation. In short, they became more '*sharī'ah*-oriented *ṭarīqah*s'.

One should also be aware that, despite their close relations, there was a great deal of diversity among scholars involved in the networks. They were different from each other in terms of not only their places of origin but also their *madhhab*s and *ṭarīqah* affiliations. While a certain teacher might be a Ḥanafī in terms of his adherence to Islamic legal doctrine, his student might be a Shāfi'ī. While a teacher might be a Shaṭṭāriyyah *ṣūfī*, his student might follow the path of the Naqshbandiyyah. Despite all these differences, however, they shared a general tendency towards Islamic reformism. This is discussed in greater detail in chapter 2.

2

Reformism in the Networks

A number of studies have been conducted on intellectual trends developed through scholarship in particular periods of Islamic history. However, never before has a study been done which examines the intellectual trends that grew out of the numerous *'ulamā'* who were linked to each other in loose scholarly networks such as those under discussion. They were different from one another not only in terms of their geographical backgrounds, which had their own 'little' Islamic traditions, but more importantly in their intellectual preferences, as reflected by their legal (*madhhab*) and *ṭarīqah* affiliations.

Furthermore, leading scholars in the networks, before settling down in the Ḥaramayn or elsewhere, had been peripatetic scholars, travelling from one centre of Islamic learning to another, studying with and learning from various teachers who had their own personal traditions of religious scholarship. Thus, scholars were influenced not by one single teacher but by many; they were exposed to and absorbed various lines of thought and intellectual tendencies. Because of this, describing the contents of teachings developed and transmitted by the scholarly networks is not easy. At this stage we will attempt to draw the broad outlines of the intellectual trends of the networks; this will perhaps help us comprehend the nature and characteristics of these scholarly networks.

In a certain sense the Ḥaramayn was a 'melting pot', where various 'little' traditions of Islam melded to form a 'new synthesis' which was strongly in favour of the 'great' tradition.[1] We have seen previously how scholars from the Indian subcontinent, for instance, carried their mystical traditions to the Ḥaramayn, while those from Egypt and North Africa came with an inheritance of *ḥadīth* scholarship. These traditions interacted with each other as well as with the tradition already established in the Ḥaramayn itself.

It must be kept in mind at the outset that what we call a 'new synthesis' is not entirely a new development in the history of Islamic social and intellectual traditions. Even though it has some distinctive characteristics, compared with the previous tradition, in many respects it also contains elements of continuity with earlier traditions. The return to the Sunnī orthodoxy that gained momentum after the twelfth century appears to reach its culmination in the period under discussion. This can be seen not only in the intellectual contents of the networks but also in their 'organisational' aspects, or more precisely the linkages among scholars. Thus, the revivalist spirit that inspired the establishment of *madrasah*s everywhere in the Middle East after the founding of the Niẓāmiyyah *madrasah* in 459/1066 continued to flourish in a variety of ways.

The salient feature of the scholarly networks is that the rapprochement between the *sharī'ah*-oriented *'ulamā'* (more specifically, the *fuqahā'*) and the *ṣūfī*s reached its climax. The long-standing conflict between these two groups of Muslim scholars appears to have greatly diminished; the rapprochement or reconciliation between them, which had been preached insistently by such scholars as al-Qushayrī and al-Ghazālī several centuries earlier, became a common goal among our scholars. Most of them were *ahl al-sharī'ah* (*fuqahā'*) and *ahl al-ḥaqīqah* (*ṣūfī*s) at the same time; thus, they were learned not only in the intricacies of the *sharī'ah* but also in the *ḥaqīqah* (mystical or Divine Realities). However, we should be very careful not to conclude that they took this reconciliation for granted; instead, they continued to nurture it.

The rapprochement between the *sharī'ah* and Sufism and the enrolment of the *'ulamā'* in the *ṭarīqah* resulted in the rise of 'neo-Sufism'. There has been considerable discussion on the meaning and use of the term 'neo-Sufism', which was coined by the late Fazlur Rahman.[2] According to Rahman, neo-Sufism is the reformed Sufism largely stripped of its ecstatic and metaphysical character and content, these being replaced by a content that was nothing other than the postulates of the orthodox religion.[3] As he explained, this new 'type' of Sufism emphasises and renews the original moral factor and puritanical self-control in Sufism at the expense of the extravagant features of the popular unorthodox Sufism. Neo-Sufism brings to the centre of attention the moral reconstruction of Muslim society, as contrasted with the earlier Sufism, which had primarily stressed the individual and not society.[4] As a consequence, Rahman concludes, the overall character of neo-Sufism is undoubtedly puritanical and activist.[5] We will now see more clearly how neo-Sufism developed in the networks.

NEO-SUFISM AND *ḤADĪTH* STUDY

Fazlur Rahman maintains that the most important group of Muslim scholars responsible for helping to crystallise the rise of neo-Sufism were the 'people of tradition' (*ahl al-ḥadīth*). He further argues that after the *ṣūfī* movement captured much of the Muslim world emotionally, spiritually and intellectually during the sixth/twelfth and seventh/thirteenth centuries, the traditionists found it impossible to neglect the *ṣūfī* forces entirely. Therefore, as Rahman puts it:

> they tried, in their methodology, to incorporate as much of the *ṣūfī* legacy as could be reconciled with orthodox Islam and could be made to yield a positive contribution towards it. First, the moral motive of Sufism was emphasised and some of its technique of *dhikr* or *murāqabah*, 'spiritual concentration', adopted. But the object and the content of this concentration were identified with the orthodox doctrine and the goal redefined as the strengthening of faith in dogmatic tenets and the moral purity of the spirit. This type of neo-Sufism tended to regenerate orthodox activism and reinculcate a positive attitude to this world.[6]

The Ḥaramayn, from the early years of Islam, had been known as the main centre of the *ḥadīth*. This is not hard to understand, as the Prophet, the source of the *ḥadīth*, lived and initiated Islam there. Furthermore, two of the four major schools of Islamic law, the Mālikī and the Ḥanbalī, known as *ahl al-ḥadīth*, had in fact initially developed and gained their stronghold in the Arabian Peninsula. It is true that the Mālikī *madhhab*, introduced by Mālik b. Anas (d. 179/795) in Medina, later became more dominant in North and West Africa and Upper Egypt, but the Ḥanbalīs also came to exercise a predominance in the Arabian Peninsula. Although the Ḥanbalīs are known for their strong reliance on *ḥadīth* and their refusal of rational philosophy and speculative mysticism, many accepted Sufism as long as it was practised in accordance with the *sharī'ah*. There is no evidence that such prominent Ḥanbalī scholars as Ibn Taymiyyah (d. 728/1328) and Ibn al-Qayyim al-Jawziyyah were opposed to all types of Sufism; what they fiercely attacked was unorthodox ecstatic and antinomian Sufism—that is, Sufism which regards itself free from injuction of *sharī'ah* or *fiqh*. For this reason, Fazlur Rahman considers them pioneers of neo-Sufism.[7]

There was also reluctance to accept Sufism among the *ahl al-ḥadīth* of the Mālikī *madhhab* in the North African region and Upper Egypt. The Maghribī Mālikīs in particular were more puritanical and, in some cases, also aggressive. It is well known that the early Egyptian (Nubian) *ṣūfī* Dhū al-Nūn al-Miṣrī (d. 245/859) was persecuted by the Egyptian Mālikī jurist 'Abd Allāh b. 'Abd al-Ḥakam;[8] al-Ghazālī's books were condemned and banned by the Mālikī *fuqahā'* of Spain,[9] and one of the fiercest attacks on Sufism in Egypt, particularly of the extravagant type, came from Ibn al-Ḥājj al-'Abdarī, a leading Mālikī *faqīh* in the fourteenth century.[10]

Again it is important to note that not all Mālikī scholars were hostile to Sufism. Some of them were even zealous *ṣūfī*s. A good example of this is 'Alī b. Maymūn (854–917/1450–1511), a noted Moroccan Mālikī, who was responsible for spreading a revivalist version of the Shādhiliyyah order in Syria. He regenerated the decadent Syrian Sufism by not allowing his disciples to isolate themselves in *khalwah* (seclusion) at the *khānqāh*.[11] It appears that when scholarly contacts and linkages between the Maghribī Mālikīs and scholars of other *madhhab*s gained momentum after the sixteenth century, some began to soften their tone of opposition to Sufism and joined other scholars in preaching neo-Sufism.

Despite these exceptions among the Ḥanbalī and Mālikī *muḥaddith*s, the majority did not make use of their expertise in *ḥadīth* for accelerating the reform of Sufism on any larger scale. These *muḥaddith*s generally continued to concentrate their *ḥadīth* studies on maintaining, reorganising and interpreting the six canonical books of the *ḥadīth* in light of their *madhhab*'s point of view. However, they increasingly established contacts and connections with scholars of the intellectual traditions. In this way they were exposed to other 'little traditions' of Islam. At the same time they played an important role in connecting scholars living in various regions of the Middle East through their *ḥadīth* scholarship.

This is particularly true among the leading Mālikī *muḥaddith*s, who lived mostly in Egypt and the North African region. As we will see shortly, they were among the scholars most responsible for transmitting *ḥadīth*s, and thus for establishing crucial linkages between various traditions of *ḥadīth* scholarship in the Middle East. The material shows that most *isnād*s in the networks were transmitted through the major fifteenth and early sixteenth century *muḥaddith*s in Egypt, namely Ibn Ḥajar al-'Asqalānī (d. 853/1449),[12] Jalāl al-Dīn al-Suyūṭī[13] and Zakariyyā al-Anṣārī,[14] noted earlier. These prominent scholars in fact constituted a group of networks among themselves.[15] They were considered the most superior *ḥadīth isnād*s, and therefore became the most sought-after *isnād*s by later scholars in the networks.[16]

As a result of this development, beginning in the late sixteenth century, connections among scholars in the Ḥaramayn resulting from *ḥadīth* scholarship increasingly widened in scope. In addition to the Egyptian *isnād*s above, we find the *isnād*s of North Africa coming into the picture. The North African *isnād*s in many cases also had strong linkages with the Egyptian *isnād*s. Being possessors of superior *isnād*s, major *muḥaddith*s from the two regions not only became crucial links among scholars but more importantly stimulated new intellectual trends in the networks. This is perhaps best illustrated by the experience of such prominent *muḥaddith*s as 'Alā' al-Dīn al-Bābilī, 'Isā al-Maghribī and Sulaymān al-Maghribī.

One of the most superior *isnād*s these three brought to the Ḥaramayn was that of Shams al-Dīn al-Ramlī, the tenth century renewer of Islam, also known as the 'little Shāfi'ī' (*al-Shāfi'ī al-Ṣaghīr*).[17] As a superior *isnād*, Shams al-Dīn received *ḥadīth*s from his father, Shihāb al-Dīn al-Ramlī (d. 957/1550),[18] who in turn received them directly from his renowned teacher, Zakariyyā al-Anṣārī. Although Shihāb al-Dīn al-Ramlī was not as famous as al-Anṣārī, he was undoubtedly one of the prominent Shāfi'ī *muḥaddith*s of his generation.

Even major scholars in the networks, who have been mainly identified as *ṣūfīs*, such as al-Qushāshī, al-Kūrānī, al-Nakhlī or 'Abd Allāh al-Baṣrī, had in fact extensive linkages with the Egyptian and North African traditions of *ḥadīth* scholarship. There is no doubt that *ḥadīth* studies constituted the most important subject in these scholars learning. Al-Kūrānī, in his accounts of his *isnād*s in various Islamic disciplines, devotes more than 40 pages to disclosing his *ḥadīth isnād*s before going on to those in *fiqh*, *sharī'ah* and *taṣawwuf*. His *ḥadīth isnād*s mostly go back through al-Qushāshī to al-Shinnāwī and further to Egyptian *isnād*s, or directly in ascending order from Shams al-Dīn al-Ramlī to Shihāb al-Ramlī to Zakariyyā al-Anṣārī to Ibn Ḥajar al-Asqalānī and so forth to Mālik.

But Ibrāhīm al-Kūrānī also possessed a *ḥadīth isnād*, beginning with 'Abd Allāh al-Lahūrī (d. 1083/1672), who migrated from Lahore, India, to Medina. Al-Lahūrī, by way of this *isnād*, connected him with Quṭb al-Dīn al-Nahrawālī. This *isnād* also includes Ibn Ḥajar at its apex, and has names not in the Egyptian and North African *isnād*s. By way of this *isnād*, al-Kūrānī is directly connected to the Indian tradition of *ḥadīth* studies.[19]

It is interesting to note that al-Kūrānī has also an interesting *ḥadīth isnād*, which runs through *ṣūfī* shaykhs that connect him to Ibn 'Arabī. It went from al-Qushāshī, who received it from al-Shinnāwī, who took it from his father, 'Alī b. 'Abd al-Quddūs 'Abbāsī al-Shinnāwī, who got it from his master, al-Sha'rānī, who got it from Zakariyyā al-Anṣārī, who got it from Abū al-Fatḥ Muḥammad al-Marāghī, who got it from Sharaf al-Dīn b. Ibrāhīm al-Jabartī al-Zabīdī from Abū al-Ḥasan 'Alī al-Wānī, who got it from the great master Ibn 'Arabī, who got it from 'Abd al-Wahhāb b. 'Alī al-Baghdādī, who got it from Abū al-Fatḥ al-Karūkhī, who got it from Abū Ismā'īl al-Anṣārī al-Ḥarawī, who finally got it from 'Abd al-Jabbār al-Jarrāḥī.[20] This *isnād* was inherited by al-Kūrānī's disciples, such as 'Abd Allāh al-Baṣrī. Al-Baṣrī tells us in his *Kitāb al-Imdād bi Ma 'rifah 'Uluw al-Isnād* that he studied al-Tirmidhī's *Sunan* and al-Nasā'ī's *Sunan* with al-Kūrānī on the authority of this *isnād*.[21]

The importance of stating Ibrāhīm al-Kūrānī's long *isnād* above is that it will enable us to see how chains of transmission can increasingly become orthodox and, by extension, how Ibn 'Arabī, often accused of being an 'unorthodox' *ṣūfī*, was a source of authority to scholars who were mostly known as *muḥaddith*s.[22]

On the above list of names, three are perhaps most important: Ibn 'Arabī, Zakariyyā al-Anṣārī, and 'Abd al-Wahhāb al-Sha'rānī. For some Muslims it may be a shock to learn that a major *muḥaddith* such as al-Anṣārī possessed a *ḥadīth isnād* that went back through Ibn 'Arabī, who had been condemned by many other *muḥaddith*s. It is important to note that, although Zakariyyā al-Anṣārī was widely known as a great *muḥaddith* and chief qāḍī, he was in fact also a *ṣūfī*. He studied with and received *taṣawwuf* from, among others, Muḥammad al-Ghamrī. Al-Anṣārī also wrote several treatises on Sufism, including a commentary on al-Qushayrī's *Risālat al-Taṣawwuf*, which is known for its insistence on the conformity of Sufism to the *sharī'ah*. Therefore, it is not a mere historical coincidence that al-Anṣārī initiated the young al-Sha'rānī (d. 973/1565) into Islamic mysticism.[23] The fruit of the master-disciple relation of this type of scholar was the emergence of al-Sha'rānī's 'neo-Sufism' or, as Trimingham[24] calls it, the 'middle course', that is, a combination of *taṣawwuf* and *fiqh*.

The connection between the leading Ḥaramayn scholars and the neo-*ṣūfī* al-Sha'rānī was far from simply a chain in the transmission of particular *ḥadīth*s or authority in studying *ḥadīth* books. Instead, their linkages were crucial to the transmission of the doctrines of neo-Sufism. Aḥmad al-Qushāshī, for instance, traces his teachings on the obligation of disciples of the *ṭarīqah* to move (*hijrah*) from negligence and ignorance to enlightenment, to wage jihād against inward and outward enemies, and to persevere in facing hardships, or on the permissibility of women to be initiated into the mystical ways, to al-Sha'rānī. Al-Sha'rānī taught them to 'Alī al-Shinnāwī, who taught them to his son, Aḥmad al-Shinnāwī, who in turn taught them directly to al-Qushāshī. But it is important to note that al-Sha'rānī derived his teachings from the authority of al-Suyūṭī.[25] Al-Qushāshī also attributes similar teachings to Zakariyyā al-Anṣārī through Aḥmad al-Shinnāwī, who got them from Shams al-Dīn al-Ramlī, who received them by way of 'general *ijāzah*' (*al-ijāzah al-'āmmah*) from al-Anṣārī.[26]

Similarly, Ibrāhīm al-Kūrānī had connections with al-Sha'rānī, which appear in more ways than simply by way of *ḥadīth isnād*: he read al-Sha'rānī's works with Aḥmad al-Shinnāwī, who received them from his father, 'Alī al-Shinnāwī, who acquired them directly from the author, al-Sha'rānī.[27] Therefore, it is clear that al-Kūrānī was fully aware of al-Sha'rānī's neo-Sufism.

Another example of the scholars in our networks who treated *ḥadīth* scholarship with particular regard is Aḥmad al-Nakhlī. He presents his *isnād*s in the search of exoteric (*ẓāhir*) and esoteric (*bāṭin*) sciences in his *Bughyat al-Ṭālibīn li Bayān al-Mashā'ikh al-Muḥaqqiqīn al-Mu'tamidīn*.[28] He possessed, for instance, an Egyptian *ḥadīth isnād* which began directly from 'Alā' al-Dīn al-Bābilī, who in turn connected him with Shams al-Dīn al-Ramlī, Zakariyyā al-Anṣārī and Ibn Ḥajar. He also acquired a North African and Egyptian *isnād* by way of 'Isā al-Maghribī as well as an Indian *isnād* that went back through Ṣibghat Allāh to al-Anṣārī. In addition to the 'Kutub al-Sittah', he studied numerous other *ḥadīth* books, such as the *al-Muwaṭṭā'* of Mālik b. Anas, *al-Sunan al-Kubrā* of al-Bayhaqī and *al-Jāmi' al-Ṣaghīr* of al-Suyūṭī.[29]

The particular importance placed by these scholars on *ḥadīth* reflects their conscious attempts to make the way of the Prophet, besides the Qur'ānic teachings, not only a source of law but also a boundless inspiration towards proper moral conduct. Therefore, as a rule, in their *ḥadīth* studies they did not confine themselves to studying standard *ḥadīth* books.

We have cited several books, outside the 'Kutub al-Sittah', studied by al-Nakhlī. It is also clear from al-Kūrānī's accounts that the six canonical *ḥadīth* books constituted only a small portion of his *ḥadīth* studies. Many lesser-known *ḥadīth* books, such as the *Musnad al-Dārimī*, *Musnad al-Bazār*, *Musnad al-Kisī* and *Musnad 'Alī al-Tamīmī al-Mawṣulī*, in fact constituted a substantial portion of his *ḥadīth* scholarship.[30] There were indeed serious efforts on the part of our scholars to go beyond the traditional study of the 'Kutub al-Sittah'.

Thus, these scholars did not view *ḥadīth* studies in the traditional way that is, for the sake of the *sharī'ah* as such. Ḥadīth studies were directed to achieving other, higher, pious purposes. Aḥmad al-Nakhlī, for example, believes that the *ḥadīth* will lead to real intimacy with the Prophet, who was second only to God as the essence of faith.[31] According to Aḥmad al-Qushāshī, the Prophet was the most important figure for the *ṭarīqah* people, as he was the source of the *sharī'ah* after God himself.[32] So attached were our scholars to the *ḥadīth* that Ibrāhīm al-Kūrānī asserts, 'I have no doubt that it [*ḥadīth*] will be everlasting on earth'.[33]

Our scholars were also aware of the fact that there were scholars who fabricated *ḥadīth* in order to pursue their own ends in the name of the Prophet. For that reason, in their *ḥadīth* studies, they preferred what these scholars called the 'high *isnād*s' or the superior *isnād*s (*'uluw al-isnād or al-isnād al-'ālī*), namely, those consisting of scholars of renowned integrity. According to 'Abd Allāh al-Baṣrī, a superior *isnād* for a scholar is much like a sharper sword for a fighter: it is a more effective tool. He gives another illustration: a scholar without the superior *isnād* is like a wood gatherer who comes in the night into a forest that has venomous snakes without light.[34]

Thus, a superior *isnād* is essential to scholars in the networks in order for them to be able to receive the true *ḥadīth*s, not the fabricated ones. Al-Nakhlī takes special note of those scholars who fabricated or advertently abused the *ḥadīth*s by citing a tradition of the Prophet which states that whoever says something the Prophet does not say, then his seat in the hereafter will be of fire.[35] In a different tone, al-Kūrānī appeals to his fellow *ṣūfī*s to interpret the *ḥadīth* only with sufficient knowledge and understanding of all teachings of Islam; to do otherwise would lead only to the elimination of *fanā'* ('annihilation' or 'passing away' of physical consciousness), an important stage of the mystical journey.[36]

There is no doubt that the special emphasis placed by these scholars on *ḥadīth* studies had considerable impact not only in linking the scholars together, as well as the various Islamic 'little traditions', but also in bringing changes in their view of Sufism, especially in its relation to the *sharī'ah*.

NEO-SUFISM AND THE *SHARĪ'AH*

The emphasis on the study of *ḥadīth* or the way of the Prophet, the second source of Islamic law, led our scholars to a greater appreciation of the significance of the *sharī'ah* in Sufism. It is interesting to take Aḥmad al-Qushāshī as an example in this respect. Al-Qushāshī was initiated by Aḥmad al-Shinnāwī into the Shaṭṭāriyyah order, often associated with Indian Sufism, which tended to transgress the rules of the *sharī'ah*—at least in the earlier growth of this order.

Aḥmad al-Qushāshī played an important part in the reorientation of the Shaṭṭāriyyah order by emphasising the importance of Islamic legal doctrines in the mystical way. In his opinion, both exoteric (legal/*sharī'ah*) and esoteric (mystical/*ḥaqīqah*) aspects of Islam should be in harmony and not in conflict with each other. Citing the *Mīzān* [*al-Kubrā*] of al-Sha'rānī,[37] he believes that there must be loyal adherence to the precepts of the *sharī'ah* on which the doctrine and practice of the *ḥaqīqah* would be built. Therefore, all mystical aspirants must practise the whole doctrine of the *sharī'ah* before they can hope to gain God's trust.[38]

Al-Qushāshī recognises certain differences between the two 'ways'—indeed 'way' or 'path' is among the meanings of both *sharī'ah* and *ṭarīqah*. He maintains that they originated from the same sources—namely, the Qur'ān and the *ḥadīth*. Basically, Muslims could attain certain stages of the *ḥaqīqah* while ignoring doctrines of the *sharī'ah* laid down by the Qur'ān and the *ḥadīth*, but they could not 'feel' the real blessing of God. Therefore, the *ṣūfī* needs to travel the mystical path with the guidance of the *sharī'ah*. According to al-Ḥamawī, 'When he [al-Qushāshī] speaks about the *ḥaqīqah*, he always supports it with Qur'ānic verses and the tradition of the Prophet'.[39] Johns rightly concludes that, in contrast to a few other *ṣūfī*s who devoted most of their exegetical skill to the Qur'ān, al-Qushāshī always presented his views by citing both the Qur'ān and the *ḥadīth*.[40]

With a clear vision of the proper relation between the sharī'ah and Sufism, it is not surprising that al-Qushāshī was an ardent supporter of neo-Sufism. He holds that there would be no real *maqām* nor *aḥwāl* (stages of mystical progress) without having sufficient knowledge (*'ilm*) and good deeds (*'amal*) as taught by the Qur'ān and the *ḥadīth*. *'Ilm* alone is not enough; there simply would be no real mystical progress for those who did not fulfill the obligatory *'ibādah*, such as prayers, fasting or alms, and other recommended actions.

Al-Qushāshī takes the Prophet Muhammad as the exemplary figure of the perfect man of Ṣufism. As a *ṣūfī*, the Prophet did not alienate himself from society; he not only asked people to enjoin good and prohibit evil but also intermingled with their brethren, and performed his 'mundane' duties. Al-Qushāshī, on the authority of the scholar and historian al-Sakhāwī, refutes the belief held in certain *ṣūfī* circles that the Prophet used to take from his companions what later became known among *ṣūfī*s as *'al-khirqat* *al-ṣūfiyyah*' (lit. '*ṣūfī*'s rag').[41] He simply could not accept the inclusion of the Prophet in specific *ṭarīqah*s, which would have supported the often-heard claim that it was sanctioned by the Prophet himself.

Similarly, Ibrāhīm al-Kūrānī emphasises the paramount importance of the *sharī'ah* without necessarily putting aside his attachment to Sufism. He argues that *ṣūfī*s should not allow their views and actions to conflict with the *sharī'ah* and other religious duties. The *ahl al-kashf*, people of intuitive revelation, have their own understanding of the meanings of the Qur'ān and the Prophetic *ḥadīth*. He reminds them, however, that each verse of the Qur'ān or *matn* (text) of the *ḥadīth* has not only esoteric (*bāṭin*) meanings—as understood by the *ahl al-kashf*—but also exoteric (*ẓāhir*) meanings. As a consequence, the *ṣūfī*s must not put their understanding of the Qur'ān in opposition to that of the *ahl al-sharī'ah*. He takes as an example the issue of *fanā'* ('annihilation') in the Qur'ān (55: 25). He explains that, according to its exoteric meaning, *fanā'* is clearly not natural death (*al-mawt al-ṭabī'ī*), but esoterically it is a kind of 'death' (*al-mawt al-ma'nawī*).[42]

It is clear that for al-Kūrānī the reconciliation between the *sharī'ah* and Sufism is not to be taken lightly. In dealing with this matter, his argument is subtle and philosophical. This is not surprising because, as al-Ḥamawī tells us in detail, he was familiar with various kinds of intellectual discourses, ranging from Mu'tazilite and Ash'arīte kalām to Ibn 'Arabī's philosophical mysticism and the Greek philosophy of Plato and Aristotle.[43] In this regard he was a scholar of distinctive stature in the networks. But it must be borne in mind that his tone was always conciliatory and all-embracing. Thus, in addition to emphasising total obedience to the *sharī'ah*, he makes appeals for the recognition of the *kashf* as a valid path to understanding the inner meaning of the Qur'ān and the *ḥadīth*.

For common Muslims, the intricate realm of Islamic philosophical interpretation could lead them to confusion and even lead them astray. Many scholars in the networks realised this. They shared a sense of responsibility for preventing their fellows from being heretical through a misunderstanding of the mystical doctrines and practices of Islam. This concern is shown by some scholars in the networks not simply by issuing fatwās but more importantly by devoting special works to the subject.

There are several outstanding examples of this. Prominent among them is Ibrāhīm al-Kūrānī. He seems to have been very responsive to answering questions either directly or indirectly posed to him. At least nine out of his 49 works listed by al-Baghdādī were devoted to responding to a variety of difficult issues, ranging from the relation of Sufism to the *sharī'ah* and the question of whether man will be able to see God, to the issue of *taqlīd* (blind imitation).[44] His most important work of this type is *Itḥāf al-Dhakī bi Sharḥ al-Tuḥfat al-Mursalah ilā Rūḥ al-Nabī*, which has been cited several times earlier. Johns[45] claims that it was al-Kūrānī's most important single work.

Al-Kūrānī wrote the *Itḥāf al-Dhakī* in response to Faḍl Allāh al-Burhānpūrī's *al-Tuḥfat al-Mursalah ilā Rūḥ al-Nabī*. As Johns concludes,[46] in this succinct work, complemented by its short commentary, *al-ḥaqīqat al-Muwāfiqah li al-Sharī'ah*, al-Burhānpūrī essentially attempts to restrain the extravagant type of Sufism by emphasising the essential elements of Islam, such as the absolute Being (*Wujūd*) of God and the importance of the *sharī'ah*. Apart from this, I would argue, the author's basic concepts, such as the seven grades of being and his arguments to explain them, are absolutely philosophical. These in turn might or could obscure the real intention of the author, especially if the work was read by the *awwām* (common believers).

The *Tuḥfat al-Mursalah* was written in 1000/1590, and in 1030/1619 or earlier it was already known in the Malay-Indonesian world. The effects of this book on Islam in the archipelago were recorded by al-Kūrānī and his disciple, al-Ḥamawī. The latter tells us that he first met and studied with al-Kūrānī in 1086/1675. The *Itḥāf al-Dhakī* had obviously been completed before that year, for al-Ḥamawī read it together with other books, such as the *Saḥīḥ al-Bukhārī* (and other 'Kutub al-Sittah'), the *Jāmi' al-Ṣaghīr* of al-Suyūṭī, the *Iḥyā' 'Ulūm al-Dīn* of al-Ghazālī and the *Futūḥāt al-Makkiyyah* of Ibn 'Arabī.[47] In his account of Faḍl Allāh al-Burhānpūrī, al-Ḥamawī relates that: [48]

> Our Shaykh *al-Khātimat al-Muḥaqqiqīn* Ibrāhīm al-Kūrānī told me, while we were reading the *Tuḥfat al-Mursalah* with him, that some of our *Jāwī* companions (*ba'ḍ aṣḥābinā al-Jāwiyyīn*) informed him that this treatise and matters it treats was popular and famous in their land and that it is read in their religious schools, and that youth study it as one of the minor treatises in their rudimentary studies.

Al-Kūrānī himself, in his introductory notes to the *Itḥāf al-Dhakī*, provides further background to his writing of the commentary:[49]

> We have had reliable information from a group (*jamā'ah*) of the *Jāwiyyīn* that there have spread among the population of the lands of *Jāwah* some books on the *ḥaqīqah* [Divine Realities] and gnostic knowledge (*'ulūm al-asrār*) passed from hand to hand by those attributed with knowledge because of their study and the teaching of others, but who have no understanding of the *'ilm al-sharī'ah* of the Prophet [Muhammad], the Chosen, the Elect [by God], peace be upon him, nor the *'ilm al-ḥaqā'iq* bestowed upon those who follow the path of God, the Exalted; those who are close to Him, those admirable ones, or those who have set their foot on any path of their paths founded on the *Kitāb* [Qur'ān] and the Sunnah [Tradition] through perfect obedience both outwardly (*al-ẓāhir*) and inwardly (*al-bāṭin*), as is done by the devout and pure. This is the reason for the deviation of many of them [the *Jāwiyyīn*] from the right path, for the rise of impure belief: in fact they have entered into the crooked camp of atheism (*al-zandaqah*) and heresy (*al-ilḥād*).

> It is mentioned [by the *Jāwiyyīn*] to me that among the famous books was the compendium named *al-Tuḥfat al-Mursalah ilā [Rūḥ] al-Nabī*, peace be upon him, written by the adept by God's help, Shaykh Muḥammad ibn Shaykh Faḍl Allāh al-Burhānpūrī, may God the Almighty render him of service. More than one of them have repeatedly asked my poor self (*al-faqīr*) to write a commentary on it to make clear of the questions [it discusses] to the principles of religion, confirmed by the Noble Book and the Sunnah of the Master of the apostles, peace be upon him.

While Drewes[50] points out that al-Kūrānī wrote the work on the orders of al-Qushāshī, the accounts of both al-Kūrānī and al-Ḥamawī provide no evidence to substantiate his view. If it is true, the work must have been conceived before the death of al-Qushāshī in 1071/1660. Whether he wrote it after having been asked directly by his *Jāwī* students or whether it was recommended by al-Qushāshī, or both, what is important is that al-Kūrānī took the task very seriously. He made special prayers for guidance (*istikhārah*) at the tomb of the Prophet in Medina, and he began the work only after he was sure that his prayers were answered and that it was appropriate for him to do the work.[51] What follows in the *Itḥāf al-Dhakī* is a long presentation on the mystical interpretation of Islam based on the Qur'ān and the *ḥadīth*.

Ibrāhīm al-Kūrānī seems not to have been satisfied with writing only a single work on the '*al-Masā'il al-Jāwiyyah*' (the questions of the *Jāwī* people). He wrote another work entitled *al-Jawābāt al-Gharāwiyyah 'an al-Masā'il al-Jāwiyyat al-Jahriyyah*,[52] in which he once again attempted to clear the matter up. It is unfortunate that we can find no trace of it; we hardly have any concept of it beyond what its title indicates.

The religious problems of the *Jāwī* evidently persisted for some time in al-Kūrānī's circle. 'Abd al-Shukūr al-Shāmī, very likely one of his students, wrote a work called *Ziyādah min 'Ibārat al-Mutaqaddimīn min Ahl al-Jāwī*. This work, like the *Tuḥfat al-Mursalah*, deals with the question of the Being and Unity of God.[53] The name 'Abd al-Shukūr occurs in one of al-Sinkilī's silsilahs of the Shaṭṭāriyyah *ṭarīqah*. Al-Sinkilī, according to this silsilah, received the *ṭarīqah* from 'Abd al-Shukūr, who took it from al-Kūrānī, who in turn received it from al-Qushāshī.[54] Al-Kūrānī also wrote a work for 'Abd al-Shukūr entitled *Kashf al-Mastūr fī Jawāb As'ilah 'Abd al-Shukūr*, which could indicate their close relationship[55] (see chapter 4).

Despite controversy around the *Tuḥfat al-Mursalah*, it was used as an important reference by virtually all major Malay-Indonesian scholars throughout the seventeenth and eighteenth centuries. From Shams al-Dīn al-Samatrānī (d. 1039/1630), al-Rānīrī, al-Sinkilī[56] and al-Maqassārī[57] to al-Palimbānī and Muḥammad Nafīs al-Banjārī, all referred to the *Tuḥfat al-Mursalah* in their writings.

Another prominent scholar who wrote a work of this nature in order to meet the special religious needs of the *Jāwī* was Tāj al-Dīn b. Aḥmad, better known as Ibn Ya'qūb. He also devoted a special work to answering problems originating from the '*Bilād al-Jāwah*'. The problem concerned the concept of the *waḥdāniyyah* (Unity of God). The title of the work is *al-Jādat al-Qawīmah ilā Taḥqīq Mas'alat al-Wujūd wa Ta'alluq al-Qudrat al-Qadīmah fī al-Jawāb 'an al-As'ilat al-Wāridah min [Bilād] Jāwah*.[58] It is doubtful whether the work is available today, as I found no trace of this very important text on the intellectual relations between the Malay-Indonesian world and the Middle East. It seems probable that it was al-Sinkilī, who asked Ibn al-Ya'qūb to write this work, as he was included among the scholars coming into contact with him in Mecca.

The fact that at least three works are devoted by leading Ḥaramayn '*ulamā'*' in the seventeenth century to what our sources call '*al-Masā'il al-Jāwiyyah*' indicates the nature of the relationships between the *Jāwī* students and scholars in Mecca and Medina. As we will see later, in the second half of the eighteenth century Sulaymān al-Kurdī, a leading Ḥaramayn scholar who was also the teacher of a group of Malay-Indonesian students, wrote a work of the same nature, entitled *al-Durrat al-Bahiyyah fī Jawāb al-As'ilat al-Jāwiyyah*. All of this indicates the existence of an intense intellectual discourse between Malay-Indonesian students and scholars in the centres of the Ḥaramayn. It also shows us the concern among the Ḥaramayn scholars about, and commitment to, intellectual reform among their fellow Muslims in the Malay-Indonesian world. They simply would not allow them to go astray because of any misunderstanding of the proper relationship between the *sharī'ah* and Sufism.

Ibrāhīm al-Kūrānī was fully aware of this danger. He thus insists that those who aspire to follow the mystical path should prepare themselves for this journey by a correct understanding of the Qur'ān and the *ḥadīth* and by total attachment both outwardly and inwardly to *sharī'ah* doctrines. To do otherwise, he believes, will only result in deviation from the right path and, worse still, to unbelief and heresy.[59] Furthermore, as related by al-Ḥamawī, al-Kūrānī maintains that young students should initially be taught articles of faith, the exoteric meaning of the Qur'ān and the *ḥadīth*, and the teachings and practices of the righteous predecessors (*al-Aslāf al-Ṣāliḥīn*) *before* they are exposed to mystical doctrines by masters who are learned not only in Sufism but also in *sharī'ah*.[60]

Aḥmad al-Qushāshī's daily practice also demonstrated his concern with common believers going astray because of their inability to comprehend the correct significance of the mystical way. Citing al-Kūrānī, al-Ḥamawī relates that al-Qushāshī usually would not allow his friends to read and discuss with him certain difficult and problematic passages of Ibn 'Arabī's *al-Futūḥāt al-Makkiyyah*, except in a very restricted manner. He would discuss them only when uneducated people were not present, and then only in a special room with locked doors. Al-Qushāshī believed that great *ṣūfīs*, such as al-Junayd, never discussed anything about the *ḥaqā'iq* except with select (*khawwāṣ*) friends or disciples. He then goes on to cite some examples from the Prophet Muhammad, who never said anything that could lead to confusion among his companions, and who indeed made distinctions between the common believers (*al-'awwām*) and the select (*al-khawwāṣ*).[61]

NEO-SUFISM AND ACTIVISM

Another striking intellectual tendency characteristic of the networks is the emphasis on the use of reason and, by extension, on the exercise of individual judgment (*ijtihād*) in religious matters. There is no evidence, however, that they actually employed the familiar slogan 'open the *bāb al-ijtihād*' ('the gate of individual judgment'), which has, since the early twentieth centry, been declared by modern Muslim scholars.

Aḥmad al-Qushāshī is reported to have urged Muslims who possessed sufficient *'ilm* (knowledge) to understand both outward and inward meanings of the verses of the Qur'ān and the *ḥadīth*. He appealed to those who devoted themselves to religion (*faqaha fī al-Dīn*) to exercise *ijtihād*. He takes Ibn 'Arabī as an example of this. According to al-Qushāshī, Ibn 'Arabī made use of *ḥadīth* extensively in order to make his own *ijtihād*. Although many traditionists opposed Ibn 'Arabī's judgment, al-Qushāshī believes that he had brought all his learning together in his attempts to produce his own *ijtihād*. Ibn 'Arabī's *ijtihād* essentially constituted a new interpretation of the mystical doctrine of Islam. Al-Qushāshī then cites his own experience of having changed his *madhhab* from Mālikī to Shafi'i, after he exerted himself to produce his own *ijtihād*. As for those who have little knowledge, al-Qushāshī considers it better for them to take others' *ijtihād*s and simply become *muqallid*s ('followers').[62]

Al-Qushāshī places emphasis not only on the exercise of reason but also on activism. Time after time he urges Muslims to abandon their negligence and ignorance by searching for *'ilm*, and by using their time to good purpose. He also insists that Muslims fully perform their worldly duties in order to support their lives by teaching, trading or farming. In his opinion, a real *ṣūfī* is not one who alienates himself from society but one who enjoins good and prohibits evil, and lends his helping hand to the oppressed, the sick and the poor. Furthermore, a real *ṣūfī* is one who can mutually cooperate (*ta'āwun*) with other Muslims for the betterment of society. These are some examples given of good deeds that should be done by those who aspire to be perfect men (*al-insān al-kāmil*) as ideally envisioned by Sufism.[63]

In contrast to most *ṣūfī*s, who would simply emphasise the total emotional commitment to God without the interference of reason, Ibrāhīm al-Kūrānī, like Aḥmad al-Qushāshī, encourages Muslims to exercise their reason. Speaking in a more philosophical way, he promotes an intellectual understanding of God and His role as Creator and the relation of the Creator to creation. In bringing up the issue of reason here, he evokes the classic heated discussion between the *mutakallimūn* ('theologians') and the *ahl al-ḥadīth* ('traditionists'). It is beyond the scope of our discussion to dwell on the long analysis in his *Itḥāf al-Dhakī* on such hotly debated topics as the Realities of God, the obscure meaning (*mutashābihāt*) of some verses of the Qur'ān and the nature of stages of mystical journeys.[64] I do not feel, however, that by bringing back these issues he intends to reactivate controversies among scholars. Rather, as al-Ḥamawī tells us, all he wants to do is to promote mutual understanding among scholars by emphasising their points of agreement.[65] After all, as al-Kūrānī reminds the Muslims, by citing al-Shāfi'ī, al-Ghazālī and Ibn 'Arabī, the power of reason is not without limit.[66]

It is worth noting, however, that not all scholars involved in the networks were ready to present long and complicated arguments to promote activism in their societies. An exception to this trend was Sulaymān al-Maghribī, who was indeed a 'radical' scholar. Although he was a *ṣūfī* himself, and founded the famous Ibn Sulaymān *ribāṭ* in Mecca, he was opposed to the extravagant type of Sufism which permitted drum-beating and dancing in the *ribāṭ*s, and to those *ṣūfī*s who alienated themselves from mainstream society. In his opinion, this type of Sufism was not sanctioned by the Qur'ān and *ḥadīth*. Taking the law into his own hands, he expelled the *aṣḥāb al-khalāwī* (secluded people) who had carried on those practices from those *ribāṭ*s affiliated with the *madrasah*s of Qayt Bey and Shārabiyyah in Mecca. In so doing, he made more room for resident students (*al-mujāwirūn*), who, he believed, better deserved them. Sulaymān al-Maghribī, who had endowed a number of *madrasah*s and *ribāṭ*s in the Ḥaramayn, also challenged misappropriation of the *waqf* properties by the Sharīfian family. These things brought him into open conflict with the Meccan Sharīfs. After several failed attempts, they were finally able to expel him from Mecca in 1093/1682 with the reluctant help of the Ottoman authorities. A year later he died in Damascus.[67]

The reformism of the networks, as we have seen thus far, is clearly centred on the social, moral and intellectual reconstruction of Muslim society. Although we find little evidence to indicate that specific discussion occurred among scholars about the regression of Muslim society, they apparently realised that society needed to be revitalised. The most logical way to achieve that end, it seemed to them, was by engendering a more balanced comprehension of each of the aspects of Islam itself: emphasising all its teachings in a unified fashion, such as legal and mystical, intellectual and practical, and social and individual. Thus, none of our scholars rejected Sufism or dismissed the importance of the *sharī'ah*. Their stress is clearly reformist, purificationist and activist in tone. In short, they sought to bring about changes in their society by their own efforts rather than waiting for eschatological intervention. There is no evidence to suggest that there were any among the scholars who adhered to such ideas as millenarianism or Mahdism. In fact, they strongly rejected these views.

The best-known example of the rejection of millenarianism is the polemic concerning the claim among the Indian subcontinent scholars that Aḥmad al-Sirhindī (971–1034/1564–1624) was the renewer of the second millennium (*mujaddid-i alf-i thānī*) of Islam. The strongest refutation to such a claim came from the *'ulamā'* involved in the networks. The most prominent among them, Muḥammad b. 'Abd al-Rasūl al-Barzanjī, devoted two works to the issue, entitled *Qadḥ al-Zand wa Qadaḥ fī Radd Jahālāt Ahl al-Sirhindī*, completed on 15 Rajab 1093/20 July 1682, and *al-Nāshirat al-Nājirah li al-Firqat al-Fŭjirah*, completed on 7 Muharram 1095/26 December 1683.[68] Ḥasan al-'Ajamī wrote another work called *al-'Aṣab al-Hind li Istīṣāl Kufriyāt Aḥmad al-Sirhindī*.[69] It is reported that al-Kūrānī also wrote a treatise on the subject, but we cannot find any trace of it in various lists of his works. Meanwhile, al-Qushāshī is said to have written a treatise after he engaged in a long discussion with Adam Banuri (d. 1053/1643), a leading follower of al-Sirhindī, who preached his master's doctrine in the Ḥaramayn.[70]

Al-Sirhindī claimed that his age was full of darkness. A thousand years after the death of the Prophet Muhammad, Islam had regressed; at the same time, infidelity and *bid'ah* (unwarranted innovations) held sway among the Muslims. He believed that he himself was a scholar of perfect knowledge, who was capable of fulfilling the task of the steadfast prophet to renew and revive Islam. Friedmann[71] shows us that eschatological speculations are in the background of al-Sirhindī's view of his times. His eschatology, however, does not anticipate the ultimate end of the world but rather the arrest of the process of decline at its nadir by means of *tajdīd* (renewal). By attributing the necessity of *tajdīd* to the period of 1000 years, he evidently adheres to the concept of millenarianism.

The crux of the issue attacked by al-Barzanjī was the very concept of and belief in the second millennium. He poses the following rhetorical questions:

> What is the meaning of the Renewer of the Second Millennium? Does a second millennium remain from the time allotted to this community so that he [al-Sirhindī] can be its renewer? Did the *'ulamā'* not agree unanimously and did *al-ḥāfiẓ* al-Suyūṭī not say in his epistle (called) *al-Kashf* [*'an Mujāwazah Hādhihi al-Ummah al-Alf*] that not even five hundred years will elapse after the Millennium and that the Day of resurrection will take place four hundred old years after it.[72]

Unlike the concept and belief in the centennial renewal of Islam widely accepted by Muslim scholars, al-Sirhindī's views on the millennial renewal imply the abolition of Muhammad's prophecy and of his law. This becomes clearer when he asserts that the Ka'bah is superior to the Prophet; that the Prophet reached perfection only 1000 years after his death, the time when the *ḥaqīqat-i muḥammadī* was changing to *ḥaqīqat-i aḥmadī*; and that he had a direct relationship with God without Muhammad's prophetic mediation.[73] With regard to these teachings, al-Barzanjī, after mentioning al-Kūrānī, who discussed these issues in the light of the Qur'ān and the *ḥadīth*, concludes that al-Sirhindī was an infidel.[74] It is not very clear whether al-Kūrānī, who was known for his conciliatory nature, really shares al-Barzanjī's conclusion. Al-Qushāshī, however, supports al-Barzanjī when he points out that it was infidelity to state that the reality of the Ka'bah was superior to the reality of the Prophet Muhammad.[75]

NEO-SUFISM AND ORGANISATION OF THE *ṬARĪQAHS*

What was the impact of all the above doctrinal changes in Sufism on the organisational aspect of the *ṭarīqah*s? In attempting to assess the organisation of the *ṭarīqah*s, we will take a comparative perspective.[76]

The most striking feature of the *ṭarīqah*s in the period under discussion is that they appear to have been loosely organised; there were no clear cut boundaries between the numerous *ṭarīqah*s in either their doctrines and practices (ritual and ceremonies) or their 'membership'. *Ṣūfī* shaykhs and *murīd*s (disciples) did not necessarily owe their loyalty to a single *ṭarīqah*; they could become masters and disciples of a number of *ṭarīqah*s. Furthermore, they could be affiliated not only with certain *ṭarīqah*s originating from or mostly developing in one particular area of the Muslim world but also with those coming from other regions. This fact undoubtedly explains further the cosmopolitanism of our scholars in the networks.

Aḥmad al-Qushāshī is a good example to support this observation. As he tells us, he was affiliated with almost a dozen *ṭarīqah*s: the Shaṭṭāriyyah, Chishtiyyah, Firdawsiyyah, Kubrawiyyah all of which he received from Aḥmad al-Shinnāwī or directly from Ṣibghat Allāh. He also took the Suhrawardiyyah order from Ṣibghat Allāh, and from al-Shinnāwī by way of a silsilah which included al-Sha'rānī. As for the Qādiriyyah *ṭarīqah*, he took it from his father, and al-Shinnāwī and Ṣibghat Allāh. He was also affiliated with the orders of Tayfūriyyah, Awīsiyyah, Khalwatiyyah and Naqshbandiyyah, all of which he received from al-Shinnāwī and Ṣibghat Allāh. Then he took the Bāṭiniyyah order through a silsilah which went back to Ḥasan al-Baṣrī. Finally he received the Shādhiliyyah order and *ṭarīqah* of Ibn 'Arabī from al-Shinnāwī by a silsilah which included al-Sha'rānī.[77]

Al-Qushāshī's *isnād*s of these orders tell us how the Indian and North African traditions of Sufism had their meeting points initially in al-Shinnāwī and later in al-Qushāshī. They also indicate how Ibn 'Arabī's mystical tradition passed through generations down to the scholars in the networks. Similarly, al-Nakhlī received several *ṣūfī* orders from various traditions. He took the Naqshbandiyyah order from Tāj al-Hindī and Mīr Kilān, the Qādiriyyah order from Ni'mat Allāh al-Qādirī, the Shādhiliyyah order from 'Alā' al-Dīn al-Bābilī, and the Khalwatiyyah order from Muḥammad 'Isā b. Kinān al-Ḥanbalī.[78]

Although affiliation with numerous *ṭarīqah*s was widely practised, once a disciple declared his allegiance (*bay'ah*) to a certain Shaykh he was required to obey his orders. As al-Qushāshī maintains, allegiance to the shaykh would lead him to the real meaning of the mystical way.[79] However, al-Qushāshī appears to have opposed the teachings of most *ṭarīqah*s in earlier periods, which required disciples to behave vis-à-vis their masters as 'a dead body in the hands of its washer'.[80] He asked disciples to leave their masters and their *ṭarīqah*s if they transgressed Islamic legal doctrines as laid down by the Qur'ān and the *ḥadīth*. This is because al-Qushāshī believes that the essence of joining the *ṭarīqah* is entering the *sharī'ah*.[81]

Thus, the rules of the *sharī'ah* become the norms for disciples wishing to be initiated into the *ṭarīqah*s. Among the most important requirements for the acceptance of disciples is maturity (*bulūgh*), which makes them accountable for practising all the pillars of Islam; in short, a total obedience to the *sharī'ah* both outwardly and inwardly.[82] With such stringent requirements, the membership of the *ṭarīqah* becomes quite restricted. These restrictions go even further in the adoption of such divisions among disciples as *'awwām* (lay) and *khawwāṣ* (elite). Both al-Qushāshī and al-Kūrānī believed that only the khawwāṣ disciples could be taught the real substance of the mystical ways. Exposing all secrets of the *ṭarīqah* doctrines to the *'awwām* would result only in religio-intellectual confusion and heresy.[83] All these restrictions make it clear that the *ṭarīqah* organisation was intended more as a vehicle for intensifying religious beliefs and devotional practices than for recruiting mass followings.

Although membership in the *ṭarīqah*s was quite restricted, disciples in the Ḥaramayn were far from homogeneous. In contrast to, for instance, the disciples of Muḥammad al-Shinnāwī—a master of al-Sha'rānī—who were mostly fellahs,[84] the Ḥaramayn *ṣūfī*s and disciples were heterogeneous in many respects. The Ḥaramayn *ṣūfī*s geographically came from various parts of the Muslim world; religiously they adhered to different *madhhab*s; and socially they occupied various positions in society, from teachers and traders to rulers. The heterogeneity in the membership of the *ṭarīqah*s in the Ḥaramayn undoubtedly comes from the existence of cosmopolitanism in the area.

Partly also because of their cosmopolitanism, the succession in the Ḥaramayn *ṭarīqah*s is ascriptive rather than descriptive. There was a tendency among certain orders in Egypt in the fifteenth and sixteenth centuries to make the post of *ṣūfī* shaykh a hereditary position.[85] However, the Ḥaramayn *ṣūfī* shaykhs, as a rule, designated their best disciples to lead their *ṭarīqah*s. We have numerous examples of this. Aḥmad al-Shinnāwī designated al-Qushāshī his successor in several *ṭarīqah*s. The latter, in turn, appointed al-Kūrānī to succeed him as the Shaṭṭāriyyah shaykh. Al-Qushāshī also appointed al-Sinkilī as his Shaṭṭāriyyah *khalīfah* for one of its branches in the Malay-Indonesian world. It is not very clear whether this pattern of succession in the Ḥaramayn *ṭarīqah*s was in one way or another influenced by al-Sha'rānī's opposition to the principle of automatic hereditary succession among his fellow Egyptian *ṣūfī* shaykhs.[86]

Furthermore, the Ḥaramayn *ṣūfī* shaykhs appear to have been free from the image of 'holy men' that we often find in the accounts of earlier *ṭarīqah*s.[87] The image of the wandering dervish is almost entirely absent in the accounts of the Ḥaramayn *ṣūfī*s. This is related to the special emphasis put by scholars involved in the networks on the importance of the *sharī'ah* in the *ṭarīqah* practices and of following the example of the Prophet Muhammad. They generally believe that the real *ṣūfī* is not the one who distinguishes himself from the rest of society by wearing distinctive clothes.

In this respect, according to al-Qushāshī, the real *ṣūfī* is the one who dresses well in accordance with the rules of the *sharī'ah*. The clothes a *ṣūfī* wears should be clean, for cleanliness reflects the purity of the soul.[88] As for al-Kūrānī, al-Qannūjī vividly narrates that despite his reputation as a great scholar and *ṣūfī*, he wore only the clothes of ordinary people, disregarding the style of dress of certain *'ulamā'* who lengthened their sleeves and enlarged their turbans in order to command people's respect, or of some *ṣūfī*s who wore dervish clothes to raise their aura of sanctity.[89]

Another important organisational aspect of the *ṭarīqah*s concerns their centre of activities. If most *ṭarīqah*s in other parts of the Muslim world carried out their activities mainly in the *ribāṭ*s, *khānqāh*s or zāwiyahs, the Ḥaramayn *ṣūfī*s were centred in the Holy Mosques, teachers' houses and *ribāṭ*s. However, the Ḥaram Mosque in Mecca and the Nabawī Mosque were the most important centres of devotional and learning activities. Most of our *ṣūfī* scholars studied and later taught as well as practised their Sufistic rituals there. The accounts of Aḥmad al-Nakhlī, cited earlier, demonstrate this.

Furthermore, those scholars who had settled in the Ḥaramayn had their own houses, which sometimes also had large libraries.[90] Thus, the *ṣūfī* shaykhs, in most cases, did not live in the *ribāṭ*s but in their own houses, where they also held learning sessions.[91] This significantly reduced the tendency among the *ṣūfī* shaykhs to style themselves in a more dervish fashion if they lived in the *ribāṭ*s. The *ribāṭ*s were, of course, also important centres of learning and devotional activities for the Ḥaramayn *ṣūfī*s. But they were occupied mainly by disciples, who stayed there temporarily until they returned to their homelands or travelled elsewhere. These *ribāṭ*s were usually led by an appointed head who was an administrator rather than a *ṣūfī* shaykh.[92]

CONTINUITY AND CHANGE

It is important to keep in mind that with the emergence of neo-Sufism the old paradigm of Sufism did not completely disappear. Extravagant Sufism was still practised by some people in Mecca, as we have seen in the experience of Sulaymān al-Maghribī. In spite of this, there is no evidence that our scholars attempted to remove all aspects of the earlier tradition of the *ṭarīqah*s. Therefore, it is appropriate to describe this phenomenon as one of continuity and change. While the scholars in the networks substantially reduced the extravagant and ecstatic features of earlier Sufism and emphasised loyal adherence to the *sharī'ah*, at the same time they maintained their doctrinal links with, for instance, Ibn 'Arabī. However, in maintaining their connection with Ibn 'Arabī they tended to disengage themselves from some points of his controversial doctrines.

Johns[93] has pointed out that Ibrāhīm al-Kūrānī was one of the last great exponents of the school of Ibn 'Arabī, so far as his philosophical and theological ideas are concerned. But we should be careful not to conclude that his thought was dominated by Ibn 'Arabī's teachings. It is true that, in his *Itḥāf al-Dhakī*, he often cites Ibn 'Arabī, but at the same time he puts forward his own arguments by citing al-Ghazālī, al-Qushayrī and even Ibn Taymiyyah.[94] Furthermore, he studied not only Ibn 'Arabī's philosophical doctrines but also his legal teachings. As he tells us, he learned this often neglected aspect of Ibn 'Arabī's teachings not from a *ṣūfī* but from a prominent Meccan scholar, Zayn al-'Ābidīn al-Ṭabarī, who was known as a *muḥaddith*.[95]

The same is true of Aḥmad al-Nakhlī. In the same vein he expresses a great appreciation of al-Ghazālī and Ibn 'Arabī. He tells us that he studied al-Ghazālī's *Iḥyā' 'Ulūm al-Dīn* with Sayyid Aḥmad al-Ḥusnī al-Maghribī al-Mālikī, better known as *al-Maḥjūb*, who later issued him an *ijāzah* to teach al-Ghazālī's teachings. But from the same teacher he studied the rules of fasting in a chapter of Ibn 'Arabī's *al-Futūḥāt al-Makkiyah*. In another passage he relates that he studied the *Iḥyā' 'Ulūm al-Dīn* with al-Kūrānī, who told him that this book was very popular in his homeland, Kurdistan. Interestingly enough, al-Nakhlī also learned the *Iḥyā' 'Ulūm al-Dīn* from al-Qushāshī, who studied it with Aḥmad al-Shinnāwī, who received it by way of an *isnād* which included al-Sha'rānī, Zakariyyā al-Anṣārī and Ibn 'Arabī.[96]

With this evidence it is clear that there was a conscious effort among scholars in the networks to reconcile different streams of thought that had often been seen as in conflict with each other by scholars before them. There seems to have been no bias against scholars who had been the subject of controversies, such as al-Ghazālī or Ibn 'Arabī. On the contrary, scholars in the networks studied them in order to understand their teachings and later attempted to reconcile them. An example of this had been set earlier by the neo-*ṣūfī* al-Sha'rānī, who sought to reconcile doctrines of the speculative theologians (*ahl al-fikr*) and the mystics (*ahl al-kashf*) by taking care not to associate himself entirely with Ibn 'Arabī, despite his admiration for him, and linking himself to famous *fuqahā'* and *muḥaddith*.[97]

Although such a scholar in the networks as Ibrāhīm al-Kūrānī was by nature a conciliator, who preferred to reconcile two opposing points of view rather than choose one or the other of them, he was bitterly criticised by a number of scholars, such as the Algerian Ibn al-Ṭayyib and Yaḥyā al-Shāwī. Ibn al-Ṭayyib writes a short biography of al-Kūrānī in the *Nashr al-Mathānī*.[98] In this work, Ibn al-Ṭayyib recognises al-Kūrānī's high reputation. Despite this, he attacks him on various issues: that he was in favour of the Qadariyyah interpretation of the ability of created power to be responsible for the acts of human beings; that he leaned to the Mu'tazilite point of view by writing a treatise on the material character of non-being; that he accepted the historicity of the report that the Prophet Muḥammad had uttered the so-called 'Satanic verses', allegedly interpolated into the Qur'ān (53:21); and that he wrote a treatise on the faith of Pharaoh according to Ibn 'Arabī's philosophical framework. Meanwhile al-Shāwī (fl. 1096/1685), in his work entitled *al-Nabl al-Raqīq fī Ḥulqūm al-Sābb al-Zindīq*, goes even further by accusing al-Kūrānī of atheism and demanding his death. Al-Shāwī's accusation, in turn, was answered by al-Barzanjī, in his work *al-'Iqāb al-Hāwi 'alā al-Tha'lab al-'Āwī wa al-Nushshāb al-Kāwī li al-A'shā al-Ghāwī wa al-Shihāb al-Shāwī li al-Aḥwāl al-Shāwī*.[99]

The fact that Ibrāhīm al-Kūrānī was attacked on such a wide range of issues is, as Johns points out,[100] an index of his learning. He had sufficient status in various Islamic disciplines to provoke disagreements. He was a master of various disciplines of Islam, and on the basis of his learning made his own *ijtihād*s. Eclectic and original, he was the kind of scholar about whom others must have divided views and who thus exercises a creative role among his contemporaries. To sum up, these attacks on al-Kūrānī indicate the dynamics of intellectual discourse in the networks, which continued to gain momentum in the succeeding periods.

3

Seventeenth Century Malay-Indonesian Networks I: Nūr al-Dīn al-Rānīrī

Two of the three major chains of networks in the Malay-Indonesian world, those stemming from al-Rānīrī and al-Sinkīlī, flourished in the Sultanate of Aceh, while the originator of the other, al-Maqassārī, was born in Sulawesi (Celebes) and established his career in Banten, West Java. In this chapter we will deal with al-Rānīrī (d. 1068/1658), discussing particularly his role in transmitting the reformism of the networks to this part of the Muslim world.

The importance of Aceh or North Sumatra as a whole in the early history of Islam in the region is unquestionable. However, in order to understand the proper socio-historical context of al-Rānīrī's reforms specifically, it is appropriate to give a brief account of the dominant Muslim intellectual discourse in Aceh prior to al-Rānīrī's time. This in turn leads us to two major scholars, Ḥamzah al-Fanṣūrī and Shams al-Dīn al-Samatrānī, who played a crucial role in shaping the religious thought and practice of the Malay-Indonesian Muslims in the first half of the seventeenth century.

Despite their prominence, many things about the life of Ḥamzah and Shams al-Dīn are still obscure. There is still disagreement on the birthplace of Ḥamzah al-Fanṣurī as well as his life span, as his dates of birth and death are unknown. However, there is evidence that he lived and flourished in the period preceding and during the reign of Sulṭān 'Alā' al-Dīn Ri'āyat Shāh (r. 997–1011/1589–1602); it has been suggested that he died before 1016/1607.[1] Apart from this it is clear that Ḥamzah was a Malay of Fanṣūr, an old centre of Islamic learning in southwest Aceh.[2]

Ḥamzah was obviously a great scholar. He is reported to have travelled to the Middle East, visiting some important centres of Islamic learning, including Mecca, Medina, Jerusalem and Baghdad, where he was initiated into the Qādiriyyah *ṭarīqah*. He also travelled to Pahang, Kedah and Java,[3] where he preached his teachings. Ḥamzah mastered Arabic, Persian and possibly also Urdu. He was a prolific writer, producing not only religious treatises but also prose works laden with mystical ideas.[4] In view of his works, he is regarded both as one of the most important early Malay-Indonesian *ṣūfī*s and a prominent precursor of the Malay literary tradition.

The nature of Ḥamzah al-Fanṣūrī's relationship with Shams al-Dīn (d. 1040/1630) is not very clear either. Most scholars are of the opinion that they were friends.[5] This may imply a sort of teacher–disciple relationship, as suggested by Hasjmi and Abdullah; both assert that Shams al-Dīn was a disciple of Ḥamzah.[6] Whatever the case, Shams al-Dīn and Ḥamzah certainly met. Sir James Lancaster, the British special envoy to Aceh in 1011/1602, tells us that he negotiated a treaty of peace and friendship between England and Aceh with two notables appointed by Sulṭān 'Alā' al-Dīn Ri'āyat Shāh to discuss this matter on his behalf:

> The one of these noblemen was the chiefe bishope of the realme, a man of great estimation with the King and all the people; and so he well deserved, for he was a man very wise and temperate. The other was one of the most ancient nobilitie, a man of very good gravitie but not so fit to enter into these conferences as the bishop was. And all the Conferences passed in the Arabicke tongue, which both the bishop and the other nobleman well understood.[7]

Schrieke[8] and Hasjmi[9] maintain that the 'chiefe bishope' was Ḥamzah al-Fanṣūrī, as he, by that time, had gained prominence. Van Nieuwenhuijze[10] and Iskandar,[11] on the other hand, are of the opinion that the 'chiefe bishope' was Shams al-Dīn. The first opinion seems to be more plausible, as Shams al-Dīn during this time was in the middle of his career; it was only under the next Sulṭān, namely Iskandar Muda (r. 1015–1046/ 1607–1636), that he became 'chiefe bishope'. Like Ḥamzah, Shams al-Dīn was a prolific writer and a master of several languages. He wrote in both Malay and Arabic, and most of his works deal with *kalām* and Sufism.[12] But, unlike Ḥamzah, he never wrote any mystical poetry.

Ḥamzah and Shams al-Dīn have been categorised as belonging to the same stream of religious thought. We are not going to describe in detail their thoughts, but the two were the leading proponents of the *waḥdat al-wujūd* philosophical interpretation of Sufism.[13] Both were deeply influenced in particular by Ibn 'Arabī and al-Jīlī, and strictly followed their elaborate system of *wujūdiyyah*. For instance, they explain the universe in terms of a series of neo-Platonic emanations and consider each of the emanations an aspect of God himself.[14] These are the very concepts that led their opponents, prominent among them al-Rānīrī, to accuse them of being pantheists and, therefore, of having gone astray.

So far as this accusation is concerned, scholars are divided into two groups. Winstedt,[15] Johns,[16] Van Nieuwenhuijze[17] and Baried[18] maintain that the teachings and doctrine of Ḥamzah and Shams al-Dīn are 'heretical' or 'heterodox'. Therefore, they were 'heretics' or 'heterodox' mystics as opposed to the 'orthodox' *ṣūfī*s such as al-Rānīrī and al-Sinkīlī. On the other hand, al-Attas maintains that the teachings of Ḥamzah, Shams al-Dīn and al-Rānīrī are essentially the same; one cannot categorise the first two as heretics. Al-Attas, in turn, accuses al-Rānīrī of distorting the thought of Ḥamzah al-Fanṣūrī and Shams al-Dīn and of conducting a 'smear campaign' against them.[19] Al-Attas, however, seems to change his assessment of al-Rānīrī in his later book,[20] in which he praises al-Rānīrī as 'a man gifted with wisdom and adorned with authentic knowledge', who succeeded in making clear the false doctrines of *wujūdiyyah* scholars, whom he calls the 'pseudo-*ṣūfī*s'.

In any case, the period before the coming of al-Rānīrī in 1047/1637 was the time during which mystical Islam, particularly that of the *wujūdiyyah*, held sway not only in Aceh but in many parts of the archipelago. Although there were attempts to apply the precepts of the *sharī'ah*, the mystical doctrine and practices, the salient feature of Malay-Indonesian Islam from the earliest period, continued to enjoy supremacy. Ḥamzah and Shams al-Dīn's writings give further impetus to this tendency. With their position as *Shaykh al-Islām* of the Acehnese Sultanate, they were able to exercise considerable influence. All the sources, local and foreign, are in agreement that the two scholars dominated the religious and intellectual life of the Malay-Indonesian Muslims before the rise of al-Rānīrī.

AL-RĀNĪRĪ'S BIOGRAPHY AND NETWORKS

A good number of studies have been devoted to al-Rānīrī. However, they mostly deal with his thought; very little attention is paid to the wider context of his scholarly milieu and to his role in Islamic discourse in the Malay-Indonesian world. There is no single study devoted to assessing the religious changes he brought about in the Malay-Indonesian world. Therefore, al-Rānīrī is mostly considered a *ṣūfī* rather than a renewer (*mujaddid*). In fact, he was obviously one of the most important early *mujaddid*s in the archipelago.

Nūr al-Dīn Muḥammad b. 'Alī b. Ḥasanjī al-Ḥamīd (or al-Ḥumayd) al-Shāfi'ī al-Ash'arī al-'Aydarūsī al-Rānīrī was born in Rānīr (modern Randir), an old harbour on the Gujarat coast. Despite his birthplace, al-Rānīrī is generally regarded as a Malay-Indonesian *'ālim* rather than Indian or Arab one. His birth date is unknown, but it was probably towards the end of the sixteenth century. It has been suggested that his mother was a Malay,[21] but his father was of Ḥaḍramī immigrants with a long tradition of migrating to South and Southeast Asia. Most of these South Arabian people settled in the harbour towns on the coast of the Indian Ocean and of the Malay-Indonesian archipelago.[22] His ancestors probably belonged to the al-Ḥamīd family of the Zuhra, one of the 10 clans of the Quraysh.[23] Among the prominent members of the Zuhra clan was 'Abd al-Raḥmān b. 'Awf, a close companion of the Prophet.[24] But it is also possible that al-Rānīrī's ancestors were of the Ḥumayd family, often associated with Abū Bakr 'Abd

Allāh b. Zubayr al-Asadī al-Ḥumaydī (d. 219/834), known as one of the prominent native scholars of Mecca.[25] Al-Ḥumaydī was among the most famous disciples of al-Shāfi'ī. He was also the *Muftī* of Mecca and a leading traditionist (*muḥaddith*) in the Ḥijāz.[26]

In the first half of the sixteenth century, Rānīr was an important and busy harbour that attracted Arabs, Persian, Turks and Malays to trade or settle there. In 1040/1530, the Portuguese attacked and colonised it. As a result, Rānīr experienced a severe blow and was replaced in eminence by Surat. Although Rānīr has since that time been under Portuguese rule, most Ḥaḍramī immigrants appear to have continued to live there. However, they maintained their contacts with Ḥaḍramawt, Yemen and the Ḥaramayn as well as with the Malay-Indonesian world. Ḥaḍramī scholars, in fact, travelled back and forth to these places, contributing significantly to the maintenance of close contacts and relations among these Muslim societies. Furthermore, the Ḥaḍramīs generally sent their children and youth to their ancestral home and to the Ḥaramayn to pursue their religious studies. When they completed their studies, most of them returned to their birthplaces or travelled elsewhere in the Muslim world.

This pattern of life among Ḥaḍramī immigrants can be observed clearly in the experience of al-Rānīrī's own uncle. In his *Bustān al-Salāṭīn fī Dhikr al-Awwalīn wa al-Ākhirīn*,[27] he tells us that his paternal uncle, Muḥammad Jīlānī b. Ḥasan Muḥammad al-Ḥumaydi, came from Gujarat to Aceh between 988/1580 and 991/1583, where he taught *fiqh*, *uṣūl al-fiqh*, ethics and logic (*manṭiq*) and rhetoric. However, people were more interested in studying mysticism (*taṣawwuf*) and theology (*kalām*). As al-Rānīrī further relates, his uncle was no expert in mysticism and was therefore not prepared to meet the people's demand to learn about it. Muḥammad Jīlānī then decided to cancel his teaching, and went to Mecca instead to pursue more advanced studies in mysticism and other related subjects. Having mastered these, he returned to Aceh during the reign of Sulṭān 'Alā' al-Dīn Ri'āyat Shāh (r. 997–1011/1589–1602) to teach people in the subjects they wanted to study. It appears that he succeeded to some extent in unraveling the intricacies of mysticism and *kalām*, especially of the nature of the archetypes (*al-a'yān al-thābitah*).

The account shows us how a Ḥaḍramī teacher from Gujarat played an important role in the development of Islam in Aceh. The events surrounding him indicate intense contacts and relations among Muslim scholars and communities in various parts of the Muslim world. As al-Rānīrī relates, the interest of the Acehnese Muslims in mysticism was generated by a deadlock in public discussion and debates between two scholars, coming from Mecca to Aceh in 947/1540, on mystical and philosophical matters, in particular concerning the permanent archetypes.

The first was Abū al-Khayr b. Shaykh b. Ḥajar, the author of a book entitled *al-Sayf al-Qāṭi'*,[28] which deals with difficult issues concerning the nature of the third metaphysical category between being and non-being:

the fixed essences, or the permanent archetypes. It seems that in addition to teaching *fiqh*, Ibn Ḥajar discusses matters contained in his book that were very difficult for the common people to grasp. The other scholar was Muḥammad al-Yamanī, an expert in *fiqh* and *uṣūl al-fiqh* as well as in *'ulūm al-ḥadīth* and sciences related to the Qurān. Both scholars were later involved in a heated discussion on these topics, but neither gained the upper hand by satisfactorily explaining these complicated matters, leaving the audience in confusion and with an abiding intellectual curiosity. To make the situation even worse, both Shaykhs left Aceh. And people had to wait for the coming of Al-Rānīrī's uncle to attempt a conclusion.

Al-Rānīrī followed in the footsteps of his uncle and many other Ḥaḍramī scholars. He acquired his early education in Rānīr, and later continued his study in the Ḥaḍramawt region. We have no information on the time he spent there, or on the teachers with whom he studied. It is not very clear either whether or not he returned to his home town when he left Ḥaḍramawt. But, most probably, he went directly to the Ḥaramayn, as, according to al-Ḥasanī, he was in Mecca and Medina in 1030/1620 or 1031/1621, when he performed the *ḥajj* pilgrimage.[29] And it is very likely that he also came into contact with the *Jāwī* students and pilgrims there before returning to Gujarat.[30]

Al-Rānīrī's most prominent teacher in India was Abū Ḥafṣ 'Umar b. 'Abd Allāh Bā Shaybān al-Tarīmī al-Ḥaḍramī (d. 1066/1656), who was also known in the Gujarat region as Sayyid 'Umar al-Aydarūs.[31] There is no information on his dates of birth or death, but he was born in the Gujarat region. Bā Shaybān was, like al-Rānīrī, of Ḥaḍramī origin, more precisely of the Aydarūsiyyah of Tarīm, one of the most important centres of Islamic learning in South Arabia. According to al-Rānīrī, it was Bā Shaybān who initiated him into the Rifā'iyyah order, an old Arab *ṭarīqah*.[32] He appointed al-Rānīrī his *khalīfah* of the *ṭarīqah* and was therefore responsible for spreading it in the Malay-Indonesian world.[33] But the Rifā'iyyah was not the only order al-Rānīrī was affiliated with. He also had chains of initiation of the Aydarūsiyyah[34] and Qādiriyyah[35] orders.

Bā Shaybān first studied in his land of birth but later travelled to Tarīm, where he studied with such well-known *'ulamā'* as 'Abd Allāh b. Shaykh al-Aydarūs (d. 1073/1662), a disciple of Aḥmad al-Qushāshī, and 'Abd al-Azīz al-Zamzamī, and his son, Zayn al-'Ābidīn; Qāḍī 'Abd al-Raḥman b. Shihāb al-Dīn al-Saqqāf (945–1014/1538–1605);[36] Abū Bakr b. Shihāb (d. 1061/1651);[37] and his two brothers, Muḥammad al-Hādī and Aḥmad Shihāb al-Dīn. After several years in Tarīm, Bā Shaybān continued his studies in Mecca and Medina for four years, studying with and taking *ṭarīqah*s from many Ḥaramayn *'ulamā'*. Prominent among these were Sayyid 'Umar b. 'Abd Allāh al-Raḥīm al-Baṣrī (d. 1037/1638),[38] Aḥmad b. Ibrāhīm b. 'Alān (d. 1033/1624)[39] and 'Abd al-Raḥmān al-Khaṭīb al-Sharbaynī (d. 1014/1605).[40] All these scholars and their connections, as their biographies inform us, were involved in the networks in the seventeenth century and, through others in addition to Bā Shaybān, also had connections with the archipelago.

Bā Shaybān returned to Tarīm and married. Later he went to *'Diyār al-Hind'* (the Hindī region=Surat?) to study with *Shaykh al-Islām* Sayyid Muḥammad b. 'Abd Allāh al-'Aydarūs, who also initiated him into the 'Aydarūsiyyah order. Muḥammad al-'Aydarūs[41] who was considered by al-Rānīrī as his spiritual grandfather,[42] was born in 970/1561 in Tarīm where he studied various branches of Islamic thought. When he was 19 years old he went to Ahmadabad to meet his grandfather, Sayyid 'Abd Allāh al-'Aydarūs (d. 990/1582), a celebrated *ṣūfī* and theologian of the Gujarat region. Muḥammad then established himself in Surat, following in the footsteps of his grandfather as a great *ṣūfī* and *'ālim*, and was known as the *'Ṣaḥīb Surat'* (Master of Surat). He died there in 1030/1621.

Another important figure related to Bā Shaybān was his uncle, 'Abd al-Qādir al-'Aydarūs, whose mother was an Indian. Born in Ahmadabad, he wrote a number of books on *taṣawwuf* and biography. After travelling extensively he returned to Ahmadabad, where he died in 1038/1638.[43] 'Abd al-Qādir had another nephew, who later became a prominent figure in the religious and political realm in Bijapur. 'Abd Allāh b. Shaykh al-Aydarūs (d. 1041/1631) was born in Tarīm. Before migrating to Gujarat in 1025/1616 he studied in Yemen and the Ḥaramayn, where he was initiated into a number of *ṭarīqah*s including the 'Aydarūsiyyah, Qādiriyyah, Shādhiliyyah and Suhrāwardiyyah orders. He was also recognised as a *muḥaddith*. After getting spiritual blessings from his uncle in Ahmadabad, 'Abd Allāh soon launched his Islamic renewal in the region.[44]

The importance of mentioning these major scholars of the Aydarūsiyyah family is to put al-Rānīrī and his renewal in the proper context, for it is certain that the 'Aydarūs scholars played an important role in channelling religious ideas from the Middle East to India and further to the Malay-Indonesian world. Al-Muḥibbī, for instance, lists no fewer than 30 prominent scholars of the 'Aydarūs family, who were centred in Tarīm. Many of them travelled back and forth from Tarīm to the Ḥaramayn to India and the archipelago throughout the tenth-eleventh/sixteenth-seventeenth centuries.[45] Bā Shaybān was one of the crucial links, connecting various traditions of Islamic learning. By way of his main disciples, like al-Rānīrī and al-Maqassārī, he transmitted religious ideas from Tarīm and the Ḥaramayn to India and the Malay-Indonesian world (see Chart 3). Bā Shaybān lived mainly in Bijapur, one of the leading centres of Islamic learning and Sufism in India.[46] There he enjoyed the patronage of Sulṭān 'Ādil Shāh (r. 1037–68/1626–1656) of the Bahmānī Sultanate. Later he moved to Burhānpūrī, where he produced several books, but he died in Bilgram.[47]

Having studied Islamic sciences and been appointed as a khalīfah of both the 'Aydarūsiyyah and Rifā'iyyah orders, the time had come for al-Rānīrī to begin his career. Some of his works indicate that he was well acquainted

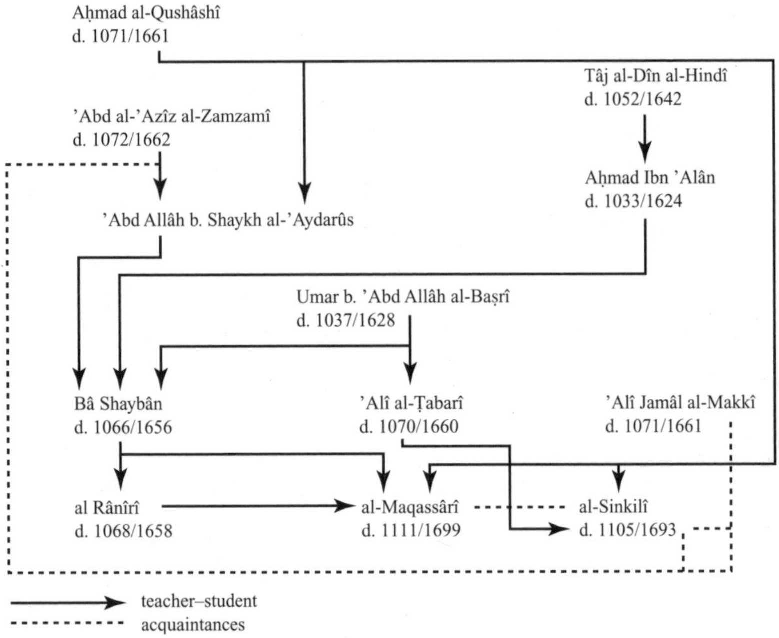

Chart 3 Al-Rānīrī's networks

with the Malay world even before coming to the archipelago. It appears that he acquired information on it from his involvement in the *Jāwī* community in Mecca. But there is little doubt that his uncle, Muḥammad Jīlānī, who used to travel back and forth to Aceh, provided him with much information on Malay cultural and religious tradition.

Al-Rānīrī was certainly the most prominent predecessor of the 'Aydarūsiyyah scholars in the Malay-Indonesian archipelago. We have mentioned that 'Abd al-Raḥman b. Muṣṭafā al-'Aydarūs (d. 1194/1780 in Egypt), a teacher of Murtaḍā al-Zabīdī, also travelled to the Malay-Indonesian world. But unlike al-Rānīrī, who left a substantial impact on the archipelago, Muṣṭafā al-'Aydarūs apparently only passed through it in his travels to many parts of the Muslim world. However, it is not impossible that he came into contact and established networks with Ḥusayn b. Abū Bakr al-'Aydarūs (d. in 1213/1798 in Batavia, now Jakarta), another leading scholar and *ṣūfī* of the 'Aydarūs family in the Malay-Indonesian archipelago.[48]

There is no information as to when al-Rānīrī travelled for the first time to, and lived in, the Malay world. But it is likely that, during the period between his completion of the pilgrimage in 1029/1621 and 1047/1637, he lived for some time in the archipelago, probably in Aceh or Pahang in the Malay Peninsula or both. His sudden rise to the office of *Shaykh al-Islām* of the Sultanate of Aceh in 1047/1637 indicates that he had been known before among the Malay rulers or circles, especially those of the Pahang Sultanate. The son of Sulṭān Aḥmad of Pahang was seven years of age when he was taken to Aceh by Sulṭān Iskandar Muda, who later married him to his daughter and treated him as his own son;[49] he was later known as Iskandar Thānī. Thus, when he succeeded his father-in-law to the throne of the Acehnese Sultanate, al-Rānīrī was not new to the Sulṭān circle. It is hard to believe that al-Rānīrī could win the patronage of the Sulṭān and the office of *Shaykh al-Islām* as soon as he arrived in Aceh without having been in close contact beforehand.

If al-Rānīrī had already been in the archipelago before 1047/1637, why then did he not establish himself in Aceh? To answer this question one should consider the political and religious situation in Aceh during the reign of Sulṭān Iskandar Muda (r. 1015–1046/1607–1636). In this period it was Shams al-Dīn al-Samatrānī who occupied the office of *Shaykh al-Islām*. Under the patronage of Iskandar Muda, the doctrines of *wujūdiyyah* preached by Ḥamzah al-Fanṣūrī and Shams al-Dīn enjoyed their heyday. Therefore, the time was not yet ripe for al-Rānīrī to challenge the established political and religious order; he had to wait until the situation became more favourable to him.

When Shams al-Dīn and Iskandar Muda successively died, al-Rānīrī came to Aceh, precisely on 6 Muharram 1047/31 May 1637.[50] He was soon appointed *Shaykh al-Islām*, one of the highest posts in the Sultanate below the Sulṭān himself, becoming perhaps even more influential than the other two highest officials, the *Qāḍī Malik al-'Ādil* and the *Orang Kaya Maharaja Srimaharaja*. The Dutch trade representatives to Aceh called him 'the Moorish Bishop'.[51] He was, of course, responsible for religious matters, but Dutch records make it clear that he also played an important role in economic and political affairs. So when the Gujarat traders once again tried to dominate trade in Aceh, the Dutch fiercely protested, but to no avail. It is only through al-Rānīrī's goodwill and mediation that Sulṭānah Ṣafiyyat al-Dīn (1051–86/1641–75), the widow of Iskandar Thānī, withdrew policies favourable to the Gujarat traders and detrimental to the Dutch.[52]

Gaining a firm foothold in the court of the Acehnese Sulṭān, al-Rānīrī began to launch Islamic renewal in Aceh. In his view, Islam in this region had been corrupted by misunderstanding of the *ṣūfī* doctrine. Al-Rānīrī lived for seven years in Aceh as an *'ālim*, *muftī* and prolific writer, spending much of his energy in refuting the doctrines of *wujūdiyyah*. He even went so far as to issue a *fatwā*, which led to a kind of heresy-hunting: killing those who refused to dismantle their beliefs and practices, and reducing to ashes all of their books. He succeeded in retaining the favour of the court until 1054/1644, when he abruptly left Aceh for his town of birth, Rānīr. This is recorded by one of his disciples in the colophon of al-Rānīrī's work, *Jawāhir al-'Ulūm fī Kashf al-Ma'lūm*:[53]

> And when he has thus far completed this work it came about by [God's] decree that he was prevented [from completing it altogether], whereat he set out for his native town of Rānīr.

This short passage provides no clear explanation as to why al-Rānīrī suddenly returned to Rānīr. This leads Daudy[54] to speculate that al-Rānīrī's abrupt departure had something to do with his dislike of the policies of Sulṭānah Ṣafiyyat al-Dīn, designed to persecute people who refused to be ruled by a woman. These people believed that, according to the local tradition as well as the *sharī'ah*, it was inappropriate for a woman to be the ruler. As a result, there was opposition to her rule; and al-Rānīrī's departure represented such an opposition. This explanation does not seem plausible. One may expect some kind of opposition or resistance from a more *sharī'ah*-oriented Muslim society to the rule of a woman; however, as far as al-Rānīrī's departure is concerned, it is unlikely that his return to his native town was caused by his alleged dislike of rule by a woman who had shown favour to him. In fact, many of his works were written to satisfy the command of the Sulṭānah, including those written in the last minutes before his departure.

The enigma of al-Rānīrī's sudden departure was solved when Ito published a short but very important article,[55] based on the diary of the *opperkoopman* ('higher trader') Peter Sourij, who in 1053/1643 was sent by the VOC (Verenigde Oost-Indische Compagnie) as a trade commissioner to Jambi and Aceh. In an entry of his diary for 8 August 1643, Sourij reports that the coming of a 'Moorish Bishop' from Surat, India, to Aceh gave rise to endless debates between him and al-Rānīrī, for the latter had branded the newcomer's doctrines as 'heretical'. The debates put the Sulṭānah in an awkward and difficult situation. She had up to then shared the views of al-Rānīrī, but the newcomer's teachings soon gained momentum.

Two weeks later Sourij provides us with more background information. In the entry of 22 August, he again reports the continuing debates between the two *'ulamā'*, now in the presence of the chairman of the Joint Councillors of the Sultanate or *Orang Kaya Maharajalela*. More importantly, Sourij informs us that the new person was Sayf al-Rijāl, a Minangkabau, who used to study in Aceh with a certain Shaykh Maldin (Jamāl al-Dīn?). The latter was banished from Aceh after the coming of al-Rānīrī because of his allegedly unorthodox views. Sayf al-Rijāl soon won the hearts of many Acehnese through his erudition and piety. He even made his entire house and adjoining lands into a pious foundation. Al-Rānīrī himself gives a vivid account of the whole situation:

> Then came Sayf al-Rijāl, and he held debates with us over the matters which had been discussed before. We ask: 'How could you approve of the people who assert that *wa Allāh bi Allāh tā Allāh*, man is Allāh and Allāh is man

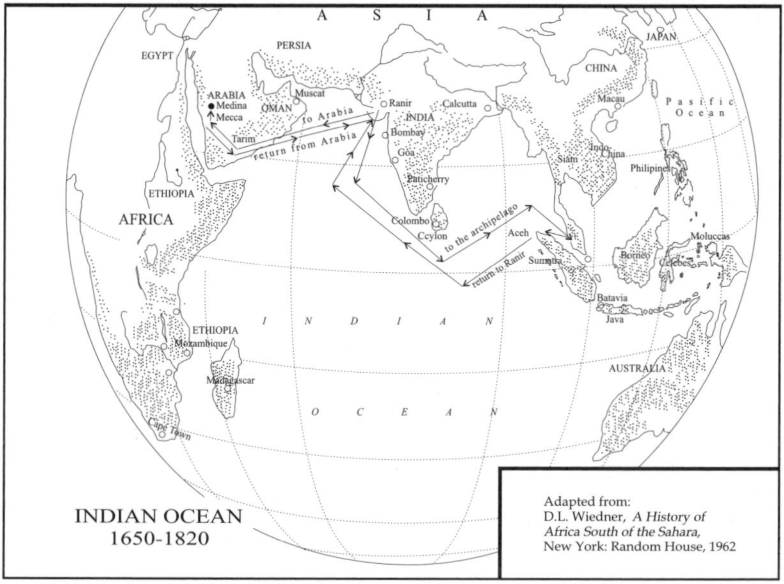

Map 1 Al-Rānīrī's itinerary

> [sic]?' He [Sayf al-Rijāl] answers: 'This is my belief and that of the people of Mecca and Medina.' Then his words prevail, and many people return to this wrong belief.[56]

It is clear that the bitter debates between al-Rānīrī and Sayf al-Rijāl became a divisive political issue. The *Orang Kaya* failed to settle the issue, so the Joint Councillors of the Sultanate and the *bentaras* (ministers) had to meet again and again to resolve the controversy. But they too failed. The only thing they could do was to recommend that the case be settled by Sulṭānah Ṣafiyyat al-Dīn, who wisely refused to do so, for she acknowledged not having knowledge on religious matters. So she left the case in the hands of the *uleebalangs* (*adat* functionaries).

With the Sulṭānah's refusal to use her authority to end the bitter disagreement between the two scholars, some kind of religious and political confusion soon prevailed among the population. So confused had the situation been that Sourij complained about the delay in his business. Finally, Sayf al-Rijāl gained the upper hand. Sourij, in his notes for 27 August 1643, writes that Sayf al-Rijāl was finally summoned to the court by the Sulṭānah herself, during which time he received honourable treatment. With this, the door was shut to al-Rānīrī, and he was forced to leave the arena.

There is no further information on Sayf al-Rijāl, who won the struggle. But what is clear is that he represents a strong counter-attack against al-Rānīrī, who for about seven years persecuted the followers of Ḥamzah al-Fanṣūrī and Shams al-Dīn. Another important point to note is the international nature of the success of Sayf al-Rijāl. In order to win the struggle, he travelled a long way to Surat, studying. We do not know with whom he studied there. When he returned, he possessed enough distinction to enable him to challenge al-Rānīrī and not easily be defeated by him in their bitter debates.

Al-Rānīrī returned to his native town in 1054/1644–45, as was mentioned in the colophon of his *Jawāhir al-'Ulūm fī Kashf al-Ma'lūm*. He spent the remaining 14 years of his life in Rānīr. Although he was now far from Aceh or the archipelago, he maintained his concern for Muslims in the 'lands below the wind'. Al-Ḥasanī relates that after returning to his native town al-Rānīrī wrote at least three works,[57] dealing with the matters he used to encounter in Aceh. One of the works was written as his answer to questions put forward by the Bantenese Sulṭān, Abū al-Mafākhir 'Abd al-Qādir al-'Alī. Al-Rānīrī died on Saturday, 22 Dhū al-Ḥijjah 1068/21 September 1658.[58]

AL-RĀNĪRĪ'S WORKS AND RENEWAL

Al-Rānīrī was a prolific and erudite writer. According to various sources he wrote no fewer than 29 works. But not all were written during his seven-year sojourn in Aceh. For instance, one of his most studied works, the *Ṣirāṭ al-Mustaqīm*, was prepared at least partly before he came to Aceh. His works mainly deal with *taṣawwuf*, *kalām*, *fiqh*, *ḥadīth*, history and comparative religion.

As he wrote much on *kalām* and *taṣawwuf*, apparently al-Rānīrī considers one of the basic questions among Malay-Indonesia Muslims to be their *'aqā'id* (fundamentals of belief). Therefore, he attempts to make clear, among other things, the relation between the Realities of God and the universe and man.[59] He delineates the Ash'arī doctrine of difference (*mukhālafah*) between God and the universe, the origin of the world in time (*iḥdāth*), and God's absolute transcendence vis-à-vis man. With his loyal adherence to the Ash'ariyyah it is not hard to understand why he was so bitter towards Ḥamzah al-Fanṣūrī and Shams al-Dīn, both of whom maintained the immanence of God in His creation.

As far as al-Rānīrī's Sufism is concerned, although he is generally known as belonging to the Rifā'iyyah order, he was also affiliated with the 'Aydarūsiyyah and Qādiriyyah orders. His affiliation, particularly with the 'Aydarūsiyyah *ṭarīqah*, appears to have been crucial in developing his radical tendencies. Eaton[60] has shown us that the 'Aydarūsiyyah, with its strong Arabian roots, is one of the most important reformist *ṭarīqah*s in the Indian subcontinent. It strongly emphasises the harmony between the mystical way and total obedience to the *sharī'ah*. It is also noted for its non-ascetic and activist attitude.

With these characteristics, the 'Aydarūsiyyah is clearly a *ṭarīqah* of neo-*ṣūfī* type. The prominent *ṣūfī* scholars of the 'Aydarūsiyyah attempted to impart in India not only the teachings of a more *sharī'ah*-oriented Islam but also certain symbols of Arab culture. 'Abd Allāh b. Shaykh al-'Aydarūs (d. 1041/1631), for instance, went so far with his reform as to 'convert' Sulṭān Ibrāhim II ('Ādil Shāh) from Shī'ism to Sunnī Islam. Although the Sulṭān was tolerant of the Shī'is, he had never been a Shī'ī himself. 'Abd Allāh also persistently attempted to persuade the Sulṭān to wear Arab clothing.

Joining in the general tendency in these networks, al-Rānīrī insisted on the importance of the *sharī'ah* in mystical practices by writing the *Ṣirāt al-Mustaqīm* in Malay.[61] In this work he explicates the basic but fundamental duties of each Muslim in his life. Using the familiar outline of any *fiqh* book, he goes on in detail to explain various matters concerning ablution (*wuḍū'*), prayers (*ṣalāt*), 'alms' (*zakāh*), fasting (*ṣawm*), pilgrimage (*ḥajj*), sacrifice (*qurbān*) and the like. Although the book would seem to be a simple exposition of basic *fiqh* rules, one should not underestimate its importance to Malay-Indonesian Muslims during the time when an extravagant Sufism was prevalent.

Most of the al-Rānīrī works are polemical, and to some extent apologetical. But this should not conceal the important fact that he always makes good use of standard books and leading authorities. He was certainly an avid reader. On *kalām* and *taṣawwuf* he eloquently quotes al-Ghazālī, Ibn 'Arabī, al-Qunyawī, al-Qāshānī, al-Fīrūzābādī, al-Jīlī, 'Abd al-Raḥmān al-Jāmī, Faḍl Allāh al-Burhānpūrī and other leading scholars.[62] As for his *fiqh*, he based himself on the standard Shāfi'ī books, including *Minhāj al-Ṭālibīn* of al-Nawawī, *Fatḥ al-Wahhāb bi Sharḥ Minhāj al-Ṭullāb* of Zakariyyā al-Anṣārī, *Hidāyat al-Muḥtāj Sharḥ al-Mukhtaṣār* of Ibn Ḥajar, *Kitāb al-Anwār* of al-Ardābilī or *Nihāyat al-Muḥtāj* (*ilā Sharḥ al-Minhājŏ* —of al-Nawawī) of Shams al-Dīn al-Ramlī.[63] Considering al-Rānīrī's works and their sources, it is clear that he was more than simply a zealous *Shaykh al-Islām*, using his religious and political influence to persecute *wujūdiyyah* followers. He was a man of erudition and argument, exploring the intricacies of the mystical doctrines in order to put those he regarded as having gone astray on the right track.

In his polemical works, al-Rānīrī vigorously charges *wujūdiyyah* followers with heresy and even with polytheism. Thus, as a consequence, they could be condemned to death if they refused to repent.[64] Furthermore, he challenges protagonists of the *wujūdiyyah* doctrine to debate the matter. Al-Rānīrī tells us that debates were held at the court of the Sultanate in the presence of the Sulṭān or Sulṭānah. In some instances the debates were fierce and lasted for several days. However, they obviously failed to settle the differences. Sulṭān Iskandar Thānī repeatedly ordered the *wujūdiyyah* followers to change their minds and repent to God for their misbelief, but this was also fruitless. Finally, the Sulṭān had them all killed and their books burned in front of the Banda Aceh grand mosque, Bayt al-Raḥmān.[65] Al-Rānīrī tells us vividly:

> Again they say: '*al-'ālam huwa Allāh, huwa al-'ālam*—the universe is God and He is the universe. After that the King orders them to repent for their wrong belief. He appeals several times, yet they are not willing [to change their mind]; they even fight the messengers of the King. Finally, the King gives orders to kill them all and to gather and burn their books in the field at the front of the Mosque Bayt al-Raḥmān.[66]

Scholars have tried to explain why al-Rānīrī used his position as the *Shaykh al-Islām* of the Sultanate to issue a *fatwā* declaring the *wujūdiyyah* people unbelievers (*kāfirs*). Daudy[67], for instance, asserts that al-Rānīrī's uncompromising personality has something closely to do with his past experience of living in the hostile Hindu environment of India. The long-standing social and religious conflicts between the Muslim minority and the Hindu majority created little tolerance within segments of both societies; and al-Rānīrī was a product of such a society.

Looking at al-Rānīrī's case in this rather wider perspective, this kind of interpretation has its own validity. However, I would argue that al-Rānīrī's uncompromising personality is to a great extent related to the reformism in the networks. In other words, as Drewes[68] correctly points out, al-Rānīrī's radical opposition to Ḥamzah al-Fanṣūrī and Shams al-Dīn al-Samatrānī, together with their followers, was not an isolated case of 'orthodox reaction' to unorthodox mysticism. Al-Rānīrī's sojourn in Aceh occurs during the period in which the doctrines of *wujūdiyyah* met serious theological opposition or were reinterpreted by many scholars in the centres, in a stricter way in light of the *sharī'ah*. In this sense, al-Rānīrī's attitude is a good example of how the reformism of the networks was translated into renewalism in the Malay-Indonesian world.

The persecution against *wujūdiyyah* followers left an everlasting mark on the intellectual life of Islam in the archipelago. It gave rise to a reassessment among the *'ulamā'*, in particular al-Sinkīlī, of such concepts as 'Muslim', '*kāfir*' (unbeliever), *tasāmuḥ* (religious tolerance), and the like, all of which will be discussed further. More importantly, al-Rānīrī's *fatwā* of *takfīr* and the killing of *wujūdiyyah* Muslims reached the Ḥaramayn, where an anonymous manuscript written in 1086/1675[69] tells us that it was the writer's answer to questions coming from an island of the Jāwah region (*min ba'ḍ jazā'ir Jāwah*). The problem put forward was that an *'ālim* coming from 'above the wind'[70] accused a *wujūdiyyah ṣūfī* of being a kāfir. The case was brought to the attention of the Sulṭān. The *'ālim* strongly demanded that he repent, but he refused. The *ṣūfī* maintained that he could not repent as his argument was not understood. But nobody took his words seriously; and finally the Sulṭān issued an order to kill him, together with all the people who followed his teachings. All of them were put into the fire. Was it permissible to do that?

The author of the treatise explains the danger of arguing with people who cannot comprehend the matter. However, the *ṣūfī*'s statements that he was not properly understood were indications of his following certain intricate interpretations of a particular religious doctrine that he himself was not able to explicate to the *'ālim*, who labelled him unbeliever. Whatever the case, the treatise's writer argues that it was terribly wrong to kill him and his followers. He further elaborates that the accusation was obviously based on a literal understanding of *wujūdiyyah* doctrine; yet this attitude was not permissible in Islam. He goes on to quote the Prophet that any statement of Muslims could not be considered wrong as long as others were able to interpret it in any other way.

It comes as no surprise that the writer was Ibrāhīm al-Kūrānī.[71] The *'ālim* from 'above the wind' was obviously al-Rānīrī; the Sulṭān was Iskandar Thānī; and the one who transmitted the problem to the Ḥaramayn was al-Sinkīlī. As we describe in greater detail in chapter 4, al-Sinkīlī apparently could not accept the way al-Rānīrī launched his reform. Therefore, without any hesitation he brought the matter to his teacher's attention across the Indian Ocean in Medina. And finally he received the teacher's response. This event tells us how the intellectual and religious networks of teacher–disciple played their role in the historical course of Islam in this part of the Muslim world.

AL-RĀNĪRĪ'S ROLE IN MALAY-INDONESIAN ISLAM

Al-Rānīrī was primarily a *ṣūfī*, a theologian and a *faqīh* (jurist). But he was also a man of letters, a preacher and a politician. His multifaceted personality could lead to misunderstanding, particularly if one viewed only a certain aspect of his thought. As a result, until now he has often been considered more as a *ṣūfī* who was probably occupied only with mystical practices, whereas he was in fact also a *faqīh*, whose main concern was the practical application of the very basic rules and regulations of the *sharī'ah*. Therefore, to understand him entirely one should take into consideration all aspects of his thought, personality and activity.

Although al-Rānīrī's sojourn in the archipelago was relatively short (for seven years only, 1047–1054/1637–1644), he had a significant role in the development of Islam in the Malay-Indonesian world. He played a key role in bringing the great tradition of Islam to the region, reducing substantially the tendency to uncontrolled intrusion of local tradition on Islam. Without underestimating the role of the earlier carriers of Islam from the Middle East or elsewhere, one can say that al-Rānīrī had a much stronger network of the *'ulamā'*, connecting the Islamic tradition in the Middle East with that of the archipelago. He was indeed one of the most important transmitters of Islamic reformism and renewals to this part of the Muslim world.

We do not know much about al-Rānīrī's network of disciples, but there is little doubt that his most prominent disciple in the archipelago was al-Maqassārī. The latter, in a work entitled *Safīnat al-Najāh*, gives his *silsilah* of the Qādiriyyah *ṭarīqah* from al-Rānīrī. Al-Maqassārī explicitly states that al-Rānīrī was his shaykh and teacher (*guru*).[72] Despite this evidence, there are problems concerning the date and place they met (which are discussed in chapter 5). We have no names for the disciples of al-Rānīrī, except al-Maqassārī. After returning to Rānīr, he apparently devoted himself to teaching and writing; he even ordered his disciples to complete his *Jawāhir al-'Ulūm fī Kashf al-Ma'lūm*, but he mentioned no names for these disciples.[73]

Despite the obscurity surrounding the identity of his disciples, al-Rānīrī's role in the transmission of reformism through his works is undeniable. His habit of citing numerous well-known authorities and standard works to support his arguments throughout his writings was a crucial means of their transmission. In so doing, he introduced these authorities to the Muslims in the archipelago. Furthermore, by introducing into and disseminating in the archipelago the interpretation of Islam held by the mainstream of *'ulamā'* and *ṣūfī*s in the centres of Islam, he stimulated a strong impetus for renewal among Malay-Indonesian Muslims. Al-Rānīrī's mastery of Arabic, Persian, Urdu, Malay and Acehnese was of great importance to him in building his scholarly reputation.

With his polemical works against what he regarded as the 'heretical' *wujūdiyyah*, al-Rānīrī was the first in the archipelago to clarify the distinction between the true and the false interpretation and understanding of *ṣūfī* doctrines and practices. There were, of course, attempts by such scholars as Faḍl Allāh al-Burhānpūrī to clarify this distinction. But al-Burhānpūrī failed to achieve the intended aim.[74] On the contrary, his work led to religious confusion among Malay-Indonesian Muslims, so that Ibrāhīm al-Kūrānī felt it necessary to write a commentary on it, as mentioned earlier. Further attempts were also carried out by Ḥamzah al-Fanṣūrī and Shams al-Dīn. But, as al-Attas points out, their works again failed to draw a clear distinction, particularly between God and the universe, or relations between God and Creation.[75] Al-Rānīrī therefore paved the way towards the rise of neo-Sufism in the archipelago.

A further consequence of his clarification of the types of Sufism was the intensification of the Islamisation process in the Malay-Indonesian world.[76] The process was pushed further by al-Rānīrī's writings on the *sharī'ah* and *fiqh*, particularly by his *Ṣirāt al-Mustaqīm*. Al-Rānīrī was the first *'ālim* in the archipelago ever to take the initiative to write a sort of standard manual for people's basic religious duties. Even though the precepts of *sharī'ah* and *fiqh* had to an extent been known and practised by some Malay-Indonesian Muslims, there was no single work in Malay to which to refer. Therefore, it is not hard to understand why the work became very popular and seems to be still in use to this day in certain parts of the Malay-Indonesian world, particularly in Southern Thailand and the Malay Peninsula.[77]

Al-Rānīrī's concern about the application of the detailed rules of the *fiqh* led him to extract sections of his *Ṣirāt al-Mustaqīm* and issue them as separate works. The most famous among these extracts are *Kaifiyat al-Ṣalāh* and *Bāb al-Nikāḥ*; the latter together with the *Ṣirāt al-Mustaqīm* were sent by al-Rānīrī himself to Kedah in about 1050/1640. This appears to be of particular importance in furthering the Islamisation of Kedah.[78] For that reason it has been claimed that his contribution to the process of Islamisation of Kedah was of equal magnitude to that of the first preachers who directly brought Islam to the people of Kedah.[79]

The role of al-Rānīrī in the intensification of the process of Islamisation is also clear in the political field. During his sojourn in Aceh, in his position as the *Shaykh al-Islām* of the Sultanate, among his duties was that of counselling the newly enthroned Sulṭān Iskandar Thānī in various matters, either religious or political. In his *Bustān al-Salāṭīn*, he tells us how he counselled the Sulṭān in his function as a ruler and *khalīfah* (representative) of God on earth. Quoting various verses of the Qur'ān (e.g. 4:59; 6:165; 38:26), he makes clear to the Sulṭān his responsibility for and duty towards his people; protecting the weak and providing goodness to the people make him protected and blessed by God. Probably because of his counsel, Sulṭān Iskandar Thānī abolished un-Islamic punishments for criminals, such as the 'immersing into hot oil' (*mencelup minyak*) and 'licking the burning steel' (*menjilat besi*).[80] The Sultān also prohibited his subjects from discussing the issues surrounding God's Being with reason.[81]

According to al-Rānīrī, the application of the *sharī'ah* could not be intensified without a deeper knowledge of the tradition (*ḥadīth*) of the Prophet. Therefore, he compiled in his *Hidāyat al-Ḥabīb fī al-Targhīb wa al-Tartīb* some traditions of the Prophet which he translated from Arabic into Malay so that the Muslim population would be able to understand them correctly. In this concise compendium, he interpolates *ḥadīth*s with citations of the Qur'ānic verses in order to support the arguments attached to the *ḥadīth*s. This work was the pioneer in the field in the archipelago and introduced the importance of *ḥadīth* in the life of Muslims.

Apart from clarifying the distinction between unorthodox and orthodox Sufism and emphasising the importance of the *sharī'ah*, al-Rānīrī took on the arduous task of making Muslims understand correctly the articles of belief (*al-'aqā'id*). It is true that one of the standard works of the 'Ash'arīs, the *Mukhtaṣar al-'Aqā'id* by Najm al-Dīn al-Nasafī, was already in use among certain circles of Malay-Indonesian Muslims. However, this is not a simple text: in addition to the subject being difficult to comprehend, its Arabic was hard for the Malays in general to understand. Realising the need for this kind of text, al-Rānīrī prepared its Malay translation or a partial translation, called *Durrat al-Farā'id bi Sharḥ al-'Aqā'id.*[82] He does not in fact simply translate it; he adds some commentary, so that it is easier for his Malay readers to understand.

Al-Rānīrī played a crucial role, not only in clarifying to the Malay-Indonesian Muslims the very basis of Islamic beliefs and practices but in revealing the truth of Islam in a comparative perspective with other religions. He was the first *'ālim* ever in the Malay world to write a work on comparative religion, called *Tibyān fī Ma'rifat al-Adyān*,[83] as well as substantial passages touching on the same subject in his other works.[84] The *Tibyān*, which has been discussed by scholars,[85] was apparently planned according to the *Kitāb al-Milal wa al-Niḥal*, the well-known work on comparative religion by al-Shahrastānī. But for much of its contents al-Rānīrī depends on Abū Shahūr al-Salimī's *Kitāb al-Tamhīd*. In the first part of the *Tibyān* he begins his discussion with non-scriptural religions, to conclude with the scriptural religions of Christianity and Judaism. The second part deals with Islam, including the 72 Muslim splinter groups considered heretical or outside the true Sunnī tradition. As one might expect, he includes the followers of Ḥamzah al-Fanṣūrī and Shams al-Dīn among these 'heretics'.

The influence of al-Rānīrī in the field of history was no less profound. Again, he was the first writer in Malay to present history in a universal context, and to initiate a new form of Malay historical writing. His history books, collectively called the *Bustān al-Salāṭīn*, are his most voluminous work, reflecting the author's special interest in the field. These seven books show us how he successfully made use of several traditions of the historiography of Islam and introduced them to Malay audiences. The first two books present the history of the world, mostly from a theological point of view. While the first book is written following the pattern of al-Kisā'ī's *Qiṣaṣ al-Anbiyā'*, dealing with the creation of the Pen, the Tablet, the Light of Muḥammad and the like, the second book is planned according to al-Ṭabarī's *Tārīkh al-Rusul wa al-Mulūk*. Thus, he begins with the history of the Persian, Greek and Arabian people in the pre-Islamic period, followed by an annalistic history of Islam until the year of the execution of al-Ḥallāj in 309/921. The second book later goes on to describe the history of the kings of India and the Malay-Indonesian world. The remaining five books of the *Bustān al-Salāṭīn* follow the pattern of al-Ghazali's *Nasīḥat al-Mulūk*, and therefore were intended to be guiding books for the court families.

The *Bustān al-Salāṭīn* is one of the most important early Malay-Indonesian histories. It has been an indispensable source for the reconstruction of the early history of Islam in the Malay-Indonesian world. Its significance becomes enormous in view of the fact that the history of Islam in the region is mostly written on the basis of Western sources. Al-Rānīrī's acquaintance with the history of the archipelago is clearly extraordinary. It seems that one of his major sources for the *Bustān al-Salāṭīn* was the *Sejarah Melayu*.

In fact, he was apparently an expert in the detailed description of the *Sejarah Melayu*, because he probably was well acquainted with its author, Tun Seri Lanang. He was also familiar with the genealogy of the Sulṭāns of Pahang.[86]

Not least important is al-Rānīrī's role in stimulating further development of the Malay language as the lingua franca of the Malay-Indonesian world. He is even acclaimed as one of the first *pujanggas* (men of letters) of Malay. Although al-Rānīrī was not a native speaker of Malay, his mastery of the language was undisputed. A. Teeuw, a Dutch scholar who was one of the prominent experts in the Malay-Indonesian language, maintains that his classical Malay indicates none of the awkwardness often found in classical Malay before the seventeenth century.[87] Thus, works in Malay are also considered literary works, and contributed substantially to the development of Malay as a language of learning.

4

Seventeenth Century Malay-Indonesian Networks II: ‘Abd al-Ra’ūf al-Sinkīlī

We have seen how al-Rānīrī sparked the momentum for renewal in the Malay-Indonesian world. Although the reform he launched underwent a significant political setback with his fall, there is no doubt that al-Rānīrī had an irreversible impact. Before long the renewal again gained a crucial stimulus in al-Sinkīlī (1024–1105/1615–93), one of the most important early *mujaddid*s in the archipelago. We have already established that al-Rānīrī in one way or another had connections with the core of networks in the Ḥaramayn. Al-Sinkīlī surpassed al-Rānīrī in this respect. He possessed direct and undisputed links with the major scholars of the networks. For the first time we find, in al-Sinkīlī, a clear picture of intellectual and spiritual genealogies, putting Islam in the Malay-Indonesian world on the map of the global transmission of Islamic reformism.

Al-Sinkīlī has been the subject of several important studies. However, these mainly concentrate on his teachings. Some of them do mention in passing his teachers in the Middle East, but no attempt has been made to trace further his intricate intellectual connections with the cosmopolitan scholarly networks centred in Mecca and Medina. There is no study either that seeks to examine how his involvement in the networks influenced his thought and intellectual disposition. Furthermore, no critical study has been done to assess his role in stimulating Islamic renewal in the Malay-Indonesian world. An attempt will be made in this chapter to deal with all these questions. In that way we shall be able to gain a better understanding not only of his position in the historical course of Islam in the archipelago but also of the interplay between Islam in the Malay-Indonesian world and Islam in the Middle East.

AL-SINKĪLĪ’S EARLY LIFE

‘Abd al-Ra’ūf b. ‘Alī al-Jāwī al-Fanṣūrī al-Sinkīlī, as his name indicates, was a Malay of Fanṣūr, Sinkil (modern Singkel), on the southwestern coastal region of Aceh. His birth date is unknown, but Rinkes, after calculating backwards from the date of his return from the Middle East to Aceh, suggests that he was born around 1024/1615.[1] This date has been accepted by most scholars of al-Sinkīlī.[2] We do not have very reliable accounts of his familial background. According to Hasjmi, ancestors of al-Sinkīlī came from Persia to the Sultanate of Samudra-Pasai at the end of the thirteenth century. They later settled in Fanṣūr (Barus), an important old harbour on the coast of western Sumatra. He further argues that al-Sinkīlī's father was the older brother of Ḥamzah al-Fanṣūrī.[3] We are not sure whether al-Sinkīlī was really a nephew of Ḥamzah, as there is no other source to corroborate it. It appears that he did have some familial relationship with him, for in some of his extant works al-Sinkīlī's name is followed by the statement: 'who is of the tribe of Ḥamzah Fanṣūrī' (*'yang berbangsa Ḥamzah Fanṣūrī'*).[4]

Daly,[5] on the other hand, maintains that al-Sinkīlī's father, Shaykh 'Alī [al-Fanṣūrī], was an Arab preacher who, after marrying a local woman of Fanṣūr, took up residence in Singkel, where their child, 'Abd al-Ra'ūf, was born. There is of course the possibility that al-Sinkīlī's father was non-Malay, as we know that Samudra-Pasai and Fanṣūr had been frequented by Arab, Persian, Indian, Chinese and Jewish traders from at least the ninth century.[6] But as far as the accounts of al-Sinkīlī's father are concerned, there is no other source to substantiate them.

It appears that al-Sinkīlī acquired his early education in his native village, Singkel, mainly from his father, a supposed *'ālim*, who, Hasjmi[7] believes, also founded a *madrasah* that attracted students from various places in the Acehnese Sultanate. It is also very likely that he continued his studies in Fanṣūr, as it, as Drakard[8] points out, was an important Islamic centre and a point of contact between Malays and Muslims from western and southern Asia. According to Hasjmi, al-Sinkīlī later travelled to Banda Aceh, the capital of the Acehnese Sultanate, to study with, among others, Ḥamzah al-Fanṣūrī and Shams al-Dīn al-Samatrānī. It is clear that al-Sinkīlī could not have met Hamzah, as the latter died around 1016/1607, at which time al-Sinkīlī was not even born.[9] However, we cannot rule out the possibility of al-Sinkīlī's studying with Shams al-Dīn. If we assume that he studied with Shams al-Dīn (d. 1040/1630) in his final years, al-Sinkīlī must have been in his teens at that time.

Despite these problematic accounts, there is no doubt that in the period before al-Sinkīlī departed for Arabia, around 1052/1642, Aceh was marked by controversies and struggles between the followers of the *wujūdiyyah* doctrine and al-Rānīrī, as discussed in chapter 3. There is no indication whatsoever that al-Sinkīlī met and had personal contact with al-Rānīrī, who was in Aceh in the period 1047/1637 to 1054/1644–45. However, he must have been aware of the teaching of Ḥamzah al-Fanṣūrī and Shams al-Dīn as well as of al-Rānīrī's persecution of their followers. Al-Sinkīlī, as we will see later, apparently attempted to disengage himself from the controversies.

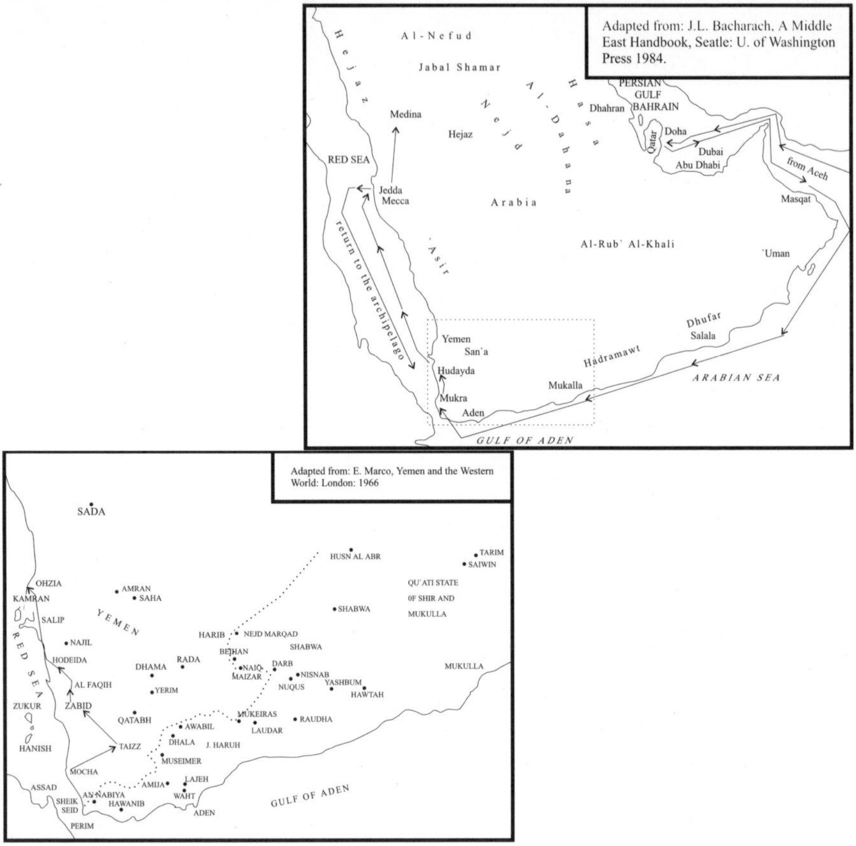

Map 2 Al-Sinkīlī's itinerary

Even though the spirit of al-Sinkīlī's writings shows that he differs from Ḥamzah and Shams al-Dīn, we find no evidence in his teachings that explicitly opposes their teaching.[10] He also has the same attitude towards al-Rānīrī. Only implicitly does he criticise the way al-Rānīrī carried out his renewal; he has no dispute with his teachings in general.

AL-SINKĪLĪ'S ARABIAN NETWORKS

Although al-Sinkīlī's early years were obscure, we are fortunate that he has left us a biographical codicil of his studies in Arabia. In the codicil attached to the colophon of one of his works, *'Umdat al-Muḥtājīn ilā Sulūk Maslak al-Mufridīn*,[11] he provides us with information on the *ṭarīqah*s he was affiliated with, the places where he studied, the teachers from whom he learned, and the scholars he met. Although the account is rather concise, it nonetheless gives us a good picture of how a Malay-Indonesian *'ālim* travelled in search of *'ilm* (religious knowledge). It discloses not only the crisscrossing of our scholarly networks but also the process of transmission of Islamic learning among Muslim scholars.

Al-Sinkīlī most probably left Aceh for Arabia in 1052/1642.[12] He lists 19 teachers from whom he learned various branches of Islamic discipline, and 27 other *'ulamā'* with whom he had personal contacts and relations. We are not going to give accounts of all his teachers; we will examine only the most prominent among them. Al-Sinkīlī studied in a number of places, scattered along the *ḥajj* routes, from Ḍuḥā (Doha) in the Persian Gulf region, Yemen, Jeddah, finally to Mecca and Medina (see Map 2). Thus he began his studies in Ḍuḥā, Qatar, where he studied with 'Abd al-Qādir al-Mawrīr,[13] but it appears that he stayed there for only a short time.

Leaving Ḍuḥā, al-Sinkīlī continued his studies in Yemen, chiefly in Bayt al-Faqīh [ibn 'Ujayl] and Zabīd, although he also had several teachers in Mawza', Mukhā, al-Luḥayyah, Hudaydah and Tā'izz. Bayt al-Faqīh and Zabīd were certainly the most important centres of Islamic learning in this region.[14] In Bayt al-Faqīh he studied mostly with scholars of the Ja'mān family, such as Ibrāhīm b. Muḥammad b. Ja'mān,[15] Ibrāhīm b. 'Abd Allāh b. Ja'mān and Qāḍī Isḥāq b. Muḥammad b. Ja'mān. In addition, he established relations with *Faqīh* al-Ṭayyib b. Abī al-Qāsim b. Ja'mān, the Mufti of Bayt al-Faqīh, and another *Faqīh*, Muḥammad b. Ja'mān.[16] The Ja'māns, an eminent *ṣūfī-'ulamā'* family in Yemen or, as al-Muḥibbī puts it, 'a prop of the people of Yemen', initially lived in Zabīd before finally moving to Bayt al-Faqīh.[17] Several of the Ja'mān scholars, mentioned earlier, were students of Aḥmad al-Qushāshī and Ibrāhīm al-Kurānī.

Among al-Sinkīlī's teachers from the Ja'mān family, the most important was Ibrāhīm b. 'Abd Allāh Ibn Ja'mān (d. 1083/1672). Mostly known as a *muḥaddith* and *faqīh*, he appears to have studied largely in the Yemen region before settling down in Bayt al-Faqīh. He was a prolific author of fatwās and, therefore, one of the most sought-after scholars in the area. He also had connections with leading *'ulamā'* in the networks.[18] al-Sinkīlī relates that he spent most of his time with Ibrāhīm b. 'Abd Allāh Ja'mān studying what he calls '*'ilm al-ẓāhir*' (exoteric sciences), such as *fiqh*, *ḥadīth* and other related subjects. It was 'with his blessing that this *faqīr*, poor [al-Sinkīlī] was able to continue his studies under the feet [*tapak*] of the enlightened *walī* (saint] who was the authority and Quṭb of his time; that is, Shaykh Aḥmad al-Qushāshī in the City of the Prophet, peace be upon him'.[19]

Isḥāq b. Muḥammad b. Ja'mān (d. 1014–1096/1605–1685) was another major scholar of the Ja'mān family with whom al-Sinkīlī studied. Born in Zabīd, he got his early education, in Yemen, from his uncle, Ibn al-Ṭayyib b. Ja'mān, among others. Later he travelled to the Ḥaramayn, where he became a student or rather a friend of Ibrāhīm al-Kūrānī, 'Isā al-Maghribī and Ibn 'Abd al-Rasūl al-Barzanjī. Returning to Bayt al-Faqīh, he gained fame as a leading *faqīh* and *muḥaddith* in the region. He died in Zabīd.[20] Even though al-Sinkīlī mentions only 'Abd Allāh b.

Ja'mān, who introduced him to al-Qushāshī, it is not unlikely that Isḥāq b. Ja'mān also recommended him to study with al-Qushāshī as well as with al-Kurānī.

The network of al-Sinkīlī's clearly becomes more complex on the continuation of his studies in Zabīd. Among his teachers in Zabid were 'Abd al-Raḥīm b. al-Ṣiddīq al-Khāṣṣ;[21] Amīn b. al-Ṣiddīq al-Mizjājī, who was also a teacher of Muḥammad al-Qushāshī;[22] and 'Abd Allāh b. Muḥammad al-'Adanī, whom al-Sinkīlī calls the best reciter of the Qur'ān in the region. He also came into contact with prominent Zabīdī or Yemeni scholars such as 'Abd al-Fattāḥ al-Khāṣṣ, the *Muftī* of Zabīd; Sayyid al-Ṭāhir b. al-Ḥusayn al-Ahdal; Muḥammad 'Abd al-Bāqī al-Mizjājī, a celebrated Naqshbandī shaykh (d. 1074/1664),[23] who was also a teacher of al-Maqassārī; Qāḍī Muḥammad b. Abī Bakr b. Muṭayr (d. 1086/1675);[24] and Aḥmad Abū al-'Abbās b. al-Muṭayr (d. 1075/1664).[25] Most of these scholars, especially of the Ahdal and Mizjājī families, as we have shown, played an important role in linking scholars in the networks.

Al-Sinkīlī does not inform us as to when he left Yemen. Following the pilgrimage route we now find him in Jeddah, where he studied with its *Muftī*, 'Abd al-Qādir al-Barkhalī.[26] He then continued his travels to Mecca, where he studied with Badr al-Dīn al-Lahūrī and 'Abd Allāh al-Lahūrī. Al-Sinkīlī's most important teacher in Mecca was 'Alī b. 'Abd al-Qādir al-Ṭabarī. Al-Sinkīlī was introduced to 'Alī al-Ṭabarī by one of his teachers in Zabīd, 'Alī b. Muḥammad al-Dayba', a *muḥaddith* who had close relationships with the Ṭabarī family and other Ḥaramayn leading scholars.[27] 'Alī al-Ṭabarī, like his brother Zayn al-'Ābidīn,[28] was a leading Meccan *faqīh*. 'Alī, or the Ṭabarī family, had extensive networks with other Yemeni scholars, especially of the Ja'mān family, who may also have recommended al-Sinkīlī to study with 'Alī al-Ṭabarī and other prominent Ḥaramayn scholars.[29]

In addition to studying with scholars whom he mentioned specifically as his teachers, al-Sinkīlī established contacts and relations with other prominent scholars in Mecca, both resident and visiting. He does not specify the nature of his relations with them, but there is little doubt that he gained great advantages from them. They can be assumed, at least, to have inspired him and brought him a much wider intellectual perspective. Most of these scholars are familiar names in the networks: they include 'Isā al-Maghribī, 'Abd al-'Azīz al-Zamzamī, Tāj al-Dīn Ibn Ya'qūb, 'Alā' al-Dīn al-Bābilī, Zayn al-'Ābidīn al-Ṭabarī, 'Alī Jamāl al-Makkī and 'Abd Allāh b. Sa'īd Bā Qashīr al-Makkī (1003–1076/1595–1665).[30]

The last leg of al-Sinkīlī's long journey in his search of knowledge was Medina. It was in the City of the Prophet that he felt satisfied that he had completed his studies. He studied in Medina with Aḥmad al-Qushāshī until the latter's death in 1071/1660, and with his *khalīfah*, Ibrāhīm al-Kūrānī. With al-Qushāshī, al-Sinkīlī learned what he calls the 'interior' sciences (*'ilm al-bāṭin*); that is, *taṣawwuf* and other related sciences. As a sign of his completion of studying the mystical way, al-Qushāshī appointed him his Shaṭṭāriyyah and Qādiriyyah *khalīfah*. Al-Sinkīlī's relationship with al-Qushāshī was apparently very cordial. An account of the Shaṭṭāriyyah *silsilah* in West Sumatra tells us that al-Sinkīlī studied with and served al-Qushāshī for several years. One day the teacher ordered him to return to *Jāwah*, for he considered that al-Sinkīlī possessed sufficient knowledge to enable him to carry out further Islamisation in his homeland. Having heard the order, al-Sinkīlī burst into tears, as he felt the need to learn more. As a result, al-Qushāshī changed his mind and allowed him to stay with him as long as he wished.[31]

Intellectually, al-Sinkīlī's largest debt was to Ibrāhīm al-Kūrānī. This is obvious not only in his thought, reflected in his writings, but also in his personal demeanour, as we will elaborate shortly. In his accounts, al-Sinkīlī makes it clear that it was with al-Kūrānī that he completed his education after the death of al-Qushāshī.[32] He had no *ṭarīqah silsilah* with al-Kūrānī; therefore, what he learned from him apparently were sciences, promoting an intellectual understanding of Islam rather than a spiritual or mystical one. In other words, for al-Sinkīlī, al-Qushāshī was a spiritual and mystical master, while al-Kurānī was an intellectual one.

There is no doubt that al-Sinkīlī's personal relationship with al-Kurānī was very close. We have mentioned earlier that Ibrāhīm wrote his masterpiece, the *Itḥāf al-Dhakī*, on the request of his unnamed '*aṣḥāb al-Jāwiyyīn*'. Considering their close intellectual and personal ties, it is no surprise that Johns[33] suggests that it was al-Sinkīlī who asked al-Kūrānī to write it. This suggestion becomes more plausible if one takes into account the fact that al-Sinkīlī, after returning to Aceh, asked al-Kūrānī's opinion on the way al-Rānīrī launched his reform in Aceh. Furthermore, it was apparently not the only question sent across the Indian Ocean by al-Sinkīlī to al-Kūrānī. In the concluding notes to his *Lubb al-Kashf wa al-Bayān li mā yarāhu al-Muḥtaḍar bi al-'Iyān*, which deals with the best type of *dhikr* for the dying, he writes:

> Let it be known, my disciples, that after I wrote this treatise, I sent a letter to the City of the Prophet, to our enlightened Shaykh in the science of Realities (*'ilm al-ḥaqā'iq*) and in the science of secret details of things (*'ilm al-daqā'iq*), i.e., Shaykh Mawlā Ibrāhīm [al-Kūrānī], asking [his opinion] about all matters described in the beginning of this treatise whether it is correct in the opinion of the [leading] *ṣūfīs*, and whether this matter on the best *dhikr* is discussed in *ḥadīth* books or in any [other] books. After a while, his treatise entitled *Kashf al-Muntaẓar* was sent by [our] Shaykh, in which he answers all the questions.[34]

Although al-Sinkīlī obviously spent most of his time in Medina studying with al-Qushāshī and al-Kūrānī, he also established contacts and scholarly relations with several other leading scholars there (see Chart 4). He

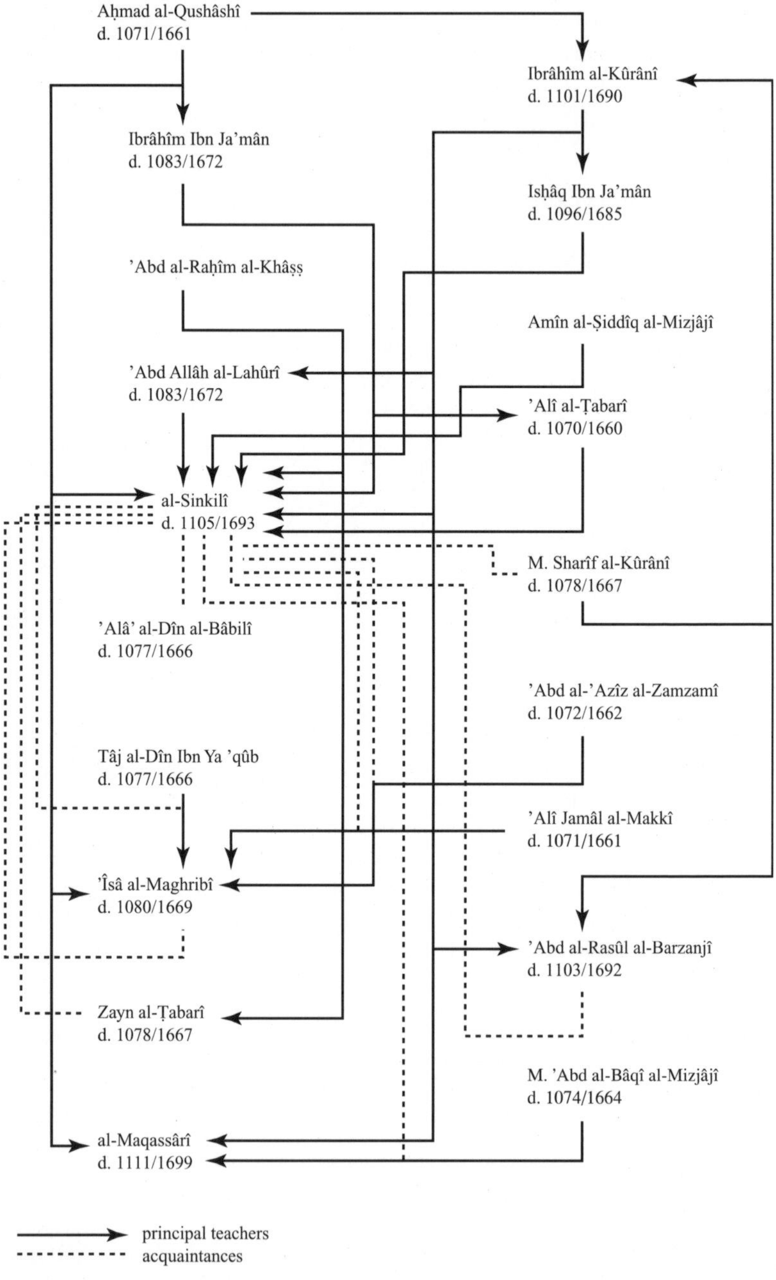

Chart 4 Al-Sinkīlī's partial networks

includes in his list[35] such scholars as Mullā Muḥammad Sharīf al-Kūrānī; Ibn ʻAbd al-Rasūl al-Barzanjī; Ibrāhīm b. ʻAbd al-Raḥmān al-Khiyarī al-Madanī (1037–83/1638–72), a student of ʻAlāʼ al-Dīn al-Bābilī, Ibrāhīm al-Kūrānī and ʻIsā al-Maghribī;[36] and ʻAlī al-Baṣīr al-Mālikī al-Madanī (d. 1106/1694), a *muḥaddith*.[37]

Al-Sinkīlī notes that he spent 19 years in Arabia. The fact that most of his teachers and acquaintances are recorded in Arabic biographical dictionaries indicates the incontestable prominence of al-Sinkīlī's intellectual milieu. Coming from a fringe region of the Muslim world, he entered the core of the scholarly networks and won the favour of the major scholars in the Ḥaramayn. His education was undeniably complete from *sharīʼah*, *fiqh*, *ḥadīth* and other related exetoric disciplines to *kalām*, and *taṣawwuf* or esoteric sciences. His career and works after his return to the archipelago were the history of his conscious efforts to implant firmly the idea of harmony between *sharīʼah* and *taṣawwuf*.

Like many other scholars in the networks, al-Sinkīlī appears to have begun his teaching career in the Ḥaramayn. This is no surprise, as by the time he came to Mecca and Medina he already possessed sufficient knowledge to be transmitted to his fellow Malay-Indonesian Muslims. It appears that al-Sinkīlī also initiated *Jāwī* disciples into the Shaṭṭāriyyah *ṭarīqah*. But there were also Shaṭṭāriyyah *silsilah*s in Java which went straight back to Aḥmad al-Qushāshī, instead of by way of al-Sinkīlī. Snouck Hurgronje[38] maintains that al-Qushāshī appointed his Malay-Indonesian *khalīfah*s during the pilgrimage. If we accept this, then we can believe that al-Sinkīlī played a crucial role in introducing them to al-Qushāshī.

AL-SINKĪLĪ'S TEACHINGS AND RENEWAL

Al-Sinkīlī supplies no date for his return to his homeland. However, he indicates that he returned not long after the death of al-Qushāshī, and after al-Kūrānī issued him an *ijāzah* to transmit what he had received from him. Therefore, most scholars of al-Sinkīlī are in accord that he returned to Aceh about 1072/1661.[39] It is useful to recall that Sulṭānah Ṣafiyyat al-Dīn, who had patronised al-Rānīrī for about two and a half years before turning to Sayf al-Rijāl, still occupied the throne of the Acehnese Sultanate. We do not know for sure whether Sayf al-Rijāl, powerful exponent of the *wujūdiyyah* type of Sufism, was still alive nor how far the doctrine could be revived by him.

In any case, the arrival of al-Sinkīlī from Arabia naturally created curiosity, particularly among court circles. Before long al-Sinkīlī was attended by a court official, Kātib Seri Raja b. Ḥamzah al-Āshī, who put unspecified religious questions to him. Voorhoeve[40] points out that al-Āshī's office was '*Reureukon Katiboy Mulo*'; that is, the Secret Secretary of the Sulṭānah. Therefore, Voorhoeve believes that al-Āshī was assigned by the Sulṭānah to assess al-Sinkīlī's religious views. It is clear that al-Sinkīlī passed the 'examination', as he soon won the favour of the court. He was appointed by the Sulṭānah to the office of the *Qāḍī Malik al-'Ādil* or *Muftī* who was responsible for administering religious affairs.

Before we proceed with al-Sinkīlī's teachings and his renewal, it is appropriate to discuss briefly the political developments in the Acehnese Sultanate during his career. The most striking feature of the period was that the Sultanate was ruled by four successive Sulṭānahs, well until the close of the seventeenth century. We already know that the first sulṭānah was Ṣafiyyat al-Dīn, who succeeded her husband, Iskandar Thānī, in 1051/1641. Under her long rule until 1086/1675, the Sultanate's authority substantially dwindled; much territory under its control in the Malay Peninsula and Sumatra soon broke away.[41] In addition to its political decline, the Sultanate under Ṣafiyyat al-Dīn was marked by religious turmoil.

The next Sulṭānah, Nūr al-'Ālam Naqīyyat al-Dīn, after reigning for only three years (1086–88/1675–8), was succeeded by Zakiyyat al-Dīn (1088–98/1678–88). Despite the Acehnese political troubles, the Sultanate was still apparently a respected Muslim political entity in the region. Thus in 1096/1683 Sulṭānah Zakiyyat al-Dīn received a delegation from the *Sharīf* of Mecca. The delegation was initially dispatched by the Sharīf Barakat to meet the Moghul Sulṭān Aurangzeb, who reportedly refused to entertain them. As a result, the delegation came to Aceh instead, bringing letters and gifts for the Sulṭānah. Feeling very pleased, she asked them to stay for a while in the capital city, while preparing gifts for the *Sharīf* of Mecca. It is reported that the Acehnese sent gifts and *ṣadaqah* (charitable gifts), consisting of, among other things, a statue made of gold taken from the ruins of the palace and the Bayt al-Raḥmān Mosque, which had both been destroyed by fire during the period of Sulṭānah Naqiyyat al-Dīn.[42]

It is clear that al-Sinkīlī was involved in events surrounding the delegation. However, we have no information on his exact role in entertaining the envoys of the *Sharīf* of Mecca. The delegation finally returned to Mecca, bringing numerous gifts to be presented not only to the *Sharīf* of Mecca, and the Prophet Mosque in Medina, but also to the poor population in the Ḥaramayn. There was dispute among the sons of the deceased Sharīf Barakat concerning the distribution of the gifts. The events surrounding the delegation, the coming of the gifts from '*Bandār Āshī*' (Banda Aceh) and the dispute among members of the Sharīfian family are not ignored by Arab historians. Based on a chronicle written about 1700, Aḥmad Daḥlān, an eminent scholar and historian of Mecca, gave a detailed account of the events.[43]

The coming of the delegation from Mecca was to a certain extent a boost to the prestige of the Sulṭānah. But it was also taken as a good opportunity for some Acehnese to ask for an opinion on the question of whether it was permissible according to Islamic law for a woman to be a ruler.[44] The question had long been an unsolved problem among the Acehnese. Al-Sinkīlī himself appears to have failed to answer it explicitly. In his *fiqh* work *Mir'āt al-Ṭullāb*, he does not address the issue directly. Discussing the requirements for the *ḥākim* (judge—by extension, the ruler), al-Sinkīlī seems deliberately to provide no Malay translation for the word *dhakar* (male).[45] He could possibly be accused of compromising his intellectual integrity, not only by accepting the rule of a woman but also by not addressing the issue more properly. On the other hand, this case could be a further indication of his personal tolerance, a trait al-Sinkīlī certainly possessed.

Similarly, the Meccan delegation gave no answer to the matter but apparently brought the question to the attention of the Ḥaramayn *'ulamā'*. The answer finally came from Mecca to the Acehnese court during the reign of Sulṭānah Kamālat al-Dīn (1098–1109/1688–99). The Chief *Muftī* of Mecca reportedly sent a *fatwā*, declaring that it ran contrary to *sharī'ah* for an Islamic kingdom to be ruled by a woman. As a result, Kamālat al-Dīn was deposed from the throne, and 'Umar b. Qāḍī al-Malik al-'Ādil Ibrāhīm was installed as Sulṭān Badr al-'Ālam Sharīf Hāshim Bā al-'Alawī al-Husaynī, establishing the 'Arab Jamāl al-Layl dynasty in Aceh.[46]

Thus, in his entire career in Aceh, al-Sinkīlī was patronised by the Sulṭānahs. He wrote about 22 works, dealing with *fiqh*, *tafsīr*, *kalām*, and *taṣawwuf*.[47] He wrote in both Malay and Arabic. He appears to have preferred to write in Arabic rather in Malay, acknowledging that his Malay was not very good because of his long sojourn in Arabia. Therefore, he was helped by two teachers of the Malay language to write his works in Sumatran Malay or, as he puts it: 'in the *lisān al-Jāwiyyat al-Samatra'iyyah*.'[48] Throughout his writings al-Sinkīlī, much like Ibrāhīm al-Kūrānī, demonstrates that his main concern is the reconciliation between the *sharī'ah* and *taṣawwuf*, or in his own terms, between the *ẓāhir* and *bāṭin* sciences.

The major work of al-Sinkīlī in *fiqh* is *Mir'āt al-Ṭullāb fī Tashīl Ma'rifat al-Al-Aḥkām al-Shar'iyyah li al-Malik al-Wahhāb*.[49] Written on the request of Sulṭānah Ṣafiyyat al-Dīn, it was completed in 1074/1663. Unlike the *Ṣirāṭ al-Mustaqīm* of al-Rānīrī, which deals solely with *'ibādat* (devotional services), the *Mir'āt al-Ṭullāb* sets out the *mu'āmalat* aspect of *fiqh*, including the political, social, economic and religious life of the Muslims. Covering so many topics, it is a substantial work in the field. Its main source was the *Fatḥ al-Wahhāb* of Zakariyyā al-Anṣārī, a major predecessor in the networks discussed earlier.[50] But al-Sinkīlī also derives materials from such standard books as: *Fatḥ al-Jawwād* and *Tuḥfat al-Muḥtāj*, both of Ibn Ḥajar al-Haytamī (d. 973/1565); *Nihāyat al-Muḥtāj* of Shams al-Dīn al-Ramlī; *Tafsīr al-Bayḍāwī* of Ibn 'Umar al-Bayḍāwī (d. 685/1286); and *Sharḥ Ṣaḥīḥ Muslim* of al-Nawawī (d. 676/1277).[51] With these sources al-Sinkīlī makes clear his intellectual connections with the networks.

Al-Sinkīlī was the first scholar in the Malay-Indonesian world who wrote on the *fiqh mu'āmalat*. By way of the *Mir'āt al-Ṭullāb* he shows his fellow Muslims that Islamic legal doctrines are not confined to purely devotional services (*'ibādat*) but include all aspects of their daily life. The *Mir'āt al-Ṭullāb* is no longer used in the archipelago today, although in the past the work was widely circulated. Hooker[52] has pointed out that the *Luwaran*, 'Selections', used by the Muslims of Maguindanao, the Philippines, since the middle of the nineteenth century, made the *Mir'āt al-Ṭullāb* one of its main references. Another work of al-Sinkīlī in *fiqh*, *Kitāb al-Farā'iḍ*, presumably taken from the *Mir'āt al-Ṭullāb*, was apparently used by some Malay-Indonesian Muslims until more recent times.[53]

The significance of Al-Sinkīlī to the development of Islam in the archipelago is irrefutable in the field of Qur'ānic commentary (*tafsīr*). He was the first *'ālim* ever in this part of the Muslim world to take on the enormous task of preparing *tafsīr* of the whole Qur'ān in Malay. A number of studies have discovered that before him there was only a fragment of commentary on *sūrah* 18 (al-Kahf). That work, supposedly written during the period of Ḥamzah al-Fanṣūrī or Shams al-Dīn al-Samatrānī, follows the tradition of al-Khāzin's commentary. But the style of translation and interpretation was different from that of Ḥamzah or Shams al-Dīn who, as a rule, interpreted passages of Qur'ānic verses cited in their works in a mystical sense.[54]

Although al-Sinkīlī gives no date for the completion of his acclaimed *tafsīr* work, entitled *Tarjumān al-Mustafīd*, there is no doubt that he wrote it during his long career in Aceh. Hasjmi[55] maintains that it was written in India, when he allegedly travelled there. This is a wild supposition, as there is no indication whatsoever that al-Sinkīlī ever set foot in India. Furthermore, it would have been impossible for him to undertake such a huge work while travelling. The patronage he enjoyed from the Acehnese rulers makes it more plausible that he wrote the work in Aceh.

Being the earliest *tafsīr*, it is not surprising that his work was widely circulated in the Malay-Indonesian world. Editions are found to be among the Malay community as far away as South Africa. Of various MSS available in many collections, Riddell[56] has established that the earliest extant copy of the *Tarjumān al-Mustafīd* dates back to the late seventeenth and early eighteenth centuries. More importantly, the *Tarjumān al-Mustafīd* lithograph and printed editions were published not only in Singapore, Penang, Jakarta and Bombay but also in the Middle East. It was published in Istanbul by the Maṭba'ah al-'Uthmāniyyah as early as 1302/1884 (and in 1324/1906); and later also in Cairo (by Sulaymān al-Marāghī) and Mecca (by al-Amīriyyah).[57] The fact that the *Tarjumān al-Mustafīd* was published in the Middle East at various times reflects the importance of the work as well as the intellectual stature of al-Sinkīlī. Its latest edition was published in Jakarta as recently as 1981. This indicates that the work is still in use among Malay-Indonesian Muslims today.

The *tafsīr* has long been regarded as simply a translation into Malay of the *Anwār al-Tanzīl* of Bayḍāwī. Snouck Hurgonje,[58] apparently without having studied the work in greater detail, concludes in his typically cynical way that it was merely a bad rendering of al-Bayḍāwī's commentary. With this conclusion Snouck was responsible for leading astray two other Dutch scholars, Rinkes and Voorhoeve. Rinkes, a student of Snouck, creates additional errors by stating that al-Sinkīlī's works, in addition to the *Tarjumān al-Mustafīd*, include a translation of the Bayḍāwī *Tafsīr* and a translation of a section of the Jalālayn *Tafsīr*.[59] Voorhoeve, after following Snouck and Rinkes, finally changed his conclusion by stating that the sources of the *Tarjumān al-Mustafīd* were various Arabic exegetical works.[60]

Riddell and Harun,[61] in their studies, have shown convincingly that the work is a rendering of the Jalālayn *Tafsīr*. Only in rare instances did al-Sinkīlī make use of the commentaries of al-Bayḍāwī and al-Khāzin (d. 41/1340). This identification is important, not only for disclosing the line of transmission from the centres, but for showing the approach al-Sinkīlī used in transmitting what he received from his teachers in the networks to his Malay-Indonesian audience.

The Jalālayn *Tafsīr*, it is worth noting, was written by the two Jalāls; that is, Jalāl al-Dīn al-Maḥallī (d. 864/1459) and Jalāl al-Dīn al-Suyūṭī (d. 911/1505), a major figure to whom most of our leading scholars in the networks traced their intellectual and spiritual genealogies. Al-Sinkīlī's selection of this *tafsīr* as the major source of his own commentary, therefore, must be because he possessed *isnād*s connecting him to Jalāl al-Dīn al-Suyūṭī through both al-Qushāshī and al-Kūrānī. Having had *ijāzah*s to transmit from al-Kūrānī all the sciences he received through successive chains of transmission, which included al-Suyūṭī, al-Sinkīlī could be expected to prefer the Jalālayn *Tafsīr* to other commentaries of the Qur'ān. This argument becomes more plausible when we take into account the fact that al-Sinkīlī also took the *Fatḥ al-Wahhāb* of Zakariyyā al-Anṣārī as the main source for his *Mir'āt al-Ṭullāb*. His tendency to rely heavily on the works by scholars in the networks is also clear in his works on *kalām* and *taṣawwuf*.

Furthermore, as Johns argues,[62] although the Jalālayn *Tafsīr* was often considered as contributing little to the development of the tradition of Qur'ānic commentary, it is a masterly, lucid and succinct exegesis of the Qur'ān. Furthermore, it provides *asbāb al-nuzūl* (the backgrounds to revelation) of the verses, which are very helpful for a fuller comprehension of the commentary. With these characteristics, the Jalālayn is a good introductory text for novices in the science of *tafsīr* among the Malay-Indonesian Muslims. In rendering the Jalālayn into Malay, al-Sinkīlī makes it simple or comprehensible to his fellow Malays in general. As a rule, he translates the Jalālayn word for word, and restrains himself from giving his own additions. Furthermore, he leaves out the Arabic grammatical explanations and long commentaries that might distract the attention of his audience. Thus, it is clear that his intention is that the *Tarjumān al-Mustafīd* should be easily understood by his readers and, as a consequence, become a practical guide for life.

One can hardly overestimate the role of the *Tarjumān al-Mustafīd* in the history of Islam in the archipelago. Johns[63] maintains that 'it is in more than one way a landmark in the history of Islamic learning in Malay'. It has contributed significantly to the study of Qur'ānic commentary in the archipelago. It lays the foundation for a bridge between *tarjamah* (translation) and *tafsīr*,[64] and thus stimulates further study on the *tafsīr* works in Arabic. For almost three centuries it was the only full rendering of the Qur'ān in Malay; only in the past 30 years have new commentaries in Malay-Indonesian made their appearance, but without necessarily detracting from the *Tarjumān al-Mustafīd*. Therefore, this work continues to play an important role in promoting a better understanding of the teachings of Islam.

We need no long argument to prove that al-Sinkīlī inherits the tendency from the scholarly networks of emphasising the importance of the *ḥadīth*. He wrote two works in this field. The first was a commentary on the *Arba'ūn Ḥadīth* of al-Nawawī, written at the request of Sulṭānah Zakiyyat al-Dīn.[65] The second was *al-Mawā'iẓ al-Badī'ah*, a collection of *ḥadīth qudsī*—that is, God's revelation communicated to the believers by the Prophet's own words. Again, al-Sinkīlī's selection of these works reflects his genuine concern for his fellow Muslims at the grassroots level; all he wants is to lead them to a better understanding of the teachings of Islam. It is worth noting that the Forty Ḥadīth of al-Nawawī, a small collection of *ḥadīth*s concerning the basic and practical duties of Muslims, is clearly intended for a general audience rather than specialists pursuing religious studies.

Al-Sinkīlī's collection of the *ḥadīth qudsī* possesses a similar nature. It delineates 50 teachings (*pengajaran*) concerning God and His relation to creation, hell and paradise, and the proper ways for the individual to achieve God's favour. Al-Sinkīlī particularly emphasises the need for each Muslim to find harmony between knowledge (*'ilm*) and good deeds (*'amal*); knowledge alone will not make a better Muslim: he must do good deeds as well. He thus appeals to Muslim activism.[66] The *Mawā'iẓ al-Badī'ah* was published in Mecca in 1310/1892 (fourth or fifth edition).[67] It was also reissued in Penang in 1369/1949, and it is still used by Muslims in the archipelago.[68] With these works, al-Sinkīlī set an example for later Malay scholars to undertake works on small collections of the *ḥadīth*, as since the nineteenth century such works have been very popular in the archipelago.[69]

Al-Sinkīlī writes not only for common Muslims (*al-'awwām*) on the *ẓāhir* sciences but also for the elite (*al-khawwāṣ*) on topics related to the *bāṭin* sciences, such as *kalām* and *taṣawwuf*. He wrote several works dealing with these topics.[70] But the works are still not sufficiently studied, and, as Johns [71] lamented more than three decades ago, there is a lack of interest among scholars in exploring them. The works of Ḥamzah al-Fanṣūrī and Shams al-Dīn al-Samatrānī, however, whom Johns calls 'the foremost exponents of heterodox pantheistic mysticism', have been published. Al-Sinkīlī's orthodoxy, he laments further, appeals less to the imagination of scholars than heresy.[72]

To begin our discussion of his mystical teachings, al-Sinkīlī, in his *Kifāyat al-Muḥtajīn ilā Mashrab al-Muwaḥḥidīn al-Qā'ilīn bi Waḥdat al-Wujūd*,[73] insists on the transcendence of God over His creation. He refuses to adhere to the notion of the *wujūdiyyah*, which emphasises the immanence of God in His creation. This teaching reminds us of the doctrines developed by the leading scholars discussed earlier. Al-Sinkīlī argues that before God created the universe (*al-'ālam*) He always thought of Himself, which resulted in the creation of the *Nūr Muḥammad* (the Light that is Muhammad). It is from the *Nūr Muḥammad* that God created permanent archetypes (*al-a'yān al-thābitah*), namely, the potential universe, which became the source of the exterior archetypes (*al-a'yān al-khārijiyyah*), the creation in its concrete form. Al-Sinkīlī concludes that although the *a'yān al-khārijiyyah* are the emanation of the Absolute Being, they are distinct from God Himself: it is like a hand and its shadow. Although the hand can hardly be separated from its shadow, the latter is not identical to the former. With this explanation, al-Sinkīlī establishes the transcendence of God over His creation.

The same argument is presented in his short treatise entitled *Daqā'iq al-Ḥurūf*. The work is a commentary on the so-called 'two pantheistic verses' of Ibn 'Arabī.[74] There is no need to dwell on al-Sinkīlī's discussion of the verses, as Johns has shown us that al-Sinkīlī knowledgeably interprets them in an orthodox sense,[75] proving that God and the universe are not identical. Although al-Sinkīlī also makes use of the quasi neo-Platonic emanation system, also closely associated with the pantheism of Shams al-Dīn, he carefully distances himself from an unorthodox interpretation.[76] Johns concludes:

> He [al-Sinkīlī] affirms at once the intuition of the mystics and the rights of orthodoxy, recognising the incapacity of human words to express adequately the dependence of the world upon God and its existence through Him, and the unspeakable reality of the Divine transcendence.[77]

Al-Sinkīlī's interpretation is clearly reminiscent of Ibrāhīm al-Kūrānī, who emphasises the importance of intuition (*kashf*) in the mystical way, while recognising the limit of reason in understanding the Realities of God. Al-Sinkīlī expresses his intellectual links with al-Kūrānī in a more than implicit way. In discussing the Unity of God in the *Daqā'iq al-Ḥurūf*,[78] he relies heavily on al-Kūrānī's concepts of *Tawḥīd al-Ulūhiyyah* (Divine Unity), *Tawḥīd al-Af'āl* (Unity of God's Act), *Tawḥīd al-Ṣifāt* (Unity of Attributes), *Tawḥīd al-Wujūd* (Unity of Being), *Tawḥīd al-Dhāt* (Unity of Essence) and *Tawḥīd al-Ḥaqīqī* (Unity of Absolute Reality).[79]

Like Ibrāhīm al-Kūrānī, al-Sinkīlī proposes that the most effective way to feel and grasp the Unity God is by performing *'ibādat*, particularly *dhikr* ('remembrance' of God), both silently (*sirr*) and vocally (*jahr*). According to al-Sinkīlī, the aim of the *dhikr* more specifically is to achieve *al-mawt al-ikhtiyārī* ('voluntary' death), or what is called by al-Kūrānī *al-mawt al-ma'nāwī* ('ideational' death), as opposed to *al-mawt al-ṭabī'ī* (natural death).[80] In his detailed method of *dhikr*, however, al-Sinkīlī, largely follows that of Aḥmad al-Qushāshī, as described in his work *al-Simṭ al-Majīd*.[81] He also follows al-Qushāshī's teachings on the obligation of disciples towards their master, as he shows in his two treatises called respectively *Risalah Adab Murid akan Syaikh* and *Risālah Mukhtaṣarah fī Bayān Shurūṭ al-Shaykh wa al-Murīd*.[82]

Having discussed al-Sinkīlī's teachings, it is clear that he transmitted the doctrines and tendencies in the scholarly networks in order to renew the Islamic tradition in the Malay-Indonesian archipelago. The most salient feature of his teachings indicates that what he transmitted is neo-Sufism: his works make it clear that *taṣawwuf* should go hand in hand with the *sharī'ah*. Only with total obedience to the *sharī'ah* can aspirants of mystical ways gain the true experience of the *ḥaqīqah* (realities).

It is important to keep in mind, however, that al-Sinkīlī's approach to renewal was different from that of al-Rānīrī: he was a *mujaddid* of an evolutionary type, not a radical. Therefore, like Ibrāhīm al-Kūrānī, he preferred to reconcile opposing views rather than to take sides. Even though he was against the doctrines of *wujūdiyyah*, only implicitly does he make clear his views. Similarly, he shows his dislike for the radical approach of al-Rānīrī's renewal quite simply and not explicitly. Again, without mentioning al-Rānīrī's name, he wisely reminds Muslims in the *Daqā'iq al-Ḥurūf* of the danger of accusing others of unbelieving by citing a *ḥadīth* of the Prophet, stating 'let no man accuse another of leading a sinful life or of infidelity, for the accusation will turn back if it is false'.[83] Considering al-Sinkīlī's gentleness and tolerance, Johns[84] rightly concludes that he was a mirror image of his teacher, Ibrāhīm al-Kūrānī.

AL-SINKĪLĪ'S MALAY-INDONESIAN NETWORKS

The Acehnese have long been proud of their country; they have always called their country, with pride, '*Serambi Mekkah*', or the front yard or gate to the Holy Land, not only because of its crucial role in Islamic learning but also for its position as the most important transit point for the Malay-Indonesian pilgrims in their journey to and from the Ḥaramayn.[85] Aceh's special position was among the main reasons why works of scholars like Ḥamzah al-Fanṣūrī, Shams al-Dīn al-Samatrānī, al-Rānīrī and al-Sinkīlī became widely circulated in the archipelago. The fact that all these scholars lived in Aceh, together with extensive relations and contacts between the Acehnese and foreign Muslim scholars, contributed substantially to the establishment of the identity of the Acehnese as one of the most ardent Muslim ethnic groups in the archipelago.

Al-Sinkīlī appears to have begun teaching while he was in the Ḥaramayn, but we have no information on his disciples there. It is only after he returned to Aceh that we are able to trace his Malay-Indonesian network of disciples. These disciples, in turn, were responsible for spreading al-Sinkīlī's teachings and *ṭarīqah*s, particularly the Shaṭṭāriyyah order, in many parts of the archipelago.

There is no doubt that the type of the Shaṭṭāriyyah order, so often associated with the Indian type of Sufism, that was implanted by al-Sinkīlī in the archipelago was the one that had been reformed by such leading scholars in our networks as Aḥmad al-Shinnāwī and Aḥmad al-Qushāshī. Archer,[86] in his classical study, calls the Shaṭṭāriyyah introduced by al-Sinkīlī the 'orthodox way'. Although in his *silsilah* al-Sinkīlī refers to the *ṭarīqah* as the Shaṭṭāriyyah, he also calls it the 'Qushāshiyyah' *ṭarīqah*.[87] The Shaṭṭāriyyah *ṭarīqah* was also known as the 'Ishqiyyah in Iran and as the Bisṭāmiyyah in Ottoman Turkey, but is not generally known as the Qushāshiyyah.[88] The Qushāshiyyah *ṭarīqah* was another name for the reformed Shaṭṭāriyyah and became a unique Malay-Indonesian phenomenon. This can be taken as an indication of al-Sinkīlī's attempts to disengage his *ṭarīqah* from the early Shaṭṭāriyyah. The Qushāshiyyah *ṭarīqah* was and can still be found in certain parts of the archipelago.[89]

The most celebrated of al-Sinkīlī's disciples in Sumatra was Burhān al-Dīn, better known as the Tuanku of Ulakan,[90] a village on the coast of the Minangkabau region (now West Sumatra). Local accounts of the development of Islam in Minangkabau relate that Burhān al-Dīn (1056–1104/1646–92) studied with al-Sinkīlī for several years before returning to his home region.[91] Burhān al-Dīn was, of course, not the first scholar to introduce Islam to the Minangkabau area, but he undoubtedly played a crucial role in the intensification of Islamisation among its population.

Soon after his return, Burhān al-Dīn established his Shaṭṭāriyyah *surau*, a *ribat*-type educational institution, in Ulakan. Before long it gained fame as the sole religious authority in Minangkabau.[92] The Ulakan surau attracted numerous students from throughout the region; they specialised in various branches of Islamic discipline, and in turn established their own suraus when they returned to their home villages.[93] By the fourth quarter of the eighteenth century several leading students of Burhān al-Dīn began in earnest to launch their reforms, which reached a climax at the turn of the century.[94]

Another eminent student of al-Sinkīlī was 'Abd al-Muḥyī of West Java. It is through the latter's efforts that the Shaṭṭāriyyah gained a large following in Java. Although our sources provide no date of birth, they are in accord in reporting that 'Abd al-Muḥyī studied with al-Sinkīlī in Aceh before embarking on a pilgrimage to Mecca. He was reported also to have travelled to Baghdad in order to visit the tomb of 'Abd al-Qādir al-Jaylānī.

Returning from the *ḥajj* pilgrimage, on the request of the local leader he settled in Karang, Pamijahan, West Java, where he played a substantial role in converting people from animistic beliefs to Islam. 'Abd al-Muḥyī was also very active in preaching the Shaṭṭāriyyah *ṭarīqah*, for many *silsilah*s of the order in Java and the Malay Peninsula went through him which he received directly from al-Sinkīlī.[95]

Al-Sinkīlī also had a prominent student in the Malay Peninsula: he was 'Abd al-Mālik b. 'Abd Allāh (1089–1149/1678–1736), better known as Tok Pulau Manis, of Trengganu. Abdullah points out that 'Abd al-Mālik studied with al-Sinkīlī in Aceh, and later continued his studies in the Ḥaramayn. According to local tradition, he studied there also with Ibrāhīm al-Kūrānī. But this is hardly plausible, because at the time of the latter's death (1101/1690) 'Abd al-Mālik had not even been born. At best, he may have met with al-Kūrānī's students. Apart from this problematic account, 'Abd al-Mālik was obviously a scholar of some distinction. His works deal mainly with the *sharī'ah* or *fiqh*; he was also very active in teaching.[96]

The closest disciple of al-Sinkīlī, without doubt, was Dāwūd al-Jāwī al-Fanṣūrī b. Ismā'īl b. Aghā Muṣṭafā b. Aghā 'Alī al-Rūmī. The importance of citing his long full name is to indicate that he was most likely of Turkish origin. His father was probably one of the Turkish mercenaries who came in large numbers to assist the Acehnese Sultanate in their contest with the Portuguese in the early sixteenth century. The attribution al-Jāwī indicates that his mother was probably a Malay, or that he was born in the archipelago.

Despite the obscurity surrounding his origin, Dāwūd al-Jāwī al-Rūmī was the most favoured student of al-Sinkīlī. There is a strong indication in the colophon of al-Sinkīlī's *Tarjumān al-Mustafīd* that he was ordered by the teacher to make some addition to the *tafsīr*. And there is also a suggestion that he did so under the supervision of al-Sinkīlī himself before the latter's death.[97] Hasjmi[98] maintains that Dāwūd al-Jāwī al-Rūmī was the main *khalīfah* of al-Sinkīlī. Together with his master, he founded a *dayah*, a traditional Acehnese Islamic educational institution, in Banda Aceh. He was also reported to have written several works.

Al-Sinkīlī died around 1105/1693 and was buried near the *kuala*, or the mouth, of the Aceh River. The site also became the graveyard for his wives, Dāwūd al-Rūmī and other disciples. It is after the site of his tomb that al-Sinkīlī later came to be known as the Shaykh of *Kuala*. Al-Sinkīlī's tomb has become the most important place of religious visitation (*ziyārah*) in Aceh until the present time.[99]

It is important to note that al-Sinkīlī was also associated with al-Maqassārī. They were in fact friends, studying together with, among others, al-Qushāshī and al-Kūrānī. It is to al-Maqassārī that we now turn.

5

Seventeenth Century Malay-Indonesian Networks III: Muḥammad Yūsuf al-Maqassārī

Our discussion of the Malay-Indonesian connection of the networks of *'ulamā'* up to now has centred mainly on Aceh. The third figure of Islamic renewal in the archipelago, Muḥammad Yūsuf al-Maqassārī (1037–1111/1627–99), brings our discussion into a vast region, from South Sulawesi (Celebes) and West Java to Arabia, Srilanka and South Africa. In order to get a better grasp of al-Maqassārī's role in Islamic development in these places, we must also deal in passing with the religious and intellectual life of the Muslims in these respective areas.

There have been a number of studies devoted to al-Maqassārī, in both Indonesia and South Africa.[1] But most of them centre only on his career in the archipelago or when he was in exile in South Africa; very little attention has been given to his scholarly connections within the international networks of *'ulamā'*. This fails not only to trace the origins of al-Maqassārī's teachings but also to recognise his role as one of the early transmitters of Islamic reformism to the region where he lived.

FROM SULAWESI TO BANTEN AND ARABIA

Muḥammad Yūsuf b. 'Abd Allāh Abū al-Maḥāsin al-Tāj al-Khalwātī al-Maqassārī, also known in Sulawesi as '*Tuanta Salamaka ri Gowa*' (Our Gracious Master from Gowa), according to the Annals of Gowa, was born in 1037/1627.[2] Despite myth and legends concerning the parents and events surrounding the birth of al-Maqassārī, probably fabricated after his death, his family was among those which had been fully Islamised.

As a result, from his early years of life, prior to his departure to Arabia, al-Maqassārī was educated according to Islamic tradition. He initially learned to read the Qur'ān with a local teacher named Daeng ri Tasammang. Later he studied Arabic, *fiqh*, *tawḥīd* and *taṣawwuf* with Sayyid Bā

'Alwī b. 'Abd Allāh al-'Allāmah al-Ṭāhir, an Arab preacher who lived in Bontoala at that time. When he was 15 years of age he continued his studies in Cikoang, where he studied with Jalāl al-Dīn al-Aydid, a peripatetic teacher who was reported to have come from Aceh to Kutai, Kalimantan, before finally settling down in Cikoang.[3]

The accounts of al-Maqassārī's initial religious education again emphasise the nature of Islamic development in Sulawesi, as in many parts of the archipelago, namely, that wandering scholars, many of them *ṣūfī*s, played a crucial role in converting and teaching the native population. However, they came to Sulawesi much later than to the western part of the archipelago; only after the second half of the sixteenth century do we find evidence of their presence in the region. It was in the early seventeenth century that these peripatetic teachers, from Aceh, Minangkabau, South Kalimantan (Borneo), Java, the Malay Peninsula and the Middle East, succeeded in converting large numbers of the population of Sulawesi. They had much greater success after the local rulers embraced Islam.[4]

Thus, in the period of al-Maqassārī's birth, Islam was gaining firmer roots in South Sulawesi. By the third decade of the seventeenth century the newly Islamised rulers made their attempts to translate some doctrines of the *sharī'ah* into the political organisation of their kingdoms. Religious posts such as *imām* (prayer leader), *khaṭīb* (reciter of the Friday sermon) and *qāḍī* (judge) were created, and their holders became included among the nobility.[5] With the creation of these offices, many wandering scholars were encouraged to stay. Al-Maqassārī was able to acquire a rudimentary Islamic education in his own region. However, it is important to note that doctrines of Islamic law were adopted only to a limited degree, especially those concerning familial matters, which were incorporated in local customs variously called *pangaderreng* or *panngadakkang*.

Returning from Cikoang, al-Maqassārī married a daughter of the Sulṭān of Gowa, 'Alā' al-Dīn, also known locally as Mangarangi Daeng Maurabiya (r. 1001–46/1591–1636). Al-Maqassārī had apparently long cherished an ambition to pursue further studies in the Middle East; it can be expected that his teachers of Arab origin gave him a further incentive towards Islamic learning there. Al-Maqassārī left Makassar for Arabia in the month of Rajab 1054/September 1644.[6] Makassar, it is worth noting, was an important harbour in the eastern part of the archipelago, and from the second half of the fifteenth century it had been frequented by Malay-Indonesian and foreign traders. It had links, in the interinsular trading networks, with Banten and other harbours on northern Java as well as with Malacca and Aceh. Al-Maqassārī took advantage of the trading networks. He boarded a Malay ship, and we soon find him in Banten.[7]

The Sultanate of Banten (Bantam) was one of the most important Muslim kingdoms on Java. When al-Maqassārī arrived in Banten, the reigning ruler was Abū al-Mafākhir 'Abd al-Qādir (r. 1037–63/1626–51), who was granted the title of Sulṭān by the Sharīf of Mecca in 1048/1638. He evidently had a special interest in religious matters; he sent inquiries about religious matters not only to al-Rānīrī but also to scholars in the Ḥaramayn, which resulted in special works written by those scholars, answering his questions.[8] As a result, Banten became known as one of the most important Islamic centres on Java, and it is highly possible that al-Maqassārī also studied there. Not least importantly, he was able to establish close personal relations with the elite of the Bantenese Sultanate, especially with the Crown Prince, Pangeran Surya, who would succeed his father, Abū al-Mafākhir, as Sulṭān with the official name 'Abd al-Fattāḥ, better known as Sulṭān Ageng Tirtayasa.

Following the route of the interinsular trade, al-Maqassārī departed for Aceh. It is reported[9] that while he was in Banten he had already heard about al-Rānīrī and intended to study with him. Meanwhile, al-Rānīrī had left Aceh for his home of birth, Rānīr, in 1054/1644. As al-Maqassārī departed from Makassar in the same year, it is unlikely that they met in Aceh. However, al-Maqassārī, in his work *Safīnat al-Najāh*, before giving his complete silsilah of the Qādiriyyah *ṭarīqah*, has the following to say:

> As for the chains of initiation of the *khalīfah* al-Qādiriyyah, I take it from my Shaykh and prop (*sandaran*), the learned and prominent, the wise and inimitable, who possesses the sciences of *sharī'ah* and *ḥaqīqah*, exploring *ma'rifah* and *ṭarīqah*, my master and teacher (*guru*), Shaykh Nūr al-Dīn b. Ḥasanji b. Muḥammad Ḥumayd al-Qurayshī al-Rānīrī; may God purify his spirit and illuminate his tomb.[10]

Considering this account, it is likely that al-Maqassārī followed al-Rānīrī to India, where, as al-Attas points out, he studied also with 'Umar b. 'Abd Allāh Bā Shaybān, al-Rānīrī's teacher.[11] If this is so, he must have been introduced to Bā Shaybān by al-Rānīrī; and they must have met only in the Gujarat region as, so far as we are aware, Bā Shaybān never travelled to the Malay-Indonesian world.

In all probability it is from the Gujarat coast that al-Maqassārī continued his travels to the Middle East. His first destination was the Yemen, where he studied mostly in Zabīd, with Muḥammad b. 'Abd al-Bāqī al-Naqshbandī, Sayyid 'Alī al-Zabīdī and Muḥammad b. al-Wajīh al-Sa'dī al-Yamanī.[12]

We have mentioned earlier that Muḥammad b. 'Abd al-Bāqī al-Mizjājī al-Naqshbandī (d. 1074/1664), probably the most important scholar of the Mizjājī family in the seventeenth century, was one of the scholars al-Sinkilī came into contact with in the Yemen. 'Abd al-Bāqī was in fact the predecessor of the Mizjājī scholars, who played an increasingly important role in the expansion of the networks to many parts of the Muslim world.

Voll[13] has suggested that by the beginning of the eighteenth century the Mizjājīs had been identified with the Naqshbandiyyah order. The association certainly began with 'Abd al-Bāqī, for, as al-Muḥibbī points out,[14] he was initiated into the order by Tāj al-Dīn al-Hindī, the leading shaykh of the Naqshbandiyyah in Mecca. Al-Maqassārī tells us that he took the Naqshbandiyyah *ṭarīqah* from 'Abd al-Bāqī.[15] He does not make mention of other sciences he learned from 'Abd al-Bāqī; therefore, we can assume that al-Maqassārī primarily studied *taṣawwuf* with him.

The second major teacher of al-Maqassārī in Yemen was simply named Sayyid 'Alī al-Zabīdī or 'Alī b. Abī Bakr, according to al-Maqassārī's silsilah of the Bā 'Alwiyyah *ṭarīqah*.[16] It is difficult to identify this scholar in Arabic sources, because his is a very common name. But his identification with Zabīd helps us in some way. Al-Muḥibbī mentions two 'Alīs, one of whom could be a teacher of al-Maqassari, because of his connection not only with al-Sinkilī but also with the larger networks; he is 'Ali bin Muhammad b. al-Shaybani al-Zabidi, as described later.

To take al-Maqassārī's silsilah of the Bā 'Alwiyyah into account, it is possible that Sayyid 'Alī was 'Alī b. Muḥammad b. Abī Bakr b. Muṭayr, who died in Zabīd in 1084/1673. The Muṭayr scholars had played some role in the networks; two of the Muṭayr scholars, have already been mentioned namely, Muḥammad b. Abī Bakr and Aḥmad Abū al-'Abbās, in connection with al-Sinkilī. 'Alī b. Muṭayr [al-Zabīdī] was known as a *ṣūfī* and *muḥaddith*. Al-Muḥibbī, however, simply mentions that 'Alī adhered to the *ṭarīqah* of the *Ahl al-Sunnah wa al-Jamā'ah* (the people of the Sunnah and community, or the mainstream of the Sunnī); no explicit mention is made of the Bā 'Alwiyyah *ṭarīqah*, although the order can surely be included among the *ṭarīqah*s with which the Ahl al-Sunnah wa al-Jamā'ah was affiliated.[17]

It is also possible that Sayyid 'Alī was actually 'Alī b. Muḥammad b. al-Shaybānī al-Zabīdī (d. 1072/1661). Al-Muḥibbī, citing Muṣṭafā b. Fatḥ Allāh al-Ḥamawī, his colleague, tells us that 'Alī al-Zabīdī was a great *muḥaddith* of Yemen and the leader of men of learning in Zabīd. He initially studied in his home town with Muḥammad b. al-Ṣiddīq al-Khāṣṣ al-Zabīdī or Isḥāq Ibn Ja'mān—both mentioned earlier in connection with al-Sinkilī. 'Alī continued his studies in the Ḥaramayn, receiving *ṭarīqah*s from Aḥmad al-Qushāshī. He was also active in teaching *ḥadīth*; among those who studied *ḥadīth* with him were Ibrāhīm al-Kūrānī, Ibn 'Abd al-Rasūl al-Barzanjī and Ḥasan al-'Ajamī. He died in Zabīd.[18] 'Alī al-Zabīdī's connections with these scholars, who were teachers of Jāwī students, including al-Maqassārī himself, made it possible for 'Alī to come into contact with and teach al-Maqassārī. We cannot go further, as there is no indication that he was a shaykh of the Bā 'Alwiyyah *ṭarīqah*.

Al-Maqassārī does not inform us of the date of his sojourn in Yemen, but it probably took several years before he continued his travels to the heart of the networks in the Ḥaramayn. His period of study in Mecca and Medina coincided with that of al-Sinkilī. Therefore, it can be expected that al-Maqassārī studied with scholars who were also the teachers of al-Sinkilī. The most important among his teachers in the Ḥaramayn were familiar names in the networks, such as Aḥmad al-Qushāshī, Ibrāhīm al-Kūrānī and Ḥasan al-'Ajamī.[19]

Al-Maqassārī's relationship with al-Kūrānī was apparently close. It is known that he was entrusted by al-Kūrānī to copy *al-Durrat al-Fākhirah* and *Risālah fī al-Wujūd*, both works of Nūr al-Dīn al-Jāmī (d. 898/1492), and a commentary on the first work by 'Abd al-Ghafūr al-Lārī (d. 912/1506). Al-Kūrānī himself later wrote a commentary on *al-Durrat al-Fākhirah* called *al-Taḥrīrāt al-Bāhirah li Mabāḥith al-Durrat al-Fākhirah.*[20] All of these works attempt to reconcile opposing positions between the Muslim theologians and philosophers on several philosophical issues concerning God. It has been suggested that al-Maqassārī studied these three works under al-Kūrānī when he was copying them.[21]

Unlike al-Sinkilī, al-Maqassārī does not specify the religious sciences he studied with the above scholars. He mentions them primarily in connection with his teachings and *ṭarīqah* silsilahs or in notes towards the end of some of his works. Considering their scholarly discourse and the kind of teachings he attributed to them, it is fair to assume that, in addition to *taṣawwuf*, al-Maqassārī studied *ḥadīth*, tafsīr, *fiqh* and other branches of Islamic science with them.

Aside from the above scholars, al-Maqassārī mentions his other teachers in the Ḥaramayn: Muḥammad al-Mazrū' [al-Madanī], 'Abd al-Karīm al-Lahūrī and Muḥammad Muraz al-Shāmī.[22] While I have failed to identify the first scholar, the second was very likely 'Abd al-Karīm al-Hindī al-Lahūrī, who settled in the Ḥaramayn and flourished in the eleventh/ seventeenth century. He appears also to have been involved in the networks; he was an acquaintance of 'Abd Allāh al-Baṣrī, Aḥmad al-Nakhlī, Tāj al-Dīn al-Qal'ī and Abū Ṭāhir al-Kūrānī.[23] We may expect that through 'Abd al-Karīm for Muḥammad al-Lahūrī, al-Maqassārī learned much about the Indian tradition of Islamic learning.

As for Muḥammad Muraz al-Shāmī, he was most probably Muḥammad Mirza b. Muḥammad al-Dimashqī. This is based on the fact that the copyists of al-Maqassārī's works obviously misspelled the names of several of his teachers. They, for instance, wrote 'Muḥammad al-Zujājī al-Naqshbandī' instead of Muḥammad [b. 'Abd al-Bāqī] al-Mizjājī al-Naqshbandī, or 'Muḥammad Bāqī Allāh al-Lahūrī' instead of 'Abd al-Karīm al-Lahūrī or Muḥammad b. 'Abd al-Bāqī al-Naqshbandī.[24]

We have other reasons to identify Muḥammad Mirza as a teacher of al-Maqassārī. First of all, he was a student of Tāj al-Dīn al-Hindī al-Naqshbandī. Like Muḥammad b. 'Abd al-Bāqī al-Mizjājī, Muḥammad Mirza was initiated by Tāj al-Dīn into the Naqshbandiyyah order in Mecca; they may be expected to have been friends. As al-Maqassārī had received the order earlier from 'Abd al-Bāqī, it is possible that he later recommended al-Maqassārī to study with Muḥammad Mirza when he left Yemen for the Ḥaramayn. Muḥammad Mirza migrated from Damascus and lived in Medina for 40 years before he finally moved to Mecca, where he died in 1066/1656, after only two years there. Muḥammad Mirza, mainly known as a *ṣūfī*, attempted to reinterpret Ibn 'Arabī's doctrines in terms that people could comprehend.[25]

Unlike al-Sinkilī, who returned directly to the Malay-Indonesian world after studying in the Ḥaramayn, al-Maqassārī travelled to Damascus, another important centre of Islamic learning in the Middle East. It appears that Muḥammad Mirza recommended that al-Maqassārī study there. But it is also possible that Aḥmad al-Qushāshī encouraged him to go to Damascus and study with one of its leading scholars, Ayyūb b. Aḥmad b. Ayyūb al-Dimashqī al-Khalwatī (994–1071/1586–1661). As we have already noted, al-Qushāshī was a close friend of Ayyūb al-Khalwatī (see Chart 5).

Ayyūb al-Khalwatī was born and died in Damascus. He was a renowned *ṣūfī* and *muḥaddith* of Syria. His education included both exoteric sciences, such as *ḥadīth*, tafsīr and *fiqh*, as well as esoteric sciences like *taṣawwuf* and *kalām*. Both al-Ḥamawī and Al-Muḥibbī call him '*al-ustādh al-akbar*' (great teacher), and they claim that nobody else in Damascus was as learned as he was during his time. Sulṭān Ibrāhīm, the ruler of Syria, often consulted him in matters relating to Islamic law and mysticism.[26]

Ayyūb al-Khalwatī was also a prolific writer. His writings mainly deal with *taṣawwuf*, *kalām*, *ḥadīth* and Khalwatiyyah rituals. He attempted to give a new interpretation of Ibn 'Arabī's doctrines, particularly concerning the concept of *al-Insān al-Kāmil* ('perfect man' or 'universal man'), in light of the *sharī'ah*. Ayyūb al-Khalwatī also had extensive networks by way of *ḥadīth* studies. His scholarly reputation made his halqahs popular with students from various parts of the Muslim world, such as the Maghribi region, Arabia, and South and Southeast Asia.

Al-Maqassārī does not tell us when the period of his study with Ayyūb al-Khalwatī took place, but al-Maqassārī evidently accompanied him for some time. After exhibiting his talent for absorbing the exoteric and esoteric sciences, he was able to win the favour of Ayyūb al-Khalwatī. The latter awarded him the title of '*al-Tāj al-Khalwatī*' (the Crown of the Khalwatī). Al-Maqassārī highly praises Ayyūb al-Khalwatī in his works and mentions him in his silsilah of the Khalwatiyyah *ṭarīqah*.[27] The way al-Maqassārī refers to Ayyūb al-Khalwatī could lead one to assume that this Damascene scholar was simply a great *ṣūfī*, but in fact he was also a leading expert in Islamic law.

After studying in Damascus, al-Maqassārī is said to have continued his travels to Istanbul.[28] Traditional accounts of al-Maqassārī's life that circulate in South Sulawesi tell the story of his journey in the '*Negeri Rum*' (Turkey), but we have no other sources to corroborate them.[29]

According to Gowa sources, while he was in Mecca al-Maqassārī had begun to teach. As one might expect, most of his students were of Malay-Indonesian origin, both from the *ḥājj* pilgrims and the *Jāwah* community in the Ḥaramayn. Among his students in Mecca was 'Abd al-Bashīr al-Ḍarīr al-Rapanī (from Rappang, South Sulawesi), who later was responsible for spreading the Naqshbandiyyah and Khalwatiyyah orders in South

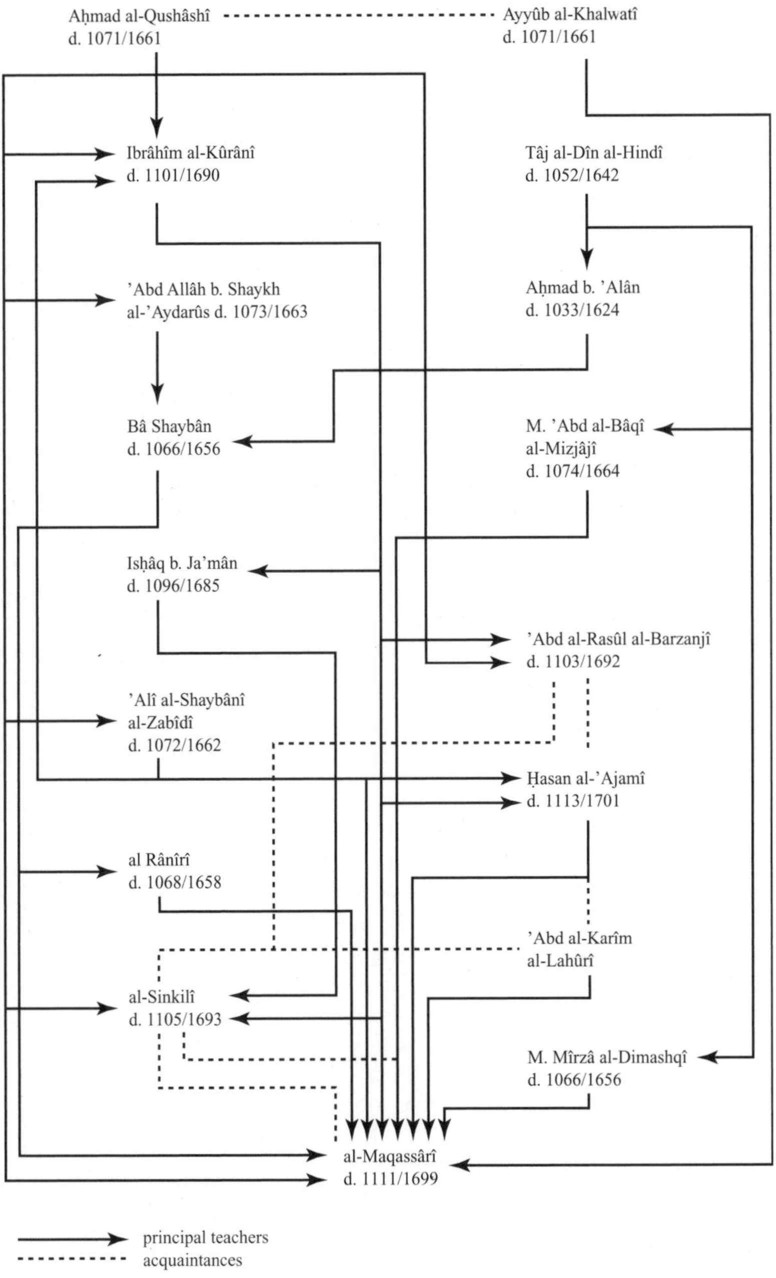
Aḥmad al-Qushâshî
d. 1071/1661
Ayyûb al-Khalwatî
d. 1071/1661
Ibrâhîm al-Kûrânî
d. 1101/1690
Tâj al-Dîn al-Hindî
d. 1052/1642
'Abd Allâh b. Shaykh
al-'Aydarûs d. 1073/1663
Aḥmad b. 'Alân
d. 1033/1624
Bâ Shaybân
d. 1066/1656
M. 'Abd al-Bâqî
al-Mizjâjî
d. 1074/1664
Isḥâq b. Ja'mân
d. 1096/1685
'Abd al-Rasûl al-Barzanjî
d. 1103/1692
'Alî al-Shaybânî
al-Zabîdî
d. 1072/1662
Ḥasan al-'Ajamî
d. 1113/1701
al Rânîrî
d. 1068/1658
'Abd al-Karîm
al-Lahûrî
al-Sinkilî
d. 1105/1693
M. Mîrzâ al-Dimashqî
d. 1066/1656
al-Maqassârî
d. 1111/1699
principal teachers
acquaintances

Chart 5 Al-Maqassārī's networks

Sulawesi.[30] Furthermore, al-Maqassārī is reported to have married the daughter of a Shāfi'ī Imām in Mecca, but his wife died when she gave birth to a child, and al-Maqassārī remarried a woman of Sulawesi origin in Jeddah before he finally returned to the archipelago.[31]

FROM BANTEN TO SRILANKA AND SOUTH AFRICA

It is not very clear when Al-Maqassārī returned to the archipelago. Hamid and Van Bruinessen respectively claim that he returned in 1075/1664 and 1083/1672,[32] but we are not able to substantiate this, for other sources do not supply us with the date of al-Maqassārī's return. However, if these dates are correct, it means that he spent between 20 and 28 years travelling in search for knowledge. There are also conflicting accounts of whether al-Maqassārī returned directly to his homeland, Gowa, or went via Banten.

Hamka,[33] Amansyah,[34] Mattulada[35] and Pelras[36] all maintain that al-Maqassārī initially returned to South Sulawesi before he proceeded to Banten. Hamid,[37] Labbakang[38] and Dangor,[39] on the other hand, believe that al-Maqassārī settled in Banten when he returned to the archipelago and never came back to Gowa. We will discuss these two conflicting accounts and attempt to determine which one is the more plausible.

According to the first opinion, when al-Maqassārī returned from Arabia to Gowa, South Sulawesi, he found that Islamic precepts were not being practised by the Muslim population; remnants of contra-Islamic local beliefs continued to hold sway. Although the ruler and nobility had long declared themselves Muslims, they were reluctant to apply the doctrine of Islamic law in their realms. They were unwilling or unable to prohibit gambling, cock-fighting, arrack drinking, opium smoking and the like. They in fact promoted superstitious practices such as giving offerings to the spirit of the ancestors in the hope that the latter would bring them prosperity.

Having witnessed such a sorry state of religious life, al-Maqassārī appealed to the Gowa ruler and notables to abolish all such practices and to implement Islamic law. However, the ruler insisted on maintaining the status quo; abolishing gambling and opium smoking, for instance, would have meant reducing financial gains.[40] As a result, al-Maqassārī departed to Banten, where he established his career. He left behind him, however, several outstanding disciples, such as Nūr al-Dīn b. 'Abd al-Fattāḥ, 'Abd al-Bashīr al-Ḍarīr and 'Abd al-Qadir Karaeng Jeno.

It is apparent that the account of al-Maqassārī's return to Gowa is based on Hamka's article, one of the earliest writings on al-Maqassārī in the Indonesian language. The problem with Hamka's article is that it relies heavily on an oral tradition that has passed through many generations. It is difficult to sift fact from myth in such oral histories, and we have no written sources to substantiate them.

The spread of al-Maqassārī's teachings and works in South Sulawesi did not necessarily require al-Maqassārī's physical presence in the region. All of his students are reported to have studied with him either in the Ḥaramayn or in Banten. Furthermore, from the middle of the seventeenth century, Muslims from South Sulawesi came to Banten in large numbers. They also played an important role in spreading al-Maqassārī's teachings and works when they returned to their own regions.[41]

It is more plausible, therefore, that al-Maqassārī returned to Banten rather than to Gowa. He may have planned to stay there temporarily on his way back to his homeland, but later developments made him change his mind. After several months in Banten he married the daughter of Sulṭān Ageng Tirtayasa.[42] It is worth remembering that al-Maqassārī and the Sulṭān had been friends before the former left for Arabia. Thus, when al-Maqassārī returned with scholarly credentials and prestige, Sulṭān Ageng attempted to keep him in Banten by any means, including marriage.

Sulṭān Ageng Tirtayasa (r. 1053–96/1651–83) was undoubtedly the last great ruler of the Bantenese Sultanate. Under his rule the Sultanate reached its golden age. Its port became an important centre of international trade in the archipelago. The Bantenese traded with traders from England, Denmark, China, Indo-China, India, Persia, the Philippines and Japan. The ships of the Sultanate sailed the archipelago, representing the last powerful trading power of the Malay-Indonesian kingdoms.[43]

Sulṭān Ageng was a fervent enemy of the Dutch; his accession to the throne resumed the long-standing conflicts between the Bantenese and the Dutch, who had fought wars in 1028/1619 and 1043–9/1633–9. Peace settlements achieved after the wars could not hold for very long. Sulṭān Ageng's fleet, modelled after those of the Europeans, attacked the Dutch posts in Sumatra. He made Banten a safe haven for fighters from elsewhere in the archipelago in wars against the Dutch, as well as for fugitives from Dutch prisons.[44] For the Dutch, who now fortified themselves in Batavia, Sulṭān Ageng was a major stumbling block in their territorial expansion in the archipelago.

Sulṭān Ageng Tirtayasa, like his father, Sulṭān Abū al-Mafākhir 'Abd al-Qādir, had a special interest in religion. The political and diplomatic relations with the Muslim rulers, particularly with the Sharīfs of Mecca, that had been established by his father continued to flourish. Contemporaneous Dutch sources[45] also note that Sulṭān Ageng was able to establish relations with Surat and other Muslim kingdoms on the coastal region of the Indian subcontinent.

Moreover, he sent his son, 'Abd al-Qahhār, on a diplomatic mission to Istanbul; this was in conjunction with the latter's *ḥājj* pilgrimages to Mecca, which were undertaken respectively from 1080/1669 to 1082/1671 and from 1085/1674 to 1087/1676. During the time of Sulṭān Ageng, scholars and students from various parts of the Muslim world continued to come to Banten. Sulṭān Ageng himself, most of the time, was accompanied by these Muslim scholars.[46] Thus, he was able to maintain the reputation of Banten as an important centre of Islamic learning in the archipelago.[47]

The political and religious situation in the Bantenese Sultanate was clearly favourable for al-Maqassārī to remain there. His marriage to the daughter of the Sulṭān created a stronger bond with the Sultanate. He rose to one of the highest positions among the court elite, and became the most influential member of the Sulṭān's Advisory Board. He was called *opper-priester* or *hoogepriester* (highest priest) by Dutch sources, and played an important role not only in religious matters but also in political ones.[48]

The news about al-Maqassārī's presence in Banten soon reached South Sulawesi. The Sulṭān of Gowa dispatched a delegation to Banten in order to induce him to return to his homeland. The Sulṭān requested that al-Maqassārī teach the royal family about Islam and thus accelerate the process of Islamisation in the region. Al-Maqassārī, however, declined the invitation. Our sources[49] cite him as stating that he would not return to Gowa until his erudition in Islamic reached perfection. He instead sent home his student 'Abd al-Bashīr al-Ḍarīr, who had apparently followed him from Mecca to Banten. Al-Maqassārī appointed al-Ḍarīr ('the blind') his *khalīfah* of the Khalwatiyyah and Naqshbandiyyah orders.

Thus, while in Banten, although al-Maqassārī was increasingly pulled into the political arena he continued to teach students in the capital city of Banten as well as to write. Later, when al-Maqassārī was involved in wars against the Dutch, he was reported to have retreated to the village of Karang, and had some connections with a man named by Dutch sources as 'Hadjee Karang'.[50] Karang was the home of 'Abd al-Muḥyī, a disciple of al-Sinkilī, and he was certainly the 'Hadjee Karang.' 'Abd al-Muḥyī took the opportunity of his meeting with al-Maqassārī to study with him, asking his commentary on certain verses of the Qur'ān that dealt with mystical doctrines. 'Abd al-Muḥyī also asked al-Maqassārī to transmit to him the silsilah of the *ṭarīqah*s he received in the Ḥaramayn.[51]

Included among the most prominent students of al-Maqassārī was the heir to the Sultanate, 'Abd al-Qahhār. There is little doubt that al-Maqassārī recommended that he travel to Istanbul after performing his pilgrimage in Mecca. Al-Maqassārī's wide contacts in the Middle East and his possible visit to Istanbul helped pave the way for the Crown Prince to carry out his diplomatic mission. We have no further information on the mission. What is clear is that when the heir Prince returned from the Middle East to Banten with the new title of Sulṭān Ḥaji, he soon appealed to the Bantenese to wear clothes of Arab style.[52]

'Abd al-Qahhār's insistence on Arab dress is reported by Sasmita[53] to have been the initial reason for the rifts between him and his father, Sulṭān Ageng. But it appears that the fundamental cause of conflict was the decision of Sulṭān Ageng to appoint his other son, Pangeran Purbaya, to succeed him to the throne while 'Abd al-Qahhār was on his pilgrimage.[54]

This decision was apparently prompted by 'Abd al-Qahhār's predilection for the Dutch, in contrast to Sulṭān Ageng's decidedly anti-Netherlands disposition. Sulṭān Ageng attempted to reach some reconciliation with 'Abd al-Qahhār: the latter was restored to his original position as heir, and was assigned to rule the Sultanate from the capital city, Banten, while the old Sulṭān moved to Tirtayasa. These policies proved to be a great blow to the old Sulṭān, for 'Abd al-Qahhār now used his position to embrace the Dutch even more closely.

Meanwhile, Sulṭān Ageng had reasserted his rule over the Cirebon Sultanate, and warned the Dutch resident in Batavia in the presence of the English, French and Danish residents that he would consider every act of hostility or interference by the Dutch East Indies Company (VOC) in the affairs of Cirebon as a *casus belli* for him.[55] 'Abd al-Qahhār did not share his father's views. He made it clear that he took the side of the Dutch. Probably with the connivance of the Dutch, 'Abd al-Qahhār declared the abdication of his father from the throne in 1091/1680, and claimed it for himself. Sulṭān Ḥāji soon dismissed supporters of Sulṭān Ageng from their official positions, and sent envoys to Batavia to negotiate a peace treaty with the Dutch.

Sulṭān Ageng refused his forced abdication; he gathered his army in Tirtayasa, and civil war appeared inevitable. Being caught in this difficult situation, al-Maqassārī, together with Pangeran Purbaya, chose to take the side of Sulṭān Ageng. The war finally broke out in the last days of 1092/early 1682, when Sulṭān Ageng's forces besieged Sulṭān Ḥāji in the capital, Banten. Realising that his position was precarious, Sulṭān Ḥāji appealed for support from Batavia. In return for Dutch help in keeping him on the throne, he promised to cede all trade benefits to the VOC.

The Dutch immediately seized this long-awaited opportunity. Reinforcements under Captain François Tack were sent from Batavia so that Sulṭān Ḥāji could escape from being humiliated by Sulṭān Ageng's army. Fresh from victories in South Sulawesi, Cirebon and Mataram, the Dutch army was able to inflict reverses on Sulṭān Ageng's forces. On 29 December 1682, Dutch troops attacked Tirtayasa, but Sulṭān Ageng, al-Maqassārī and Pangeran Purbaya escaped the siege and took refuge in the southern mountains of West Java. Persistently pursued by forces of the Dutch and Sulṭān Ḥāji, Sulṭān Ageng was finally captured in 1096/1683 and was exiled to Batavia, where he died in 1103/1692.[56]

The capture of Sulṭān Ageng, however, did not put an end to the war. His force was now led by al-Maqassārī. Conducting a guerilla warfare, al-Maqassārī's forces of 4000 men, consisting of the Bantenese, Makassarese/Buginese and Javanese, proved difficult to subdue. This attests to al-Maqassārī's dauntless courage and bravery, and to his firm determination to fight the enemy. After failing to capture al-Maqassārī on the battlefield, the Dutch finally employed the trickery that they were so often to use in their territorial expansion in the archipelago. According to one version from Dutch accounts, Van Happel, the commander of the Dutch troops, wearing Arab garb and disguised as a Muslim, was able to infiltrate al-Maqassārī's fortification, finally capturing him on 14 December 1683.[57] Another version of the capture is that Van Happel came to al-Maqassārī's hiding place with the latter's daughter, promising him the pardon of the Dutch if he surrendered. Persuaded by the promise, which was never honoured by the Dutch, al-Maqassārī and his forces joined Van Happel and followed him to Cirebon, where he was officially declared a prisoner of war and taken to Batavia. At the same time, his followers of South Sulawesi origin were sent back to their homeland.[58]

With the capture of al-Maqassārī, the Banten wars practically ended. The news of al-Maqassārī's detention spread through Batavia; he was hailed as a great hero in the struggle against the Dutch expansionism. He was highly venerated: even his *sepah* (chewed betelnut) was picked up by his followers when he spat it out, and was preserved as a relic.[59] It is not hard to understand, then, the Dutch fear that the Muslims would rise up to free him. In September 1684 they exiled him to Srilanka, together with two wives, several children, 12 disciples and a number of maids.[60]

Despite the fact that al-Maqassārī stayed in Srilanka for almost a decade, studies of the Malay-Indonesian Muslim community on that island fail to disclose his presence and role in the development of Islam there.[61] This is unfortunate, as when he was in Srilanka al-Maqassārī produced a substantial number of works, some of which bear the title of *Saylāniyyah* (or Sailan = Ceylon) or are mentioned explicitly to have been written in '*Sarandib*' (mediaeval Arabic term for Srilanka).[62] Furthermore, al-Maqassārī appears to have left some descendants in Srilanka who possess manuscripts that could be a starting point for future research.[63] Such manuscripts would certainly be useful for complementing both Indonesian accounts and Dutch records of al-Maqassārī's life in Srilanka.

It is worth noting that outside the archipelago, Srilanka, ruled by the Dutch in the period between 1050/1640 and 1211/1796, was the second centre for banishment after the Cape of Good Hope for Malay-Indonesian exiles. Due to its proximity to the archipelago, Srilanka had been preferred by the Dutch to the Cape of Good Hope, which seems to have been reserved for more dangerous exiles. The Dutch apparently began to transport a substantial number of Malay-Indonesian exiles to Srilanka as soon as they established their rule there.[64] We know very little about the life of exiles prior to the seventeenth century, but there is no doubt that al-Maqassārī was the most prominent Malay-Indonesian figure ever banished by the Dutch to Srilanka.

In a sense, al-Maqassārī's banishment to Srilanka was a blessing in disguise. While he was in Banten he experienced political turbulence, but he never abandoned his scholarly concerns; he was even able during this period to produce several works. Now in Srilanka he had the opportunity to return entirely to the scholarly world. In the introduction to his *Safīnat al-Najāh*, al-Maqassārī in retrospect expected that by the grace of God he would inherit the wisdom of Adam, the prophet, who was, in the Muslim belief, discharged on Srilanka after his fall from Heaven.[65] So al-Maqassārī devoted himself primarily to writing.

We can fairly safely assume that al-Maqassārī played an important role in nurturing the hitherto small and inchoate Malay Muslim community on the island. Al-Maqassārī himself expressly mentioned that he wrote his works in Srilanka to satisfy the requests of his friends, disciples and fellow Muslims there.[66] He also established contact with other scholars there. Among the Muslim scholars of Indian origin who became his friends were Sidi Matilaya, Abū al-Ma'ānī Ibrāhīm Minḥān and 'Abd al-Ṣiddīq b. Muḥammad Ṣādiq.

The fact that his *Safīnat al-Najāh* was written on the request of Ibrāhīm Minhan was an indication that Minhan and his fellow Indian scholars were well aware of al-Maqassārī's erudition. It is possible that through these scholars the Moghul ruler Aurangzeb (1071–1119/1659–1707) learned about the banishment of al-Maqassārī to Srilanka. The Sulṭān reportedly warned the Dutch authorities there to pay attention to the wellbeing of al-Maqassārī.[67]

Thus, the banishment had failed to cut al-Maqassārī off from outside contacts. No less important than al-Maqassārī's relations with the Indian scholars were his contacts with Malay-Indonesian pilgrims, who made Srilanka their transit point on their way to and from Mecca and Medina, or with Muslim traders who came there for business. That the contacts between al-Maqassārī and the pilgrims existed becomes obvious from an explicit mention in one of his works that he wrote it for his friends the *ḥājji*s.[68]

It was these *ḥājji*s who brought al-Maqassārī's works, written in Srilanka, to the archipelago so that we are able to read them today. They in turn brought works written by Malay-Indonesian scholars to Srilanka. The religious works found among the Malays on this island include these of al-Rānīrī, al-Sinkilī and al-Maqassārī himself.[69]

Considering the existence of such extensive relations, the Dutch were right in assuming that al-Maqassārī still exerted a considerable influence on the Malay-Indonesian Muslims. They were suspicious that through those pilgrims al-Maqassārī had established networks, consisting of various Muslim rulers in the archipelago, who would wage concerted and large-scale wars against the Dutch. Fearing further political and religious repercussions from al-Maqassārī's relations with his countrymen, the Dutch authorities decided in 1106/1693 to send al-Maqassārī even farther away, to exile in South Africa. He was already 68 years old when once again he was forced to embark on 'De Voetboog', which would take him to the Cape of Good Hope.[70]

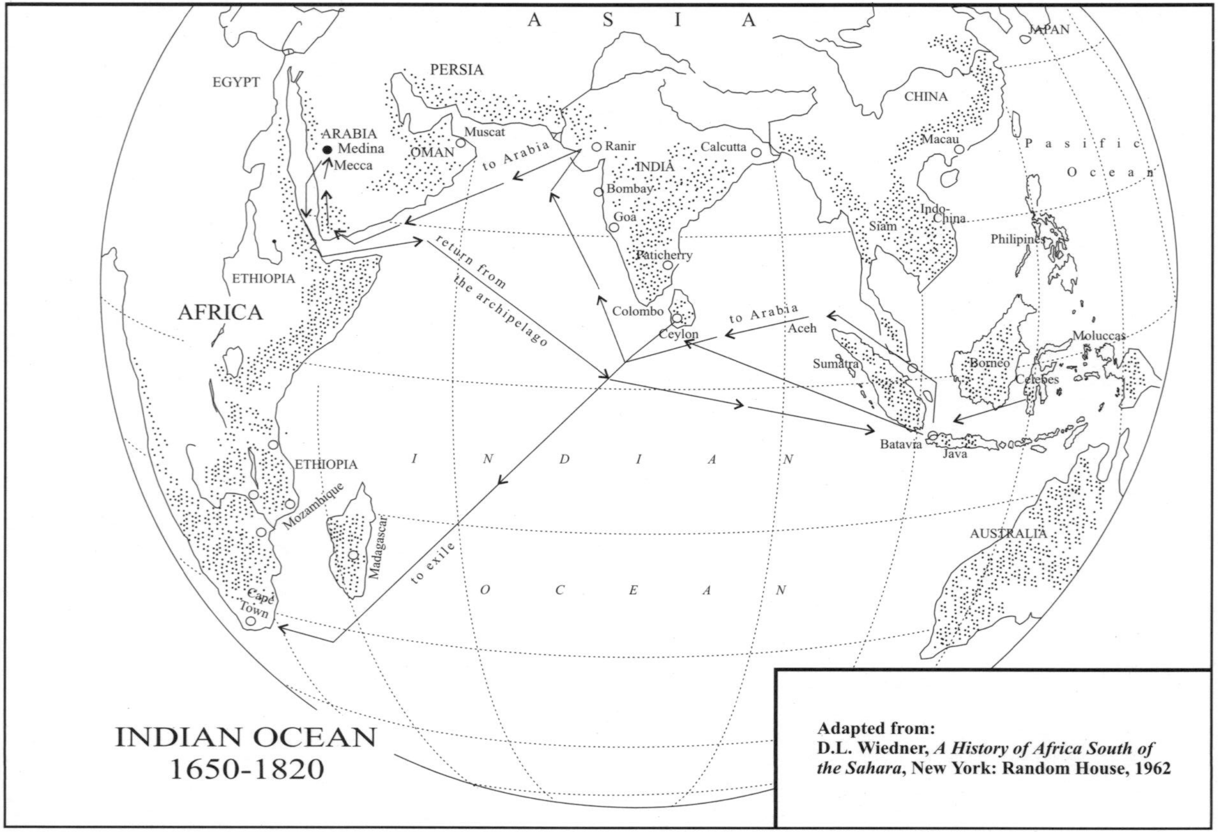

Map 3 Al-Maqassārī's itinerary

Among the Malays, the Cape of Good Hope was the most notorious place of banishment. Since colonisation by the Dutch in 1064/1652, a number of eminent Malay-Indonesian figures, considered by the Dutch to be the most dangerous, had been exiled there. But, as in Srilanka, not all Malay-Indonesians brought to the Cape of Good Hope were exiles; some of them were slaves who were used for work on Dutch farms in the region.[71] Prior to the coming of al-Maqassārī, both the early exiles and slaves constituted the nucleus of a small Muslim group known as the Cape Malays.

All writers on South African Islam are in accord that al-Maqassārī was the most important Malay-Indonesian exile ever banished to South Africa.[72] Al-Maqassārī arrived in the Cape of the Good Hope on 2 April 1694. Most of his retinue of 49 people were those who had followed him earlier to Srilanka. Two months later the Dutch authorities took him and his retinue to live in Zandvliet, a farm village at the mouth of the Eerste River, so that he, as Jeffreys points out, 'would not be in touch with any adherents of the old regime'.[73] Bearing historical connections to al-Maqassārī and his followers, this locality today is known as Macassar, and its coastal area is called Macassar beach.

Generally, al-Maqassārī received good treatment and due respect from the Dutch authorities in the Cape. Governor Simon van der Stel and later his son, Willem Adriaan, befriended him.[74] Despite this, they must have been aware that al-Maqassārī could give them problems. Therefore, the Dutch attempted to isolate him and his followers from other Malay-Indonesian exiles who had arrived before them. But their attempts apparently failed. He once again became the rallying point for the Malay-Indonesians, not to rise up against the Dutch but to intensify their Islamic beliefs and practices. Al-Maqassārī and his 12 disciples, now called *imāms*, together with other exiles, carried out teaching sessions and religious services secretly in their lodges.[75] With such activities, al-Maqassārī was able not only to preserve the Islamic belief of his fellow exiles but to gain numerous new converts.[76]

Al-Maqassārī appears to have devoted most of his time to proselytising activities; there is no evidence that he also spent his time on writing, for none among his known works contains any indication whatsoever that it was written in South Africa. This suggests that al-Maqassārī considered direct propagation through teaching to be of the utmost importance to his Malay-Indonesian community. In short, the maintenance of Islamic belief was his primary concern.

This is no surprise, as the Dutch not only prohibited Muslims from openly holding religious services but, worse still, ordered the Christianisation of all Muslim slaves in the Cape.[77] The Dutch evangelist scholar Zwemer even regrets the failure of Petrus Kalden, first minister of the Old Dutch Church at Cape Town, to convert al-Maqassārī to Christianity, despite the fact that the latter lived on land belonging to the minister. Zwemer bluntly points out that a great opportunity was lost by Kalden.[78]

Al-Maqassārī has been hailed by historians of South African Islam as the founder of Islam in the region. The term 'founder' could be misleading: Islam, or a Malay-Indonesian Muslim community, had clearly existed in the Cape before he arrived there. Therefore, I would suggest that he is more appropriately called the 'reviver' or 'revitaliser' of Islam in South Africa. His determination to preserve the belief of his fellow Muslims was one of the crucial factors contributing to the survival and further development of Islam in the region.

Furthermore, as Zwemer[79] points out, there were three *ṣūfī* orders that existed among Muslims in South Africa: the Qādiriyyah, Shaṭṭāriyyah, and Rifā'iyyah. It is highly likely that al-Maqassārī was responsible for introducing these orders there, for he was a *khalīfah* of all of them. As early as 1186/1772, Thurnberg[80] observed a ritual among the Malays that clearly constituted *dhikr*, and in the 1860s Mayson[81] gives us vivid accounts of the well-known practices among the Rifā'iyyah followers of being invulnerable to fire and weapons.

Al-Maqassārī, as Colvin[82] in his *Romance of the Empire* asserts, could not but have longed for the palms and spices of his native land, which he was fated never again to see. Colvin may be right, but al-Maqassārī himself never made clear his sense of being an old exile under his long-contested enemy. It is clear that his relatives in Gowa had never lost hope for his freedom. As early as 1103/1689, when al-Maqassārī was still in Srilanka, the Sulṭān of Gowa, 'Abd al-Jalīl (r. 1088–1121/1677–1709), and all the important local notables came to meet the Dutch Governor in Makassar, asking for the return of al-Maqassārī to his homeland. They brought with them 2000 *rijksdaalders*, which had been donated by both notables and commoners to make possible his return. Although the Governor agreed to meet the request, Batavia annulled his decision.[83] 'Abd al-Jalīl asked the Dutch to return al-Maqassārī repeatedly until 1110/1698, when the Dutch Council in Batavia issued a definite refusal to consider any such request, obviously fearing political repercussions from his return.[84]

Al-Maqassārī died at the Cape on 22 Dhū al-Qa'dah 1111/22 May 1699,[85] and was buried in Faure, on the sandhills of False Bay, not far from the farm of Zandvliet. His tomb later came to be known as the '*Karāmat*' Shaykh Yusuf (lit. 'miracle'). Between 1321/1903 and 1333/1913 the grave of al-Maqassārī was restored by Ḥāji Sulaymān Shāh Muḥammad, a rich Cape Muslim of Indian origin. A splendid domed mausoleum was erected over al-Maqassārī's grave, which later was complemented by other buildings, including tombs of four of his disciples. The 'karāmat' of al-Maqassārī is one of the most beautiful and the most important tomb buildings in the Cape Peninsula. It became a central point of the Malay-Indonesian community and the most important place of Muslim religious visitation (*ziyārah*) at the Cape; or, as Du Plessis puts it, 'the tomb has become the Mecca of the South, where thousands of pilgrims pay their respects annually to the memory of a noble exile'.[86]

The death of al-Maqassārī was a relief for the Cape Dutch authorities, both politically and financially. On 1 July 1699, they reported his death to Batavia; they asked Batavia to lift the financial burden, incurred by the Cape authorities, for the upkeep of al-Maqassārī and his retinue. As a result, the Council of Batavia decided in October 1699 to grant permission to al-Maqassārī's survivors and followers to return to the archipelago, should they want to; most of them chose to return, and they departed on board the ships 'De Liefde' and 'De Spiegel' in 1116/1704.[87]

In the meantime, the news of al-Maqassārī's death had reached South Sulawesi. Once again the Sulṭān of Gowa requested the return of al-Maqassārī—now, of course, only his remains. Finally, the remains allegedly belonging to al-Maqassārī arrived in Gowa on 5 April 1705, and were reburied the following day in Lakiung.[88] Like his tomb in Faure, this tomb of al-Maqassārī soon became one of the most important places of religious visitation in South Sulawesi.[89]

The fact that al-Maqassārī has two tombs has led to some speculation. De Haan believes that the Dutch sent the actual remains of al-Maqassārī to Gowa; therefore, his tomb in Faure is empty.[90] The Muslims in the Cape, on the other hand, believe that only the remains of a single finger of al-Maqassārī were taken to his homeland.[91] This speculation appears to contain some truth if one considers a legend in Gowa about the body of al-Maqassārī they reburied. According to the legend, initially only a handful of dust, which was probably the remains of his finger, was brought from the Cape. The dust, however, kept growing until it took the shape of the full body of al-Maqassārī when it reached Gowa.[92]

AL-MAQASSĀRĪ'S NEO-SUFISM

Al-Maqassārī was primarily a *ṣūfī*. His life experience makes it clear that his Sufism did not keep him away from worldly affairs. Unlike earlier *ṣūfī*s who exhibited strong tendencies to shun worldly life, the whole expression of al-Maqassārī's teachings and practices shows a full range of activism.

Like al-Rānīrī and al-Sinkilī in the Sultanate of Aceh, al-Maqassārī played an important role in Bantenese politics. Not only that he stepped up to the forefront of the wars against the Dutch after the capture of Sulṭān Ageng Tirtayasa. However, like most scholars in the international networks of scholars in the seventeenth century, al-Maqassārī did not employ the *ṭarīqah* organisation to mobilise the masses, especially for the purposes of war.

Al-Maqassārī wrote his works in perfect Arabic; his long sojourn in the Middle East had enabled him to write in that language. Almost all his known works deal with *taṣawwuf*, particularly in its relations with *kalām*. Like al-Rānīrī and al-Sinkilī, al-Maqassārī in developing his teachings often cites such scholars and *ṣūfī*s as al-Ghazālī, Junayd al-Baghdādī, Ibn 'Arabī, al-Jīlī, Ibn 'Atā' Allāh and other authorities.

A central concept of al-Maqassārī's *taṣawwuf* is the purification of belief (*'aqīdah*) in the Unity of God (*tawhīd*). This is his attempt to explain the transcendence of God over his creation. Such, of course, is a central theme developed by other scholars in the networks. Citing Sūrat al-Ikhlāṣ (the Qur'ān, chapter 112) and another verse of the Qur'ān that states that nothing can be compared with Him (42:11), al-Maqassārī maintains that the Unity of God (*tawḥīd*) is infinite and absolute.[93] *Tawḥīd* is the essential component in Islam; one who does not believe in *tawḥīd* is an unbeliever (*kāfir*). He further compares the immaculate *tawḥīd* with a leafy tree: gnostic knowledge (*ma'rifah*) is its branches and leaves, and devotional services (*'ibādāt*) are its fruits. One who has no *ma'rifah* is ignorant (*jāhil*), and one who does not practise *'ibādāt* is sinful (*fāsiq*).[94]

Despite his insistence on the transcendence of God, al-Maqassārī believes that God is all-encompassing (*al-iḥāṭah*) and omnipresent (*al-ma'iyyah*) over His creation.[95] But he takes great care not to associate himself with the doctrine of pantheism by maintaining that although God is present or expresses Himself in His creation, it does not necessarily mean that the creation is God himself; all creation is simply allegorical being (*al-mawjūd al-majāzī*), not the Real Being (*al-mawjūd al-ḥaqīqī*).[96] Thus, like al-Sinkilī he believes that the creation is only a shadow of God, not God Himself. According to al-Maqassārī, the 'expression' of God in His creations is not the 'physical' presence of God in them.

With the concept of *al-iḥāṭah* and *al-ma'iyyah*, God descends (*tanazzul*) while man ascends (*taraqqī*), a spiritual process that brings the two closer. It is important to note that according to al-Maqassārī the process will not take its form in the ultimate unity between man and God: while the two may be closely associated, in the final analysis man is man and God is God. With this, al-Maqassārī rejects the concept of *waḥdat al-wujūd* ('Unity of Being', or ontological monism) and *al-ḥulūl* ('Divine Incarnation'). In his opinion, God is simply incomparable to anything (*laysa ka mithlihi shay*, Qur'ān 42:11). Instead he adopts the concept of *waḥdat al-shuhūd* ('Unity of Consciousness', or phenomenological monism).[97] Thus, while he carefully disengages himself from the controversial doctrine of *waḥdat al-wujūd* of Ibn 'Arabī and of al-ḥulūl of Manṣūr al-Ḥallāj, al-Maqassārī adopts the doctrine of *waḥdat al-shuhūd*, developed mainly by Aḥmad al-Sirhindī (971–1034/1564–1624); later, this doctrine was also adopted by Shah Wali Allah (1114–76/1702–1762).

A salient feature of al-Maqassārī's theology of God's Unity is that he attempts to reconcile all Attributes or Qualities of God. According to Islamic belief, God possesses Attributes which may seem to be conflicting one with another. God is, for instance, believed to be the First (*al-Awwal*) and the Last (*al-Ākhir*); the Exterior (*al-Ẓāhir*) and the Interior (*al-Bāṭin*); the One who gives guidance (*al-Hādī*), but also the One who allows humans to go astray (*al-Muḍill*). According to al-Maqassārī, all these seemingly conflicting Attributes of God should be understood in accordance with the Unity of

God Himself. Emphasising only certain Attributes while ignoring the others will lead to wrong belief and practices. The Realities of God are the Unity of pairs of conflicting Attributes, and none will be able to comprehend their secret but those who have been granted knowledge by God Himself.[98]

As far as al-Maqassārī's theology is concerned, he adheres strictly to the Ash'arī doctrines. He thus stresses total commitment to all six articles of belief—that is, belief in the One God, the Angels, the Revelation, the Prophets, the Day of Judgment and the Will of God. Furthermore, in connection with impeccable belief in these articles of faith, he appeals to his fellow Muslims to accept the ambiguous meanings of some verses of the Qur'ān, or *al-āyāt al-mutashābihāt*.[99] Looking for or questioning the real meanings of such verses is simply an indication of not totally believing in God; only with the acceptance of the verses as such will a traveller on God's path be able to gain the blessing of God.[100]

It is well known that the theology of al-Ash'arī emphasises human predestination vis-à-vis the Will of God. Al-Maqassārī basically accepts this notion. For instance, he repeatedly asks Muslims to sincerely embrace their fate and the divine decree (*al-Qaḍā wa al-Qadar*), either good or bad.[101] He insists, however, that men must not simply surrender to them. Of particular importance, men cannot blame God for their bad deeds, for they should not simply accept them as their fate. Instead, they must make ceaseless attempts to avoid sinful behaviour and improve humanity by thinking about the creation and doing good deeds.

In this way, al-Maqassārī believes, men will be able to create a better life in this world and the next. More importantly, they will open the way to attaining the highest stage, called *al-'ubūdiyyah al-muṭlaqah* (unrestricted adoration). The one who succeeds in achieving this stage reaches the centre of his being, and is accordingly called the Universal Man (*al-Insān al-Kāmil*).[102] According to al-Maqassārī, by achieving the stage of Universal Man a slave strips his allegorical being (*al-mawjūd al-majāzī*) and gets into his real 'nothingness', non-existence (*'udum al-ḥaqīqī*). His nothingness is taken by God as a mirror (*mir'ah*) of Himself. God further reveals (*tajallī*) Himself in the slave. In other words, the slave who is absorbed (*fanā'*) in the existence of God is able to recognise the secrets of his Master—that is, God. He then sees through His Sight, hears with His Hearing, reaches with His Hands, walks with His Feet, speaks with His Word and thinks with His Mind.[103]

Al-Maqassārī's notion of the Universal Man reminds us of the similar doctrine elaborated by al-Jīlī. The latter says:

> If the servant is lifted higher and God fortifies him and conforms him, after his extinction (*fanā'*), in the state of subsistence (*baqā'*), God will reply Himself to whoever invokes this servant.
>
> When God reveals Himself to His servant in one of his Qualities, the servant soars in the sphere of this Quality until he has reached the limit by way

> of integration (*al-ijmāl*), not by distinctive knowledge, for those who realise the Divine Qualities do not have distinctive knowledge except by virtue of integration. If the servant soars in the sphere of a Quality, and he realises it entirely by (spiritual) integration, he is seated on the throne of this Quality, so that he assimilates it into himself and becomes its subject; from then on, he encounters another Quality, and so on until he realises all the Divine Qualities.
>
> To some, God reveals Himself in the Quality of the Sight (*al-baṣar*). For, revealing Himself first by the total intellectual vision which penetrates everything, God will reveal Himself more particularly in the Quality of Sight, so that the sight of the servant will become the organ of his knowledge.[104]

Again, al-Maqassārī takes pains not to be trapped in the long and heated controversy concerning the concept of Unity of Being between the servant and God. He maintains that even though the servant is able to enter the existence of God, he nevertheless remains a human being, whereas God remains God.

Like most other *ṣūfī*s, al-Maqassārī clearly holds a positive view of humankind as a whole. In his opinion, every person has an innate disposition to believe in God, and those who are closest to Him are the ones who are able to nurture that disposition in the right way.[105] Therefore, he appeals to his fellow believers not to scold or look down on those who do not believe in God and who live a sinful life; the faithful simply must have a good opinion (*ḥusn al-ẓann*) of the unbelievers. Citing Abū Madyān al-Tilimsānī, he reminds them that the flaws of the unbelievers may be better than the pitfalls of the faithful.[106] With such a view it is not suprising that nowhere in his works does al-Maqassārī accuse the Dutch, who inflicted great misery on his life.

In accordance with their degree of belief in God, al-Maqassārī classifies the believers into four categories. The first, those who simply utter the statement of faith (*shahādah*) without really believing, are called the hypocrites (*al-munāfiq*). The second group is the people who do not only utter the *shahādah* but also implant it deep in their souls; this group is called the common faithful (*al-mu'min al-'awwām*). The third category is the group of faithful who fully realise the inward and outward implication of their statement of faith in their life; they are called the people of the elite (*ahl al-khawwāṣ*). The last group is the highest category of the faithful, who come out of the third group by intensifying their *shahādah*, mainly by practising *taṣawwuf*, in order to get closer to God; they are accordingly called the select of the elite (*khāṣṣ al-khawwāṣ*).[107]

Al-Maqassārī clearly reserves the *taṣawwuf* for the select of the elite. Like other scholars in the networks, his *taṣawwuf* is the one that has been classified as neo-Sufism; he calls his *taṣawwuf* by the name the 'ṭarīqat al-Muḥammadiyyah' or 'ṭarīqat al-Aḥmadiyyah', which is familiar among scholars in the networks. This very name implicitly conveys their aim to return to the way of the Prophet Muhammad. Al-Maqassari believes the 'ṭarīqat al-Muḥammadiyyah' constitutes the right path (*Ṣirāṭ al-Mustaqīm*).[108] Throughout his writings he makes it clear that the mystical way can be trod only through a total commitment, both outwardly and inwardly, to the legal doctrine of Islam as well as to the way of the Prophet. He maintains that committing oneself simply to the *sharī'ah* is better than practising *taṣawwuf* while ignoring Islamic legal precepts.[109] He even goes so far as to classify as *zindīq* (freethinker) and *mulḥid* (heretic) those who believe that they will be able to get closer to God without practising such rituals as prayer and fasting.[110]

It appears that al-Maqassārī was rather overzealous in his reconciliation between the exoteric and esoteric aspects of Islam. In this regard, he repeatedly narrates statements of unnamed authorities who assert that those who stick only to the *sharī'ah* without the *ḥaqīqah* are *fāsiq* (sinful), and those who practise *taṣawwuf* while ignoring *sharī'ah* are *zindiq*.[111] The best that can be done is to harmonise the two. As al-Maqassārī puts it: 'Let it be known, my fellows, exoteric devotion without esoteric one is like a body without a soul (*rūḥ*), whereas esoteric occupation without exoteric devotion is like a soul without a body'.[112] Finally he cites a *ḥadīth* of the Prophet which states that the Prophet was sent by God in order to bring to the people both the *sharī'ah* and *ḥaqīqah*.[113]

Al-Maqassārī insists that every aspirant in the path of God should practise all the precepts of the *sharī'ah* before he enters *taṣawwuf*.[114] He then lists the ways to get closer to God. First is the way of the *akhyār* (best people), that is by performing numerous prayers, reading the Qur'ān and *ḥadīth*, striving in the way of God (*al-jihād fī sabīl Allāh*) and other exoteric devotion. The second is the way of the people of *mujāhādāt al-shaqā'* (those who strive against hardship), by way of rigorous training to get rid of bad habits and to purify the mind and soul. The last is the way of the people of *dhikr* (*ahl al-dhikr*), who love God both outwardly and inwardly; they take very special care of the two kinds of devotion.[115]

Al-Maqassārī, however, discourages the traveller on God's path (*sālik*) from treading his own way in seeking after truth; it will only lead him astray, for Satan will become his master. Therefore, he should look for a trusted and experienced *ṣūfī* master, even if he, as a consequence, must travel to distant places, leaving his family and homeland behind. But there is no other way; only with the guidance of a trusted *ṣūfī* master (*shaykh*) will he be able to get to God; for the master will show him the correct and surest way to achieve spiritual progress.[116] More than that, *ṣūfī* shaykhs are successors of the Prophet; they are his representatives (*khalīfah*) both outwardly and inwardly.[117]

With such an important position reserved by al-Maqassārī for the *ṣūfī* shaykh, he differentiates himself from most scholars in the networks. Unlike Aḥmad al-Qushāshī, who encourages a *sālik* to leave his master if the latter disobeys the *sharī'ah*, al-Maqassārī adheres to the earlier notion of the position of the *ṣūfī* master vis-à-vis his disciples. Thus, for al-Maqassārī, once a *sālik* pledges his allegiance (*bay'ah*) to a certain *ṣūfī* master, he must totally obey him, even if the shaykh does something that does not necessarily lead to a closer communion with God. In accordance with the traditional way, he should behave like a dead body in the hands of those who clean it. To support this view, al-Maqassārī cites Ibn 'Arabī, who maintains that a *sālik* must obey his master, even though he may observe that the shaykh does something that runs contrary to the precepts of the *sharī'ah*. The reason for this is that the shaykh is not infallible: even some prophets made mistakes.[118] However, when the shaykh makes mistakes by transgressing certain rules of the *sharī'ah*, al-Maqassārī reminds the disciple to keep up his good deeds and not to follow his master's transgression.[119]

Al-Maqassārī discusses at length some specific religious devotional services and the steps towards spiritual progress that should be undertaken by the travellers in God's path. He puts a special emphasis on *dhikr*. His *dhikr* was mainly the vocal one (*jahr*), as taught by both Ibrāhīm al-Kūrānī and Muḥammad b. 'Abd al-Bāqī al-Naqshbandī.[120] In accordance with his concept of the purification of faith, in al-Maqassārī's opinion the essence of the *dhikr* is the full recognition of the Unity of God. On the preliminary level (*al-mubtadī'*), the one who performs *dhikr* confirms that in his faith nothing should be worshipped but God. On the intermediate level (*al-mutawassiṭ*), he recognises that he seeks and loves nothing but God. On the final level (*al-muntahī*), he fully believes that there is no other being but God.[121]

Although al-Maqassārī's teachings are apparently confined to the *taṣawwuf*, this does not conceal his main concern; that is, the renewal of Muslim belief and practice in the archipelago by way of the implementation of a more *sharī'ah*-oriented Sufism. Of the various *ṭarīqah*s al-Maqassārī was affiliated with, it was the Khalwatiyyah—later known as the Khalwatiyyah Yūsuf—that found fertile ground, especially in the South Sulawesi region. If the people of South Sulawesi, and also of West Java, have been counted generally as among the most fervent Muslims in the archipelago, one can hardly underestimate the role of al-Maqassārī in developing that identity.

6

Networks of *'Ulamā'* and Islamic Renewal in the Eighteenth Century Malay-Indonesian World

So far we have attempted to give a comprehensive account of the transmission of reformist ideas from the centres of scholarly networks in the Middle East by three of the most important scholars of the Malay-Indonesian world in the seventeenth century, al-Rānīrī, al-Sinkīlī and al-Maqassārī. The career and teachings of these scholars clearly show us that Islamic developments in the archipelago were to an extent influenced by those in the Middle East. Thanks to al-Rānīrī, al-Sinkīlī and Al-Maqassārī, the reformist tendencies of the scholarly networks found their rapid translation in the archipelago.

Despite differences among modern scholars over the definition and boundaries of the terms 'reform' and 'renewal', it is clear that not all of the Malay-Indonesian scholars proposed radical doctrinal changes of Islam that can be categorised as reform. Their endeavours are more appropriately called renewal (*tajdīd*) than reform. Their central theme is a return to an orthodoxy that finds its most salient feature in the harmony between *sharī'ah* and *taṣawwuf*. With this, these *mujaddid*s contributed substantially to the strengthening of the Islamic identity of their societies. The immediate result of this process was the intensification of Islamisation in the archipelago.

I have argued that Islamic renewal began in the Malay-Indonesian world as early as the seventeenth century, rather than at the beginning of the nineteenth century or the early twentieth century, as maintained by some scholars. Hamka and Federspiel, for instance, believe that Islamic reform or renewal began in the archipelago only with the rise of the Padri Movement in West Sumatra at the beginning of the nineteenth century.[1] Although Geertz recognises that what he calls 'a more precisian Islam' (or 'scripturalist Islam') was introduced to the archipelago before the nineteenth century, he is of the opinion that it gained momentum only after the early nineteenth century with the rise, for instance in West Sumatra, of what he termed 'a band of religious zealots, outraged by the heterodoxy of local customs'.[2] In this reference to the Padri Movement, Geertz clearly views Islamic reforms very simplistically.

The Padri Movement, as we will discuss briefly later, in fact originated from the scholarly networks. The birth and growth of this movement reflect a complicated process of the transmission of reformist ideas, including a 'tug of war' between the forces of reformism and local factors such as *adat* (custom). The Padri Movement is an excellent example of how reformism generated by the networks found one of its extreme manifestations in the archipelago.

Deliar Noer,[3] on the other hand, maintains that Islamic reformism started only in the early twentieth century. Noer overemphasises Islamic reformism in the period he discusses, concluding without hesitation that Indonesian Islam before the twentieth century was dominated by *taṣawwuf* and was thus no more than a hybrid of Islamic mysticism and remnants of local Hindu-Buddhist beliefs. He does mention the influences that had come from Mecca since the eighteenth century, but by using Snouck Hurgronje's framework Noer views this influence mostly in political terms, or more precisely as pan-Islamism.

As we will see shortly, this view can no longer be maintained, because there is no evidence in the eighteenth century, among scholars in the centres of the Ḥaramayn or among our Malay-Indonesian scholars, that points to any attempt to forge a feeling of pan-Islamism in the archipelago. What they transmitted to this part of the Muslim world was for the most part, indeed, reformist or renewalist religious ideas rather than political ones.

Our three *mujaddid*s did not explicitly declare that they were launching reform, nor did they employ the organisation of the *ṭarīqah*s in order to pursue their ends, but the central theme of their teaching leaves no doubt about their commitment to renewalism. It is important to note that reformism or renewal is not an overnight process. Therefore, although by the second half of the seventeenth century reformist ideas had been introduced to the archipelago, they took root only slowly and sporadically. There is no doubt, however, that the momentum of renewalism sparked by al-Rānīrī, al-Sinkīlī and al-Maqassārī was irreversible. Thus, as Federspiel rightly points out, over the past four centuries Islam in Indonesia has slowly altered its form: 'the heterodox religious trends of the early period have slowed in momentum, and more orthodox Islamic practices and patterns have slowly gained in importance'.[4]

Federspiel recognises that contacts between the Malay-Indonesian world, by way of *Jāwī* students and pilgrims, and the Middle East greatly contributed to the rise of Islamic renewalism in the region. Again, however, like Hamka, he simply points to the famous example of the Padri Movement, which gained crucial stimulus from the return of three *ḥājji*s from Mecca in the early nineteenth century.[5] But as we have already noted, and will discuss further later, the origins of the Padri Movement can be traced back to al-Sinkīlī and to reformist movements in the centres of the networks in Mecca and Medina.

In the final analysis, the roots of Islamic renewal in the Malay-Indonesian world are to be found in the teachings of al-Rānīrī, al-Sinkilī and al-Maqassārī. Like reformism in the Ḥaramayn, the renewal is genuine and born as an internal response to prevailing religious conditions among Muslims themselves. But from the eighteenth century outside factors, especially increasing colonial encroachment, also contributed to the acceleration of Islamic renewal and reform in the archipelago.

'ULAMĀ' IN THE EIGHTEENTH CENTURY NETWORKS

If al-Rānīrī, al-Sinkīlī and al-Maqassārī have commanded much attention from scholars, the *'ulamā'* in the eighteenth century have been less studied. Furthermore, the few sources available, mainly in Malay and Indonesian, simply narrate biographies, without critical examination of their positions vis-à-vis Islamic developments in the Malay-Indonesian world or their relationship to the teachings introduced by al-Rānīrī, al-Sinkīlī and al-Maqassārī. No attempt has been made to trace their connections with the scholarly networks of the larger Muslim world, which should give us a better picture of the continuing religious and intellectual relations between the archipelago and the Middle East.

The *'ulamā'* involved in the eighteenth century scholarly networks indeed had traceable connections with earlier networks. While they did not have direct teacher-student connections with al-Rānīrī, al-Sinkīlī and al-Maqassārī, their teachers in Mecca and Medina were among the prominent figures of the networks in their period and had direct connections with earlier scholars to whom the three predecessors had also been linked. Malay-Indonesian scholars in the eighteenth century, moreover, were well aware of the teachings of their three precursors, and they established intellectual connections with them by making reference to their works.

In chapter 5 we have seen how, through al-Maqassārī and his disciples, the regions of South Sulawesi and West Java, following Aceh, came into the picture of Islamic learning in the archipelago in the seventeenth century. In the eighteenth century, South Sumatra, South Kalimantan (Borneo) and the Patani region in the northern part of the Malay Peninsula came to prominence. Therefore, I would argue that the birthplaces and ethnic origins of Malay-Indonesian scholars in a way reflect the historical course of Islam in the archipelago through centuries. This points to the fact that appreciation of the importance of Islamic learning as well as the need for renewal and reform began to gain ground among various ethnic groups in the archipelago. These scholars, having acquired substantive credentials in Islamic learning, in turn stimulated further intensification of Islamisation, particularly among their respective ethnic groups. In the eighteenth century such developments continued, so as to become one of the most distinctive features in the transmission of Islam in the archipelago.

There were several major Indonesian-Malay *'ulamā'* who came from various regions and ethnic groups in the archipelago in the eighteenth to the early nineteenth centuries. A prominent group came from the Palembang region of South Sumatra. The most important among them were Shihāb al-Dīn b. 'Abd Allāh Muḥammad, Kemas Fakhr al-Dīn, 'Abd al-Ṣamad al-Palimbānī, Kemas Muḥammad b. Aḥmad and Muḥammad Muḥyī al-Dīn b. Shihāb al-Dīn. Then came Muḥammad Arshad al-Banjārī and Muḥammad Nafīs al-Banjārī from South Kalimantan; 'Abd al-Wahhāb al-Bugisī from Sulawesi; 'Abd al-Raḥmān al-Batāwī al-Maṣrī from Batavia and Dāwūd b. 'Abd Allāh al-Faṭānī from the Patani region (South Thailand). Although information on several of these scholars is sketchy, their careers and teachings make it clear that they were involved both socially and intellectually in the networks. Taken together, they constituted the most important scholars of the archipelago in the eighteenth century.

AL-PALIMBĀNĪ AND OTHER PALEMBANG SCHOLARS

The fact that there were several scholars of the Palembang region who rose to prominence in the period under discussion is an interesting example of the relations between Middle Eastern Muslims and the growth of Islamic learning in the archipelago.

Arab migrants, particularly from the Ḥaḍramawt,[6] began to come to Palembang in increasing numbers from the seventeenth century. Al-Palimbānī's father, although he stayed in Palembang for only a relatively short time, was among the Arab sayyids who came to this region in the early seventeenth century. By the middle of the eighteenth century, some Arab scholars had gained prominent positions in the court of the Palembang Sultanate. In 1168/1754–5 a certain Sayyid al-'Aydarūs was reported to have married Sulṭān Maḥmūd's sister, and several unnamed sayyids came to control the religious hierarchy in the Sultanate: they became 'senior priests', and one of the sayyids was called 'Tuan Besar' (great lord).[7]

These Arabs clearly played an important role in the growth of the tradition of Islamic learning in the region. They stimulated and encouraged the Sulṭāns of Palembang to pay special attention to religious matters, but apparently did not go much further. They did not take any initiative, for instance, to establish religious educational institutions at the popular level, for there is no evidence that such institutions as *madrasah* or *pesantren* existed during this period. Instead, they concentrated on the court, and apparently contributed to the rise of the court as the centre of learning. As a result, the court of Palembang become the centre for an extensive collection of religious works by local scholars. This further indicates the importance of the court in the scholarly discourse in the Malay-Indonesian archipelago.[8]

Most of the Palembang scholars, such as Shihāb al-Dīn, Kemas Fakhr al-Dīn, Muḥammad Muḥyī al-Dīn and Kemas Muḥammad, are known mostly from their works, preserved initially in the court of the Palembang

Sultanate before being taken by the Dutch and the British. Drewes has correctly concluded that they lived throughout the second half of the seventeenth and the early eighteenth centuries. There is insufficient information on their lives, although it is known that Kemas Fakhr al-Dīn (1133–77/1719–63) travelled to India and spent a good deal of his life in Arabia, most probably in Mecca or Medina, where he wrote his works.[9] Most of the works of these scholars deal with mysticism and theology and are based largely on the teachings of al-Junayd, al-Qushayrī and al-Ghazālī. They clearly embraced teachings belonging to neo-Sufism.[10]

Without doubt, the most prominent among these Palembang scholars was 'Abd al-Ṣamad al-Palimbānī. He was also the most influential, especially through his works, which were widely circulated in the archipelago. We have a rather complete account of his life and career, unlike his fellow Palembang scholars, so that we are able to reconstruct his biography. So far, accounts of al-Palimbānī's life are based on the scattered information he supplied in his works, which have been supplemented by Malay accounts and Dutch sources. However, there is ample information on him in Arabic biographical dictionaries, which throw some light on this major Malay-Indonesian scholar. This is an important finding, for never before had accounts of a Malay-Indonesian scholar been given in Arabic biographical dictionaries. This also indicates that al-Palimbānī enjoyed a respected career in the Middle East.

According to Malay sources the full name of al-Palimbānī was 'Abd al-Ṣamad b. 'Abd Allāh al-Jāwī al-Palimbānī, but Arabic sources call him Sayyid 'Abd al-Ṣamad b. 'Abd al-Raḥmān al-Jāwī.[11] We have every reason to believe that 'Abd al-Ṣamad b. 'Abd al-Raḥmān al-Jāwī was indeed 'Abd al-Ṣamad al-Palimbānī. As we will show in this chapter, the picture of the career of 'Abd al-Ṣamad b. 'Abd al-Raḥmān al-Jāwī in Arabic sources almost entirely describes that of 'Abd al-Ṣamad al-Palimbānī given by other sources.

Of all the available sources, only the *Tārīkh Salāsilah Negeri Kedah* supplies the date of al-Palimbānī's birth and death. According to this work, al-Palimbānī was born about 1116/1704 in Palembang to a sayyid father and a Palembang woman. This, therefore, corroborates the Arabic sources, which mention that al-Palimbānī was a sayyid. Al-Palimbānī's father is said to have come from Sana'a, Yemen, and travelled widely in India and Java before taking up residence in Kedah, where he was appointed *Qāḍī*. About 1112/1700 he went to Palembang, where he married a local woman and returned to Kedah with his new born son, al-Palimbānī. It is believed that al-Palimbānī acquired his early education in Kedah and Patani, probably in a *pondok* (local traditional Islam educational institution), about which more follows. Later, his father dispatched him to study in Arabia.[12] We have no information on when he left the archipelago.

Although we cannot resolve the conflicting dates surrounding his life, all sources are in accord that al-Palimbānī's life span was from the first decade well into the late eighteenth century. Al-Bayṭār points out al-Palimbānī died after 1200/1785.[13] But most probably he died in 1203/1789, the date of completion of his final and most acclaimed work, the *Sayr al-Sālikīn*.[14] When he completed this work he would have been 85 years old. In the *Tārīkh Salāsilah Negeri Kedah*, it is reported that he was killed in the war against the Thais in 1244/1828.[15] It is difficult to accept this account, as there is no evidence in other sources to indicate that al-Palimbānī ever returned to the archipelago. Furthermore, he would then have been about 124 years old—too old to go to the battlefield. Although al-Bayṭār does not mention the place where al-Palimbānī died, there is a strong suggestion that he died in Arabia.[16]

Al-Palimbānī almost certainly established his career in the Ḥaramayn and never returned to the archipelago. He nevertheless maintained a deep concern for Islam and Muslims in the Malay-Indonesian world. In the Ḥaramayn, al-Palimbānī was involved in the *Jāwī* community and was a fellow student of Muḥammad Arshad al-Banjārī, 'Abd al-Wahhāb Bugis, 'Abd al-Raḥmān al-Batāwī and Dāwūd al-Faṭānī. His involvement in the *Jāwī* community kept him fully aware of the religious and political developments in the archipelago.

Al-Palimbānī and his group all had the same teachers. The most famous among them were Muḥammad b. 'Abd al-Karīm al-Sammānī, Muḥammad b. Sulaymān al-Kurdī and 'Abd al-Mun'im al-Damanhūrī.[17] Al-Bayṭār, in addition to mentioning Muḥammad [b. Sulaymān] al-Kurdī, lists other teachers of al-Palimbānī: they were Ibrāhīm al-Ra'īs, Muḥammad Murād, Muḥammad al-Jawharī and 'Aṭā' Allāh al-Maṣrī.[18] Some of these scholars were also teachers of the four friends of al-Palimbānī.

It is important to examine briefly the biographies of these last four teachers, as they further show us the connections al-Palimbānī and his fellow Malay-Indonesians had with the extensive scholarly networks.

[Abū al-Fawz] Ibrāhīm [b. Muḥammad] al-Ra'īs [al-Zamzamī al-Makkī] (1110–94/1698–1780) was evidently another important scholar from the Zamzamī family.[19] As al-Jabartī points out, Ibrāhīm al-Zamzamī al-Ra'īs was well versed in various religious sciences; one of his special subjects was *'ilm al-falak* (astronomy). Among his teachers were 'Abd Allāh al-Baṣrī, Ibn al-Ṭayyib, Aḥmad al-Jawharī, 'Aṭā' Allāh al-Maṣrī and Ḥasan al-Jabartī, the father of the historian al-Jabartī; he took the Khalwatiyyah order from Muṣṭafā al-Bakrī and the Naqshbandiyyah from 'Abd al-Raḥmān al-'Aydarūs. No less importantly, he was a student of Murtaḍā al-Zabīdī[20] and Ṣāliḥ al-Fullānī,[21] both major figures of the scholarly networks in the eighteenth century. Ibrāhīm al-Ra'īs was also closely connected with Muṣṭafā al-'Aydarūs and with scholars of the Ahdal and Mizjājī families, including the father of Sulaymān al-Ahdal, one of al-Palimbānī's students.[22]

As for Muḥammad Murād, there is strong evidence that he was Muḥammad Khalīl b. 'Alī b. Muḥammad b. Murād al-Ḥusaynī (1173–1206/1759–91). My research on Muḥammad Murād in several biographical dictionaries of the period points to Muḥammad Khalīl al-Murādī.[23] Better known as al-Murādī, primarily for his four-volume biographical dictionary *Silk al-Durar*,[24] he was a contemporary of al-Palimbānī. Al-Jabartī, his good friend, points out that al-Murādī mainly lived in Damascus but travelled extensively, including to the Ḥaramayn, in order to collect information on the scholars he would write about in his biographical dictionary. In the course of his travels, al-Murādī not only advanced his knowledge but taught students as well.[25] Therefore, it is highly probable that al-Palimbānī took the opportunity of al-Murādī's visits to the Ḥaramayn to study with him.

Although al-Murādī was renowned mostly as a historian, al-Jabartī reports that he was a 'prop of the *sharī'ah*' and a 'house of knowledge' in Syria during his time, who had mastered both exterior and interior sciences to the fullest extent.[26] As al-Baghdādī also tells us, he was the *Muftī* of the Ḥanafī school of law in Damascus, and a Naqshbandī shaykh.[27] He had wide connections with such major scholars in the networks as Murtaḍā al-Zabīdī, not only because he had met them in the course of collecting biographical data but more importantly because of *ḥadīth* scholarship; his was considered a 'superior' *isnād* in *ḥadīth* studies.[28]

The next teacher of al-Palimbānī, Muḥammad [b. Aḥmad] al-Jawharī [al-Miṣrī], was the son of a leading Egyptian *muḥaddith*, Aḥmad b. al-Ḥasan b. 'Abd al-Karīm b. Yūsuf al-Karīmī al-Khālidī al-Jawharī al-Azharī (1096–1181/1685–1767).[29] Muḥammad al-Jawharī (1132–86/1720–72), like his father, Aḥmad al-Jawharī, was known mainly as a traditionist.[30] Although he lived mostly in Egypt, Muḥammad al-Jawharī often travelled to the Ḥaramayn, where besides performing pilgrimages he taught students. In addition to receiving *ḥadīth* from his father, he possessed *isnād*s through his father which connected him with such scholars as 'Abd Allāh al-Baṣrī and Aḥmad al-Nakhlī. Therefore, he was among the most sought-after *isnād*s in the networks during this period. He had also extensive networks through *ḥadīth* studies down to more recent times.[31]

The last scholar in the list of al-Palimbānī's teachers was 'Aṭā' Allāh [b. Aḥmad] al-Azharī al-Maṣrī al-Makkī, mentioned earlier as a teacher of Ibrāhīm al-Ra'īs. 'Aṭā' Allāh was a renowned *muḥaddith*[32] and a colleague of Muḥammad al-Sammānī, Muḥammad al-Jawharī and Murtaḍā al-Zabīdī. Al-Zabīdī even lists 'Aṭā' Allāh as one of his numerous teachers.[33] It appears that after completing his education at the Azhar, later in his life 'Aṭā' Allāh migrated to Mecca or, in al-Kattānī's terms, he was '*nazīl al-Ḥaramayn*', where he was very active in teaching.[34] Among his students were Abū al-Ḥasan al-Sindī al-Ṣaghīr and Ṣāliḥ al-Fullānī, and a number of Yemeni scholars.[35] Like Muḥammad al-Jawharī, 'Aṭā' Allāh is considered a superior *isnād* in *ḥadīth* studies.[36]

Thus, as al-Sinkīlī earlier, al-Palimbānī reaped great profit from visiting scholars in the Ḥaramayn, especially during the pilgrimage season. One visiting scholar from whom al-Palimbānī gained great benefit was Aḥmad al-Damanhūrī. The latter, whose biography has been provided by Zabīdī, lived mostly in Cairo, though he often travelled to the Ḥaramayn. Based on notes he took when he attended lectures given by al-Damanhūrī in Mecca, al-Palimbānī was able to write one of his earliest works, entitled *Zuhrat al-Murīd fī Bayān Kalimat al-Tawḥīd*. The work, in Malay, deals with logic (*manṭiq*) and theology (*uṣūl al-dīn*), and it was written at the request of one of his friends, obviously a Malay, in order to better understand al-Damanhūrī's lectures.[37]

Considering the status of the scholars he studied with, it is certain that al-Palimbānī's education was a thorough one; he studied *ḥadīth*, *fiqh*, *sharī'ah*, *tafsīr*, *kalām* and *taṣawwuf*. Al-Palimbānī had a strong disposition towards mysticism, and it is evident that he studied *taṣawwuf* mostly with al-Sammānī, from whom he also took both *ṭarīqah*s of Khalwatiyyah and Sammāniyyah.[38] Abdullah[39] believes that al-Palimbānī studied with al-Sammānī for five years in Medina. During the course of his studies with al-Sammānī, he was entrusted to teach some of al-Sammānī's students of Arab origin. So far as his adherence to *ṭarīqah* is concerned, al-Palimbānī was deeply influenced by al-Sammānī. Conversely, it is through al-Palimbānī that the Sammāniyyah *ṭarīqah* found fertile ground not only in the Palembang region but in other parts of the archipelago; al-Sammānī and the Sammāniyyah *ṭarīqah* became principal subjects in the writings of later Palembang scholars.

Al-Palimbānī never returned to the archipelago. He devoted his time in the Ḥaramayn to writing and teaching. Al-Bayṭār reports that in 1201/1787 he travelled to Zabīd, where he taught students, particularly of the Ahdal and al-Mizjājī families.[40] This report is in accord with Abdullah's accounts of al-Palimbānī's travels to Zabīd and his meetings with local scholars and students.[41] One of his students in Zabīd was Wajīh al-Dīn 'Abd al-Raḥmān b. Sulaymān b. Yaḥyā b. 'Umar al-Ahdal (1179–1255/1765–1839), a *muḥaddith* who later occupied the post of *Muftī* of Zabīd. Wajīh al-Dīn al-Ahdal evidently considered al-Palimbānī one of his most important teachers, as he included his biography in his dictionary, *al-Nafs al-Yamānī wa al-Rūḥ al-Rayḥānī*.[42]

According to al-Kattānī, Wajīh al-Dīn al-Ahdal in his biographical dictionary put al-Palimbānī into his third category *(al-ṭabaqat al-thālithah)*; that is, major scholars who visited Zabīd and spent their time there primarily as teachers.[43] It is interesting to note that, in addition to studying with al-Palimbānī, Wajīh al-Dīn learned from such scholars as Aḥmad b. Ḥasan al-Muqrī al-Zabīdī, Amr Allāh b. 'Abd al-Khāliq b. Muḥammad al-Bāqī al-Mizjājī, Sulaymān al-Kurdī, 'Abd al-Raḥmān Muṣṭafā al-'Aydarūs and Murtaḍā al-Zabīdī.[44] Thus, through Wajīh al-Dīn al-Ahdal, al-Palimbānī was connected to a much wider networks of scholars.

Because of his scholarly connections, al-Palimbānī was, without doubt, the most prominent Malay-Indonesian scholar in the eighteenth century networks. However, his importance in light of Islamic development in the archipelago lies not only in his involvement in the scholarly networks but more importantly in his writings, which were widely read in the Malay-Indonesian world, particularly in the *'ulamā'* circles, in the *pesantren, pondok* and other Islamic educational institutions. In his works al-Palimbānī disseminated the teachings of neo-*ṣūfī*s, but he also appealed to his fellow Muslims to launch a *jihād* against Europeans, particularly the Dutch, who had intensified their attempts to subdue Muslim political entities in the archipelago.

AL-BANJĀRĪ

With Muḥammad Arshad al-Banjārī we now come to South Kalimantan (Borneo), a region where the development of Islam is still insufficiently studied. As elsewhere in the archipelago, studies of Islam in South Kalimantan have so far mainly concentrated on the questions of when, how and whence Islam came to this region; there is almost no discussion of the growth of Islamic institutions and the tradition of learning among its Muslim population. With regard to this, the importance of Muḥammad Arshad lies not simply in his involvement in the scholary networks but also in the fact that he was the first scholar to establish new Islamic institutions as well as to introduce new religious ideas to South Kalimantan.

Islam came to South Kalimantan at a much later period than, for instance, North Sumatra or Aceh. It is assumed that there had been some Muslims in the coastal region since the early sixteenth century, but Islam gained momentum only after the Demak Sultanate's troops in Java came to Banjarmasin to assist Pangeran Samudra in his struggles with the court elite of the Daha Kingdom. On his victory, Pangeran Samudra converted to Islam around 936/1526 and was installed as the first Sulṭān of the Banjar Sultanate. He was given the name of Sulṭān Surian Shāh or Surian Allāh by an Arab teacher.[45]

With the establishment of the Sultanate of Banjar, Islam appears to have been officially regarded as the religion of the state, although Muslims constituted a minority of the population. Adherents to Islam, by and large, were confined to the Malay population; Islam only very slowly made inroads among the tribal population, commonly called the Dayaks.[46] Even among Malay Muslims, the adherence to Islam was evidently nominal and did not go beyond the utterance of the confession of faith. Under successive Sulṭāns down to the period of al-Banjārī, it is evident that there was no substantial attempt made by the rulers to advance Islamic life. However, they did adopt the Arabic script for the Sultanate's correspondence with other Malay-Indonesian rulers, the Dutch and the British. There are also accounts of attempts by wandering scholars to further Islamisation in the region, but apparently they made little progress.[47]

A substantial drive for further Islamisation was launched by Muḥammad Arshad b. ʻAbd Allāh al-Banjārī (1122–1227/1710–1812), one of the best-known scholars of Kalimantan. Born in Martapura, South Kalimantan, Muḥammad Arshad acquired a rudimentary religious education in his own village, apparently from his father and local teachers, for there is no evidence that *surau* or *pesantren* existed during this period in the region. When he was seven years old he is reported to have been able to read the Qur'ān perfectly. He became famous for this, which led Sulṭān Tahlīl Allāh (1112–58/1700–45) to take him and his family to live in the court of the Sultanate. Later the Sulṭān married him to a woman, but almost immediately he sent Muḥammad Arshad to the Ḥaramayn in order to pursue further studies at the Sultanate's expense. The Sulṭān seems to have financed him generously; Muḥammad Arshad was even able to buy a house in the Shamiyyah quarter of Mecca, which is still maintained by the Banjar immigrants even today.[48]

As we noted earlier, Muḥammad Arshad studied with al-Palimbānī and several other Malay-Indonesian students. However, while al-Palimbānī had a good number of teachers, Muḥammad Arshad's known teachers included only al-Sammānī, al-Damanhūrī, Sulaymān al-Kurdī and ʻAṭā' Allāh al-Maṣrī. It is possible that he studied with other teachers, especially with Ibrāhīm al-Ra'īs al-Zamzamī, from whom Muḥammad Arshad most likely studied *ʻilm al-falak* (astronomy), a field in which he was a leading authority among Malay-Indonesian scholars.

With regard to his works and activities after his return to the archipelago, one might assume that Muḥammad Arshad was simply an expert in *fiqh* or *sharī'ah*, especially due to the fact that his best-known text, entitled *Sabīl al-Muhtadīn*, is a *fiqh* book. But this does not necessarily mean that he was not learned in Sufism; it is known that he also wrote a work entitled *Kanz al-Ma'rifah*, dealing with *taṣawwuf*. Thus Muḥammad Arshad was well versed in the exterior (*al-ẓāhir*) and interior (*al-bāṭin*) sciences or, as Steenbrink writes,[49] he was an expert in *fiqh* as well as in *taṣawwuf*. Muḥammad Arshad received the Sammāniyyah *ṭarīqah* from al-Sammānī, and he is considered the scholar most responsible for the spread of the Sammāniyyah *ṭarīqah* in Kalimantan.

Muḥammad Arshad studied for about 30 years in Mecca and five years in Medina before returning to the archipelago. Several years before his return it is said that he began to teach students in the Ḥarām Mosque of Mecca.[50] However, Muḥammad Arshad felt that he did not yet have sufficient knowledge. Together with al-Palimbānī, ʻAbd al-Raḥmān al-Batāwī and ʻAbd al-Wahhāb al-Bugisī, he asked permission of their teacher, ʻAṭā' Allāh al-Maṣrī, to advance their education in Cairo. While appreciating their good intention, ʻAṭā' Allāh suggested that it would be much better for them to return to the the archipelago, as he believed they already possessed more than sufficient knowledge to be effective as teachers in their homeland. They decided to travel to Cairo anyway, but simply for a visit, not to study.[51] It was probably a sign of their connection with 'Aṭā' Allāh and their visit to Cairo that one of Muḥammad Arshad's friends, 'Abd al-Raḥmān al-Batāwī, added the *laqab* (surname) of 'al-Maṣrī' to his name.

Like other Malay-Indonesian scholars, Muḥammad Arshad maintained constant contact and communication with his homeland while he was in the Ḥaramayn, so that he was well informed about the developments of Islam there. In this connection he is reported to have asked the opinion of his teacher, Sulaymān al-Kurdī, about the religious policies of the Sulṭān of Banjar. The Sulṭān, he had heard, imposed heavy fines on his Muslim subjects for failing to perform the *Jum'ah* (Friday) prayer. Muḥammad Arshad also asked Sulaymān al-Kurdī to explain the differences between *zakāh* (obligatory 'alms') and tax, for the Banjar Sulṭān had required the population to pay tax instead of *zakāh*.[52] It is unfortunate that we have no information on Sulaymān al-Kurdī's responses to these questions, but this account reflects the genuine concern on the part of Muḥammad Arshad about the correct application of the *sharī'ah*.

Muḥammad Arshad, together with 'Abd al-Raḥmān al-Batāwī al-Maṣrī and 'Abd al-Wahhāb al-Bugisī, returned to the archipelago in 1186/1773. Before he proceeded to Banjarmasin, at the request of al-Batāwī, Muḥammad Arshad stayed in Batavia for two months. Although in Batavia for a relatively short time, he was able to launch an important reform for the Batavian Muslims. He corrected the *qiblah* (the direction Muslims face when performing prayers towards the Ka'bah in Mecca) of several mosques in Batavia. According to his calculation, the *qiblah* of mosques in Jembatan Lima and Pekojan, Batavia, were not directed correctly at the Ka'bah, and therefore had to be changed. This created controversy among Muslim leaders in Batavia, and as a result the Dutch Governor summoned Muḥammad Arshad to explain the matter. The Governor, impressed by Muḥammad Arshad's mathematical calculations, happily presented him with several gifts.[53] Later, the correction of the direction of the *qiblah* was proposed by 'Abd al-Raḥmān al-Batāwī in Palembang when he travelled there around 1800; this incited heated discussion as well.[54]

The reformist impulse in Muḥammad Arshad's personality to introduce new religious ideas and institutions is obvious after his return to Martapura, South Kalimantan. One of the first things he did after his arrival was to establish an Islamic educational institution, which was crucial to the education of Muslims in advancing their understanding of Islamic teachings and practices. To that end Muḥammad Arshad asked Sulṭān Taḥmīd Allāh II (r. 1187–1223/1773–1808) to grant him a large plot of wasteland outside the capital of the Sultanate. He and 'Abd al-Wahhāb al-Bugisī, who was now married to Muḥammad Arshad's daughter, built a centre for Islamic education, which was similar in characteristics to the *surau* in West Sumatra or *pesantren* in Java. Like many *surau*s and *pesantren*s, Muḥammad Arshad's centre of learning consisted of lecture halls, students' hostels, teachers' houses and libraries. This centre was economically self-sufficient, as Muḥammad Arshad together with other teachers and students transformed nearby lands into productive rice fields and vegetable gardens. Before long, the centre had established itself as the most important locus for the training of students, who later became leading scholars in Kalimantan society.[55]

Muḥammad Arshad took another important step in intensifying Islamisation in his region by reforming the administration of justice in the Sultanate of Banjar. In addition to making Islamic legal doctrines the most important reference in criminal courts, Muḥammad Arshad, with the support of the Sulṭān, established separate Islamic courts to deal with more purely civil legal matters. He also initiated the establishment of the office of *Muftī*, who was responsible for issuing *fatwā*s on religious and social matters.[56] With these initiatives, Muḥammad Arshad managed to put Islamic law into effect in the realm of the Sultanate of Banjar.

Another important Kalimantan scholar is Muḥammad Nafīs b. Idrīs b. Ḥusayn al-Banjārī. Although we do not have much information on his life, there is no doubt that he was second only to Muḥammad Arshad in terms of the influence he exerted on the Kalimantan Muslims, especially in the field of *taṣawwuf*. If Muḥammad Arshad was known primarily as an expert in *sharī'ah*, Muḥammad Nafīs was famous as a *ṣūfī* scholar by virtue of his well-known work, *al-Durr al-Nafīs fī Bayān Waḥdat al-Af'āl al-Asmā' wa al-Ṣifāt wa al-Dhāt al-Taqdīs*, which circulated widely in the archipelago. This work was printed several times in Cairo by Dār al-Ṭabā'ah (as recently as 1347/1928) and by Muṣṭafā al-Ḥalabī (1362/1943), in Mecca by Maṭba'at al-Karīm al-Islāmiyyah (1323/1905), and in various places in the archipelago.[57]

Muḥammad Nafīs was born in 1148/1735 in Martapura into the Banjar royal family. Thus, he lived in the same period as Muḥammad Arshad. There is no evidence of the date of his death, although it is known that he died and was buried in Kelua, a village about 125 kilometres from Banjarmasin.[58] His early education is not known, but he was most probably taught the basic principles of Islam in his own region. Later, we find him studying in Mecca, as he writes in his introductory notes to his *al-Durr al-Nafīs*: '. . . he who writes this epistle . . . that is Muḥammad Nafīs b. Idrīs b. al-Ḥusayn, who was born in Banjar and lives in Mecca'.[59] There is no hard evidence that he studied together with al-Palimbānī, Muḥammad Arshad or their colleagues, but it is highly probable that his period of study in the Ḥaramayn coincided with that of al-Palimbānī and others. I would suggest that they studied together at one time or another, particularly if we consider the following list of Muḥammad Nafīs' teachers.

Abdullah mentions that Muḥammad Nafīs studied with a number of scholars in the Ḥaramayn, the most famous of whom were al-Sammānī, Muḥammad al-Jawharī, 'Abd Allāh b. Ḥijāzī al-Sharqāwī, Muḥammad Ṣiddīq b. 'Umar Khān and 'Abd al-Raḥmān b. 'Abd al-Azīz al-Maghribī.[60] Muḥammad Ṣiddīq b. 'Umar Khān was a student of al-Sammānī and 'Abd al-Azīz al-Maghribī, and was apparently a close friend of al-Palimbānī. The latter even includes the titles of several works of Muḥammad Ṣiddīq in the list of works that he recommends to be read by aspirants of the *ṣūfī* path.[61]

We have already mentioned both al-Sammānī and Muḥammad al-Jawharī, who were among the teachers of al-Palimbānī and his fellows. The fact that Muḥammad Nafīs studied with al-Sammānī, al-Jawharī and Muḥammad Ṣiddīq indicates that he was indeed a fellow student of al-Palimbānī, Muḥammad Arshad and their other Malay-Indonesian counterparts.

As for 'Abd Allāh b. Ḥijāzī [b. Ibrāhīm] al-Sharqāwī al-Azharī (1150–1227/1737–1812), he was Shaykh al-Islām and Shaykh of the Azhar from 1207/1794.[62] Al-Sharqāwī was two years younger than Muḥammad Nafīs. As al-Sharqāwī mostly lived in Cairo, it is very likely that Muḥammad Nafīs studied with him during his frequent visits to the Ḥaramayn.[63] We are not so certain whether al-Palimbānī, Muḥammad Arshad, 'Abd al-Raḥmān al-Batāwī and 'Abd al-Wahhāb al-Bugisī also studied with al-Sharqāwī. But, as we will see shortly, al-Sharqāwī had another important Malay-Indonesian student, namely Dāwūd al-Faṭānī.

Al-Sharqāwī, it is worth mentioning briefly, was himself a student of important scholars in the networks, including Aḥmad al-Damanhūrī, Maḥmūd al-Kurdī and Aḥmad al-Jawharī. Maḥmūd al-Kurdī appointed him as the khalīfah of the Khalwatiyyah *ṭarīqah* in Cairo. Al-Sharqāwī then established himself among reformists of the order. He was well versed in various branches of Islamic discipline, although he was mainly known as a leading expert in the *sharī'ah* and *ḥadīth*. Like most scholars in the networks, he emphasised the importance of *ḥadīth*, in terms of its position not only as the second source of Islamic legal doctrines but also as the indispensable source of proper moral conduct.[64] Therefore, in addition to being a reformist, and a *ṣūfī* with numerous khalīfahs, al-Sharqāwī was among the most respected *isnād*s in the networks.[65] It is important to note in passing that Muḥammad Maḥfūẓ al-Tarmisī (from Termas, East Java—1285–1338/1842–1920), an important Malay-Indonesian *ḥadīth* scholar who lived and died in Mecca, traced his *isnād*s to al-Sharqāwī, among others.[66] Having studied with al-Sharqāwī as well as with al-Sammānī and Muḥammad al-Jawharī, Muḥammad Nafīs clearly had strong links with the networks in the period under discussion.

Muḥammad Nafīs al-Banjārī, like all Malay-Indonesian scholars, followed the Shāfi'ī school of law and Ash'arī theological doctrines. He was affiliated with several *ṭarīqah*s: Qādiriyyah, Shaṭṭāriyyah, Sammāniyyah, Naqshbandiyyah and Khalwatiyyah.[67] Muḥammad Nafīs was an expert in *kalām* and *taṣawwuf*. His *Durr al-Nafīs*, while stressing the absolute transcendence and Unity of God, refused the notion of the Jabariyyah, who maintained fatalistic determinism as opposed to free will (Qadariyyah). In Muḥammad Nafīs' opinion, Muslims must strive to achieve a better life by doing good deeds and avoiding evil.[68] Thus,

Muḥammad Nafīs was clearly a proponent of activism, one of the basic characteristics of neo-Sufism discussed earlier. With its strong emphasis on Muslim activism, it is no surprise that his book was banned by the Dutch, who feared that it would incite people to launch a *jihād*.[69]

There is no information on when Muḥammad Nafīs al-Banjārī returned to the archipelago. It appears that he proceeded straight to South Kalimantan. Like Muḥammad Arshad, who was the pioneer of the Islamic educational institution, Muḥammad Nafīs devoted himself to the pioneering work of propagating Islam in the interior of the South Kalimantan region. He was indeed a typical wandering *ṣūfī* teacher and played a crucial role in expanding Islam in Kalimantan.[70]

DĀWŪD B. 'ABD ALLĀH AND THE RISE OF PATANI SCHOLARSHIP

To conclude this chapter, we will examine the Patani scholars who by the end of the eighteenth century increasingly came into the picture of Islamic learning in the archipelago. With the rise of Patani scholars, we can observe not only the proliferation of the tradition of Islamic learning but also the further dissemination of renewal and reformism in the Malay-Indonesian world.

The conversion of the Patani region in South Thailand to Islam took place from roughly the twelfth to the fifteenth century. The Patani Sultanate was a populous and prosperous Muslim kingdom in the Malay Peninsula until it fell under Thai control in 1202/1786. Its harbour was also an important centre of trade for Asian and European traders.[71]

There have been numerous studies on Patani Muslim separatism after World War II but little attention has been paid to the growth of Islamic tradition and institutions among the Patani Muslims in the earlier period.[72]

Despite Patani's political weakness as a border state, wandering teachers, mainly *ṣūfī*s, continually frequented the Patani region. The *Hikayat Patani* reports the coming of scholars such as Shaykh Gombak and his student 'Abd al-Mu'min from Minangkabau,[73] and Shaykh Faqīh Ṣafī al-Dīn from Pasai in the second half of the sixteenth century. They played a crucial role in the religious life of the Sultanate. Ṣafī al-Dīn, for instance, urged the construction of a royal mosque and later became adviser to Sulṭān Muẓaffar Shāh on religious matters.[74] Again, in the middle of the seventeenth century, a number of scholars came to Patani: Sayyid 'Abd Allāh from Jerusalem via Trengganu, Ḥāji 'Abd al-Raḥmān from Java, Faqīh 'Abd al-Manān, a Minangkabau from Kedah, and Shaykh 'Abd al-Qādir from Pasai.[75] They are reported to have carried out concerted efforts to spread the *hukum Allah* (*sharī'ah*) into Patani.[76]

An important point conveyed by these accounts is that the Patani Muslims were not isolated among their fellow Muslims in the archipelago. With the coming of scholars to their region, Patani Muslims were made aware of developments in religious ideas and institutions in other parts of the Malay-Indonesian world. It is highly plausible that it was such scholars who stimulated the establishment of the traditional Islamic educational instititution known in Patani as *pondok*.[77] Furthermore, it is suggested that the *pondok* system, which also developed in other parts of the Malay Peninsula, originated from Patani.[78] Al-Palimbānī, as mentioned earlier, is said to have had his early education in Patani, probably in the *pondok*s there, but little is known about them in the period before the nineteenth century. Matheson and Hooker point out that the *pondok*s in Patani were very prestigious and that their more advanced students were welcomed as teachers elsewhere.[79] I would argue, however, that this was true only in the nineteenth century, when native Patani scholars increasingly came onto the scene and contributed significantly to the growth of the *pondok*s.

Shaghir Abdullah, a grandson of Aḥmad Zayn al-'Ābidīn al-Fatānī, a leading Patani scholar,[80] lists Muḥammad Ṭāhir b. 'Alī al-Faṭānī (914–78/1508–78), the author of the famous *Tadhkirāt al-Mawḍū'āt*,[81] as among the earliest and most famous scholars of Patani. This is incorrect, as Muḥammad Ṭāhir also had a *laqab* (nickname) of al-Hindī (from India), to be exact, from Patan in the Gujarat region.[82] If this claim were true, Muḥammad Ṭāhir al-Faṭānī would have been the earliest Malay scholar involved in the scholarly networks of the Ḥaramayn; that is, a century ahead of al-Rānīrī, al-Sinkīlī and al-Maqassārī.

The best-known Patani scholar was Dāwūd b. 'Abd Allāh b. Idrīs al-Faṭānī; but he was neither the earliest nor the only scholar from this region involved in the networks. At least from Dāwūd al-Faṭānī's silsilah of the Sammāniyyah *ṭarīqah* we know that he received the order not directly from Muḥammad al-Sammānī but by way of two other Patani scholars, namely 'Alī b. Isḥāq al-Faṭānī and Muḥammad Ṣāliḥ b. 'Abd al-Raḥmān al-Faṭānī.[83] They probably came to the Ḥaramayn earlier than Dāwūd al-Faṭānī, but Abdullah suggests that the three were contemporaries, with Dāwūd al-Faṭānī the youngest among them.[84]

Thanks to research done by Abdullah, published in his *Syeikh Daud bin Abdullah al-Fatani*, we know more about Dāwūd al-Faṭānī's life and career. According to Abdullah, records kept by families related to Dāwūd al-Faṭānī give the date of birth of this great scholar differently; that is, 1724, 1153/1740 and 1183/1769. He died in Ṭā'if, and one of the records gives his date of death as 1265/1847.[85] There is no way we can be certain which of the dates is the correct one. But because of his studying with the teachers listed below, I think al-Faṭānī was most probably born in 1153/1740; he is reported to have studied with al-Barrāwī (d. 1182/1768), as will be seen shortly. Furthermore, his earliest dated work was completed in Mecca in 1224/1809, when he was 69 years old and had established himself as a learned scholar. The date of his last work is 1259/1843.[86] This means that he lived a relatively long life. The height of his career was certainly in the early decades of the nineteenth century—beyond the period of our discussion. However, as he had direct connections with the eighteenth century scholarly networks, he must be included in this discussion.

According to Abdullah, Dāwūd al-Faṭānī was born in Kresik (also spelled Gresik), an old harbour in Patani, where Mawlānā Malik Ibrāhīm, one of the famous Wali Sanga, reportedly preached Islam before he proceeded to East Java. There he built a centre of Islamic propagation also named Gresik. It said that Dāwūd al-Faṭānī had ancestral relations with Malik Ibrāhīm.[87] Abdullah believes that Dāwūd al-Faṭānī's grandfather was a certain Faqīh 'Alī or Datuk Andi Maharajalela, a prince of the Bone Sultanate, South Sulawesi, who came to Patani in 1047/1637 from the court of Bone as a result of political unrest. Later he married a Patani woman and rose to influence in the Patani Sultanate.[88] Although it is difficult to substantiate these accounts, they at least indicate that, in addition to intellectual connections in the various Muslim ethnic groups in the archipelago, there existed some kind of blood relations among them.

Dāwūd al-Faṭānī acquired his early education in his own region, apparently from his father. But Abdullah suggests that Dāwūd al-Faṭānī also studied in the *pondok*s in Patani.[89] He later travelled to Aceh, where he studied for two years with Muḥammad Zayn b. Faqīh Jalāl al-Dīn al-Ashī.[90] Muḥammad Zayn al-Ashī, as Hasjmi tells us, was a leading scholar of the Acehnese Sultanate during the period of Sulṭān 'Alā' al-Dīn Maḥmūd Shāh (r. 1174–95/1760–81). Al-Ashī appears to have inherited his father's expertise in *fiqh*, for he wrote several works in this field. There is strong evidence that al-Ashī also studied in the Ḥaramayn. Two of al-Ashī's known works, the *Bidāyat al-Hidāyah* and *Kashf al-Kirām*, were prepared in Mecca in 1170/1757 and 1171/1758 respectively, and were apparently completed in Aceh.[91]

In all probability, Dāwūd al-Faṭānī travelled from Aceh directly to the Ḥaramayn, but we have no information on when he reached the Holy Land. In the Ḥaramayn, he immediately joined the circle of *Jāwī* students already there. Among them were Muḥammad Ṣāliḥ b. 'Abd al-Raḥmān al-Faṭānī, 'Alī b. Isḥāq al-Faṭānī, al-Palimbānī, Muḥammad Arshad, 'Abd al-Wahhāb al-Bugisī, 'Abd al-Raḥmān al-Batāwī and Muḥammad Nafīs. Abdullah tells us that Dāwūd al-Faṭānī was the youngest of these scholars.[92] All the older students were also teachers of Dāwūd al-Faṭānī, or at least assisted him in his studies with non-Malay teachers.

Abdullah argues that Dāwūd al-Faṭānī, like al-Palimbānī, Muḥammad Arshad, 'Abd al-Raḥmān al-Batāwī and 'Abd al-Wahhāb al-Bugisī, studied directly with al-Sammānī.[93] He is also reported to have learned from 'Isā b. Aḥmad al-Barrāwī,[94] who died in 1182/1768, seven years earlier than al-Sammānī (d. 1189/1775). In other words, when Dāwūd al-Faṭānī studied with al-Barrāwī, presumably in the last years of his life, al-Sammānī was at the height of his career. Because of his studying with al-Barrāwī and al-Sammānī, Dāwūd al-Faṭānī must have reached the Ḥaramayn in the second half of the 1760s, or when he was in his late 20s.

'Isā b. Aḥmad [b. 'Isā b. Muḥammad al-Zubayrī al-Shāfi'ī al-Qāhirī al-Azharī], better known as al-Barrāwī, was a *muḥaddith* and *faqīh* who had a special expertise in legal *ḥadīth*s and in the comparative study of schools of Islamic law.[95] He lived mainly in Cairo, where he died in 1182/1768. He was also a frequent visitor to the Ḥaramayn, performing pilgrimage and involving himself in scholarly activities. He received *ḥadīth* through *isnād*s which included 'Abd Allāh al-Baṣrī. Al-Barrāwī was also a teacher of Murtaḍā al-Zabīdī and Muḥammad b. 'Alī al-Shanwānī.[96] Al-Shanwānī, as we will see shortly, was also a teacher of Dāwūd al-Faṭānī. Al-Faṭānī mostly studied *uṣūl al-Dīn* (lit. 'roots of religion') with al-Barrāwī. He possessed an *isnād* in this science, which ran from al-Barrāwī to include such major network scholars as 'Abd Allāh al-Baṣrī, 'Alā' al-Dīn al-Bābilī, Shams al-Dīn al-Ramlī and Zakariyyā al-Anṣārī.[97] Considering the fact that al-Faṭānī wrote a number of works on *fiqh*, it is highly probable that he also learned this science mostly from al-Barrāwī.

More than any other Malay scholar who preceded him, al-Faṭānī had many teachers either of Egyptian origin or with a strong Egyptian connection. As there is no evidence that al-Faṭānī ever travelled to Cairo, he must have studied with them during their visits to the Ḥaramayn. In addition to studying with al-Barrāwī, al-Faṭānī continued his studies with al-Sharqāwī,[98] the Shaykh of Azhar and celebrated Khalwatiyyah reformist mentioned earlier as a teacher of Muḥammad Nafīs. As al-Sharqāwī was an expert in *ḥadīth*, *sharī'ah*, *kalām* and *taṣawwuf*, it is probable that al-Faṭānī also learned these sciences from him.

The next teacher Dāwūd al-Faṭānī studied with was the successor of al-Sharqāwī as the Shaykh of al-Azhar. He was Muḥammad b. 'Alī Al-Shanwānī (d. 1233/1818), better known simply as Al-Shanwānī, who was elected President of the Azhar University on al-Sharqāwī's death.[99] During his youth, Al-Shanwānī studied with most of the leading scholars of Egypt, including Aḥmad al-Damanhūrī, al-Barrāwī, al-Sharqāwī and Murtaḍā al-Zabīdī. He was an outstanding scholar of *ḥadīth*, *fiqh*, *tafsīr* and *kalām*. Although he taught mostly in Cairo, he had a number of students in Mecca, who studied with him during his visits there.[100] With Al-Shanwānī, al-Faṭānī advanced his studies in *fiqh* and *kalām*.

In addition to studying with the scholars mentioned above, al-Faṭānī learned from Muḥammad As'ad, Aḥmad al-Marzūqī and Ibrāhīm al-Ra'īs al-Zamzamī al-Makkī.[101] The latter, as we have seen, was also a teacher of al-Palimbānī. Dāwūd al-Faṭānī studied various branches of Islamic discipline with Ibrāhīm al-Ra'īs as well as receiving the Shādhaliyyah *ṭarīqah* from him. It is interesting that Ibrāhīm al-Ra'īs in turn took this *ṭarīqah* from Ṣāliḥ Al-Fullānī, who got it from his teacher, Ibn Sinnah.[102]

'Muḥammad As'ad' was most probably Muḥammad As'ad al-Ḥanafī al-Makkī, a *muḥaddith* who is said to have been very proud of having a *ḥadīth isnād* that went back to 'Abd Allāh al-Baṣrī.[103] Interestingly enough, al-Faṭānī did not take the *isnād* but instead took the Shaṭṭāriyyah *ṭarīqah* from Muḥammad As'ad al-Makkī, who took it from Muḥammad Sa'īd b. Ṭāhir, who took it from his father, Abū Ṭāhir, who in turn took it from his father, Ibrāhīm al-Kūrānī, who took it from Aḥmad al-Qushāshī, who took it from Aḥmad al-Shinnāwī, who took it from Ṣibghat Allāh.[104] This silsilah is different from that of al-Sinkilī, who received the *ṭarīqah* not from al-Kūrānī but from al-Qushāshī.

We do not have much information on 'Aḥmad al-Marzūqī', the last in the list of al-Faṭānī's teachers. This scholar very likely was Aḥmad al-Marzūqī [al-Makkī al-Mālikī], a student of Al-Shanwānī. Aḥmad al-Marzūqī was known as a *muḥaddith* who taught mostly in Mecca.[105] Both Muḥammad As'ad al-Ḥanafī and Aḥmad al-Marzūqī al-Mālikī were al-Faṭānī's teachers of non-Shāfi'ī *madhhab*s. This indicates that the differences among scholars in their adherence to schools of Islamic law, as in the previous century, were not barriers in the networks of *'ulamā'* in the eighteenth century.

Considering all the teachers he studied with and the sciences he got from them, it is clear that Dāwūd al-Faṭānī's education was complete and comprehensive. He possessed more than sufficent knowledge to earn him fame as a major Malay-Indonesian scholar in the period of transition between the eighteenth and nineteenth centuries. Al-Faṭānī seems never to have returned to Patani or elsewhere in the Malay-Indonesian archipelago. Instead he devoted himself to teaching and writing in the Ḥaramayn until he died in Ta'if. His numerous Malay-Indonesian students came from all over the archipelago.[106] He has been claimed as a pivotal figure in the history of Islam in Patani.[107]

There can be no question that al-Faṭānī was one of the most prolific among Malay-Indonesian scholars. He wrote at least 57 works, dealing with almost all branches of the Islamic disciplines.[108] The works themselves, however, some printed in various places in the Middle East and the Malay-Indonesian world, have not been sufficiently studied.

The careers of Malay-Indonesian scholars in the eighteenth century, from al-Palimbānī to al-Faṭānī, have shown us that the networks among Middle Eastern and Malay-Indonesian scholars continued to gain momentum. More importantly, these indicate the incessant transmission of reformism from the centres of learning in the Middle East to various parts of the archipelago. The wide circulation of the writings of these Malay-Indonesian scholars pushed Islamic reformism in this part of the Muslim world even further.

7

Renewal in the Network: The European Challenge

We have seen how 'Abd al-Ṣamad al-Palimbānī, Muḥammad Arshad al-Banjārī, Muḥammad Nafīs al-Banjārī, Dāwūd al-Faṭānī and other scholars in the eighteenth century had definite connections with a number of important scholars in the centres of networks in the Ḥaramayn and in Cairo. Not only were they the crucial channels of transmission of Islamic reformism from the Middle East to the archipelago, they also served as connections for later Malay-Indonesian scholars, who came in ever-increasing numbers to the Ḥaramayn. Their links with *Jāwī* students in the nineteenth century, which involved a number of leading scholars in the Ḥaramayn, created similarly complex webs of scholarly networks.[1]

The connections of al-Palimbānī and his group with earlier scholars were more than simply student–teacher relations; throughout their writings they showed their intellectual lineage to earlier major scholars by giving their works as major sources of their thought. It is no surprise to find that they developed equally reformist teachings.

Al-Palimbānī and his fellow Malay-Indonesian scholars also played an important role in preserving the morale of their fellow Muslims in facing the continuing encroachment of European colonial powers. This period marked a painful transition in the history of Malay-Indonesian Muslims: one after another, the Malay Muslim kingdoms fell into the hands of foreign powers.

These encounters with European powers added a new dimension to the development of Islam in the archipelago. We should not, of course, overemphasise the European factor, but there is little doubt that it contributed to the growing concern among our Malay-Indonesian scholars about the future of Islam in this region. This concern is, in turn, reflected in their writings. We will first attempt to discuss their teachings, particularly in relation to the intellectual currents in the wider networks. Then we will assess their impact on Islamic development in the archipelago. Lastly we will examine their response to the intensification of the European attempts to incorporate the Malay-Indonesian world ino their realm.

SHARĪ'AH AND *TAṢAWWUF*: RECONCILING AL-GHAZĀLĪ WITH IBN 'ARABĪ

In previous chapters we have examined the central theme of al-Rānīrī, al-Sinkīlī and al-Maqassārī, which was the harmony between the legal and mystical aspects of Islam. This harmony also became the central theme in the writings of al-Palimbānī and his group. Throughout their writings, they were eager to reconcile Ibn 'Arabī's philosophical mysticism and al-Ghazālī's *taṣawwuf*. At the same time, the importance of the *sharī'ah* was repeatedly emphasised.

This tendency in the development of Islamic thought is best seen in Palembang. As Drewes has shown,[2] local religious literature in this region at the end of the eighteenth and beginning of the nineteenth century did not include works of Ḥamzah al-Fanṣūrī or Shams al-Dīn al-Samatrānī, nor any writings that had been considered 'unorthodox' or that even contained some 'heterodox' teachings. On the other hand, works of al-Rānīrī and al-Sinkīlī circulated widely. Prominent Palembang scholars such as Shihāb al-Dīn b. 'Abd Allāh Muḥammad preached neo-Sufism as taught by al-Junayd, al-Qushayrī and al-Ghazālī. Shihāb al-Dīn even went so far as to condemn the reading of works on the *martabat tujuh* (seven grades of being). He opposed this doctrine, it appears, simply because he feared that it would lead his fellow Muslims astray. He assumed they would misunderstand it because of their lack of solid grounding in Islamic knowledge, particularly of the *sharī'ah*.[3] As we will see, most Malay-Indonesian scholars in the period, from al-Palimbānī to al-Faṭānī, in fact adopted the very same concept of the seven grades of being.

Of all the Malay-Indonesian scholars in the eighteenth century, it was Muḥammad Arshad al-Banjārī and Dāwūd al-Faṭānī who fostered the entrenchment of the *sharī'ah* in the archipelago. We have seen how Muḥammad Arshad played a crucial role in the establishment in the Banjar Sultanate of the administration of justice in accordance with Islamic law. His role in the spread of Islamic legal doctrines in the archipelago, however, was far greater through his works on *fiqh*, which were widely circulated in the archipelago.[4]

Muḥammad Arshad's principal work was the *Sabīl al-Muhtadīn li al-Tafaqquh fī Amr al-Dīn*. Without doubt it is one of the major works on *fiqh* in Malay after the completion of the *Ṣirāṭ al-Mustaqīm* of al-Rānīrī and the *Mir'āt al-Ṭullāb* of al-Sinkīlī. As Muḥammad Arshad states in his introductory notes, he began to write the *Sabīl al-Muhtadīn* in 1193/1779 at the request of Sulṭān Taḥmīd Allāh. It was completed in 1195/1781. The work is in two volumes, consisting of some 500 pages. It deals with detailed rules of the *'ibādah* (ritual) aspect of *fiqh*. It is basically an elaboration, or to some extent a revision, of al-Rānīrī's *Ṣirāṭ al-Mustaqīm*, which used many Acehnese words hardly understood by Malay-Indonesians in other areas of the archipelago.[5]

The *Sabīl al-Muhtadīn*, printed several times in Mecca, Cairo, Istanbul and various places in the archipelago, was highly popular in the Malay-Indonesian world, and is still used in many parts of the region. Later, descendants of Muḥammad Arshad composed a collection of his teachings on the fundamentals of belief (*'aqā'id*) and *fiqh*, entitled *Perukunan Besar al-Banjārī* or *Perukunan Melayu*. The work enjoyed similar success and was subsequently translated into other languages of the archipelago, such as Javanese and Sundanese.[6] The popularity of Muḥammad Arshad's writings indicates that works explicating Islamic legal precepts were needed by Malay-Indonesian Muslims as practical guides in their daily life. It attests to the fact that Muslims in the archipelago also exhibited a deep interest in the legal aspect of Islam. They were not solely interested in Islamic mysticism, as had been supposed by some scholars.[7]

The main sources of the *Sabīl al-Muhtadīn* are Zakariyyā al-Anṣārī's *Sharḥ Minhāj al-Ṭullāb*, Shams al-Dīn al-Ramlī's *Nihāyat al-Muḥtāj* [*ilā Sharḥ al-Minhāj of al-Nawawī*], Ibn Ḥajar al-Haytamī's *Tuḥfat* [*al-Muḥtāj li Sharḥ al-Minhāj*], and Khaṭīb al-Sharbaynī's *Mughnī al-Muḥtāj*.[8] Both al-Rānīrī and al-Sinkīlī also made extensive use of these sources. Al-Rānīrī's *Ṣirāṭ al-Mustaqīm*, which was printed in the margin of *Sabīl al-Muhtadīn*, was Muḥammad Arshad's starting point; he then made the works of the scholars mentioned above his major references. Muḥammad Arshad thereby strengthened his intellectual connections with some important scholars in the networks. Because of its popularity, the *Sabīl al-Muhtadīn* played an important role in establishing the dominance of the above works as standard references of the Shāfi'ī school of law in the archipelago.

A substantial contribution to the further spread of Islamic legal doctrines was made by Dāwūd al-Faṭānī, the most prolific among the Malay-Indonesian scholars in the eighteenth century. He is the best example of a scholar successful in his attempts to reconcile the legal and mystical aspects of Islam. We discuss Dāwūd al-Faṭānī's main works on *taṣawwuf* later, focusing our attention now on those works dealing with various aspects of the *sharī'ah* or *fiqh*. The most important among them are the *Bughyat al-Ṭullāb li Murīd Ma'rifat al-Aḥkām bi al-Ṣawāb*, which discusses religious observances (*fiqh al-'ibādah*), and *Furū' al-Masā'il wa Uṣūl al-Wasā'il*, which deals with rules and guidelines in daily life. Smaller epistles then follow, such as the *Jam' al-Fawā'id*, on various obligations of a Muslim towards his fellows and others; *Hidāyat al-Muta'allim wa 'Umdat al-Mu'allim*, on *fiqh* in general; *Munyat al-Muṣallī*, on prayer (*ṣalāt*); *Nahj al-Rāghibīn fī Sabīl al-Muttaqīn*, on commercial transactions; *Ghāyat al-Taqrīb*, on inheritance (*farā'iḍ*), *Īḍāḥ al-Bāb li Murīd al-Nikāḥ bi al-Ṣawāb*, on matters relating to marriage and divorce; and a number of other shorter writings on particular sections of *fiqh*.[9]

Coming out of the same intellectual milieu, it is hardly surprising that al-Faṭānī also derived most of his teachings from the important scholars referred to earlier. His major sources for *Bughyat al-Ṭullāb* are, among others, the *Minhāj al-Ṭālibīn* of al-Nawawī, *Fatḥ al-Wahhāb* of Zakariyyā al-Anṣārī, *Tuḥfat al-Muḥtāj* of Ibn Ḥajar al-Haytamī, and *Nihāyat al-Muḥtāj* of Shams al-Dīn al-Ramlī. Al-Faṭānī's *Bughyat al-Ṭullāb* consists of two volumes of 244 and 236 pages, and was printed several times in Mecca, Istanbul, Cairo and various places in the archipelago. Delineating the details of various Muslim religious obligations (*'ibādah*), this work has been acclaimed as the most complete book on this particular aspect of *fiqh*. The *Bughyat al-Ṭullāb* was as popular as the *Sabīl al-Muhtadīn* of Muḥammad Arshad, and it is still used in many parts of the Malay-Indonesian world.[10]

The *Furū' al-Masā'il* is another ample work on *fiqh*; a reprinted Meccan edition (1257/1841), based on an earlier edition published in Cairo (n.d.), consists of two volumes of 275 and 394 pages. The work is an adaptation of both Shams al-Dīn al-Ramlī's *al-Fatāwā* and Ḥusayn b. Muḥammad al-Maḥallī's *Kashf al-Lithām*, and was written in the form of questions and answers. By adopting this style of writing, al-Faṭānī introduced a new method of delineating the intricacies of *fiqh* in what he considered an attractive and effective vehicle for teaching *fiqh* to his Malay-Indonesian audience.

Al-Faṭānī, through his works listed above, played a major role in the history of *fiqh* in the archipelago. Although the works bore Arabic titles, they were in fact written in Malay. This reflects al-Faṭānī's concern that his Malay-Indonesian co-religionists should be able to understand the precepts of the *sharī'ah*. He underlines the importance of the *sharī'ah* or *fiqh* for Muslims by citing a *ḥadīth* of the Prophet, which states that a good *faqīh* can better defend himself against evils than a thousand Muslims who perform religious obligations without sufficient knowledge of *fiqh*.[11] It must be kept in mind, however, that al-Faṭānī was not simply a great *faqīh* or an expert on the *sharī'ah*; he was also a *ṣūfī par excellence*, devoting a number of writings to *taṣawwuf* and *kalām*.

So far as the eighteenth century is concerned, al-Palimbānī was the scholar most responsible for the further spread of neo-Sufism in the archipelago. He was particularly an expert on the Ghazālian *taṣawwuf*. As Al-Bayṭār informs us, al-Palimbānī was renowned among his fellow scholars in the Ḥaramayn for his outstanding expertise on al-Ghazālī's *Iḥyā' 'Ulūm al-Dīn*. He not only taught his students the *taṣawwuf* of al-Ghazālī, appealing to them to study and practise it seriously, but he also wrote several works about it, including the *Faḍā'il al-Iḥyā' li al-Ghazālī*.[12] It is known that al-Rānīrī, al-Sinkīlī and al-Maqassārī referred to al-Ghazālī in their works, but al-Palimbānī more than all of them made the *Iḥyā' 'Ulūm al-Dīn* the basis for his works. Therefore, he can appropriately be considered the most prominent 'translator' of al-Ghazālī among Malay-Indonesian scholars. The immense popularity of the Ghazalian *taṣawwuf* in the archipelago can to a great extent be attributed to al-Palimbānī.

Al-Palimbānī's masterpieces, widely circulated in the archipelago, were two works that have been closely associated with al-Ghazālī's writings, the *Hidāyat al-Sālikīn fī Sulūk Maslak al-Muttaqīn* and *Sayr al-Sālikīn ilā 'Ibādah Rabb al-'Ālamīn*. Both works were written in Malay and were thus intended to be read by the wider Malay-Indonesian audience. The *Hidāyat al-Sālikīn*, completed in Mecca in 1192/1778, was printed at various times in Mecca (1287/1870 and 1303/1885), Bombay (1311/1895), Cairo (1341/1922), Surabaya (1352/1933) and Singapore (n.d.). The *Sayr al-Sālikīn,* consisting of four parts, was written in Mecca and Ṭā'if between 1193/1780 and 1203/1788. Like the *Hidāyat al-Sālikīn*, the *Sayr al-Sālikīn* was printed in Mecca (1306/1888) and Cairo (1309/1893 and 1372/1953), and later also reprinted in Singapore, Malaysia and Indonesia.

The *Hidāyat al-Sālikīn* deals mostly with rules of the *sharī'ah* interpreted in a mystical way. As al-Palimbānī himself points out, it is a translation of al-Ghazālī's *Bidāyat al-Hidāyah.* But this work can more appropriately be termed an adaptation of the *Bidāyat al-Hidāyah*, as, according to al-Palimbānī, 'it renders several topics found in al-Ghazālī's [*Bidāyat al-Hidāyah*] into the *Jāwī* language, while at the same time it introduces a number of appropriate additional [topics which] are not addressed in it'.[13]

Al-Palimbānī, of course, depends heavily on the *Bidāyat al-Hidāyah*, but at the same time he takes material from other works of al-Ghazālī, such as the *Iḥyā' 'Ulūm al-Dīn, Minhāj al-'Ābidīn* and *al-Arba'īn fī Uṣūl al-Dīn.* Of particular importance, he makes numerous references to works by several prominent scholars in the networks, such as the *Yawāqīt al-Jawāhir* of al-Sha'rānī,[14] *al-Durr al-Thamīn* of 'Abd Allāh al-'Aydarūs,[15] *al-Bustān al-'Ārifīn* of al-Qushāshī[16] and *Nafḥat al-Ilāhiyyah* of al-Sammānī.[17]

In many respects al-Palimbānī's *Sayr al-Sālikīn* is a further elaboration of the teachings contained in the *Hidāyat al-Sālikīn.* According to al-Palimbānī, the *Sayr al-Sālikīn* is a rendering of the *Lubāb Iḥyā' 'Ulūm al-Dīn,* an abridged version of the *Iḥyā' 'Ulūm al-Dīn,* written by al-Ghazālī's brother, Aḥmad b. Muḥammad.[18] But the *Sayr al-Sālikīn* is not just a translation of the *Lubāb Iḥyā'*. As in the *Hidāyat al-Sālikīn*, al-Palimbānī in the *Sayr al-Sālikīn* takes additional material from works of such scholars as Ibn 'Arabī, al-Jīlī, Ibn 'Aṭā' Allāh, al-Sha'rānī, al-Burhānpūrī, al-Shinnāwī, al-Qushāshī, al-Kūrānī, al-Nabulūsī, al-Bakrī and al-Sammānī. Al-Palimbānī also makes references to works of his Malay-Indonesian predecessors, such as al-Sinkīlī and even Shams al-Dīn al-Samatrānī,[19] who had been considered by many an unorthodox scholar.

All this again underlines the fact that al-Palimbānī possessed not only teacher–disciple connections but also intellectual links to many important scholars in the networks.

We are not going to dwell on the detailed contents of the *Hidāyat al-Sālikīn* and *Sayr al-Sālikīn*. It suffices to say that both works elucidate the principles of Islamic faith and religious duties to which every aspirant of the mystical way should commit himself. Like many scholars in the networks, al-Palimbānī believes that the grace of God can be attained only through correct faith in the absolute Unity of God and total obedience to the *sharī'ah* precepts. Although he accepts certain notions of Ibn 'Arabī or al-Jīlī, particularly concerning the doctrine of the Universal Man, al-Palimbānī interprets them in light of al-Ghazālī's teachings. He puts emphasis in his *taṣawwuf* more on purification of mind and moral conduct than on the exploration of speculative and philosophical mysticism.[20]

With such an emphasis, al-Palimbānī adopted the central teaching of other scholars in the networks. He maintained that the fulfilment of the doctrines of the *sharī'ah* concerning rituals and good deeds was the surest way to achieve spiritual progress. At a higher level, further progress would be attained through the intensification of the *dhikr*. Al-Palimbānī outlines seven kinds of *dhikr*, each of which is designed to uplift the *nafs* (human soul), which has seven corresponding stages.[21] He then goes on to describe in detail various requirements of the *dhikr* that will enable the person who performs it to achieve the intended aims.[22]

As far as his *dhikr* is concerned, although al-Palimbānī was mostly known as a Sammāniyyah shaykh, he followed the teachings of the Khalwatiyyah *ṭarīqah*. This is not surprising, as he received this order from al-Sammānī.[23] In fact, al-Palimbānī's teaching of seven kinds of *dhikr* and seven stages of the soul was originally developed among the circle of the Khalwatīs, and later incorporated by al-Sammānī in the body of Sammāniyyah teachings.[24]

However, in contrast to the tendency among the Khalwatiyyah shaykhs to encourage a certain degree of individualism and freedom among their disciples, al-Palimbānī subscribes to the older teachings, which emphasise the absolute position of masters vis-à-vis their disciples. Al-Palimbānī, in accord with al-Maqassārī, also a Khalwatiyyah shaykh, requires total obedience of disciples to their master. In order for disciples to succeed, they must pledge their allegiance (*bay'ah*) to their master and obey him totally, for he is an heir or representative of the Prophet.[25] In the final analysis, the disciples must submit themselves to the master like 'a dead body in the hands of its washers'.[26]

From these teachings one may gain the impression that al-Palimbānī encourages some kind of passivity, at least in the realm of mysticism, but it would be unfair to view him only from those teachings. Al-Palimbānī, like al-Maqassārī, who was an exemplary activist against Dutch colonialism, encouraged activism among his fellow Muslims, such as the *jihād* against the Dutch.[27] It appears that it was al-Palimbānī's concern for disciples who might be led astray if they embarked on the mystical path on their own that inspired him to adopt these teachings. Therefore, he insisted that disciples be guided by trusted masters, who would shield them from confusion about the mystical doctrines.

Al-Palimbānī categorises the travellers on the mystical path into three groups: the beginners (*al-mubtadī*), the intermediates (*al-mutawassiṭ*), and the advanced (*al-muntahī*). For each group, al-Palimbānī recommends a number of readings. His list of readings is interesting indeed. For the beginnners he lists no fewer than 56 works: among others, six works of al-Ghazālī, two works of al-Anṣārī, seven works of al-Sha'rānī, three works of 'Abd al-Qādir al-'Aydarūsī, one work each of al-Qushāshī, al-Kūrānī, Tāj al-Dīn al-Hindī and al-Sinkīlī, some 13 works of al-Bakrī and al-Sammānī or their students concerning doctrines and practices of the Khalwatiyyah and al-Sammāniyyah orders, and several works by other scholars.[28] Most of these works were simple elucidations of the fulfilment of the *sharī'ah* in connection with the aim of achieving spiritual progress in the mystical way. With his selection of such works by these scholars, al-Palimbānī clearly intends to show to every aspirant of the mystical way that the *sharī'ah* constitutes the fundamental basis of Islamic mysticism.

At the intermediate level, al-Palimbānī brings the seekers after truth to a deeper exploration of Sufism. He lists no fewer than 26 works, most of which are more philosophical and theological.[29] He includes the *Ḥikam* of Ibn 'Aṭā' Allāh, which must be read along with commentaries by Muḥammad b. Ibrāhīm b. al-'Ibād, al-Qushāshī and Aḥmad b. 'Alān. He then lists the *Ḥikam* of Raslān al-Dimashqī. This work is most probably the same work as the *Risalah fī al-Tawḥīd*, for al-Palimbānī mentions its commentary entitled *Fatḥ al-Raḥmān* by al-Anṣārī.[30] Al-Palimbānī points out that he read the *Ḥikam* and the *Risālah fī al-Tawḥīd* together with the latter's commentaries by al-Nabulūsī and al-Sammānī. Al-Palimbānī also includes theological works such as *al-Yawāqīt al-Jawāhir* of al-Sha'rānī, *Miftāḥ al-Ma'iyyah fī al-Ṭarīqat al-Naqshbandiyyah* of al-Nabulūsī, and several works of al-Bakrī and al-Sammānī.[31]

At the advanced level, the travellers in God's path are exposed to more complicated and, therefore, somewhat more controversial works.[32] At the top of the list are the works of Ibn 'Arabī, including the *Fuṣūṣ al-Ḥikam*, *Futūḥāt al-Makkiyyah* and *Mawāqi' al-Nujūm*. Then follows the *al-Insān al-Kāmil* of al-Jīlī, the *Iḥyā' 'Ulūm al-Dīn* of al-Ghazālī, the *Tuḥfat al-Mursalah* of al-Burhānpūrī together with its commentaries written by al-Kūrānī and al-Nabulūsī, the *Lawāqih al-Anwār al-Qudsiyyah* of al-Sha'rānī, the *Mir'āt al Ḥaqā'iq* of al-Shinnāwī and the *Maslak al-Mukhtār* of al-Kūrānī. Finally he includes works by Malay-Indonesian scholars: the *Jawāhir al-Ḥaqā'iq* and *Tanbīh al-Ṭullāb fī Ma'rifat al-Malik al-Wahhāb* of Shams al-Dīn al-Samatrānī,[33] the *Ta'yīd al-Bayān Ḥāshiyyah*

Īḍāḥ al-Bayān fī Taḥqīq Masā'il al-A'yān [sic] of al-Sinkīlī,[34] and finally al-Palimbānī's own work, *Zād al-Muttaqīn fī Tawḥīd Rabb al-'Ālamīn*.[35] Al-Palimbānī states that *Zād al-Muttaqīn* was written as an exposition of the doctrine of *waḥdat al-wujūd* as he received it from al-Sammānī and his student Ṣiddīq b. 'Umar al-Khān.[36]

Al-Palimbānī, undoubtedly, was fully aware of the possibility that such works might lead to intellectual and religious confusion. Therefore, the above works were reserved for advanced disciples only. Those who did not totally comprehend and practise the *sharī'ah* and its proper relations with the *ḥaqīqah* might be led astray or even to heresy by such works.[37]

With regard to the works he recommends, al-Palimbānī again demonstrates his intellectual linkage to the tendencies in earlier networks. Following the lead of al-Sha'rānī, al-Qushāshī, al-Kūrānī, al-Sinkīlī and al-Maqassārī, who took great care not to sever their intellectual and spiritual links with the philosophical-mystical doctrines of Ibn 'Arabī, al-Palimbānī made his own attempts to reconcile Ibn 'Arabī's teachings with those of al-Ghazālī, emphasising the importance of the purification of mind and of the fulfilment of religious obligations in the mystical way. Al-Palimbānī was opposed to the uncontrollable speculative notion of mysticism; he denounced the doctrines of the so-called *wujūdiyyah mulḥid* (lit. atheistic unity of being) as well as the practice of religious offerings to the ancestors' spirits.[38] These religious beliefs and practices appear to have had some followers in South Sumatra during the times of al-Palimbānī, which inspired him to try to end them.

In the same way as al-Rānīrī, al-Palimbānī divides the doctrines of *wujūdiyyah* into two kinds: the *wujūdiyyah mulḥid* (atheistic unity of being), and the *wujūdiyyah muwaḥḥid* (unitarianism of unity of being). Al-Palimbānī points out that according to the followers of the doctrine of *wujūdiyyah mulḥid*, the first article of belief—that is, *lā ilāh illā Allāh* (there is no god but God)—means that 'there is no such thing as our being, but only God's Being, that is, we are God's Being'.[39] Al-Palimbānī moreover explains:

> They further said *innā al-ḥaq subḥānahu wa ta'ālā laysa bi mawjūd illā fī ḍimn wujūd al-kā'ināt* [sic], that is, the Reality of God does not exist but in the beings of all created things. Thus they insist that the Unity of God exists only in the beings of creation. They, in addition, say that 'we are of the similar nature (*sebangsa*) and similar being (*sewujud*) with God and that the Essence of God is knowable, for He exists in the external world (*khārij*) in time and place'. Such a belief is infidelity (*kufr*).[40]

Al-Palimbānī apparently did not cite al-Rānīrī for his denunciation of the followers of *wujūdiyyah mulḥid*. But both scholars share the same teaching. Al-Rānīrī, for instance, states that:

> Now I would like to explicate and make you all aware of the falsity of the belief of *wujūdiyyah mulḥid* and *zindīq*. They maintain that our beings and that of the universe are God's Being, and [conversely] God's Being is the being of us and the universe. Let it be known if such a belief of *wujūdiyyah* [*mulḥid*] is correct, then every thing is God. And if we kill a man and cut him into pieces, then what [we] kill and cut is God.[41]

Again reminding us of al-Rānīrī, al-Palimbānī includes the followers of *wujūdiyyah mulḥid* among the group of people whom he calls pseudo-*ṣūfī*s (*kaum yang bersufi-sufian dirinya*). Another group of pseudo-*ṣūfī*s, according to al-Palimbānī, were the followers of *ḥulūliyyah* (the doctrine of God's incarnation). He maintains that their error was their belief that God incarnates Himself into the beings of man and other creations.[42]

Muḥammad Arshad al-Banjārī is known to have written only one work on Sufism. But because he studied together with al-Palimbānī in the same social and intellectual milieu, there is little doubt that he shared al-Palimbānī's views on the subject. Muḥammad Arshad opposed the doctrine of *wujūdiyyah mulḥid*. According to local tradition, several years after his return a scholar named Ḥājī 'Abd al-Ḥamīd Abulung came to South Kalimantan. Despite the obscurity surrounding his life, what is clear is that he introduced to the local Muslims the kind of teachings that have been categorised by both al-Palimbānī and al-Rānīrī as *wujūdiyyah mulḥid*. 'Abd al-Ḥamīd reportedly taught people that 'there is no being but God. There is no 'Abd al-Ḥamīd but God; He is I and I am Him'.[43]

As a result, religious confusion spread among the population and 'Abd al-Ḥamīd was summoned to the royal court. But he fiercely held fast to his belief. This led Muḥammad Arshad to issue a *fatwā* declaring 'Abd al-Ḥamīd's teachings heretical and led Sulṭān Taḥmīd Allāh to order his execution.[44] This is reminiscent of the heresy hunting and killing of Wujūdiyyah followers in Aceh during the time of al-Rānīrī.

In al-Palimbānī's opinion, the true *ṣūfī*s were followers of the doctrine of *wujūdiyyah muwaḥḥid*. These *ṣūfī*s affirmed the absolute Unity of God in Himself. They were called the *wujūdiyyah* because 'their belief and intellectual disposition centre on the absolute Unity of God'.[45] Al-Palimbānī does not elaborate his teachings about true *ṣūfī*s. However, it is clear from al-Palimbānī's short statement that true *ṣūfī*s put more stress on the transcendence of God than on His immanence. Although they accept the notion that God is immanent in creation, it is anathema for them to hear any statement saying that God is identical with creation.

Al-Palimbānī shares the view of many scholars in the networks that God and the universe are two different entities: each possesses distinct realities. At this stage, al-Palimbānī and many scholars in the networks accept the view of Ibn 'Arabī that the universe is the exterior expression (*al-a'yān al-khārijiyyah*) of God. As such, the exterior expression of God is not God Himself; it is simply a shadow of God's Being.

In such a view, the doctrine of *wujūdiyyah muwaḥḥid* is basically similar to that of *waḥdat al-wujūd* of Ibn 'Arabī, according to which all created beings come into existence only when God reveals Himself. Men and other creatures, in essence, are separate from the Self of God, and it is only through revelation, as a way opened up by God Himself, that they are able to reunite with God. This reunion requires purification and total conformity to the Divine norm on the part of men. All this finally leads to a stage where men fully realize the Unity of Being. This stage of *waḥdat al-wujūd* is also called by al-Palimbānī the stage of *tawḥīd al-Ṣiddīqīn*—that is, the stage of the *tawḥīd* of the truthful whose spiritual progress makes them occupied solely with God; they come to realise that there is no other being but God. As al-Palimbānī points out:

> At the fourth stage of *tawḥīd*, he [who seeks after truth] sees nothing in the existence of the universe but *Dhāt* (Essence) of the One Supreme God, who is the Necessary Being (*al-wājib al-wujūd*) this is the vision of those *Ṣiddīqīn* (who fully believe), those *'ārifīn* (who are adept); the *ṣūfī* master calls them people who experience *fanā'* (perish) in the *tawḥīd* they then will not realize themselves, for their spirit is occupied with the *shuhūd* (vision) of God, the Real Being.[46]

At this point al-Palimbānī apparently succeeds in his attempt to reconcile the tradition of Ibn 'Arabī with that of al-Ghazālī. The concept of the fourth stage of *tawḥīd* of the Ṣiddīqīn, taken from al-Ghazālī,[47] is equated by al-Palimbānī with Ibn 'Arabī's *waḥdat al-wujūd*. But this does not mean they are identical.

To explicate the revelation of God in accordance with the concept of *waḥdat al-wujūd* or to achieve *fanā'* in the fourth stage of *tawḥīd*, al-Palimbānī adopts the doctrine of the seven stages of revelation or seven grades of being (*martabat tujuh*). This doctrine was originally developed by Ibn 'Arabī but was later reinterpreted in a more orthodox sense by al-Burhānpūrī. According to al-Burhānpūrī, God reveals (*ta'ayyun* or *tajallī*) Himself through seven stages of being. The creation of man is the last stage of God's revelation.[48] While al-Burhānpūrī believes that nobody will be able to grasp the essence of the Real Being,[49] al-Palimbānī maintains that it can be known through *ma'rifah* (gnostic knowledge), centred in the *qalb* (lit. heart = intuition).[50] Emphasising the teachings of al-Ghazālī, al-Palimbānī considers that *ma'rifah* can be attained through spiritual purification and concentration, all of which will result in, as al-Ghazālī puts it, 'the vision of the Essence of God'.[51]

An attempt to reconcile the tradition of al-Ghazālī's *sharī'ah*-oriented *taṣawwuf* with that of Ibn 'Arabī's philosophical Sufism was also made by Muḥammad Nafīs in his *Durr al-Nafīs*. This work, completed in Mecca in 1200/1785, apparently enjoyed wide circulation. Printed several times in various places in the Middle East and the archipelago, it is still used in many places in the Malay-Indonesian world. The *Durr al-Nafīs* was written in the '*Jāwī* language, so that it can be read by those who do not read Arabic.' [52]

A glance at the *Durr al-Nafīs* attests to the fact that Muḥammad Nafīs made a conscious attempt to reconcile the tradition of al-Ghazālī and that of Ibn 'Arabī. In preparing this work, aside from using the oral teachings of his masters in the Ḥaramayn he makes extensive use of the *Futūḥāt al-Makkiyyah* and *Fuṣūṣ al-Ḥikam* of Ibn 'Arabī, the *Ḥikam* of Ibn 'Aṭā' Allāh, the *al-Insān al-Kāmil* of al-Jīlī, the *Iḥyā' 'Ulūm al-Dīn* and *Minhāj al-'Ābidīn* of al-Ghazālī, the *Risālat al-Qushayriyyah* of al-Qushayrī, the *Jawāhir wa al-Durar* of al-Sha'rānī, the *Mukhtaṣar al-Tuḥfat al-Mursalah* of 'Abd Allāh b. Ibrāhīm al-Mirghānī and the *Manḥat al-Muḥammadiyah* of al-Sammānī.[53]

According to Muḥammad Nafīs, the Unity of God (*tawḥīd*) falls into four stages: the *tawḥīd al-Af'āl* (Unity of the Acts of God), *tawḥīd al-Ṣifāt* (Unity of God's Attributes), *tawḥīd al-Asmā'* (Unity of God's Names), and *tawḥīd al-Dhāt* (Unity of God's Essence). At the highest stage, the *tawḥīd al-Dhāt*, seekers after truth will experience *fanā'*, during which they will be able to have a vision (*mushāhadah*) of God. Like al-Palimbānī, Muḥammad Nafīs believes that the Essence of God cannot be known through the five senses and reason: only with *kashf* (direct intuition) will one be able to grasp the Essence of God.[54]

Muḥammad Nafīs stresses the importance of the fulfilment of the *sharī'ah* both outwardly and inwardly in order to attain the stage of *kashf*. It is impossible for anybody to reach that stage without intensifying his spiritual power through performing the religious rituals and obligations laid down by the *sharī'ah*.

A comprehensive study of Dāwūd al-Faṭānī's mystical teachings is not yet available, but it is clear that he was a great proponent of al-Ghazālī's *taṣawwuf* as well as a prominent defender among Malay-Indonesian scholars of Ibn 'Arabī's tradition. Al-Faṭānī is known to have written several works along the same lines as the doctrines of al-Ghazālī, bearing such titles as the *Tarjamah Bidāyat al-Hidāyah* and *Minhāj al-'Ābidīn*.[55] For al-Faṭānī, al-Ghazālī was the greatest *ṣūfī*. As he puts it: 'Imām al-Ghazālī is like a very deep sea, containing precious pearls which cannot be found in other seas'.[56]

In al-Faṭānī's view, the greatest *ṣūfī* next to al-Ghazālī was al-Sha'rānī. He points out in the introductory notes to his Malay translation of al-Sha'rānī's *Kashf al-Ghummah* that al-Sha'rānī was his '*penghulu*' (master), who guided him in the path of God.[57] It is no surprise, therefore, that al-Faṭānī, like al-Sha'rānī, staunchly defends the doctrine of Ibn 'Arabī's *waḥdat al-wujūd* and the seven grades of being in a little-known but important work entitled *Manhal al-Ṣāfī fī Bayān Zumar Ahl al-Ṣūfī*.[58]

Al-Faṭānī was very critical of people who styled themselves as *ṣūfīs* while in fact being simply pseudo-*ṣūfīs* (*berlagak seperti sufi*) and ignorant of the true teachings of Sufism. According to al-Faṭānī, among the groups of pseudo-*ṣūfī*s were people who claimed to have complete union (*ittiḥād*) with God. He bitterly denounces them:

> The people of *ittiḥād* believe that their essence (*dhāt*) becomes the Essence of God. This is a gross infidelity (*kufr*). Those who worship idols are much better than they are, they think that they gain the true vision, [in contrast] they have come to the presence of *iblīs* (devil).[59]

In connection with this view, al-Faṭānī conceives the *Manhal al-Ṣāfī* as an answer and explanation of various concepts and terms in *taṣawwuf*. In addition to discussing such concepts as *waḥdat al-wujūd*, *martabat tujuh* and other mystico-theological matters, al-Faṭānī complements the work with a list of some key terms in *ṣūfī* vocabularies and their meanings. In the introductory notes to the *Manhal al-Ṣāfī*, the author again criticises pseudo-*ṣūfī*s who misunderstood the concept of, for instance, *waḥdat al-wujūd* because they simply embraced its literal meaning. For that reason, he reminds the Muslims that books dealing with such topics should be read only by experts or by those who have solid grounding in the '*ṭarīqah* Muḥammadiyyah'.[60]

The fact that the Malay-Indonesian scholars in the eighteenth century continued to cling to the central doctrine of Ibn 'Arabī is hardly surprising. Despite criticism of the concept of *waḥdat al-wujūd*, it is in fact the fundamental and central doctrine of all kinds of Sufism. Criticism of this doctrine by such scholars as Ibn Taymiyyah, al-Subkī (d. 745/1344) and Ibn Khaldūn (d. 780/1378) is essentially based on the fact that it can be easily misunderstood. It may lead to the belief that there is a continuity, or a total unity, between the creation and God. In other words, it could bring one to a pantheistic belief, which is anathema to legal scholars (*ahl al-shar'ī*).

It is important to note that the doctrine of *waḥdat al-wujūd*, quite surprisingly, was defended by several eminent legal and *ḥadīth* scholars, including Muḥy al-Dīn al-Nawawī (d. 676/1278), Jalāl al-Dīn al-Suyūṭī and Zakariyyā al-Anṣārī. We have shown how al-Anṣārī, for example, possessed *ḥadīth* isnād which can be traced to Ibn 'Arabī. The staunchest defender of Ibn 'Arabī among neo-*ṣūfī*s was, of course, al-Sha'rānī, to whom many scholars in the networks traced their mystical teachings.[61]

It is of particular importance to keep in mind that many scholars in the networks, from al-Qushāshī, al-Kūrānī, 'Uthmān b. Fūdī, al-Sinkīlī, al-Maqassārī, al-Palimbānī and Muḥammad Nafīs to al-Faṭānī, responded in a similar fashion to controversy surrounding Ibn 'Arabī's doctrines. Much like al-Sha'rānī, they insisted that Ibn 'Arabī's doctrines should not be taken at face value: they must be understood in connection with other mystical concepts.

In order to avoid misinterpretation of Ibn 'Arabī's doctrines, these scholars unanimously urged disciples in the mystical path to read Ibn 'Arabī's books only after they had achieved the degree of the '*khāṣṣ*' (elite). Disciples must have firm grounding in all aspects of mystico-philosophical doctrines and understand fully their relations with the legal teachings of Islam before they can understand the teachings of Ibn 'Arabī in their proper contexts. It is equally important to note that these scholars took great care not to associate themselves entirely with Ibn 'Arabī; they cited other authorities, unanimously known as 'orthodox' scholars, such as al-Ghazālī, as their central sources.

JIHĀD AND THE RADICAL COURSE OF REFORMISM

Sufism, particularly among modernist Muslims, has been regarded as one of the main causes of regression of the Muslim world. Religiously it has been accused of being the source of *bid'ah* (unwarranted innovation) and *takhayyul* (delusion) or *khurāfat* (superstitions). Socially, Sufism has been blamed for pulling the Muslim masses into 'passivity' and withdrawal (*'uzlah*) from worldly affairs. It allegedly promoted escapism from the socioeconomic and political ills of their societies. As a result, so the accusation goes, Muslim societies failed to cope with the advanced but hostile Western world, which from the early seventeenth century increasingly penetrated the *Dār al-Islām*.[62]

Most of the accusations are ill-founded. There is no need to repeat the arguments and evidence presented throughout this book: that the central teaching of the reformed Sufism or neo-Sufism was puritanical in its nature. It called for the total obedience, both outwardly and inwardly, of Muslims to orthodoxy, or more precisely to the sharī'ah. The scholars in the networks agreed that it was simply impossible for the *ṣūfī*s to achieve their spiritual goal without committing themselves fully to the orthodox doctrine of Islam. There were, of course, deviant manifestations of Sufism, particularly at the level of the masses, but these were generated mostly by a lack of understanding of the correct teachings of Sufism. Therefore, Sufism as such could not be held responsible for all *bid'ah*s and *khurāfat*s found in Muslim societies.

Similarly, the modernists' accusation that Sufism encouraged passivity and withdrawal from worldly affairs was based mostly on ignorance or misunderstanding of the whole teachings of Sufism. We have shown throughout this discussion that none of the scholars in the networks taught passivity and withdrawal. On the contrary, they appealed to Muslim activism; for them, the fulfilment of Muslims' worldly duties was an integral part of their spiritual progress in the mystical journey.

In the case of Malay-Indonesian scholars in the seventeenth century, we have seen that al-Sinkīlī and al-Maqassārī presented themselves as exemplary *ṣūfī*s, who were absorbed not only with their own spiritual journeys but also with worldly affairs, holding the office of *Muftī* in their respective Sultanates. Al-Maqassārī went so far as to become one of the most important leaders and heroes of the Bantenese war against the Dutch.

This was also true of Malay-Indonesian scholars in the eighteenth century. We have already mentioned Muḥammad Arshad's reformism and activism; he was the pioneer of the establishment of the office of *Muftī* and of Islamic educational institutions in the Sultanate of Banjar. Even though the Sultanate was, from 1021/1612 onwards, continually harassed by the Dutch before they finally subdued it in 1237/1860, it is surprising to find how little Muḥammad Arshad had to say about the struggle against the Dutch; neither his own works nor other sources indicate that he ever preached the doctrine of *jihād* (holy war) against the Dutch.[63]

Appeals for *jihād*, strangely enough, came from al-Palimbānī and al-Faṭānī, who spent most of their lives and died in the Ḥaramayn. This is strong evidence of their very close attachment to and concern for Islam in their homelands. It indicates that they were not the *ṣūfī*s pictured by modernist Muslims merely occupied with their spiritual journeys and alienated from their societies. This also suggests that contacts and communications between the Malay-Indonesian world and the Ḥaramayn were well maintained, so that the *Jāwī* scholars were well informed about the development of Islam in the archipelago, particularly in connection with the continued encroachment by unbelievers.

On more than one occasion al-Palimbānī urged his Malay-Indonesian fellows to wage *jihād* against European colonialists. Voorhoeve and Drewes[64] even argue that *jihād* was one of al-Palimbānī's specialties. This seems to be an exaggeration, which has led to a misunderstanding and distortion of al-Palimbānī's teachings as a whole.

The major work of al-Palimbānī on *jihād* is *Naṣīḥat al-Muslimīn wa Tadhkīrat al-Mu'minīn fī Faḍā'il al-Jihād fī Sabīl Allāh wa Karāmat al-Mujāhidīn fī Sabīl Allāh*.[65] The work is unquestionably the first of this type known widely in the archipelago. However, the *Faḍā'il al-Jihād* was apparently intended to be read not only by a Malay-Indonesian audience, but by a much wider one, for it was written in Arabic. He appears to have deliberately not written it in Malay, so that, he might have assumed, the Dutch would not understand it. The work, consisting of seven chapters delineating the virtues of the holy war according to the Qur'ān and the *ḥadīth*, was a concise but substantial writing on the subject. After explaining that it was obligatory for Muslims to wage holy war against hostile unbelievers, al-Palimbānī concludes the *Faḍā'il al-Jihād* with a short supplication (*du'ā'*), which would make the *mujāhidīn* (those who carry out *jihād*) invulnerable.

Snouck Hurgronje has maintained that al-Palimbānī's *Faḍā'il al-Jihād* was the main source of various works on *jihād* in the long Acehnese wars against the Dutch. It became the model of the Acehnese version of admonition to Muslims to fight the unbelievers.[66] Known collectively as the *Hikayat Prang Sabi*, such works played an important role in sustaining the fighting spirit of the Acehnese throughout the protracted wars fought between 1873 and the early twentieth century. Roff[67] rightly points out that the Acehnese resistance to Dutch aggression from the early stages assumed the character of *jihād* led by the independent *'ulamā'* who were best fitted to organise and prosecute a holy war.

Al-Palimbānī's appeal to Malay-Indonesian Muslims for *jihād* was not confined to writing the *Faḍā'il al-Jihād*. He is said to have written letters, three of which were intercepted by the Dutch. They contained exhortations to Javanese rulers and princes to wage holy wars against the infidels. The letters were written in Arabic and later translated into Javanese and then into Dutch. The writer of the letter called himself Muḥammad, but in the text of the Javanese translation he is referred to as 'Abd al-Raḥmān, a Palembang scholar in Mecca. Drewes[68] has established that the writer was 'Abd al-Ṣamad al-Palimbānī; according to Arabic sources, al-Palimbānī was also called Ibn 'Abd al-Raḥmān.

The first letter, translated into Dutch in Semarang, Central Java, on 22 May 1772, was addressed to the Sulṭān of Mataram, Hamangkubuwana I, previously known as Pangeran Mangkubumi. After a quite lengthy doxology in praise of God, al-Palimbānī writes:

> A sample of God's goodness is that He has moved the heart of the writer [al-Palimbānī] to despatch a letter from Mecca, the Lord has assured that those Sulṭāns shall enter it [paradise] whose magnanimity, virtue and prowess against enemies of other religion [sic] are without equal. Among these is the king of Java, who maintains the religion of Islam and is triumphant over all potentates, and furthermore excels in good works in the war against those of other religion [sic]. The Lord reassures those who act in this way by saying 'Do not think that those who fell in the holy war are dead; certainly not, they are still alive' [Qur'ān 2:154, 3:169]. The Prophet Muhammad says: 'I was ordered to kill anyone but those who know God and me, His Prophet' [sic]. Those who are killed in the holy war are in odour of sanctity beyond praise; so this is a warning to all followers of Muhammad.[69]

The conclusion of the letter then follows, which recommends two *ḥājji*s for religious positions in the Mataram and mentions that the writer has sent with them a small quantity of Zemzem (Zamzam) water (from Mecca) for the Sulṭān.

While the contents and addressee of the second letter were almost identical to the first letter, the third one was sent to Pangeran (Prince) Paku Nagara, or Mangkunagara, together with a banner reading *al-Raḥmān al-Raḥīm, Muḥammad Rasūl Allāh 'Abd Allāh*, meaning 'the Merciful and Compassionate [God], His apostle and servant Muhammad'. After praising God and the Prophet in the opening, the letter runs as follows:

God will forgive the sins of the most pious people like Pangeran Mangkunagara, whom He has created to win such repute in the world, and also because Your Highness is a scion of the House of Mataram, upon whom God has bestowed Abundant mercy beside Muhammad the Prophet, considering that Your Highness' justice is a matter of common knowledge. Furthermore, Your Highness should bear in mind the words of the Qur'ān, to the effect that a small host is capable of gaining the victory over a mighty force.

Will it please Your Highness to also keep in mind that it says in the Qur'ān: 'Do not say that those who fell in the holy war are dead' [Qur'ān 2:154, 3:169]. God has said that the soul of such a one enters into a big pigeon and ascends straight up to the heaven. This is a thing all devout people surely know in their hearts, and more particularly this will be the case with Your Highness, who is comparable to a flower which gives forth its fragrance from sunrise to sunset, nay all Mecca and Medina and the Malay countries are wondering at this fragrance, and pray to God that Your Highness may triumph over all his enemies. Please think of the word of Muhammad, who has said: 'Kill those who are not of the Islamic faith, one and all, unless they go over to your religion'.

Be confident of permanent good fortune and exert yourself in the fear of the Lord; do not fear misfortune and eschew all evil. One doing so will see the sky without cloud and the earth without squalor. Derive comfort from the following words of the Qur'ān: 'Those who have believed and worked the works of righteousness, shall obtain the grace of the Lord [in the paradise]', [Qur'ān 2:25] for the Prophet Muhammad has said: 'If a man can live forever in this world, he will also live forever and enjoy eternal bliss in the hereafter'.

This is to notify Your Highness that I am directed, to deliver to Your Highness the accompanying *jimat* [amulet, in the form of banner], the potency of which is such that when it is used by Your Highness, when campaigning against your enemies, [with God's blessing Your Highness] will always be victorious, which will lead to the protection of the Muslim faith and the extermination of all its malevolent adversaries.

The reason why this banner has been sent to you is that we in Mecca have heard that Your Highness, being a truly princely leader, is much feared in battle. Value it and make use of it, please God, in exterminating your enemies and all unbelievers. Good wishes and greetings are conveyed to Your Highness on behalf of the old Godfearing people of Mecca and Medina: Ibrāhīm, Imam Shāfi'ī, Imām Ḥanafī, Imām Mālikī and Imām Ḥanbalī, and furthermore on behalf of all the other people here, whose unanimous wish is that the blessings of the Prophet and his four great companions Abū Bakr, 'Umar, 'Uthmān and 'Alā, may abide with Your Highness'person.[70]

Ricklefs[71] concludes that these letters were a significant historical landmark in the history of the struggles of Malay-Indonesian Muslims against the Dutch. In his opinion, they are the first evidence to come to light of an attempt from the world of international Islam to foment holy war in Java in the second half of the eighteenth century. On the other hand, Drewes[72] argues that the letters had only modest purposes: recommending two scholars for religious posts in the Mataram Sultanate, and sending a banner to a Javanese prince. Even though Drewes recognises that *jihād* was one of al-Palimbānī's concerns, he suspects that the letters were simply a display of the writer's learning in religious matters, particularly in the holy war, not really exhortations to wage the *jihād*.

Even though I do not subscribe to Ricklefs' view that the letters contained the spirit of pan-Islamism, I accept the notion that the main purpose of the letters was indeed to encourage the adressees to lead the *jihād*. Al-Palimbānī evidently devoted the larger part of the letters to the virtues of *jihād* against the unbelievers to incite the Javanese rulers to take the lead in holy wars. The letters, as Ricklefs believes, reinforced potential indigenous antagonism towards the Dutch.[73]

It is worth noting that al-Palimbānī did not criticise the Javanese ruling house for division and quarrels among themselves, nor did he question their attachment to Islam. For that reason, it is clear that he did not wish to exacerbate their conflicts by criticising any one among them. Instead, he recalled the greatness of the Mataram Sultanate and, therefore, appealed to its rulers to once again revive it by way of *jihād*. Although al-Palimbānī made no explicit mention of the Dutch in the letters, what he calls unbelievers or infidels were undoubtedly the Dutch, who had intensified their attempts to subdue the Mataram Sultanate: it is the Dutch who were to be the target of the *jihād*.

Al-Palimbānī failed in his attempts to instigate Javanese rulers to wage the *jihād*, for the Dutch intercepted the letters before they reached their destination. The original letters were subsequently destroyed by order of the Dutch authorities in Batavia. But it is not impossible that the central message of the letters was conveyed orally to the addressees by scholars recommended by al-Palimbānī. If so, as Ricklefs argues, the oral communication of the contents of the letters did not immediately affect the course of events in Java. The 1770s marked the beginning of major steps towards political stability on the part of the Javanese monarchs. The incendiary message from al-Palimbānī in Mecca did not impede this progress.[74]

Another leading proponent of the *jihād* among Malay-Indonesian scholars in the eighteenth century was Shaykh Dāwūd ibn 'Abd Allāh al-Faṭānī. In his case, his period saw the increasing attempts of the Thais to tighten their grip over the Muslim region of Patani. It is hardly surprising, therefore, that this sorry political situation in his homeland also became a main concern for al-Faṭānī.[75] Abdullah[76] even asserts that al-Faṭānī returned home to lead *jihād* himself against the Thais before he finally returned and settled permanently in the Ḥaramayn. We cannot support this assertion, as there is no evidence to corroborate it. Al-Faṭānī never returned to Patani from the time he left it in search of knowledge: he spent the rest of his life teaching and writing in the Ḥaramayn.

Al-Faṭānī appeals to Muslims, especially those in Patani, through his writings. However, he did not write a special work on the *jihād*, nor did he send letters to the Muslim rulers of Patani. He delineated his ideas on the *jihād* in his various works. It is known, for example, that his work on prayer (*ṣalāt*), entitled *Munyat al-Muṣallī* in Malay, completed in Mecca in 1242/1827, has some political overtones. Matheson and Hooker[77] suggest that the work was written particularly for the Muslims in Patani in order to support them in their struggles against the Thais.

Al-Faṭānī's teachings on *jihād* appear to bear some relation to his idea of the Islamic state. In his opinion, an Islamic state (*dār al-Islām*) should be based on the Qur'ān and the *ḥadīth*; otherwise it would be called a state of unbelievers (*dār al-kufr*).[78] We have no details on his notion of the Islamic state, particularly with regard to its system and administration. However, an Islamic state must function to protect Islam and the Muslims. Therefore, apostasy (*murtadd*) from Islam is not allowed, and those who so deviate should be killed.[79]

In connection with the protection of Islam and the Muslims, according to al-Faṭānī, it is an essential obligation (*farḍ al-'ayn*) for every Muslim to wage *jihād* against hostile unbelievers (*kāfir al-ḥarb*). If an Islamic state is attacked and annexed by unbelievers, the Muslims are obliged to fight them until they regain their freedom. As for the *jihād* to expand the realm of Islam, which involves the subduing of the unbelievers, it is only a *farḍ al-kifāyah*, an obligation which is acquitted in the name of all as long as it is performed by some. In both cases of the obligation of *jihād*, al-Faṭānī stresses the need for Muslims to have fighting strategies; they must not wage *jihād* if they are ill-prepared militarily.[80]

Having seen such teachings of Malay-Indonesian scholars, known as *ṣūfī* scholars, it is no surprise that the Dutch in particular considered these teachings and *ṭarīqah* highly dangerous to their rule. Snouck Hurgronje, the most prominent adviser on Islamic affairs to the Dutch authorities, points out that *ṣūfī* shaykhs were the most dangerous enemies of Dutch rule in the archipelago. He claims that the menace of Malay-Indonesian *ṣūfī* scholars to the Dutch was no less than that of the Sanūsiyyah to the French in Algeria.[81] For the Dutch, *ṣūfī* scholars, whom they also called 'independent teachers', were very difficult to control. It is thus not hard to understand why the Dutch did whatever they possibly could to contain their influence, including the banning of their books and interception of their letters.

One of the best-known examples of Islamic renewal and reformism originating among *ṣūfī* and *ṭarīqah* circles, which resulted in long wars between the Dutch and the native population, was the Padri Movement in Minangkabau or West Sumatra. We have discussed in chapter 4 how al-Sinkīlī's renewalist teachings and *ṭarīqah*, mainly by way of his student Burhān al-Dīn, spread to this region. Burhān al-Dīn in turn, through his famous surau of Ulakan, established himself as the most important Minangkabau scholar towards the end of the seventeenth century, with whom most of the next generation of Minangkabau scholars studied. After his death, the tomb of Burhān al-Dīn became a centre of religious visitation, where pilgrims performed what Hamka[82] calls some strange religious practices but which were in fact the rituals of the *ṭarīqah* people, such as *dhikr* followed by dancing or singing.

Despite such practices, Shaṭṭāriyyah writings, such as those of al-Sinkīlī and the teachings of Burhān al-Dīn himself, again and again emphasised the need for the *taṣawwuf* followers to commit themselves totally to the precepts of the *sharī'ah*.[83] It appears that *ṭarīqah* practices in Ulakan, particularly at the popular level, had become uncontrolled and tended to be excessive and extravagant; this in turn invited criticism among ex-students of the Ulakan *surau*. From this it is evident that the embers of reformism did not die out.

In the late years of the eighteenth century, clearer signs of religious reform came to the forefront in Minangkabau society. For instance, among the Shaṭṭāriyyah *surau*s, mainly located in the Minangkabau inner highland (*darek*), there were conscious attempts to revive al-Sinkīlī's teachings, particularly on the importance of the *sharī'ah* in the practice of *taṣawwuf*.[84] Furthermore, as Jalāl al-Dīn, a contemporary Minangkabau who also took part in this new wave of renewal and reform, tells us, there were constant arrivals in Minangkabau of scholars from Mecca, Medina and Aceh, who contributed to reformism. Jalāl al-Dīn makes no mention of their names, but he does state that scholars from the Ḥaramayn were experts in *manṭiq* (logic) and *ma'ānī* (ideal realities), both sciences being crucial to understanding *sharī'ah* as well as *taṣawwuf*. Meanwhile, an Acehnese scholar came to teach such sciences as *ḥadīth*, *tafsīr* and *farā'iḍ* (inheritance).[85]

The leading scholar in Minangkabau in this period was Tuanku Nan Tuo, the principal teacher of Jalāl al-Dīn. The latter tells us that Tuanku Nan Tuo (1136–1246/1723–1830) of Ampat Angkat was a student of Tuanku Mansiangan Nan Tuo, who was in turn a student of Burhān al-Dīn.[86] Tuanku Nan Tuo was also reported to have studied in the Ulakan *surau* with other students of Burhān al-Dīn. Later he established his own *surau* in Cangking, Ampat Angkat, and gained fame as a scholar of both *sharī'ah* and *taṣawwuf*.[87] For his expertise in these two aspects of Islam, Tuanku Nan Tuo earned the title of 'Sulṭān 'Ālim Awliyā' Allāh', who was the 'leader of all Minangkabau *'ulamā'* of the *Ahl al-Sunnah wa al-Jamā'ah*' ('people of the approved way and community').[88]

The *surau* of Tuanku Nan Tuo accordingly became the best-known centre for the study of *fiqh* and *taṣawwuf* in Minangkabau.[89] Similarly, the students of Tuanku Nan Tuo, when they later returned to their own villages and devoted themselves to teaching in the *surau*s or in society in general, stressed the importance of the *sharī'ah*. Jalāl al-Dīn, the foremost disciple of Tuanku Nan Tuo, for instance, established his surau in Kota Lawas, which was already the home of another, older, Shaṭṭāriyyah *surau*. The aim of Jalāl al-Dīn in establishing his *surau* was to create a genuine Muslim community in Minangkabau by way of total commitment to the implementation of the Islamic way of life as prescribed by the *sharī'ah*. For that purpose, Jalāl al-Dīn taught his students the various aspects of Islamic law.[90]

Tuanku Nan Tuo committed himself to the cause of the reform of Minangkabau society. He made clear to the people the differences between good and evil, as well as between the conduct of Muslims and kāfirs. He impressed on his students the need for the Minangkabaus to follow the path of the *Ahl al-Sunnah wa al-Jamā'ah*, who based their lives on the Qur'ān and the *ḥadīth*. At the same time, he warned them that failure to do so would only lead to social insecurity and disruption.[91]

Tuanku Nan Tuo was not content with simply lecturing his students in his *surau* on the importance of the *sharī'ah*; he himself, together with his students, led the way to the field where un-Islamic practices such as robbery, arrack drinking and slavery held sway.[92] According to Jalāl al-Dīn, Tuanku Nan Tuo visited places where robbery occurred and people were held captive to be sold as slaves, or where the precepts of the *sharī'ah* were violated. He appealed to those who were involved in such things to rid themselves of those wrongdoings; otherwise they would be attacked and punished. As a result, peace returned to the region and trade once again revived in the region; Tuanku Nan Tuo, himself a well-to-do merchant, was renowned as a '*tempat pernaungan*' (protector) of the traders.[93]

The Shaṭṭāriyyah *ṭarīqah* was not the only *ṣūfī* order in Minangkabau. It is known that the Naqshbandiyyah *ṭarīqah* was introduced to the region in the first half of the seventeenth century by Jamāl al-Dīn, a Minangkabau who initially studied in Pasai before he proceeded to Bayt al-Faqīh, Aden, the Ḥaramayn, Egypt and India. On his way home he stopped in Aceh before finally reaching his homeland in West Sumatra, where he was active in teaching and preaching the Naqshbandiyyah *ṭarīqah*. Jamāl al-Dīn's travels remind us of al-Sinkīlī's earlier. Even though Jamāl al-Dīn provides lively accounts of his travels to these places, unlike al-Sinkīlī, he makes no mention of his teachers, so we are not able to trace his scholarly connections. Both Van Ronkel and Johns[94] have suggested that Jamāl al-Dīn was the author of a Naqshbandī *fiqh* text entitled *Lubāb al-Hidāyah*, which was based on the teachings of Aḥmad Ibn 'Alān al-Ṣiddīqī al-Naqshbandī. By the late eighteenth century, the Naqshbandiyyah and the Qādiriyyah *ṭarīqah*s had made substantial inroads on Minangkabau. Both *ṭarīqah*s, like the Shaṭṭāriyyah, contributed significantly to Islamic renewal in the period.[95]

The renewalism of the Shaṭṭāriyyah, Naqshbandiyyah and Qādiriyyah, best represented by Tuanku Nan Tuo and Jalāl al-Dīn, met strong opposition from the *penghulu*s (*adat*, custom chiefs) as well as from the followers of the extravagant type of Sufism. More importantly, some disciples of Tuanku Nan Tuo himself considered his reform simply a piecemeal one. The most prominent among such students was Tuanku Nan Renceh, who envisaged a more thorough and radical reform.

Having failed to persuade Tuanku Nan Tuo to change his evolutionary and peaceful approach to Islamic renewal, Tuanku Nan Renceh found strong supporters in the famous three *ḥājji*s who returned from Mecca in 1218/1803: Haji Miskin, Haji Sumanik, and Haji Piobang. Their pilgrimage coincided with the capture of Mecca by the Wahhābīs. Therefore, they are considered to have been influenced by the Wahhābī teachings, such as opposition to *bid'ah*s, the use of tobacco and silk clothing, which they attempted to spread by force in the Minangkabau region.

Tuanku Nan Renceh, together with the three *ḥājji*s, now known as the Padris, declared *jihād* against those Muslims who declined to follow their teachings. As a result, civil war erupted among the Minangkabau; the suraus, considered the bastion of *bid'ah*s, were attacked and burned to the ground, including those of Tuanku Nan Tuo and Jalāl al-Dīn. The royal family and the *penghulu*s, who also became a major target, soon asked the help of the Dutch. With the intervention of the Dutch, the Minangkabau struggles for reform led to the famous Padri wars, which ended at the close of the 1830s.[96]

It is beyond the scope of this book to discuss the teachings of the Padris and the course of events surrounding the Padri wars. Important for our purpose here is that Islamic renewal and reform in the Minangkabau region, whether initiated by Tuanku Nan Tuo and the *ṭarīqah* cirles or launched by Tuanku Nan Renceh and the Padris, found their origins in the scholarly networks. The differences in their approach to renewal and reform, peaceful or evolutionary on the one hand and radical on the other, reveal that the course of reform was not a simple one.

Muhammad Ibn 'Abd al-Wahhāb (1115–1201/1703–87), the pioneer of the radical wahhābi movement, despite his connection with the networks, was also influenced by other factors that substantially determined his approach to renewal and reform. Similarly, although most of the leading proponents of the Padris in Minangkabau derived their inspiration for renewal and reform from the *ṭarīqah* circles, at a later stage they were influenced by a string of other factors, such as the 'success' of the Wahhābīs in Arabia and the local conditions in Minangkabau that led them to adopt radicalism.

Despite its excesses, the Padri Movement was a major landmark in the history of Islamic renewal and reform in the archipelago. Its impact on the development of Malay-Indonesian Islam was tremendous. The Padri Movement, in restrospect, not only questioned the degree of renewalism among the *ṭarīqah* circles but more importantly challenged the established formulation of relations between the 'great tradition' of Islam in the centres and an Islamic 'little tradition' that mixed with the *adat* (customs) at the local level. The transmission of reformist ideas and teachings through all Malay-Indonesian scholars, as we have shown throughout our discussion, constituted a conscious attempt to bring the great tradition of Islam to supremacy in the archipelago. This also becomes one of the most distinctive features of Islamic development in the Malay-Indonesian world in later periods.

Epilogue

THE LEGACY OF THE SEVENTEENTH AND EIGHTEENTH CENTURY NETWORKS; THE NINETEENTH CENTURY AND BEYOND

This book has been concerned with the transmission of the reformist tradition from the seventeenth and eighteenth century Ḥaramayn to Southeast Asia. The nature and form of transmission is fundamental to our understanding of tradition—the latter defined broadly as a body of knowledge. The data, the traditions in this book, are the Arab biographical dictionaries (*tarājim*) of the period. The primary research on which this book is based was completed a decade ago, and during that time knowledge about many of the outstanding Muslim scholars of the seventeenth and eighteenth centuries has grown considerably. It has not been possible to include references to all the new contributions to the fields since the time I prepared my dissertation. However, in this Epilogue I draw on that research to offer some preliminary notes on the persistence of the reformist tradition into the nineteenth century and beyond to the formation of new traditions originating from the reform movements at the end of the nineteenth century.

Some preliminary comment on transmission is, however, apposite at this stage. 'Transmission' means to hand on through time, and we thus need some basic understanding of time in Islam and in Indonesian Islam.

TIME: THE SEVENTEENTH AND EIGHTEENTH CENTURY

From the linear view, time gives us a past, a present and a future; for Islam the Torah was revealed, as was the Injil, and Islam has completed revelation. Similarly, the networks of transmission are completed transmissions, datable in historical time. This last phrase is clearly referring to linear time, but it also creates two difficulties.

First, from the internal point of view, the Arab biographies are in the present. By this I mean they are a continuing and present authority in the *pesantren* (traditional Muslim boarding schools) and circles of Muslim scholarship in the fifteenth/twenty-first century in Indonesia. They exist now and have meaning and authority now because they are how we know original Islam. Their time is present. This can be seen for instance in the case of Shaykh Muḥammad Yāsin al-Padanī (originally from Padang, West Sumatra, died in Mecca in 1990), who had a number of students that are now *kiyai*s of the *pesantren*s and *'ulamā'* at the same time. His students proudly maintain the chain of authority (*isnād*) from al-Padanī, who was regarded as one of the most important authorities of the *ḥadīth* in the contemporary times. Al-Padanī himself produced a manuscript entitled *Tarājim 'Ulamā' al-Jāwī*, in which he gave an account of the *isnād* he and his students possessed.

Second, the truths of Islam, which is transmitted, are timeless. This is not to propose that they are ahistorical, alhough this was the view of much nineteenth century European historiography. Such a view is to comprehensively misunderstand revelation. Unfortunately, remnants of this position persist in occasional social science accounts of Indonesian Islam, which fail to realise that time is historical but that networks are both in the historical past and in the present.

Transmission through time is achieved by *isnād* and *silsilah* (chains of transmission). Indeed, Islam may be described (up to a point) as a religion and law formulated by chains of transmission. Accuracy of linkage is thus fundamental. Here time must be historically demonstrable. However, linkages are not solely linear, as the Arab biographies show; historical links are equally important. They indicate sometimes a variability in the material being transmitted. There are many examples of these, not only in the *isnād 'ilmiyyah* (chain of transmission of Islamic learning) but also in the *ṭarīqah silsilah* (chain of transmission of esoteric sciences of *taṣawwuf*). Among the *isnād*s—both *isnād 'ilmiyyah* and *isnād taṣawwuf*—there exist what are called as the *isnād 'ālī* (supreme *isnād*s), which indicate that the sources of authority occupied a higher or even highest position, but also that the sciences they had transmitted were of the highest values. This can clearly be seen in some of the *isnād*s of al-Sinkīlī (seventeenth century), al-Palimbānī (eighteenth century), Muḥammad Nawawī al-Bantānī (nineteenth century) and Muḥammad Yāsin al-Padanī (twentieth century).[1]

NEW TIMES, NEW AUTHORITIES: THE NINETEENTH AND TWENTIETH CENTURIES

By 1800, the Malay-Indonesian world or, more correctly, the various parts of what later became Indonesia and Malaysia, no longer drew authority, sovereignty or legitimacy primarily from Islam. While it is true that some areas, such as Aceh, maintained an ethic of Muslim authority (and still do, though in a different form) until the end of the nineteenth century, Islam itself began to be redefined in European (Dutch and English) terms. The colonial period saw the introduction of a new sort of authority, which essentially reduced Islam to a private and personal religion and justified itself in secular terms (treaties, the colonial state). This was the context for nineteenth and twentieth century Islam. That was a real context, as it remains today, but this does not mean that seventeenth and eighteenth century *isnād*s and *silsilah*s became irrelevant; of course they did not, and they persist. What it does mean is that we have to recognise two streams of authority: the traditional *isnād* and *silsilah*, and the new 'reform' *isnād* and *silsilah* of the nineteenth and twentieth centuries.

THE TRADITIONAL *ISNĀD* AND *SILSILAH*

The time is the nineteenth century and the material is the Malay[2] scholarship of this period. That scholarship is extensive, and there is space here only for some illustrative examples, all from the northeast Malayan Peninsula (Kelantan-Patani), a somewhat neglected area.

There are 15 or so major authors, plus a number of others in the mid to late nineteenth century. In terms of time, the context is important. These scholars were writing in the timelessness of revealed Islam, but the context was the time of European triumphalism. The lines of transmission could no longer be taken for granted. The *zaman* Islam, while timeless and true, was also in European *zaman*, which imposed its own time. Intellectual Sufism was not self-contained, as in the past: it had to cope with a new and apparently superior way of thinking—the so-called scientific rationalism, which is even more apparent in the Islamic modernism that began to take roots. This challenge comes through in the writing of the period. The *'ulamā'* had to look over one shoulder at the past and, at the same time, to a new future in a new world.

The Patani *'ulamā'* were no exception. By the early to mid-nineteenth century, the scholarship coming from this area was overwhelmingly concerned with *fiqh* and *uṣūl al-dīn*; *taṣawwuf* is poorly represented in the surviving material. In part, this may be explained as a consequence of what was happening in Mecca where, as Snouck describes,[3] the chief branches of learning had been reduced to these two. However, there is also the local factor to take into account. Patani in the nineteenth century was a mere pawn in the power struggle between Britain and France for political control in Southeast Asia. Siam itself was desperately trying to retain its status as an independent state, and part of its success lay in convincing European powers (in this case Britain) of its actual exercise of sovereignty over its southern, and Malay-populated, possessions. The *'ulamā'* were well aware of this, and their priority became the protection of Malay Muslim identity. In this effort, *taṣawwuf* had little obvious practicality to offer. This is not to say that it was neglected—it was not—but that the prior emphasis was elsewhere.

An excellent example is Shaykh Dāwūd ibn 'Abd Allāh al-Faṭānī discussed above. But we can also give an illustration in the life and work of Shaykh Aḥmad Muḥammad Zain (1856–1906), one of the greatest Patani *'ulamā'* in post-Dāwūd ibn 'Abd Allāh period. His grandfather, two of his three uncles and two cousins were all well-known scholars.[4] In Mecca, Shaykh Aḥmad studied medicine and later became supervisor of the Malay (*Jāwī*) printing press, which published many of Shaykh Dāwūd's works. He was also a noted teacher and his students went on to fill high positions in politics, as *Muftī* in various parts of Malaya, Kalimantan and Cambodia and as teachers and founders of *pondok*. His influence has extended into the twentieth century. One of the most prominent of his students was Che Muḥammad Yūsuf, better known as Tok Kenali (1868–1933), who established the Majlis Ugama Islam in Kelantan and was a leading commentator and teacher of religion in the Malay world. Shaykh Aḥmad's own writing is distinguished, in particular his *al-Fatāwā al-Faṭāniyyah*. This is a complex collection of *fatāwā* and may be compared with those of Ahmad Hassan in the Persis collections one generation later in Indonesia. The pressures of time were clearly beginning to transform *isnād* and *silsilah* from those delivered in person to include also those transmitted from a distance through new print media.

However, this transformation has never been linear, as can be shown in the works of Muḥammad al-Nawawī al-Bantanī (1813–97). Born in Tanara, Banten, West Java, al-Nawawī settled in Mecca permanently in 1855, where he became one of the most important *Jāwī 'ulamā'* in the Ḥaramayn. Prior to his becoming an *'ālim*, he had studied with a number of prominent *'ulamā'* in the Ḥaramayn, among whom were Shaykh Aḥmad al-Nahrawī, Shaykh Sayyid Aḥmad al-Dimyaṭī, Shaykh Sayyid Aḥmad Dahlan, and Shaykh Muḥammad Khaṭīb al-Hanbalī. Many Malay-Indonesian flocked to him, and many of them later became *kiyai*s of many *pesantren*s in Java. They carried with them the *isnād*s and *silsilah*s of religious learning and tradition in the time of translation from Islamic traditionalism to modernism. Among al-Nawawī's prominent students were Kiyai Haji (KH) Hasyim Asy'ari (founder of Tebu Ireng *pesantren* and the Nahdlatul Ulama organisation); KH Khalil of Bangkalan, Madura; and KH Asnawi of Caringin, West Java. He produced 26 works, some of which are still used in many *pesantren*s in Indonesia. His most important work is the *Tafsīr al-Nūr Marah Lābid*, which, according to Riddell,[5] represents an exegetical approach in harmony with the new reformist spirit of the time.

THE NEW *ISNĀD* AND *SILSILAH*

The new *isnād* and *silsilah* could just as well be named the 'reform' *isnād* and *silsilah*, and we conventionally date them from about 1900, with the works of Egyptian reformers (Muḥammad 'Abduh and Rashīd Riḍā) plus the explosion of journals such as *al-Imām* and *al-Manār*. Internally within the Muslim reform groups (*Kaum Muda*, *Sarekat Islam* and others), there began the long debate on how to renew Islam in the face of modern challenges, chief among which was the successful Western imperialism and, even more fundamentally, secularism. In addition, from within Muslim thought arose views that were critical of *ṣūfī* scholars such as al-Bantanī and his fellow in Mecca, Shaykh Aḥmad Khaṭīb al-Minangkabawī, which were widely disseminated in the later nineteenth century. These *'ulamā'* on the surface would seem staunchly anti-Sufism; but careful examination of their works reveals that what they opposed was the excessive and escapist Sufism as practised by certain *ṭarīqah*s. On the other hand they accepted a more puritan Sufism, which was strongly oriented to the socio-moral reconstruction of Muslim society.

The twentieth century was a time of great intellectual turmoil, and this is represented in a number of authors. Hamka (1908–81) is a good example.[6] He grew up in a religious household and was educated in religious schools. By his mid-20s he had published widely on both religious and secular subjects as well as working as a journalist, including as an editor. He was also a novelist, often using religious themes, and a teacher in religious institutions. His own personal *isnād* and *silsilah*, therefore, were formed from a number of different sources which, in typical nineteenth and twentieth century fashion, included new media forms, new educational methods and new intellectual derivations. Taken together, these are perhaps a definition of modernism. His *Pelajaran Agama Islam* (1984) and *Tasawuf Moderen* (1987) are good examples, because in them he attempted to show that orthodox *ṣūfī* belief and practice were consonant with modernity, provided that the individual's response to the latter did not lead to syncretism, especially with reference to local customs. He was himself well aware of the dangers of mixing elements of different philosophical traditions.

The same is true of Harun Nasution[7] (1919–98), although the contradictions in his *isnād* and *silsilah* are much more marked. He was educated in both Western and Islamic traditions and is now remembered primarily for his reforms of the IAIN curricula in the 1960s–70s. His contribution to Islamic education was notable. But this is not the whole sum of his achievement. Nasution was a bold and constructive thinker on the place of revelation in the contemporary state, Indonesia, which was avowedly secular but populated by Muslims whose intellectual *isnād* and *silsilah* went back many centuries. While he did not dismiss that heritage, he was concerned to contextualise it in the new circumstances of the time. This took several forms.

First, he held very strongly to the view that no one of the revealed religions can be held to be prior to any other; time, as such, is not a determinant because any completion of how one knows and experiences God is impossible. All that is possible is the individual effort, the will to approach God, and each of the three monotheisms accepts this premise as fundamental. The logical consequence therefore, for Indonesia, is not an 'Islamic state'. To hold otherwise is to deny that the revealed message is outside time: that is, social, cultural, language and geographic circumstances are the determining factors in how one 'knows'.

Second, and following from this, it is true that these factors cannot either be ignored or diminished at any stage of history. Indonesia is not the Arabic Middle East, though it shares the Prophethood of Muhammad. The temporal factors, therefore, are 'natural' and this itself is God-willed. This allows different temporal expressions of truth but it is the same truth. To insist on a common or general form for truth is (a) not necessary and (b), given the diversity of Muslim cultures and societies, actually quite perverse. Harun is presenting here a form of Mu'tazilī argument, which allows even for ascetism. In his view there is no necessity to force oppositions between reason, revelation and/or Sufism. Reason, for Nasution, is a God-given capacity, but the ways in which it is exercised are various. However, variety is always limited by revelation, which imposes its own intellectual and spiritual constraints. The laws of science are an example: there is no value-free science, although science does tell us about the 'nature of things'. Scientific truths certainly do describe possible behaviour and do not deny choice.

This rationalist trend also makes the values of Islam relatively compatible with political ideologies, and Nasution himself was not unsympathetic to the ideology of Pancasila. He read it as a possible intellectual justification for modernisation and development, which also allowed space for religion. But to hold this position is to come close to a 'rational' Islam, and the danger here is that revelation itself can be made into an ideology or, worse, reduced to one ideology among others. Pancasila, in fact, becomes a manifestation of Islam for the nation-state.

There is a serious implication here: are the new *isnād* and *silsilah* in time, are they conditioned in the modern world by the state and by science? The discussion in the seventeenth and eighteenth centuries was conducted from within Islam. This is not now a possibility, because with the best will in the world it is now hard to avoid the objectification of religion. The new *isnād* and *silsilah* are responsive to secularism to the extent that they may now even be conditioned by it. Time, and hence transmission through time, is now linear, so that timeless truths in Islam are now debatable in a place and in the circumstances of that place at a given time. This is the real challenge for Islam in contemporary Indonesia. The lessons of the historical seventeenth and eighteenth century transmissions are thus still with us.

Notes

INTRODUCTION

1 See, for instance, 'Abd al-Raḥmān Badawī, *La transmission de la philosophie gresque au monde Arabe*, Paris: J. Vrins, 1964; F. Gabrieli, 'The Transmission of Learning and Literary Influences to Western Europe', in P.M. Holt et al. (eds), *The Cambridge History of Islam*, Cambridge: University Press, 1970, II, 851–89. For transmission of learning among Muslims, there are several studies, such as Jonathan Berkey, *The Transmission of Knowledge in Medieval Cairo: A Social History of Islamic Education*, Princeton: Princeton University Press, 1992; G. Vajda, *La transmission du savoir en Islam (VIIe–XVIIIe siecles)*, N. Cottart (ed.), London: Variorum Reprints, 1983; Ivor Wilks, 'The Transmission of Islamic Learning in the Western Sudan', in J. Goody (ed.), *Literacy in Traditional Societies*, Cambridge: Cambridge University Press, 1968. A recent work is Peter Riddell, *Islam and the Malay-Indonesian World: Transmission and Responses*, London & Singapore: C. Hurst & Horizon Books, 2001.

2 See, for instance, M.M. Azami, *On Schacht's Origins of Muhammadan Jurisprudence*, New York & Riyad: John Wiley & King Saud University, 1985; *Studies in Hadith Methodology and Literature*, Indianapolis: American Trust Publication, 1977; G.H.A. Juynboll, *Muslim Tradition: Studies in Chronology, Provenance, and Authorship of Early Hadith*, Cambridge: Cambridge University Press, 1983; J. Schacht, *The Origins of Muhammadan Jurisprudence*, Oxford: Clarendon Press, 1979.

3 See, J.O. Voll, *Islam: Continuity and Change in the Modern World*, Boulder, CO: Westview, 1982, esp. 82; N. Levtzion & J.O. Voll (eds), 'Introduction', in *Eighteenth-Century Renewal and Reform in Islam*, Syracuse: Syracuse University Press, 1987, 3–20.

4 See, for instance, C. Geertz, *The Religion of Java*, New York: Free Press, 1960.

5 J.O. Voll, 'Muḥammad Ḥayyā al-Sindī and Muḥammad ibn 'Abd al-Wahhāb: An Analysis of an Intellectual Group in the Eighteenth Century Madina', *BSOAS*, 38 (1975); 'Ḥadīth Scholars and Ṭarīqahs: An 'Ulamā' Group in the Eighteenth Century Ḥaramayn and Their Impact in the Islamic World', *JAAS*, 15, 3–4 (1980).

6 See, A.H. Johns, 'Friends in Grace: Ibrāhīm al-Kūrānī and 'Abd al-Ra'ūf al-Singkeli', in S. Udin (ed.), *Spectrum: Essays Presented to Sutan Takdir Alisjahbana on His Seventieth Birthday*, Jakarta: Dian Rakyat, 1978; 'Islam in Southeast Asia: Reflections and New Directions', *Indonesia*, 19 (1975).

7 See bibliography for the complete titles.

8 See, for instance, 'Umar 'Abd al-Jabbār, *Siyar wa Tarājim ba'ḍ 'ulamāinā fī al-qarn al-Rābi' 'Ashar*, Jeddah: Tihama, 1403/1982; *Durūs min Mādi al-Ta'līm wa Ḥādirih bi al-Masjid al-Ḥaram*, Cairo: n.p., 1959. For further discussion on Malay-Indonesian *'ulamā'* after the eighteenth century, see Azyumardi Azra, 'Ulama Indonesia di Haramayn: Pasang dan Surutnya sebuah Wacana Intelektual', *Ulumul Qur'an*, III, 3 (1992).

1 NETWORKS OF THE '*ULAMĀ*' IN THE SEVENTEENTH CENTURY ḤARAMAYN

1 Al-Fāsī, *Shifā' al-Gharām bi Akhbar al-Balad al-Ḥaram*, 2 vols, Makkahi Maktabat al-Nahḍat al-Ḥadithah, 1965, I, 329.

2 See al-Nahrawālī, *Kitāb al-I'lām*, in Wustenfeld (ed.), *Die Chroniken der Stadt Mekka*, Brockhaus, 1857, III, 353–4.

3 Al-Fāsī, *al-'Iqd al-Thamīn fī Tārīkh al-Balad al-Amīn*, 8 vols, Cairo, Maṭba'at al-sunnat al-Muhammadiyyah, n.d., VI, 130. For information on the Shujā' *ribāṭ*, see Al-Fāsī, *Shifā' al-Gharām*, I, 333.

4 Al-Fāsī, *al-'Iqd al-Thamīn*, II, 53–8.

5 *Ibid*, II, 293; III, 168–9.

6 *Ibid*, II, 56.

7 See R.H. Djajadiningrat, *Kesultanan Aceh: Suatu Pembahasan tentang Sejarah Kesultanan Aceh berdasarkan Bahan bahan yang terdapat dalam Karya Melayu*, trans. Teuku Hamid, Banda Aceh: Departemen Pendidikan dan Kebudayaan, 1982–3, 60. Cf. D. Crecellius & E.A. Beardow, 'A Reputed Sarakata of the Jamal al-Lail Dynasty', *JMBRAS*, 52, II (1979), 54.

8 For a discussion of *ijāzah*, see Tritton, *Materials on Muslim Education in the Middle Ages*, London, Luzac, 1957, 40–6; Jonathan Berkey, *The Transmission of Knowledge in Medieval Cairo: A Social History of Islamic Education*, Princeton, NJ: Princeton University Press, 1992, esp. 31–3, 176–8.

9 See the case of Ṣāliḥ al-Fullānī and his teacher, Ibn Sinnah, in Azyumardi Azra, *Jaringan Ulama Timur Tengah dan Kepulauan Nusantara Abad XVII dan XVIII*, Bandung, Mizan, 3rd edn, 1995, 152–4.

10 See 'Abd al-Raḥmān Ṣāliḥ 'Abd Allāh, *Tārīkh al-Ta'līm fī Makkah al-Mukarramah*, Jeddah: Dār al-Shurūq, 1403/1982, 41; Gibb & Bowen, *Islamic Society and the West*, 2 vols, Oxford: Oxford University Press, 1957, I:1, esp. 98–100. Cf. C. Snouck Hurgronje, *Mekka in the Latter Part of the 19th Century*, trans. J.H. Monahan, Leyden and London: Brill & Luzac, 1931, 173–86; W. Ochsenwald, *Religion, Society and the State in Arabia: The Hijaz under Ottoman Control*, Columbus: Ohio State University Press, 1984, 50–4.

11 Al-Fāsī, *al-'Iqd al-Thamīn*, III, 139–42.

12 *Ibid*, I, 335–63.

13 A biography of 'Abd al-Rasūl al-Barzanjī will be provided shortly. Cf. Ochsenwald, *Religion and Society*, 52.

14 A biography of Ḥasan al-'Ajamī will be given below. For the further role of scholars of the 'Ajamī family in the religious offices in Mecca, see al-Sibā'ī, *Tārīkh Makkah*, 2 vols, al-Mamlakat al-Arabiyyat al-Su'ūdiyyah, 1404/1984, II, 469–70.

15 'Abd Allāh, *Tārīkh al-Ta'līm*, 41–2; Abdullatif Abdullah Dohaish, *History of Education in the Hijaz up to 1925*, Cairo: Dār al-Fikr al-Arabī, 1398/1978, 189–90. Cf. C. Snouck Hurgonje, *Mekka*, 174–5.

16 Snouck Hurgronje, *Mekka*, 183; Dohaish, *History of Education*, 180.

17 Snouck Hurgronje, *Mekka*, 183.

18 For Ṣibghat Allāh's biography and works, see Muḥammad Amīn al-Muḥibbī (1061–1111/1651–99), *Khulāṣat al-Athar fī A'yān al-Qarn al-Ḥādī 'Ashar*, 4 vols, Cairo, 1248/1867–8, repr. Beirut: Dār Ṣādir, n.d., II, 243–4; 'Abd al-Ḥayy b. Fakhr al-Dīn al-Ḥasanī (d. 1923), *Nuzhat al-Khawāṭir fī Buhjat al-Masāmi' wa al-Nawāẓir*, 7 vols, Hayderabad: Dā'irat al-Ma'ārif al-'Uthmāniyyah, 1931–59, V, 175–7; Ṣiddīq b. Ḥasan al-Qannūjī (d. 1307/1889), *Abjad al-'Ulūm*, 3 vols, Beirut: Dār al-Kutub al-'Ilmiyyah, n.d., III, 225; Ismā'īl Bāshā al-Baghdādī, *Hadiyyat al-'Ārifīn: Asmā' al-Mu'allifīn 'Āthār al-Muṣannifīn*, 2 vols, Istanbul: Milli Egitim Basimevi, 1951, I, 425; Khayr al-Dīn al-Zarkalī (al-Zerekli), *al-A'lām: Qāmūs Tarājim*, 12 vols, Beirut: n.p., 1389/1969, III, 287. Cf. S.A.A. Rizvi, *A History of Sufism in India*, 2 vols, New Delhi: Munshiram Manoharlal, 1983, II, 329–30.

19 Rizvi, *A History of Sufism*, II, 130.

20 For a list of his works, see al-Baghdādī, *Hadiyyat al-'Ārifīn*, I, 425.

21 Al-Muḥibbī, *Khulāṣat al-Athar*, II, 234–4; al-Ḥasanī, *Nuzhat al-Khāwāṭir*, V, 185–6.

22 See T. Iskandar, *De Hikajat Atjeh*, 's-Gravenhage: Smits, 1959, 167–8; Djajadiningrat, *Kesultanan Aceh*, 47.

23 For al-Burhānpūrī's complete biography, see Muṣṭafā Fatḥ Allāh al-Ḥamawī (d. 1123/1711), *Fawā'id al-Irtiḥāl wa Natā'ij al-Safar fī Akhbār Ahl al-Qarn al-Ḥādī 'Ashar*, 3 vols, Cairo, MS. Dār al-Kutub al-Miṣriyyah, Tārīkh 1093, I, fols 166–8; al-Muḥibbī, *Khulāṣat al-Athar*, IV, 110–11; al-Ḥasanī, *Nuzhat al-Khawāṭir*, V, 352–3; al-Baghdādī, *Hadiyyat al-'Ārifīn*, II, 271.

24 See A.H. Johns, *The Gift Addressed to the Spirit of the Prophet*, Canberra: Australian National University, 1965. For its commentaries, see al-Baghdādī, *Hadiyyat al-'Ārifīn*, II, 271; Brockelmann, *GAL*, S. II, 617. In addition to Ibrāhīm al-Kūrānī, 'Abd al-Ghānī al-Nābulusī wrote another commentary on it entitled *Nuhabat al-Mas'alah*.

25 For al-Shinnāwī's biography and works, see al-Muḥibbī, *Khulāṣat al-Athar*, I, 243–6; al-Qannūjī, *Abjad al-'Ulūm*, III, 165; al-Zarkalī, *al-A'lām*, I, 174–5.

26 On Muḥammad al-Shinnāwī's and Aḥmad al-Shinnāwī's relationship with al-Sha'rānī, see M. Winter, *Society and Religion in early Ottoman Egypt: Studies in the Writings of 'Abd al-Wahhāb al-Sha'rānī*, New Brunswick: Transaction Books, 1982, 30, 51, 57, 95, 98, 99, 126, 129, 138–40. Cf. Al-Kattānī, *Fahras*, I, 319, 1052.

27 For a biography of Shams al-Dīn al-Ramlī, who played a significant role in the networks as we will see in due course, see 'Abd al-Wahhāb al-Sha'rānī (899–973/1493–1565), *al-Ṭabaqāt al-Ṣughrā*, 'Abd al-Qādir Aḥmad 'Aṭā (ed.), Cairo: Maktabah al-Qāhirah, 1390/1970, 121–3; al-Muḥibbī, *Khulāṣat al-Athar*, III, 342–7; al-Baghdādī, *Hadiyyat al-'Ārifīn*, II, 261; al-Zarkalī, *al-A'lām*, VI, 235; Brockelmann, *GAL*, II, 418.

28 For further information on Abū al-Ḥasan al-Bakrī's, see al-Sha'rānī, *al-Ṭabaqāt al-Ṣughrā*, 78–80. It is curious that, according to al-Sha'rānī, al-Bakrī died in 950/1543(?). If this is true, Aḥmad al-Shinnāwī had probably not met him. Or perhaps another Muḥammad b. 'Alī Abū al-Ḥasan al-Bakrī al-Maṣrī, died in 1087/1676, who seems to be younger than al-Shinnāwī. In any case, the Bakrī was a noted *muḥaddith* of a *ṣūfī* family in Egypt. See al-Muḥibbī, *Khulāṣat al-Athar*, III, 465–8.

29 For Aḥmad al-Shinnāwī's connections in the networks, see al-Kattānī, *Fahras*, I, 296, 319; II, 734, 865, 957, 958, 1022, 1051.

30 Al-Baghdādī, *Hadiyyat al-'Ārifīn*, I, 154-5; Brockelmann, *GAL*, II, 514; S. II, 534. See also a description of his work, entitled *Bughyat al-Iṭlāq fī al-Salāsil wa al-Khiraq*, in al-Kattānī, *Fahras*, I, 254.

31 Its complete title is *al-Simṭ al-Majīd fī Sha'n al-Bay'ah wa al-Dhikr wa Talqīnih wa Salāsil Ahl al-Tawḥīd*, Hayderabad: Dā'irat al-Ma'ārif al-Niẓāmiyyah, 1327/1909. A short description of the *al-Simṭ* is also given in al-Kattānī, *Fahras*, II, 1061. For further discussion on the *Simṭ*, see Oman Fathurahman, 'Tarekat syattariyyah di Dunia Melayu-Indonesia', doctoral dissertation, Program Pasca-Sarjana, Universitas Indonesia, 2003.

32 For al-Ḥamawī's biography, see Muḥammad Khalīl al-Murādī, *Silk al-Durar fī A'yān al-Qarn al-Thānī 'Ashar*, 4 vols, Beirut: Dār Ibn al-Ḥazm, 1408/1988, IV, 178; 'Abd al-Raḥmān al-Jabartī (1169–1239/1754–1822), *Tārīkh 'Ajā'ib al-Athār fī al-Tarājim wa al-Akhbār*, 3 vols, Beirut: Dār al-Jīl, n.d., I, 125. The last work is available in several editions, in different numbers of volumes. On the importance of the *'Ajā'ib al-Āthār* for the history of Arabia, see Muḥammad Maḥmud al-Sarwajī, 'Kitāb 'Ajā'ib al-Athār fī al-Tarājim wa al-Akhbār li al-Shaykh 'Abd al-Raḥmān al-Jabartī ka-maṣdar li Aḥdāth al-Jazīrat al-'Arabiyyah fī al-Qarn al-Thālith 'Ashar al-Ḥijrī (al-Tŭsi' 'Ashar al-Mīlādī)', in *Maṣādir Tārīkh al-Jazīrat al-'Arabiyyah*, Riyad: Maṭbū'āt Jāmi'ah al-Riyāḍ, 1279/1979, II, 279–301. It should be noted, however, that al-Jabartī also provides accounts of prominent scholars in the seventeenth and eighteenth centuries.

33 MSS Dār al-Kutub al-Miṣriyyah, Cairo, Tarikh, 1093.

34 Al-Ḥamawī, *Fawā'id al-Irtiḥāl*, I, fols 320–33.

35 Ibrāḥīm al-Kūrānī, *al-Umam li Īqāẓ al-Himam*, MS Dār al-Kutub al-Miṣriyyah, Mujāmī' Tal'at 933. For practical reasons, we cite its published edition in Hayderabad, 1328/1910. Aḥmad al-Qushāshī's biographical note is on 125–7.

36 Cf. al-Muḥibbī, *Khulāṣat al-Athar*, I, 343–6.

37 Al-Qushāshī, *al-Simṭ al-Majīd*, 181; al-Ḥamawī, *Fawā'id al-Irtiḥāl*, I, fol. 323; al-Kattānī, *Fahras*, II, 970–1; al-Zarkalī, *al-A'lām*, I, 228. The same account is also found in Shāh Walī Allāh al-Dihlawī (1114–76/1702–62), *Anfās al-'Ārifīn*, Delhi: 1315/1897, 179–80.

38 Al-Qushāshī, *al-Simṭ al-Majīd*, 181–2; al-Ḥamawī, *Fawā'id al-Irtiḥāl*, I, fol. 231; al-Muḥibbī, *Khulāṣat al-Athar*, I, 344.

39 Al-Qushāshī, *al-Simṭ al-Majīd*, 182; al-Ḥamawī, *Fawā'id al-Irtiḥāl*, I, fol. 324. On further reasons of the change of his *madhhab*, see al-Ḥamawī, *Fawā'id al-Irtiḥāl*, I, fols 324–6, 327.

40 Al-Ḥamawī, *Fawā'id al-Irtiḥāl*, I, fol. 321; al-Muḥibbī, *Khulāṣat al-Athar*, I, 344–5. For Ayyūb b. Aḥmad b. Ayyūb al-Khalwatī al-Ḥanafī's biography, see al-Ḥamawī, *Fawā'id al-Irtiḥāl*, II, fols 87–8; al-Muḥibbī, *Khulāṣat al-Athar*, I, 428–33. We provide Ayyūb al-Khalwatī's detailed biography in connection with al-Maqassārī in chapter 5.

41 Al-Baghdādī, *Hadiyyat al-'Ārifīn*, I, 161.

42 Brockelmann, *GAL*, II, 514–15; S. II, 535; Cf. 'Abd al-Salām Hāshim Ḥafiẓ, *al-Madīnat al-Munawwarah fī Tārīkh*, Cairo: Dār al-Turāth, 1381/1972, 149.

43 A.H. Johns, 'al-Kushashī, Ṣafī al-Dīn Aḥmad b. Muḥammad b. Yūnus, al-Madanī al-Dadjānī', *EI*[2], V, 525.

44 Al-Ḥamawī, *Fawā'id al-Irtiḥāl*, I, fol. 321.

45 For Aḥmad al-Qushāshī's connections and role in the networks, see al-Kattānī, *Fahras*, I, 166, 208, 254, 319, 347; 415, 449, 480, 502, 505: II, 552, 558, 583; 587; 620, 734, 811, 914, 927, 957, 958, 1022, 1027, 1053, 1082.
46 For 'Abd Allāh b. Shaykh al-'Aydarūs' biography, see al-Muḥibbī, *Khulāṣat al-Athar*, III, 51; al-Ḥasanī, *Nuzhat al-Khawāṭir*, V, 53–4. On Ba Shaybān, al-Muḥibbī, *Khulāṣat al-Athar*, III, 214–5; al-Ḥasanī, *Nuzhat al-Khawāṭir*, V, 288–9. The role of the 'Aydarūs scholars and their connections with Middle Eastern and Malay-Indonesian scholarly networks are discussed in greater detail in chapter 3.
47 Al-'Ajamī's complete biography is given shortly.
48 He later became a leading shaykh of the Chishtiyyah order in Lahore. See Rizvi, *A History of Sufism*, II, 267.
49 'Abd al-Raḥmān al-Maḥjūb was a good example of the scholars who were successful in harmonising *ḥadīth* and Sufism. He was reported to have numerous miracles (*karāmah*) in the Ḥaramayn. For his biography, see al-Muḥibbī, *Khulāṣat al-Athar*, II, 346–8; al-Qannūjī, *Abjad al-'Ulūm*, III, 166.
50 We examine 'Isā al-Maghribī's biography below.
51 Several leading scholars of these families were also teachers of al-Sinkīlī and al-Maqassārī. We discuss their role in the networks in chapter 4 and 5 respectively.
52 The complete biography of al-Barzanjī is provided below.
53 Al-Murādī, *Silk al-Durar*, I, 6.
54 Abū al-Ṭayyib Muḥammad Shams al-Ḥāq al-'Aẓīmābādī, *'Awn al-Ma'būd: Sharḥ Sunan Abī Dāwūd*, 14 vols, Medina: Maktabat al-Salafiyyah, 1389/1969, IV, 395. Cf. another 4 volume repr. ed. publ. in Delhi 1323/1905, Beirut: Dār al-Kitāb al-'Arabī, n.d., IV, 181. I am most grateful to Prof. J.O. Voll, who brought to my attention an article by Hunwick that mentions these *mujaddid*s. See J.O. Hunwick, 'Ṣāliḥ al-Fullānī (1752/3–1803): The Career and Teachings of a West African 'Ālim in Medina', in A.H. Green (ed.), *In Quest of an Islamic Humanism: Arabic and Islamic Studies in Memory of Mohamed al-Nowaihi*, Cairo: The American University Press, 1984, 139–53.
55 For an account of preference for Zakariyyā al-Anṣārī, see for instance, al-Muḥibbī, *Khulāṣat al-Athar*, III, 346. For a biography of Jalāl al-Dīn al-Suyūṭī, see al-Sha'rānī, *al-Ṭabaqāt al-Ṣughrā*, 17–36; E.M. Sartain, Jalāl al-Dīn al-Suyūṭī, 2 vols, Cambridge: Cambridge University Press, 1975. For Zakariyyā al-Anṣārī's biography, see al-Sha'rānī, *al-Ṭabaqāt al-Ṣughrā*, 37–45; *al-Ṭabaqāt al-Kubrā*, 2 vols, Cairo: Maktabah wa Maṭba'ah Muḥammad 'Alī Ṣabīḥ wa Awlāduh, (1965?), II, 111–3.
56 See al-Muḥibbī, *Khulāṣat al-Athar*, III, 242.
57 Al-Kattānī, *Fahras*, I, 494.
58 Al-Zarkalī, *al-A'lām*, I, 28.

59 Al-Ḥamawī devotes a long account to Ibrāhīm al-Kūrānī's biography. See his *Fawā'id al-Irtiḥāl*, I, fols 21–32. Al-Kūrānī's biography is also given in the colophon of his own work, *al-Umam*, 131–3; al-Murādī, *Silk al-Durar*, I, 5–6; al-Jabartī, *'Ajā'ib al-Āthār*, I, 117; al-Shawkānī, *al-Badr al-Ṭāli'*, 2 vols, Cairo: Maṭba'at al-Sa'ādah, 1348/1929, I, 11; al-Qannūjī, *Abjad al-'Ulūm*, III, 167; Ḥāfiẓ, *al-Madīnat al-Munawwarah fī al-Tārīkh*, 150; A.H. Johns, 'Al-Kūrānī, Ibrāhīm b. al-Shahrazūrī al-Ḥasan Shahrānī, al-Madanī (1023–1101/1615–90)', *EI*[2], V, 432–3; al-Kattānī, *Fahras*, I, 166–8, 493–4; al-Zarkalī, *al-A'lām*, I, 28.

60 Al-Mulā Muḥammad Sharīf al-Kūrānī appears to have been a teacher of numerous scholars in the Ḥaramayn, including Ibrāhīm al-Kūrānī. See his biography in al-Kūrānī, *al-Umam*, 128–9; al-Ḥamawī, *Fawā'id al-Irtiḥāl*, I, fols 93–3; al-Muḥibbī, *Khulāṣat al-Athar*, IV, 280–1. For a list of his works which includes a commentary on the Baiḍāwī *Tafsīr* (*Anwār al-Tanzīl*), see al-Baghdādī, *Hadiyyat al-'Ārifīn*, II, 291.

61 Al-Ḥamawī, *Fawā'id al-Irtiḥāl*, II, fol. 22; cf. Al-Murādī, *Silk al-Durar*, I, 5.

62 Al-Bābilī's biography is given shortly.

63 Mainly known as an *adīb* (man of letters) and a *qāḍī*, al-Khafājī was an important chain in the networks. He lived mainly in Cairo, though he regularly travelled to the Ḥaramayn and other centres for Islamic learning in the Middle East. He was a disciple of the *muḥaddith* Shams al-Dīn al-Ramlī, who in turn connected him, among others, to Zakariyyā al-Anṣārī. See al-Muḥibbī, *Khulāṣat al-Athar*, I, 331–43. For a list of his works, see al-Baghdādī, *Hadiyyat al-'Ārifīn*, I, 160–1.

64 Al-Mazzāḥī was professor of *fiqh* at the Azhar after studying with almost 30 scholars. He was also learned in *ḥadīth*. He wrote a commentary on the *Minhāj of Zakariyyā al-Anṣārī*. Among his prominent students were 'Alā' al-Dīn al-Bābilī and Nūr al-Dīn al-Shabrāmalisī. See al-Muḥibbī, *Khulāṣat al-Athar*, II, 210–1; al-Baghdādī, *Hadiyyat al-'Ārifīn*, I, 394.

65 Al-Kūrānī, *al-Umam*, 3–13; al-Ḥamawī, *Fawā'id al-Irtiḥāl*, I, fol. 23.

66 Al-Kūrānī, *Masālik al-Abrār ilā Ḥadīth al-Nabī al-Mukhtār*, MS. Dār al-Kutub al-Miṣriyyah, Ḥadīth 2283, Microfilm 14904.

67 Al-Ḥamawī, *Fawā'id al-Irtiḥāl*, I, fol. 25.

68 *Ibid*, I, fols 24–5; al-Qannūjī, *Abjad al-'Ulūm*, III, 167.

69 Al-Kattānī, *Fahras*, I, 494. For Ibrāhīm al-Kūrānī's connections in the networks, see *Ibid*, I, 92, 96, 115, 116, 118, 148, 166, 167, 168, 169, 170, 171, 183, 194, 203, 208, 218, 225, 226, 242, 252, 255, 301, 312, 316, 319, 326, 343, 415, 423, 427, 447, 451, 480, 493–4, 495, 496, 502, 505, 508, 512, 534; II, 555, 557, 559, 586, 588, 595, 634, 671, 679, 683, 714, 727, 734, 735, 738, 760, 767, 770, 771, 808, 878, 914, 941, 942, 948, 951–4, 957–8, 971, 1005, 1027, 1061–2, 1075–6, 1094, 1103, 1115–16, 1157–8.

70 The complete account of Al-Nakhlī is given below.

71 Nūr al-Dīn Muḥammad b. 'Abd al-Ḥādī al-Sindī, better known as Abū al-Ḥasan al-Sindī al-Kabīr, was a *muḥaddith*. He was also a student of al-Bābilī and al-Barzanjī. One of his well-known students was Muḥammad Ḥayyāt al-Sindī, an important figure of in the scholarly networks in the eighteenth century. For his life and works, see al-Murādī, *Silk al-Durar*, III, 66; al-Jabartī, *'Ajā'ib al-Āthār*, I, 135; al-Baghdādī, *Hadiyyat al-'Ārifīn*, II, 318. One of his works was a commentary on the *Kutub al-Sittah*. See al-Kattānī, *Fahras*, I, 148. Abū al-Ḥasan al-Sindī (al-Kabīr) should not be confused with Abū al-Ḥasan al-Sindī al-Ṣaghīr (or Muḥammad Ṣadīq al-Sindī, 1125–87/1713–73), a disciple of Muḥammad Ḥayyāt al-Sindī and a teacher of Ṣāliḥ al-Fullānī. See al-Kattānī, *Fahras*, I, 148–9.

72 'Abd Allāh b. Sa'd Allāh al-Lāhūrī, a *muḥaddith*, was known to be very active in introducing to Ḥaramayn *'ulamā'* the teachings of such Indian scholars as Mulā 'Abd al-Ḥakīm al-Siyalkūtī and 'Abd al-Ḥāq al-Muḥaddith Dihlawī. Among his students in the Ḥaramayn were Abū Ṭāhir b. Ibrāhīm al-Kūrānī and Shāh Walī Allāh. See Walī Allāh, *Anfās al-'Ārifīn*, 190–2. For al-Lāhūrī's connections in the networks, see al-Kattānī, *Fahras*, I, 166, 168, 495, 496; II, 948, 949, 951, 953, 957, 958, 960.

73 'Abd Allāh b. Sālim al-Baṣrī's complete biography is given shortly.

74 Abū Ṭāhir's biography is provided below.

75 The *muḥaddith* 'Alī al-Zabīdī appears to be one of the earliest Zabīd scholars involved in the networks in this period. The Zabīdī scholars increasingly played an important role in the subsequent periods. His teachers also included al-Qushāshī, al-Barzanjī and al-Nakhlī. See al-Muḥibbī, *Khulāṣat al-Athar*, III, 192–3.

76 Isḥāq b. Ja'mān al-Yamanī, a leading scholar of the Ja'mān family, was the *Qāḍī* of Zabīd. In the Ḥaramayn he also studied with 'Isā al-Maghribī and al-Barzanjī. See al-Muḥibbī, *Khulāṣat al-Athar*, I, 394–6; al-Baghdādī, *Hadiyyat al-'Ārifīn*, I, 202. Among his students in the networks was al-Sinkīlī, discussed in chapter 4

77 Al-Ḥamawī, *Fawā'id al-Irtiḥāl*, I, fol. *Silk al-Durar*, I, 6.

78 Al-Baghdādī, *Hadiyyat al-'Ārifīn*, I, 35–6.

79 Brockelmann, *GAL*, II, 505–6; S. II, 520.

80 They are: *al-Umam*, cited earlier, and Alfred Guillaume, 'Al-Lum'at al-Sanīya fī Taḥqīq al-Ilqā' fī-l-Umnīya by Ibrāhīm al-Kūrānī', *BSOAS*, XX (1957), 291–303.

81 For al-Bābilī's detailed biography, see al-Ḥamawī, *Fawā'id al-Irtiḥāl*, I, fols 201–4; al-Muḥibbī, *Khulāṣat al-Athar*, IV, 39–42; al-Qannūjī, *Abjad al-'Ulūm*, III, 166. For his works: al-Baghdādī, *Hadiyyat al-'Ārifīn*, II, 290; al-Kattānī, *Fahras*, I, 210–12; al-Zarkalī, *al-A'lām*, VII, 152.

82 Al-Kattānī, *Fahras*, I, 210.
83 For al-Bābilī's connections in the networks, see al-Kattānī, *Ibid*, I, 194; 213, 217, 219, 233, 252, 255, 327, 328, 339, 345, 405, 411, 425, 452, 457, 480, 502, 505, 521, 533, 536, 538; II, 558, 562, 583, 587, 589, 590, 592, 605, 620, 739, 784, 807, 851, 890, 916, 918, 935, 941, 942, 964, 987, 1094, 1127, 1132, 1134, 1151.
84 Al-Muḥibbī, *Khulāṣat al-Athar*, 41; al-Zarkalī, *al A'lām*, I, 152.
85 For Tāj al-Dīn al-Hindī's life and works, see al-Muḥibbī, *Khulāṣat al-Athar*, I, 464–70; al-Bagdādī, *Hadiyyat al-'Ārifīn*, I, 244. Cf. Rizvi, *A History of Sufism*, II, 336–8; Trimingham, *The Sufi Orders*, 93–4.
86 For more information on Aḥmad b. 'Alān, see chapter 3 note 39. For an account of the prominence of the 'Alān family in Mecca, see al-Sibā'ī, *Tārīkh Makkah*, II, 468.
87 On al-Nakhlī's becoming a disciple of Tāj al-Dīn al-Hindī, see Walī Allāh, *Anfās al-'Arifīn*, 188. Cf. al-Nakhlī, *Bughyat al-Ṭālibīn li Bayān al-Mashā'ikh al-Muḥaqqiqīn al-Mu'tamidīn*, Hayderabad: Dā'irat al-Ma'ārif al-Niẓāmiyyah, 1328/1910, 73–6, 80.
88 For detailed accounts of 'Isā al-Maghribī's career and works, see al-Muḥibbī, *Khulāṣat al-Athar*, III, 240–2; al-Qannūjī, *Abjad al-'Ulūm*, III, 166–7; al-Zarkalī, *al-A'lām*, V, 294–5; al-Kattānī, *Fahras*, I, 500–3; II, 589–90, 806–9; Brockelmann, *GAL*, S. II, 691, 939.
89 Tāj al-Dīn ibn Ya'qūb's career follows shortly.
90 Zayn al-'Ābidīn's biography is given below.
91 'Abd al-'Azīz al-Zamzamī was a leading scholar of the Zamzamī family, the guardian of the Zamzam well. He was a grandson of the *muḥaddith* Ibn Ḥajar in the maternal line. As a renowned scholar, he wrote a number of works. See al-Muḥibbī, *Khulāṣat al-Athar*, II, 426–7; Brockelmann, *GAL*, II, 379. On the role of the Zamzamīs in Islamic learning in Mecca, see al-Sibā'ī, *Tārīkh Makkah*, II, 470. Cf. Al-Baghdādī, *Hadiyyat 'Ārifīn*, I, 584, 737.
92 'Alī b. Abī Bakr al-Jamāl al-Makkī, also known as al-Jamāl al-Maṣrī, was born in Mecca. After studying with various teachers he taught at the Ḥarām Mosque. Among his students were Ḥasan al-'Ajamī, Aḥmad al-Nakhlī and 'Abd Allāh b. Sālim al-Baṣrī. He wrote numerous works dealing with various topics. See al-Muḥibbī, *Khulāṣat al-Athar*, III, 128–30; al-Baghdādī, *Hadiyyat al-'Ārifīn*, I, 759–80. For his connections in the network, see al-Kattānī, *Fahras*, I, 194, 252, 502; II, 583, 811.
93 Al-Muḥibbī, *Khulāṣat al-Athar*, III, 242; al-Qannūjī, *Abjad al-'Ulūm*, III, 166.
94 Al-Kattānī, *Fahras*, II, 806–7.
95 For a quite lengthy description of the contents of the *Kanz al-Riwāyat*, see al-Kattānī, *Fahras*, I, 500–3.

96 For Sulaymān al-Maghribī's complete biography, see al-Muḥibbī, *Khulāṣat al-Athar*, IV, 204–8; Daḥlān, *Khulāṣat al-Kalām*, 87–104; al-Sibā'ī, *Tārīkh Makkah*, II, 378–83; al-Kattānī, *Fahras*, I, 95, 425–9; al-Zarkalī, *al-A'lām*, VII, 22.

97 Al-Muḥibbī, *Khulāṣat al-Athar*, IV, 204–5; Daḥlān, *Khulāṣat al-Kalām*, 103–4; al-Sibā'ī, *Tārīkh Makkah*, II, 380.

98 For a description of the contents of these works, see al-Kattānī, *Fahras*, I, 95, 426–7.

99 See al-Muḥibbī, *Khulāṣat al-Athar*, IV, 207. Cf. Al-Murādī, *Silk al-Durar*, IV, 82.

100 For detailed accounts of Sulaymān al-Maghribī's connections in the networks, see al-Kattānī, *Fahras*, I, 90, 95, 97, 98, 101, 116, 131, 156, 160, 194, 209, 211, 237, 252, 298, 301, 302, 309, 326, 339, 343, 351, 378, 386, 401, 425–9, 474, 475, 496, 505, 518, II, 567, 576, 582, 583, 595, 711, 716, 736, 784, 805, 808, 811, 838, 903, 941, 942, 973, 988, 1028, 1093, 1134.

101 For Ibn Ya'qūb's detailed biography and works, see al-Muḥibbī, *Khulāṣat al-Athar*, I, 457–64; al-Baghdādī, *Hadiyyat al-'Ārifīn*, I, 245; Brockelmann, *GAL*, II, 379. For his further connections in the networks, see al-Kattānī, *Fahras*, I, 198, 501; II, 576, 587, 865.

102 Zayn al-'Ābidīn al-Ṭabarī's complete biography is given in al-Muḥibbī, *Khulāṣat al-Athar*, II, 195–6. For his connections in the networks, see al-Kattānī, *Fahras*, I, 119, 166, 169, 183, 194, 196, 209, 252, 296, 327, 415, 502; II, 583, 587, 685, 811, 992, 1022.

103 For 'Abd al-Qādir al-Ṭabarī's biography and works, see al-Muḥibbī, *Khulāṣat al-Athar*, II, 457–64; al-Baghdādī, *Hadiyyat al-'Ārifīn*, I, 600; al-Zarkalī, *al-A'lām*, IV, 168–9; Brockelmann, *GAL*, S. II, 509. For his further scholarly connections, see al-Kattānī, *Fahras*, I, 209, 518; II, 685, 781, 935.

104 For biography and works of 'Alī al-Ṭabarī, see al-Muḥibbī, *Khulāṣat al-Athar*, III, 161–6; al-Baghdādī, *Hadiyyat al-'Ārifīn*, I, 759; al-Zarkalī, *al-A'lām*, V, 115. For his scholarly connections, see al-Kattānī, *Fahras*, I, 194, 415; II, 587, 811, 941–4, 1000.

105 For further accounts of the role of the Ṭabarī family in Islamic learning in Mecca, see al-Sibā'ī, *Tārīkh Makkah*, II, 466.

106 For a biography of al-Muḥibb al-Ṭabarī, see al-Zarkalī, *al-A'lām*, VII, 189.

107 For more detail on al-'Ajamī, see al-Jabartī, *'Ajā'ib al-Āthār*, I, 123; al-Qannūjī, *Abjad al-'Ulūm*, III, 167–8. His more complete biography is provided by the editor of his work, *Ihdā' al-Laṭā'if min Akhbār al-Ṭā'if*, Yaḥya Maḥmūd Junayd Sā'ātī (ed.), Tā'if: Dār Thaqīf, 1400/1980, 9–24; al-Kattānī, *Fahras*, II, 810–3. For lists of his works, see al-Baghdādī, *Hadiyyat al-'Ārifīn*, I, 294; and *Ihdā' al-Laṭā'if*, 17–23; al-Zarkalī, *al-A'lām*, II, 223; al-Kattānī, *Fahras*, I, 209, 4479, 504–5; II, 810–13.

108 Al-Kattānī, *Fahras*, II, 810–11; al-Zarkalī, *al-A'lām*, II, 223.
109 For al-'Ajamī's further connections in *ḥadīth* studies, see al-Kattānī, *Fahras*, I, 209; II, 811–13; III, 66.
110 A short description of the contents of the *Risālat al-'Ajamī fī al-Ṭuruq* is given in al-Kattānī, *Fahras*, II, 447–9. This work is not listed either in al-Baghdādī, *Hadiyyat al-'Ārifīn*, I, 284, or in al-Zarkalī, *al-A'lām*, II, 223.
111 For a biography of Tāj al-Dīn, who was also known as Muḥammad b. 'Abd al-Muḥsin al-Qal'ī, see al-Kattānī, I, 978; al-Qannūjī, *Abjad al-'Ulūm*, III, 168–9.
112 For an account of the scholarly role of 'Ajamī family in Mecca, see al-Sibā'ī, *Tārīkh Makkah*, I I, 469–70; al-Kattānī, *Fahras*, 813.
113 For al-Barzanjī's biography and work, see the colophon of his own work, *Kitāb al-Ishā'ah li Ishārat al-Sā'ah*, Muḥammad Badr al-Dīn al-Na'sānī (ed.), Cairo: Maṭba'at al-Sa'ādah, 1325/1907; al-Murādī, *Silk al-Durar*, IV, 65–6; al-Baghdādī, *Hadiyyat al-'Ārifīn*, II, 303–4; al-Zarkalī, *al-A'lām*, VII, 75.
114 Al-Barzanjī's connections in the networks is provided in al-Kattānī, *Fahras*, I, 98, 148, 301, 302, 314, 427, 447, 451, 495; II, 767, 828, 840, 1095.
115 Further information on Ja'far al-Barzanjī is given in al-Murādī, *Silk al-Durar*, II, 9; al-Baghdādī, *Hadiyyat al-'Ārifīn*, I, 255; al-Zarkalī, *al-A'lām*, II, 117. For a history of the Barzanjī family, see C.J. Edmonds, *Kurds, Turks, and Arabs*, London: Oxford University Press, 1957, esp. 68–79.
116 For al-Nakhlī's complete biography, see his *Bughyat al-Ṭālibīn li Bayān al-Mashā'ikh al-Muḥaqqiqīn al-Mu'tamidīn*, Hayderabad: Dā'irat al-Ma'ārif al-Niẓāmiyyah, 1328/1910; al-Murādī, *Silk al-Durar*, I, 171–2; al-Qannūjī, *Abjad al-'Ulūm*, III, 177; al-Kattānī, *Fahras*, I, 251–3; al-Zarkalī, *al-A'lām*, I, 230. Among his works was *al-Tafsīrāt al-Aḥmadiyyah fī Bayān al-Āyāt al-Shar'iyyah*. See al-Baghdādī, *Hadiyyat al-'Ārifīn*, I, 167.
117 Al-Nakhlī, *Bughyat al-Ṭālibīn*, 5–9, 65–80.
118 Al-Kattānī, *Fahras*, I, 252.
119 For al-Nakhlī's connections in *ḥadīth* studies, see *Ibid*, I, 98, 101, 118, 168, 199, 211, 213, 224, 234, 251–3, 256, 302, 339, 411, 447, 487, 495, 497, 502, 511, 518, 533; II, 559, 589, 590, 607, 608, 609, 702, 734, 751, 792, 805, 809, 829, 865, 919, 942, 976, 985, 1007, 1076, 1133, 1135, 1147, 1156.
120 For 'Abd Allāh b. Sālim al-Baṣrī's biography and works, see his *Kitāb al-Imdād bi Ma'rifah 'Uluw al-Isnād*, Hayderabad: Dā'irat al-Ma'ārif al-Niẓāmiyyah, 1328/1910; al-Jabartī, *'Ajā'ib al-Āthār*, I, 132–3; al-Baghdādī, *Hadiyyat al-'Ārifīn*, I, 480; al-Qannūjī, *Abjad al-'Ulūm*,

III, 177; al-Zarkalī, *al-A'lām*, IV, 219–20; Brockelmann, *GAL*, S. II, 521; al-Kattānī, *Fahras*, I, 95–6, 193–9.

121 Al-Sibā'ī, *Tārīkh Makkah*, II, 469.

122 *Ibid.*

123 For al-Baṣrī's connections with his contemporaries and earlier scholars, see his *Kitāb al-Imdād*. For his connections with later scholars, see al-Kattānī, *Fahras*, I, esp. 95–6, 193–9; III, 113.

124 For Abū Ṭāhir's biography and works, see Al-Murādī, *Silk al-Durar*, IV, 27; al-Baghdādī, *Hadiyyat al-'Ārifīn*, II, 321; al-Qannūjī, *Abjad al-'Ulūm*, III, 168; al-Kattānī, *Fahras*, I, 494–6; al-Zarkalī, *al-A'lām*, 6, 195.

125 For Abū Ṭāhir's connections in the networks, see al-Kattānī, *Fahras*, I, 98, 101, 110, 119, 166, 167, 178, 195, 219, 253, 289, 356, 423, 427, 483, 505, 511, 514; II, 559, 605, 735, 743, 760, 770, 811, 812, 829, 850, 903, 951, 976, 986, 1048, 1070, 1076, 1111.

126 J.O. Voll, 'Hadith Scholars and Tariqahs: An Ulama Group in the 18th Century Haramayn and their Impact in the Islamic World', *JAAS*, XV, 3–4 (1980), 246–73; 'Muḥammad Ḥayyā al-Sindī and Muḥammad Ibn 'Abd al-Wahhāb: An Analysis of an Intellectual Group in Eighteenth Century Madīna', *BSOAS*, 38 (1975), 32–9.

127 Voll, 'Hadith Scholars', 267.

2 REFORMISM IN THE NETWORKS

1 For an explanation of the 'melting pot theory', see Nathan Glazer & Daniel P. Moynihan, *Beyond the Melting Pot*, Cambridge, MA: MIT Press, 1974. For a thorough discussion on the dichotomy between 'great tradition' and 'little tradition' in Islam, see D.F. Eickelman, 'The Study of Islam in Local Contexts', *Contributions to Asian Studies*, 17 (1982), 1–16.

2 See Fazlur Rahman, *Islam*, 2nd ed, Chicago: University of Chicago Press, 1979, esp. 193–6, 205–6. For further discussion on neo-Sufism, see John O. Voll, 'Hadith Scholars and Tariqahs: An Ulama Group in the 18th Century Haramayn and their Impact in the Islamic World', *JAAS*, XV, 3–4 (1980), 264–72; N. Levtzion & J.O. Voll (eds), 'Introduction', in *Eighteenth Century Renewal and Reform in Islam*, Syracuse: Syracuse University Press, 1987, 3–20; L. Brenner, 'Sufism in Africa in the Seventeenth and Eighteenth Centuries', in *Islam et Societés au sud du Sahara*, 2 (1988), 80–92; R.S. O'Fahey, 'Neo-Sufism and Ibn Idris', in his *Enigmatic Saint: Ahmad ibn Idris and the Idrisi Tradition*, Evanston, Il: Northwestern University Press, 1990, 1–26; Bernd Radtke, 'Kritik am Neo-Sufism', in Frederick de Jong & Bernd Radtke (eds), *Islamic Mysticism Contested: Thirteen Centuries of Controversies and Polemics*, Leiden: E.J. Brill, 1999, pp. 162–73.

3 Rahman, *Islam*, 205–6.

4 Fazlur Rahman, 'Revival and Reform', in P.M. Holt et al. (eds), *The Cambridge History of Islam*, 1970, II, 637.

5 Rahman, *Islam*, 194.

6 *Ibid*, 195.

7 For further discussion on this, see Rahman, *Islam*, 194–5. For arguments against the inclusion of Ibn Taymiyyah among *ṣūfī*s or neo-*ṣūfī*s, see for instance, F. Meier, 'Das Sauberste über die Vorbestimmung. Ein Stück Ibn Taymiyya', *Saeculum*, 32 (1981), 74–89. For discussion on the role of some leading Ḥanbalī scholars in Sufism, see G. Makdisi, 'The Sunni Revival', D.S. Richards (ed.), *Islamic Civilisation*, 950–1150, London: Bruno Cassirer, 1973, esp. 161–8; J.S. Trimingham, *The Sufi Orders in Islam*, 41–2.

8 L. Massignon, *Essai sur les origines du lexique de la mystique musulmane*, Paris: J. Vrin, 1954, 207. A fuller account of Dhū al-Nūn is in 'Abd al-Wahhāb al-Sha'rānī (d. 973/1565), *al-Ṭabaqāt al-Kubrā*, 2 vols, Cairo: Maktabah wa Maṭba'ah Muḥammad 'Alī, n.d., I, 59–61.

9 Trimingham, *The Sufi Orders*, 46.

10 See Ibn al-Ḥājj al-'Abdarī (d. 738/1336–7), *al-Madkhal*, 4 vols, Cairo: Muṣṭafā al-Bābī al-Ḥalabī, 1380/1960, III, 194–8, 218–20.

11 Trimingham, *The Sufi Order*, 89–90. For Ibn Maymūn's biography, see Abū al-Fallāḥ 'Abd al-Ḥayy Ibn al-'Imād (d. 1089/1678), *Shadharāt al-Dhahab fī Ahkbār man Dhahab*, 8 vols, Cairo: Maktabat al-Qudsī, 1350–1/1931–2, VIII, 81–4. This biographical chronicle covers the earlier centuries of Islam to the year 1000/1591.

12 For Ibn Ḥajar's biography, see Ibn al-'Imād, *Shadharāt al-Dhahab*, VII, 270–3.

13 *Ibid*, VIII, 51–5 for sources of al-Suyūṭī's biography.

14 *Ibid*, VIII, 134–6 for sources of Zakariyyā al-Anṣārī's biography.

15 The famous Egyptian neo-*ṣūfī* al-Sha'rānī had a common link with all of them. Zakariyyā al-Anṣārī was his direct teacher, who used to study with Ibn Ḥajar al-'Asqalānī. Al-Suyūṭī, also a student of Ibn Ḥajar, was a teacher of al-Sha'rānī's father. A month before al-Suyūṭī died, al-Sha'rānī himself met him in Cairo. See al-Sha'rānī, *al-Ṭabaqāt al-Kubrā*, II, 111–3; *al-Ṭabaqāt al-Sughrā*. (ed.) 'Abd al-Qādir Aḥmad 'Aṭā (ed.), Cairo: Maktabat al-Qāhirah, 1390/1970, 18–20. More to follow on links between al-Sha'rānī and our networks.

16 See 'Abd al-Ḥayy b. 'Abd al-Kabīr al-Kattānī (d. 1963), *Fahras al-Fahāris wa al-'Athbāt*, 3 vols, Beirut: Dār al-Gharb al-Islāmī, 1402/1982, I, 71–94, for a discussion on the importance of the *isnāds* in *ḥadīth* study and other branches of Islamic discipline, and on their ranking. Cf. M.M. Azami, *Studies in Hadith Methodology and Literature*, Indianapolis: American Trust Publication, 1977, esp. 58–67.

17 See for instance, his *Nihāyat al-Muḥtāj ilā Sharḥ al-Manhāl fī al-Fiqh 'alā Madhhab al-Imām al-Shāfi'ī*, 8 vols, Misr: Muṣṭafā al-Bābī al-Ḥalabī, 1967, which expressly introduces him by that honorific.
18 For Shihāb al-Dīn al-Ramlī's biography, see al-Sha'rānī, *al-Ṭabaqāt al-Sughrā*, 67–9.
19 Ibrāhīm al-Kūrānī, *al-Umam li Īqāẓ al-Himam*, Hayderabad: Dā'irat al-Ma'ārif al-Niẓāmiyyah, 1328/1910, 3–5; al-Kattānī, *Fahras*, II, 952.
20 Al-Kūrānī, *al-Umam*, 10–1.
21 See 'Abd Allāh b Sālim al-Baṣrī, *Kitāb al-Imdād bi Ma'rifah 'Uluw al-isnād*, Hayderabad: Dā'irat al-Ma'ārif al-Niẓāmiyyah, 1328/1910, 50–1.
22 For Ibn 'Arabī's further connections in *ḥadīth* studies, see al-Kattānī, *Fahras*, I, 99, 204, 208, 310, 449, 496; II, 596, 686, 716, 928, 991, 1055.
23 For al-Sha'rānī's accounts of Zakariyyā al-Anṣārī, see *al-Ṭabaqāt al-Kubrā*, I, 111–3; *al-Ṭabaqāt al-Sughrā*, 37–45.
24 Trimingham, *The Sufi Orders*, 220–5. For a complete discussion on the neo-*ṣūfī* al-Sha'rānī, see Michael Winter, *Society and Religion in Early Ottoman Egypt: Studies in the Writings of 'Abd al-Wahhāb al-Sha'rānī*, New Brunswick: Transaction Books, 1982, esp. 53–8, 150–200, 219–51. On his initiation into Sufism by Zakariyyā al-Anṣārī, see *Ibid*, 5.
25 Aḥmad al-Qushāshī, *al-Simṭ al-Majīd fī Sha'n al-Bay'at wa al-Dhikr wa Talqīnih wa Salāsil Ahl al-Tawḥīd*, Hayderabad: Dā'irat al-Ma'ārif al-Niẓāmiyyah, 1327/1909, 45–8, 86.
26 *Ibid*, 45.
27 Al-Kūrānī, *al-Umam*, 80.
28 Published in Hayderabad: Dā'irat al-Ma'ārif al-Niẓāmiyyah, 1328/1910.
29 Al-Nakhlī, *Bughyat al-Ṭālibīn*, esp. 10–14. He mentions here all *ḥadīth* books he studied and their *isnād*s through 28.
30 See al-Kūrānī, *al-Umam*, 4–44.
31 Al-Nakhlī, *Bughyat al-Ṭālibīn*, 31.
32 Al-Qushāshī, *al-Simṭ*, 7–8.
33 Muṣṭafā Fatḥ Allāh al-Ḥamawī, *Fawā'id al-Irtiḥāl wa Natā'ij al-Safar fī Akhbār Ahl al-Qarn al-Hādī 'Ashar*, 3 vols, Cairo, MS. Dār al-Kutub al-Miṣriyyah, Tārīkh 1093, I, fol. 21.
34 Al-Baṣrī, *Kitāb al-Imdād*, 3.
35 Al-Nakhlī, *Bughyat al-Ṭālibīn*, 12, 31.
36 Al-Kūrānī, *al-Umam*, 115.
37 This work was published in Cairo: Maktabah wa Maṭba'ah 'Alī Ṣabīḥ wa Awlāduh, n.d., 2 vols.
38 al-Qushāshī, *al-Simṭ*, 41, 83–4; al-Kūrānī, *al-Umam*, 125–6; al-Ḥamawī, *Fawā'id al-Irtiḥāl*, I, fol. 320, 329. Cf. S.A.A. Rizvi,

A History of Sufism in India, 2 vols, New Delhi: Munshiram Manoharlal, 1983, II, 330–1.

39 Al-Ḥamawī, *Fawā'id al-Irtiḥāl*, I, fol. 320; al-Kūrānī, *al-Umam*, 166.

40 EI², V, 525.

41 Al-Qushāshī, *al-Simṭ*, 106–10; al-Ḥamawī, *Fawā'id al-Irtiḥāl*, I, fol. 329.

42 Ibrāhīm al-Kūrānī, *Itḥāf al-Dhakī bi Sharḥ al-Tuḥfat al-Mursalah ilā Rūḥ al-Nabī*, Cairo, MS Dār al-Kutub al-Miṣriyyah, Taṣawwuf 2578, fols 6, 9, 11, 15.

43 Al-Ḥamawī, *Fawā'id al-Irtiḥāl*, I, fols 25–6, 28.

44 See Ismā'īl Basha al-Baghdādī, *Hadiyyat al-'Ārifīn: Asmā' al-Mu'allifīn wa 'Āthār al-Muṣannifīn*, 2 vols, Istanbul: Milli Egitim Basimevi, 1951, I, 35–6.

45 A.H. Johns, 'Islam in Southeast Asia: Reflections and New Directions', *Indonesia*, 19 (1976), 51; 'Friends in Grace: Ibrāhīm al-Kūrānī and 'Abd al-Ra'ūf al-Singkeli', in S. Udin (ed.), *Spectrum: Essays Presented to Sutan Takdir Alisjahbana*, Jakarta: Dian Rakyat, 1978, 476. The *Itḥāf al-Dhakī* is included in all lists of his works; see al-Baghdādī, *Hadiyyat al-'Ārifīn*, I, 35; Brockelmann, *GAL*, S. II, 520. This work is reserved in several libraries: Cairo, MS Dār al-Kutub, Taṣawwuf 2578, Microfilm 7651, another copy is Taṣawwuf 2954, Microfilm 10200; MS Leiden University, Or. 7050, 1892; MS India Office, no. 684, 1877.

46 See A.H. Johns, *The Gift Addressed to the Spirit of the Prophet*, Canberra: Australian National University, 1965, 5–7.

47 Al-Ḥamawī, *Fawā'id al-Irtiḥāl*, I, fol. 25.

48 *Ibid*, I, fol. 167; Cf. Johns, 'Reflections', 50.

49 Al-Kūrānī, *Itḥāf al-Dhakī*, fol. 2; Cf. Johns, 'Reflections', 51–2.

50 G.W.J. Drewes, 'Review of: A.H. Johns PhD Malay Sufism', *BKI*, 115, III (1959), 283.

51 Al-Kūrānī, *Itḥāf al-Dhakī*, fol. 2.

52 Al-Baghdādī, *Hadiyyat al-'Ārifīn*, I, 35; Muḥammad Khalīl al-Murādī, *Silk al-Durar fī A'yān al-Qarn al-Thānī 'Ashar*, 4 vols, Beirut: Dār Ibn al-Ḥazm, 1408/1988, I, 6.

53 See P. Voorhoeve, *Handlist of Arabic Manuscripts in the Library of the University of Leiden and Other Collections in the Netherlands*, The Hague: Leiden University Press, 1980, 461.

54 Leiden University, MS. F. Or. A13d (17–18); D.A. Rinkes, *Abdoerraoef van Singkel: Bijdrage tot de kennis van de mystiek op Sumatra en Java*, Heerenveen: Hepkema, 1909, 95 n. 2.

55 See al-Baghdādī, *Hadiyyat al-'Ārifīn*, I, 35.

56 Johns, *The Gift*, 8–12.

57 Al-Maqassārī, *Zubdat al-Asrār*, 47; *Tāj al-Asrār*, 72–4. Both are included in a collection of al-Maqassārī's MSS, Jakarta, National Library, KBL MS A-101. This collection consists of 20 works of al-Maqassārī.

58 The work is listed in both al-Baghdādī, *Hadiyyat al-'Ārifīn*, I, 245, and Muḥammad Amīn al-Muḥibbī, *Khulāṣat al-Athar fī 'A'yān al-Qarn al-Hādī 'Ashar*, 4 vols, Cairo: 1248/1867–8, repr. Beirut: Dār Ṣādir, n.d., I, 458. For his complete biography and works, see al-Muḥibbī, *Khulāṣat al-Athar*, I, 457–64; al-Baghdādī, *Hadiyyat al-'Ārifīn*, I, 245; Brockelmann, *GAL*, II, 379.

59 Al-Kūrānī, *Itḥāf al-Dhakī*, fol. 2.

60 Al-Ḥamawī, *Fawā'id al-Irtiḥāl*, I, fol. 167.

61 *Ibid*, I, fol. 320.I, 344.

62 *Ibid*, I, fols 326–7; al-Muḥibbī, *Khulāṣat al-Athar*, I, 344.

63 Al-Qushāshī, *al-Simṭ*, 118–20; al-Ḥamawī, *Fawā'id al-Irtiḥāl*, fol. 329.

64 Al-Kūrānī, *Itḥāf al-Dhakī*, fols 11–24; *al-Umam*, 115–18.

65 Al-Ḥamawī, *Fawā'id al-Irtiḥāl*, I, fol. 30.

66 *Ibid*, I, fol. 12.

67 Al-Muḥibbī, *Khulāṣat al-Athar*, IV, 305–7; Aḥmad Zaynī Daḥlān, *Khulāṣat al-Kalām fī Bayan Umarā' al-Bilād al-Ḥaram*, Cairo: n.p., 1305/1888, 102–3; Aḥmad al-Sibā'ī, *Tārīkh Makkah*, Riyad (?): al-Mamlakah al-'Arabiyyah al-Su'ūdiyyah, 1404/1984, II, 378–82; G. de Gaury, *Rulers of Mecca*, 1951, repr. ed. New York: Dorset Press, 1991, 148, 155–6.

68 Asafiyya State Public Library, Hayderabad, MS Kalām 224 and Kalām 223 respectively, cited in Y. Friedmann, *Shaykh Aḥmad Sirhindī: An Outline of His Thought and a Study of His Image in the Eyes of Posterity*, Montreal: Institute of Islamic Studies, McGill University Press, 1971, 7–8, 97–101, appendix C; Rizvi, *A History of Sufism*, II, 339–2. Only the *Qadḥ al-Zand* is included among al-Barzanjī's 56 works given by al-Baghdādī, *Hadiyyat al-'Ārifīn*, II, 303. I was not able to check these MSS myself.

69 Asafiyyah State Library, Kalām, 224, cited in Friedmann, 8. The work is not listed among al-'Ajamī's works listed by al-Baghdādī, *Hadiyyat al-'Ārifīn*, I, 294, nor by Yaḥyā Maḥmūd Junayd Sā'ātī, editor of al-'Ajamī's *Ihdā' al-Laṭā'if min Akhbār al-Ṭā'if*, Ṭā'if: Dār Thaqīf, 1400/1980, 17–24.

70 See Rizvi, *A History of Sufism*, 339.

71 Friedmann, *Shaykh Aḥmad Sirhindī*, esp. 13–21.

72 Al-Barzanjī, *Qadḥ al-Zand*, fols 14a[28]–14b[1], cited in Friedmann, *Shaykh Aḥmad Sirhindī*, 98. For al-Suyūṭī's work cited by al-Barzanjī, see Brockelmann, *GAL*, II, 151, no. 135, and I. Goldziher, *Zur Charakteristik Gelal ud-Din us-Suyuti's und seiner literarischen Tätigkeit*, Vienna: 1872.

73 Friedmann, *Shaykh Aḥmad Sirhindī*, 98–9; Rizvi, *A History of Sufism*, II, 340–1.

74 Friedmann, *Shaykh Aḥmad Sirhindī*, 99. See appendix C of this work, in which a portion of al-Barzanjī's treatises is given.

75 For al-Qushāshī's detailed opinion on this question, see Rizvi, *A History of Sufism*, II, 339.
76 For discussion on the organisation of *ṭarīqah*s, see for instance, Trimingham, *The Sufi Orders*, 166–93; Winter, *Society and Religion*, 126–44.
77 For al-Qushāshī's complete silsilah of the respective *ṭarīqah*, see his *al-Simṭ*, 66–135.
78 For his complete silsilah, see his *Bughyat al-Ṭālibīn*, 65–81.
79 Al-Qushāshī, *al-Simṭ*, 36.
80 This simile was first coined by al-Junayd al-Baghdādī. See Rahman, *Islam*, 137. Initially, it was employed to refer to Muslim's total submission (*tawakkul*) to God. See I. Goldziher, 'Materialien zur Entwicklungsgeschichte des Sufismus', *Gesammelte Schriften*, Hildesheim: 1967, IV, 180.
81 Al-Qushāshī, *al-Simṭ*, 83–4; al-Ḥamawī, *Fawā'id al-Irtiḥāl*, I, fol. 329. Cf. A. Janson, R. Tol and J.J. Witkam (eds), 'Mystical Illustrations from the Teachings of Shaykh Ahmad al-Qusyasyi: A Facsimile Edition of a Manuscript from Aceh (Cod. Or. 2222) in the Library of Leiden University', *Manuscripta Indonesica*, vol. 5, Leiden: INIS and Leiden University Library, 1995; Trimingham, *The Sufi Orders*, 167, on the freedom of each member, provided he adhered at the same time to regulations for communal life.
82 Al-Qushāshī, *al-Simṭ*, 27–8, 41–5; al-Ḥamawī, *Fawā'id al-Irtiḥāl*, I, fol. 322, 329.
83 Al-Ḥamawī, *Fawā'id al-Irtiḥāl*, I, fol. 167, 320; al-Kūrānī, *Itḥāf al-Dhakī*, fol. 2. Cf. Trimingham, *The Sufi Orders*, 175.
84 See Winter, *Society and Religion*, 129–30.
85 See *Ibid*, 131–9, and Trimingham, *The Sufi Orders*, 173–4, on the general tendency among *ṣūfī* shaykhs to give first priority to their descendants who will succeed them. This type of succession in some cases led to the appointment of incompetent or worldly oriented successors. But in Syria the tendency did not become universal. In some orders, notably the Khalwatiyyah and Shādhiliyyah, the shaykh was elected by disciples.
86 See Winter, *Society and Religion*, 137–41.
87 See Trimingham, *The Sufi Orders*, 22.
88 Al-Qushāshī, *al-Simṭ*, 15–6; al-Ḥamawī, *Fawā'id al-Irtiḥāl*, I, fol. 329.
89 Ṣiddīq b. Ḥasan al-Qannūjī, *Abjad al-'Ulūm*, 3 vols, Beirut: Dār al-Kutub al-'Ilmiyyah, n.d., III, 168.
90 Al-Kūrānī, for instance, is reported to have had a big library in his house. See Ibn al-Ṭayyib, *Nashr al-Mathānī*, Fes: 1310/1892, II, 130–7, cited in Johns, 'Friends in Grace', 474.
91 For an account of al-Qushāshī, who also held teaching sessions in his house, see al-Ḥamawī, *Fawā'id al-Irtiḥāl*, I, fol. 330.

92 Cf. Trimingham, *The Sufi Orders*, 168.
93 EI², V, 433.
94 See al-Kūrānī, *Itḥāf al-Dhakī*, esp. fols 7–23.
95 See al-Kūrānī's accounts of his studies of Ibn 'Arabī's works with Zayn al-'Ābidīn al-Ṭabarī, in *al-Umam*, 122–5.
96 Al-Nakhlī, *Bughyat al-Ṭālibīn*, 27, 45–6.
97 See Winter, *Religion and Society*, 165–72.
98 Ibn al-Ṭayyib, *Nashr al-Mathānī*, II, 130–7, cited in Johns, *EI²*, V, 433; 'Friends in Grace', 473–4.
99 See P.K. Hitti, N.A. Faris & B. 'Abd-al-Mālik, *Descriptive Catalogue of the Garrett Collection of Arabic Manuscripts in the Princeton University Library*, Princeton, NJ: Princeton University Press, 1938, 460–1.
100 Johns, 'Friends in Grace', 474.

3 SEVENTEENTH CENTURY MALAY-INDONESIAN NETWORKS I

1 S.M.N. al-Attas, 'New Light on the Life of Hamzah Fansuri', *JMBRAS* 40, I (1967), 40; *The Mysticism of Hamzah Fansuri*, Kuala Lumpur: University of Malaya Press, 1970, 313. Cf. Hasjmi, *Kebudayaan Aceh dalam Sejarah*, Jakarta: Beuna, 1983, 195–7.
2 A. Hasjmi, *Ruba'i Hamzah Fansuri, Karya Sastra Sufi Abad XVII*, Kuala Lumpur: Dewan Bahasa & Pustaka, 1976, 10. A recent discussion on the date of Hamzah al-Fanṣūrī, based on archeological evidence calculates that Hamzah al-Fanṣūrī died in 1527 (see C. Guillot & L. Kalus, 'La stèle funéraire de Hamzah Fansuri', *Archipel,* 2000, 3–24). The argument was disputed, however, by another article of Vladimir I. Braginsky, 'On the Copy of Hamzah Fansuri's Epitaph Published by C. Guillot & L. Kalus', *Archipel*, 2001, 20–33. In turn, this Braginsky's comment led Guillot & Kalus to write a counter-response, see Guillot & Kalus, 'En réponse à Vladimir I. Braginsky', *Archipel*, 2001, 34–8).
3 For an account of the places visited by Hamzah, see J. Doorenbos, *De geschriften van Hamzah Pansoeri*, Leiden: Batteljee & Terpstra, 1933. Cf. H. Kraemer, *Een Javaansche Primbon uit de zestiende eeuw*, Leiden: 1921, 23–30.
4 Some of his writings are romanised in Doorenbos, *De Geschriften*, 16–204; al-Attas, *Mysticism of Hamzah*, 233–353.
5 See for instance, C.A.O. van Nieuwenhuijze, *Samsu'l-Din van Pasai*: *Bijdrage tot de kennis der Sumatraansche mystiek*, Leiden: Brill, 1945, 19–20, 234–5; C. Snouck Hurgronje, *The Achehnese*, 2 vols, trans. A.W.S. Sullivan, Leyden: Brill, 1906, II, 13 and n. 2.
6 Hasjmi, *Ruba'i*, 11–3; Hawash Abdullah, *Perkembangan Ilmu Tasawuf dan Tokoh-tokohnya di Nusantara*, Surabaya: Al-Ikhlas, 1980, 41–2.

7 J. Lancaster, *The Voyages of Sir James Lancaster to Brazil and the East Indies*, Sir William Foster (ed.), London: The Hakluyt Society, 1940, 96.
8 B.J.O. Schrieke, *Indonesian Sociological Studies*, The Hague & Bandung: Van Hoeve, 1955, II, 243.
9 A. Hasjmi, *Kebudayaan*, 197–8.
10 Van Nieuwenhuijze, *Samsu'l-Din*, 18.
11 T. Iskandar, *De Hikajat Atjeh*, 's-Gravenhage: Smits, 1959, 137, 153, 168.
12 For lists of his works, see Van Nieuwenhuijze, *Samsu'l-Din*, 25–6; Abdullah, *Perkembangan Ilmu Tasawuf*, 35–49; Hasjmi, *Kebudayaan*, 198.
13 For a detailed exposition and analysis of their thought and doctrine, see al-Attas, *Mysticism of Hamzah*; *Raniri and the Wujudiyyah of the 17th Century Acheh*, Monograph of MBRAS no. 3, Singapore, 1966, 43–79; Van Nieuwenhuijze, *Samsu'l-Din*; Hasjmi, *Ruba'i*; Abdullah, *Perkembangan Ilmu Tasawuf*, 35–49.
14 A.H. Johns, 'Aspects of Sufi Thought in India and Indonesia in the first half of the 17th Century', *JMBRAS*, 28, I (1955), 72–7.
15 R.O. Winstedt, 'Some Malay Mystics, Heretical and Orthodox', *JMBRAS*, 1 (1923), 312–8.
16 Johns, 'Aspects', 73–5.
17 Van Nieuwenhuijze, *Samsu'l-Dīn*, 329–39.
18 Siti Baroroh Baried, 'Perkembangan Ilmu Tasawuf di Indonesia', in S. Sutrisno et al. (eds), *Bahasa, Sastra, Budaya*, Yogyakarta: Gadjah Mada University Press, 1985, 2908.
19 Al-Attas, *Raniri*, esp. 15–42; *Mysticism of Hamzah*, esp. Chs II, III and VI.
20 S.M.N. al-Attas, *A Commentary on the Ḥujjat al-Ṣiddīq of Nūr al-Dīn al-Rānīrī*, Kuala Lumpur: Ministry of Culture, 1986, xiii, 8–12.
21 S.M.N. al-Attas, *Raniri*, 12.
22 For a more complete account of the Ḥadramī migration to the archipelago, see L.W.C. van den Berg, *Le Hadhramout et les colonies arabes dans l'archipel indien*, Batavia: Imprimerie de Gouvernement, 1886; U. Freitag & W.G. Clarence-Smith (eds), *The Hadrami Traders, Scholars, and Statesmen in the Indian Ocean 1750–1960s*, Leiden: Brill, 1997.
23 al-Attas, *A Commentary*, 3.
24 Ibn Khalliqān, *Wafayāt al-A'yān wa Anbā' al-Zamān*. Ed. Iḥsān 'Abbās, 8 vols, Beirut: Dār al-Thaqāfah, 1968–72, IV, no. 616.
25 According to G.W.J. Drewes, if (الحميد) is read 'al-Ḥumayd', then al-Rānīrī could belong to the Bā Ḥumayd family of Ḥaḍramawt. See his 'De herkomst van Nuruddin ar-Raniri', *BKI*, 111 (1955), 149. For Abū Bakr al-Ḥumaydī's biography, see Taqī al-Dīn al-Fāsī, *'Aqd*

al-Thamīn fī Tārīkh al-Balad al-Amīn, 8 vols, Cairo: Maṭba'at al-Sunnat al-Muḥammadiyyah, 1385/1966, V, 160–1.
26 Ibn Khalliqān, *Wafayāt*, IV, no. 558.
27 Al-Rānīrī, *Bustān al-Salāṭīn Bab II*, Fasal 13, ed. T. Iskandar, Kuala Lumpur: Dewan Bahasa dan Pustaka, 1966, 25.
28 I failed to find the book and its author. But al-Kattānī mentions a book entitled *al-Sayf al-Qāṭi' wa al-Ḥiṣn al-Māni' bi Madḥ al-Rasūl al-Shāfi'* by Muḥammad b. 'Alī al-Fāsī. See 'Abd al-Ḥayy b. 'Abd al-Kabīr al-Kattānī, *Fahras al-Fahāris*, 3 vols, Beirut: Dār al-Gharb al-Islāmī, 1402/1982, I, 273.
29 'Abd al-Ḥayy b. Fakhr al-Dīn al-Ḥasanī, *Nuzhat al-Khawāṭir wa Bahjat al-Masāmi' wa al-Nawāẓir*. 7 vols. Hayderabad: Dā'irat al-Ma'ārif al-'Uthmāniyyah, 1931–59. V, 349.
30 P. Voorhoeve, 'Van en over Nuruddin ar-Raniri', *BKI*, 107 (1951), 357.
31 Al-Ḥasanī, *Nuzhat al-Khawāṭir*, V, 350; Voorhoeve, 'Van en over Nuruddin', 356; *Twee Maleische geschriften van Nūruddīn ar-Rānīrī*, Leiden: Brill, 1955, 5–6; Drewes, 'De herkomst', 149–50; For Bā Shaybān's biography, see Muḥammad al-Amīn Al-Muḥibbī, *Khulāṣat al-Athar fī A'yān al-Qarn al-Ḥādī 'Ashar*, 4 vols, Cairo: 1868, III, 214–15.
32 J.S. Trimingham, *The Sufi Orders in Islam*, Oxford: Clarendon Press, 1971, 37–40. The Rifā'iyyah *ṭarīqah*, one of the most widespread orders until the fifteenth century, was known for its transitory annihilation in Absolute Reality; its *ṣūfis* were noted for their fire-resisting and snake-charming skills.
33 For accounts of the spread of the Rifā'iyyah order in Aceh and other parts of the archipelago, see Snouck Hurgronje, *The Achehnese*, II, 249–57; Aboebakar Atjeh, *Tarekat dalam Tasawwuf*, Kota Bharu: Pustaka Aman, 1979, 95–8. For *dhikr* and litanies of the Rifā'iyyah in the archipelago, see Leiden University, MSS Or. 7617, 7618, 1994.
34 See the chains of initiation of the 'Aydarūsiyyah in his *Jawāhir al-'Ulūm fī Kashf al-Ma'lūm*, MS Marsden Collection, Text no. 12151, 21v–158r, SOAS, University of London. A microfilm of this is in Leiden University Cod. Or. A41. Another copy is in Jakarta, National Library, Ml 795.
35 Al-Rānīrī's *silsilah* of the Qādiriyyah is given in *Safīnat al-Najāh* of al-Maqassārī, cited in Hamka, *Dari Perbendaharaan Lama*, Medan: Madju, 1963, 40–1; Tudjimah et al., Syekh Yusuf Makasar: *Riwayat Hidup, Karya dan Ajarannya*, Jakarta: Departemen P&R, 1987, 22–3.
36 'Abd al-Raḥmān b. Shihāb al-Saqqāf, born and died in Tarīm, was a leading scholar in the Ḥaḍramawt region. He was well versed in *ḥadīth*, *tafsīr*, *fiqh* and *taṣawwuf*. For his biography, see Al-Muḥibbī, *Khulāṣat al-Athar*, II, 359–60.

37 Abū Bakr b. Shihāb, called by Al-Muḥibbī the 'great traditionist' (*al-muḥaddith al-kabīr*), had studied in the Yemen and the Ḥaramayn before establishing his career in Tarīm. Among his teachers in the Ḥaramayn were 'Umar b. 'Abd al-Raḥīm al-Baṣrī, 'Abd al-'Azīz al-Zamzamī and Aḥmad b. Ibrāhīm b. 'Alān. Among his prominent disciples was 'Abd Allāh b. Shaykh al-'Aydarūs. See Al-Muḥibbī, *Khulāṣat al-Athar*, I, 85–6. For his connections in *ḥadīth* studies, see al-Kattānī, *Fahras*, II.

38 'Umar al-Baṣrī, a *faqīh* and *ṣūfī*, was perhaps a major link connecting Bā Shaybān and al-Rānīrī with Egyptian *ḥadīth* scholarship, for he was a student of Shams al-Dīn al-Ramlī; he established his career in Mecca, and therefore had disciples from many parts of the Muslim world. Among them were 'Alī al-Ṭabarī and 'Alī Jamāl al-Makkī, both of whom were teachers and acquaintances of al-Sinkīlī. For his biography, see Al-Muḥibbī, *Khulāṣat al-Athar*, III, 210–12.

39 Aḥmad b. 'Alān al-Makkī was a noted Naqshbandiyyah shaykh in Mecca. He received this order from Tāj al-Hindī. His works mainly deal with the Naqshbandiyyah doctrine and with *Tawḥīd* such as *Sharḥ Risālat al-Shaykh Raslān fī Tawḥīd*. For his biography and works, see Al-Muḥibbī, *Khulāṣat al-Athar*, I, 157–8; Ismā'īl Bāshā al-Baghdādī, *Hadiyyat al-'Ārifīn*, 2 vols, Istanbul: Milli Egitim Basimevi, 1951, I, 165. Yūsuf al-Maqassārī, who was a student of Muḥammad b. 'Abd al-Bāqī al-Mizjājī, another disciple of Tāj al-Naqshbandī, apparently did not meet Aḥmad b. 'Alān while he was studying in Mecca. But his name is found in Ismā'īl al-Khalīdī al-Minangkabawī's *silsilah* of the Naqshbandiyyah in the Malay-Indonesian world in the nineteenth century. See K.F. Holle, 'Mededeelingen over de devotie der Naqsjibendijah in den Ned. Indischen Archipelago', *TBG* 31 (1886), esp. 74. Cf. Ph.S. van Ronkel, *Supplement to the Catalogue of the Arabic Manuscripts Preserved in the Museum of the Batavia Society of Arts and Sciences*, Batavia & The Hague: Albrecht & Nijhoff, 1913, 171–2, for a text of the Naqshbandiyyah *dhikr* attributed to Aḥmad b. 'Alān.

It is important to note that Aḥmad b. 'Alān should not be confused with his nephew, Muḥammad b. 'Alī b. 'Alān al-Ṣiddīqī (996–1057/1588–1647). Born in Mecca, Muḥammad b. 'Alān was a leading *muḥaddith*, who studied with, among others, Sayyid 'Umar al-Baṣrī, mentioned above. (For his biography and works, see Al-Muḥibbī, *Khulāṣat al-Athar*, IV, 184–9; al-Baghdādī, *Hadiyyat al-'Ārifīn*, II, 284–5; al-Zarkalī, *al-A'lām*, VII, 187; Brockelmann, *GAL*, S. II, 533. For his connections in *ḥadīth* studies, see al-Kattānī, *Fahras*, I, 451; II, 730, 811.) He seems to have been in close contact with Aḥmad al-Qushāshī, who wrote a work entitled *Ijābat al-Akh al-Fāḍil al-Kāmil bi Ḥall al-Abwāb al-Arba'* [sic] *min Kitāb al-Insān al-Kāmil* to answer his questions. Muḥammad b. 'Alān, a prolific writer, was quick to answer questions posed to him. Among his works was *al-Mawāhib al-Rabbāniyyah 'an al-As'ilat al-Jāwīyyah*, written as answer to a question put forward by the Sulṭān of Banten, Abū al-Mafākhir 'Abd al-Qādir (r. 1037–63/1626–51), concerning al-Ghazālī's *Naṣīḥat al-Mulūk*. See P. Voorhoeve, *Handlist of Arabic Manuscripts*, The Hague: Leiden University Press, 1980, 130–1, 204–5. The questions of the Bantenese Sulṭān were apparently brought to Mecca by his delegation in 1038/1638. The *al-As'ilat al-Jāwīyyah* is not listed in Arabic sources.

40 Al-Khaṭīb al-Sharbaynī was born in Egypt and performed pilgrimages 24 times. During these frequent visits to the Ḥaramayn he also taught disciples, especially on the subject of Shāfi'ī *fiqh*. See his biography in Al-Muḥibbī, *Khulāṣat al-Athar*, II, 378.

41 Al-Muḥibbī, *Khulāṣat al-Athar*, IV, 26–7.

42 Voorhoeve, *Twee Maleische*, 6.

43 Al-Muḥibbī, *Khulāṣat al-Athar*, II, 440–2; Brockelmann, GAL, II, 418; al-Baghdādī, *Hadiyyat al-'Ārifīn*, I, 600–1; al-Kattānī, *Fahras*, I, 340; II, 967, 1021.

44 Al-Muḥibbī, *Khulāṣat al-Athar*, II, 235–6: EI2, Art. 'Aydarūs', 780–2.

45 Al-Muḥibbī, *Khulāṣat al-Athar*, see for instance, I, 70–1, 81–8, 182, 218, 482; II, 94, 235–6, 389–90, 440–2; III, 37, 37–8, 49–50, 51, 117–18, 118, 234; IV, 20, 26, 56, 94.

46 R.M. Eaton, *Sufis of Bijapur 1300–1700: Social Roles of Sufis in Mediaeval India*, Princeton, NJ: Princeton University Press, 1978; D.C. Verma, *History of Bijapur*, New Delhi: 1974.

47 Al-Muḥibbī, *Khulāṣat al-Athar*, III, 215.

48 For Ḥusayn al-Aydarūs, see Van den Berg, *Le Hadhramout*, 162–3. For further accounts on Hadhrami *'ulamā'* in Southeast Asia, see Azyumardi Azra, 'Hadhrami Scholars in the Malay-Indonesian Diaspora', *Studia Islamika: Indonesian Journal for Islamic Studies*, 2, II (1995), 1–33; 'A Hadhrami Scholar in Indonesia: Sayyid 'Uthman', in U. Freitag & W.G. Clarence-Smith (eds), *Hadhrami Traders, Scholars and Statesmen in the Indian Ocean, 1750s–1960s*, Leiden: E.J. Brill, 1997, 249–63.

49 Al-Rānīrī, *Bustān al-Salāṭīn*, Iskandar (ed.), 36. Cf. MS. Leiden University, Cod. Or. 5443, f. 28–30.

50 Voorhoeve, 'Van en over Nuruddin', 357.

51 *Daghregister 1641–2*, 166.

52 *Daghregister 1641–2, Ibid.*

53 The Malay text was cited in Voorhoeve, 'Van en over Nuruddin', 353. Cf. A. Daudy, *Allah dan Manusia dalam Konsepsi Nuruddin ar-Raniri*, Jakarta: Rajawali, 1983, 45; H. Djajadiningrat, 'De ceremonie van het "poela batèë" op het graf van Soeltan Iskandar II van Atjeh

(1636–1641)', *TBG*, 69 (1929), 109–11. For further accounts on the controversy, see A. Vakily, 'Sufism, Power Politics and Reform: Al-Raniri's Opposition to Hamzah al-Fansuri's Teachings Reconsidered', *Studia Islamika: Indonesian Journal for Islamic Studies*, 4, I (1997), 113–35.

54 A. Daudy, *Syeikh Nuruddin ar-Raniri*, Jakarta: Bulan Bintang, 1978, 17.

55 Takeshi Ito, 'Why Did Nuruddin ar-Raniri leave Aceh in 1054 A.H.', *BKI*, 134 (1978), 489–91. Ito makes use of the Koloniaal Archief no. 1052, fols 667v–668r.

56 Al-Rānīrī, *Fatḥ al-Mubīn*, MS in the Daudy collection, 4, cited in his *Allah*, 47. A much longer passage is also cited in A. Hasjmi, *Syi'ah dan Ahlussunnah*, Surabaya: Bina Ilmu, 1983, 107–9.

57 See al-Ḥasanī, *Nuzhat al-Khawāṭir*, V, 350. For the complete list of al-Rānīrī's works, see H.N. van der Tuuk, 'Kort verslag der Maleische handschriften', *BKI*, 13 (1866), esp. 462–6; P. Voorhoeve, 'Lijst der geschriften van Rānīrī', *BKI*, 111 (1955), 152–61; Tudjimah (ed.), *Asrār al-Insān fī Ma'rifa al-Rūḥ wa 'l-Raḥmān*, Bandung: al-Ma'arif, 1961, 9–22; Daudi, *Allah*, 47–58. For a classification of his works according to the branches of Islamic discipline, see Siti Chamamah Soeratno et al., *Memahami Karya-karya Nuruddin Arraniri*, Jakarta: Departemen P&K, 1982, 16–48.

58 Al-Ḥasanī, *Nuzhat al-Khawāṭir*, V, 349.

59 For further discussion on al-Rānīrī's teachings on Sufism, see for instance, al-Attas, *Raniri; A Commentary;* Daudi, *Allah*; Siti Chamamah Soeratno, *Memahami Karya-karya*. For a comparison of his teachings with those of Ḥamzah al-Fanṣūrī and Sham al-Dīn, see Van Nieuwenhuijze, *Samsu'l-Din*; 'Nur al-Din al-Raniri als bestrijder der Wugudiya', *BKI*, 104 (1948), 337–411; al-Attas; *Mysticism of Hamzah*.

60 Eaton, *Sufis of Bijapur*, 127–9. Cf. Al-Muḥibbī, *Khulāṣat al-Athar*, II, 235–6.

61 For a detailed discussion on the *Ṣirāṭ al-Mustaqīm*, see R.S. Tjokrowinoto, *Tindjauan Kitab Ṣirāṭ'l-Mustaqīm (Karangan Nūr ad-Dīn Ar-Rānīrī)*, Unpubl. MA thesis, Universitas Gadjah Mada, Yogyakarta: 1964.

62 For al-Rānīrī's sources of *ṣūfī* doctrine, see Tudjimah, *Asrār al-Insān*, 244–87; al-Attas, *A Commentary*, 15–24; Daudy, *Allah*, 226, 247.

63 Tjokrowinoto, *Tindjauan*, 124; Abdullah, *Perkembangan Ilmu Tasawuf*, 29.

64 Al-Rānīrī, *Tibyān fī Ma'rifat al-Adyān*, in Voorhoeve, *Twee Maleische*, 5.

65 Al-Rānīrī, *Tibyān*, in *Ibid*; *Bustān al Salāṭīn*, Iskandar (ed.), 40–1.

66 Al-Rānīrī, *al-Fatḥ al-Mubīn*, MS in the Daudy collection fols 3–4,

cited in his *Allah*, 41; also in the Hasjmi collection, cited in his *Syi'ah dan Ahlussunnah*, 109.

67 Daudy, *Allah*, 44.

68 G.W.J. Drewes, 'Nūr al-Dīn al-Rānīrī's Charge of Heresy against Ḥamzah and Shamsuddīn from an International Point of View', in C.D. Grijns & S.O. Robson (eds), *Cultural Contact and Textual Interpretation*, Dordrecht: Foris, 1986, 54–9. For a comprehensive account of polemic and controversy during this period, see Azyumardi Azra, 'Opposition to Sufism in the East Indies in the Seventeenth and Eighteenth Century', in Frederick de Jong & Bernd Radtke (eds), *Islamic Mysticism Contested: Thirteen Centuries of Controversies and Polemics*, Leiden: Brill, 1999, 665–86.

69 MS Leiden University Cod. Or. 2467 (5660), fols 12–31.

70 'Lands above the wind' is a term popular in mediaeval Arabic literature referring to the 'upper' region to the West of the Malay-Indonesian archipelago. In contrast, the term 'land below the wind' is employed to designate the whole archipelago. See H. Clifford & F.A. Swettenham, *A Dictionary of the Malay Language*, I, Taiping: 1894, 63.

71 MS Leiden University Cod. Or. 2467 (5660), fols 12–21. In the colophon of the work, 'Abd Allāh al-Jāwī the copyist prays to God to give His blessing to Ibrāhīm ibn Ḥasan al-Kurdī al-Kūrānī al-Shahrānī al-Sharazūrī al-Madanī. See folio 12. Cf. Voorhoeve, 'Van en over Nuruddin', 365–8.

72 Hamka, *Dari Perbendaharaan*, 40–1; Tudjimah et al., Syekh Yusuf, 22–3.

73 See colophon of the work printed in Tudjimah (ed.), *Asrār al-Insān*, 6.

74 See Faḍl Allāh al-Burhānpūrī, *Tuḥfat al-Mursalah ilā al-Nabī*, Arabic and Javanese texts, English trans. A.H. Johns, Canberra: The Australian National University, 1965.

75 For detailed discussion, see Al-Attas, *Rānīrī*; *A Commentary*; Tudjimah (ed.), *Asrār al-Insān*; Daudy; *Allah*.

76 Al-Attas, *A Commentary*, 8, 46.

77 There are several editions of this work now available. See al-Rānīrī, *Ṣirāṭ al-Mustaqīm*, Shaykh Aḥmad b. Muḥammad Zayn Muṣṭafā al-Fatānī (ed.), Singapore: n.d.; another edition printed in the margin of Muḥammad Arshad al-Banjārī's *Sabīl al-Muhtadīn*, Singapore: Sulayman Mar'ie, n.d. For the spread and use of the *Ṣirāṭ al-Mustaqīm*, see Mohd Nor Bin Ngah, *Kitab Jawi: Islamic Thought of the Malay Muslim Scholars*, Singapore: ISEAS, 1983; Muhd Shaghir Abdullah, *Perkembangan Ilmu Fiqh*, esp. 29–31; Martin van Bruinessen, 'Kitab *Fiqh* di Pesantren Indonesia dan Malaysia', *Pesantren*, 6, I (1989), 37; 'Kitab Kuning: Books in Arabic Script used in the Pesantren Milieu', *BKI*, 146 (1990), 249–50.

78 See *Hikayat Merong Mahawangsa*, Siti Hawa Saleh (ed.), Kuala Lumpur: Dewan Bahasa & Pustaka, 1970, Ch. IV, esp. 115.
79 Al-Attas, *A Commentary*, 11.
80 Al-Rānīrī, *Bustān al-Salāṭīn*, Iskandar (ed.), 38–40.
81 Snouck Hurgronje, *The Achehnese*, I, 109–10.
82 Al-Attas, *A Commentary*, 46–7. Cf. S.M.N. al-Attas, *The Oldest known Malay Manuscript: A 16th Century Malay Translation of the 'Aqā'id of al–Nasafī*, Kuala Lumpur: University of Malaya, 1988.
83 The Malay text of the work in Arabic script is published in facsimile, with an introduction by Voorhoeve, *Twee Maleische*. A romanised part of the work is in K. Steenbrink, *Kitab Suci atau Kertas Toilet: Nuruddin Ar-Raniri dan Agama Kristen*, Yogyakarta: IAIN Sunan Kalijaga Press, 1988.
84 See for instance, *Asrār al-Insān*, Tudjimah (ed.), 17582; *Bustān al-Salāṭīn*, MS Raffles no. 8, Royal Asiatic Society, esp. Book II; *Akhbār Akhīrah fī Aḥwāl al-Qiyāmah*, esp. Ch. IV. Cf. Edwar Djamaris, 'Nuruddin ar-Raniri Khabar Akhirat dalam Hal Kiamat', in Sutrisno et al. (eds), 131–46.
85 Voorhoeve, *Twee Maleische*; Ph.S. van Ronkel, 'Raniri's Maleische geschrift: Exposé der religies', *BKI*, 102 (1943), 461–80; K. Steenbrink, *Kitab Suci atau Kertas Toilet*, 'Jesus and the Holy Spirit in the Writings of Nūr al-Dīn al-Rānīrī', *ICMR*, I, no. 2 (1990), 192–207.
86 Al-Attas, *A Commentary*, 7.
87 A. Teeuw, 'Pertumbuhan Bahasa Melayu menjadi Bahasa Dunia', in Harimurti Kridalaksana (ed.), *Masa Lampau Bahasa Indonesia: Sebuah Bunga Rampai*, Yogyakarta: Kanisius, 1991, 125–6.

4 SEVENTEENTH CENTURY MALAY-INDONESIAN NETWORKS II

1 D.A. Rinkes, *Abdoerraoef van Singkel: Bijdrage tot de kennis van de mystiek op Sumatra en Java*, Heerenveen: Hepkema, 1909, 25–6.
2 See for instance, T. Iskandar, 'Abdurrauf Singkel Tokoh Syatariyah (Abad ke-17)', in M.D. Mohamad (ed.), *Tokoh-tokoh Sastera Melayu Klasik*, Kuala Lumpur: Dewan Bahasa dan Pustaka, 1987, 72–3; P. Riddell, *Transferring a Tradition: 'Abd al-Ra'ūf al-Singkilī's Rendering into Malay of the Jalālayn Commentary*, Monograph no. 31, Berkeley: Center for South and Southeast Asia Studies, University of California at Berkeley, 1990, 4–5; Salman Harun, 'Hakekat Tafsir Tarjumān al-Mustafīd Karya Syekh Abdurrauf Singkel', unpubl. doctoral diss., Institut Agama Islam Negeri, Jakarta, 1988, 12–13; Oman Fathurahman, *Tanbih al-Masyi, Menyoal Wahdatul Wujud: Kasus Abdurrauf Singkel di Aceh Abad 17*, Bandung: Mizan & EFEO, 1999.

3 A. Hasjmi, 'Syekh Abdurrauf Syiah Kuala, Ulama Negarawan yang Bijaksana', in *Universitas Syiah Kuala Menjelang 20 Tahun*, Medan: Waspada, 1980, 370.

4 See Snouck Hurgronje, *The Achehnese*, II, 19; P. Voorhoeve, *Bayān Tajallī: Bahan-bahan untuk Mengadakan Penyelidikan lebih Mendalam tentang Abdurra-uf Singkel*, trans. Aboe Bakar, Banda Aceh: PDIA, 1980, 3. The original article is in Dutch, 'Bayān Tadjallī: Gegevens voor een nadere studie over Abdurrauf van Singkel', *TBG*, 85 (1952), also reprinted in *Madjallah untuk Ilmu Bahasa, Ilmu Bumi dan Kebudayaan Indonesia*, 85, IV (1955–7), 87–117.

5 Peunoh Daly, 'Naskah Mir'atut Thullab Karya Abdur-Rauf Singkel', in *Agama, Budaya dan Masyarakat*, Jakarta: Balitbang Depag RI, 1980, 133.

6 For accounts of Fansur or Barus, see J. Drakard, 'An Indian Ocean Port: Sources for the Earlier History of Barus', *Archipel*, 37 (1989), 53–81; L. Nurhakim, 'La Ville de Barus: Etude archéologique préliminaire', *Archipel*, 37 (1989), 4352; Cf. S.D. Goeitein, *Letters of Medieval Jewish Traders*, Princeton, NJ: Princeton University Press, 1973, 228–9.

7 Hasjmi, 'Syekh Abdurrauf', 369.

8 Drakard, 'History of Barus', 54–5; Voorhoeve, *Bayān Tajallī*, 3.

9 Hasjmi, 'Syekh Abdurrauf', 370–1. Recent discussion on the date of Hamzah al-Fanṣūrī, see chapter 3, note 2 above.

10 Cf. Snouck Hurgronje, *The Achehnese*, II, 19–20; Voorhoeve, *Bayān Tajallī*, 3.

11 For a list of MSS of this work and its location, see Voorhoeve, *Bayān Tajallī*, 42–3. For our purposes, we use MS Jakarta National Library, M1. 107 B and MS Leiden University, Cod. Or. 1933.

12 See Rinkes, *Abdoerraoef*, 25.

13 Al-Sinkīlī, *'Umdat*, MS Jakarta National Library, M1. 107, fol. 112.

14 For an identification of these places and the state of Islamic learning there, see 'Abd al-Raḥmān b. 'Alī al-Dayba', *al-Faḍl al-Mazī' 'alā Bughyat al-Mustafīd fī Madīnah Zabīd*, Yūsuf Shalhud (ed.), Sana'a: Markaz al-Dirāsat wa al-Buḥūth al-Yamanī, 1983; Ismā'īl b. 'Alī al-Akwa', *Al-Madāris al-Islāmiyyah fī al-Yaman*, Beirut: Mu'assasat al-Risālah, 1406/1986.

15 According to Al-Muḥibbī, Ibrāhīm b. Muḥammad b. Ja'mān was the grandfather of Ibrāhīm b. 'Abd Allāh b. Ja'mān, and died in 1034/1625. If this date is correct, al-Sinkīlī could not have met him. See Al-Muḥibbī, *Khulāṣat al-Athar*, I, 39; Cf. al-Kattānī, *Fahras*, I, 415.

16 Al-Sinkīlī, *'Umdat*, MS Ml. 107, fol. 112, 113.

17 Al-Muḥibbī, *Khulāṣat al-Athar*, I, 22.

18 For Ibrāhīm b. 'Abd Allāh b. Ja'mān's biography and works, see Al-Muḥibbī, *Khulāṣat al-Athar*, I, 21–2; al-Baghdādī, *Hadiyyat al-'Ārifīn*, I, 33; al-Kattānī, *Fahras*, I, 131, for his further connections in the networks.

19 Al-Sinkīlī, *'Umdat*, M1. 107, fol. 112.
20 For Isḥāq b. Ja'mān's biography and works, see Al-Muḥibbī, *Khulāṣat al-Athar*, I, 394–6, al-Baghdādī, *Hadiyyat al-'Ārifīn*, I, 202; For his further connections in the networks, see al-Kattānī, *Fahras*, I, 415.
21 For 'Abd al-Raḥīm al-Khāṣṣ' biography, see Al-Muḥibbī, *Khulāṣat al-Athar*, I, 347. It is important to note that 'Abd al-Raḥīm al-Khāṣṣ was also a teacher of Ḥasan al-'Ajami, Zayn al-'Ābidīn and 'Alī al-Ṭabarī. See al-Kattānī, *Fahras*, I, 270; II, 554, 811, 992.
22 Al-Muḥibbī, *Khulāṣat al-Athar*, IV, 281; 'Alī b. Muḥammad al-Dayba' [al-Shaybānī], a *muḥaddith* and reciter of the Qur'ān. For al-Dayba', see al-Kattānī, *Fahras*, I, 374, 415, 587, 714.
23 Al-Muḥibbī, *Khulāṣat al-Athar*, II, 283.
24 *Ibid*, III, 334–6
25 *Ibid*, I, 252–3.
26 Al-Sinkīlī, *'Umdat*, M1. 107, fol. 112.
27 See al-Kattānī, *Fahras*, II, 587.
29 For 'Alī al-Ṭabarī, see chapter 1, note 104 and accounts attached to it.
30 'Abd Allāh Bā Qashīr, a *muḥaddith* and poet, was a friend of Al-Muḥibbī. Among his teachers were 'Umar b. 'Abd al-Raḥīm al-Baṣrī, 'Abd al-Qādir al-Ṭabarī and Aḥmad b. 'Alān. He has numerous students from Mecca, Yemen, Iraq and Syria. See Al-Muḥibbī, *Khulāṣat al-Athar*, III, 42–4; al-Baghdādī, Hadiyyat *al-'Ārifīn*, I, 478; al-Kattānī, *Fahras*, I, 194, 252; II, 583.
31 See the accounts called 'Pasal pada Menyatakan *Silsilah* Tuan Syekh Abdul Ra'uf tatkala Menuntut Ilmu kepada Syekh Abdul Qusyasyi [sic]', Ph. S. van Ronkel (ed.), 'Het Heiligdom te Oelakan', *TBG*, 64 (1914), esp. 309–12. Henceforth, *Silsilah* Abdul Rauf.
32 Al-Sinkīlī, 'Umdat, M1. 107, fol. 112.
33 A.H. Johns, 'Islam in Southeast Asia: Reflections and New Directions', *Indonesia*, 19 (1975), 48–54; 'Islam in Southeast Asia: Problems of Perspective', in C.D. Cowan & O.W. Wolters (eds), *Southeast Asian History and Historiography: Essays Presented to D.G.E. Hall*, Ithaca, NY: Cornell University Press, 1976, esp. 316–9.
34 See the complete Malay text printed in Voorhoeve, *Bayān Tajallī*, 18. This text of al-Kūrānī's is not listed in various bibliographies of his works. In the Malay-Indonesian world it is known through its translation into the *Jāwī* language by Katib Seri Raja. The work begins with passages that are said to have been taken from Jalāl al-Dīn al-Suyūṭī's *Sharḥ bi Sharḥ Ḥāl al-Mawt wa al-Qubr*, giving a detailed description of events on the eve of one's death.
35 Al-Sinkīlī, *'Umdat*, M1. 107, fol. 113.
36 Al-Muḥibbī, *Khulāṣat al-Athar*, I; 25–8; Brockelmann, *GAL*, II, 393; al-Baghdādī, *Hadiyyat al-'Ārifīn*, I, 33; For his further connections in the networks, see al-Kattānī, *Fahras*, I, 169, 183, 211, 212, 386; II, 576, 587, 767, 808.

37 Al-Murādī, *Silk al-Durar*, III, 229–30.
38 See Snouck Hurgronje, *The Achehnese*, II, 10, 18-9. I was unable to inspect these *silsilah*s myself.
39 See Rinkes, *Abdoerraoef*, 25; Snouck Hurgronje, *The Achehnese*, II, 18; Voorhoeve, *Bayān Tajallī*, 2; Iskandar, 'Abdurrauf', 72–3; Johns, 'Reflections', 47.
40 Hasjmi, 'Sjekh Abdurrauf', 375; Cf. K.F.H. van Langen, 'Susunan Pemerintahan Aceh semasa Kesultanan', trans. Aboe Bakar, Banda Aceh: PDIA, 1986, 42–4, 54–9. The original article in Dutch is 'De inrichting van het Atjehsche staatsbestuur onder het Sultanaat', *BKI*, 37 (1888), 382–471.
41 R.H. Djajadiningrat, *Kesultanan Aceh*, trans. Teuku Hamid, Banda Aceh: Dep. P&K, 1982/3, 27. This is a translation of 'Critisch overzicht van de in Maleische werken vervatte gegevens over de Geschiedenis van het Soeltanaat van Atjeh', *BKI*, 65 (1911), 135–265.
42 For complete account of the delegation, see C. Snouck Hurgronje, 'Een Mekkaansch gezantschap naar Atjeh in 1683', *BKI*, 37 (1888), 545–54; Djajadiningrat, *Kesultanan*, 58–9.
43 Aḥmad Daḥlān, *Khulāṣat al-Kalām fī Bayān Umarā' al-Balad al-Ḥarām*, Cairo: n.p., 1305/1888, 104–5. Snouck Hurgronje points out that he based his accounts on Daḥlān's work. The information was also copied by Aḥmad al-Sibā'ī, *Tārīkh Makkah*, 2 vols, Riyad(?): al-Mamlakat al-'Arabiyyat al-Su'ūdiyyah, 1404/1984, II, 388.
44 Snouck Hurgronje, 'Een Mekkaansch', 144.
45 See al-Sinkīlī, *Mir'āt al-Ṭullāb*, MS Jakarta National Library, Ml 445, cited in Harun, 'Hakekat Tafsir', 27.
46 Djajadiningrat, *Kesultanan*, 60. For further accounts of the Jamāl al-Layl Dynasty, see D. Crecelius & E.A. Beardow, 'A Reputed Acehnese Sarakata of the Jamāl al-Lail Dynasty', *JMBRAS*, 52, 2 (1979), 51–66.
47 For a complete list of his works, see Voorhoeve, *Bayān Tajallī*, 35–53; Cf. Hasjmi, 'Syekh Abdurrauf', 377–8.
48 Al-Sinkīlī, *Mir'āt al-Ṭullāb*, printed in part in S. Keijzer, 'De spiegel voor leergierige wetgeleerden', *BKI*, 11 (1864), 221; Voorhoeve, *Bayān Tajallī*, 4.
49 For the locations of this work, see Voorhoeve, *Bayān Tajallī*, 36–7.
50 See al-Sinkīlī, *Mir'āt al-Ṭullāb*, MS Jakarta National Library, Ml 445, 1; cf. Zakariyyā al-Anṣārī, *Fatḥ al-Wahhāb bi Sharḥ Manhaj al-Ṭullāb*, Beirut: Dār al-Ma'rifah, 1978(?).
51 See Daly, 'Naskah Miratut Thullab', 137.
52 See M.B. Hooker, *Islamic Law in South-East Asia*, Singapore: Oxford University Press, 1984, 20, 32, 41 n. 98.
53 See 'Abd al-Ra'ūf b. 'Alī al-Fanṣūrī, *Kitāb al-Farā'id*, Singapore/ Jeddah: Ḥaramayn, n.d. Another edition is published in one volume with Ismā'īl al-Minangkabawī's *Kifāyat al-Ghulām*, Penang: n.d.

54 For further discussion on the growth of the Qur'ānic commentary tradition in the archipelago, see P. Riddell, 'Earliest Quranic Exegetical Activity in the Malay-Speaking States', *Archipel*, 38 (1989), 107–24; A.H. Johns, 'Quranic Exegesis in the Malay World: In Search of a Profile', in A. Rippin (ed.), *Approaches to the History of the Interpretation of the Qur'ān*, Oxford: Clarendon Press, 1988, 257–87; 'Islam in the Malay World: An Exploratory Survey with Some Reference to Quranic Exegesis', in R. Israeli & A.H. Johns (eds), *Islam in Asia: Volume II, Southeast and East Asia*, Boulder, CO: Westview Press, 1984, 115–61; R.M. Feener, 'Notes towards the History of Qur'anic Exegesis in Southeast Asia', *Studia Islamika: Indonesian Journal for Islamic Studies*, 5, III (1998), 47–76.

55 See Hasjmi, 'Syekh Abdurrauf', 378.

56 Riddell, *Transferring*, 20–5.

57 For complete accounts of various editions of the *Tarjumān al-Mustafīd*, see Riddell, *Transferring*, 15-33; Harun, 'Hakekat Tafsir', 38–42.

58 Snouck Hurgronje, *The Achehnese*, II, 17 n. 6.

59 Rinkes, *Abdoerraoef*, 31–2.

60 See Voorhoeve, *Bayān Tajallī*, 38; 'Abd al-Ra'ūf al-Sinkīlī', in E[1], I, 88.

61 His full name was 'Alā' al-Dīn b. Muḥammad b. Ibrāhīm al-Baghdādī al-Khāzin. For an edition of his commentary, see *Tafsīr al-Khāzin*, Cairo: Muṣṭafā al-Bābī al-Ḥalabī, 1375/1955. The original title of the commentary is *Lubāb al-Ta'wīl fī Ma'ānī al-Tanzīl*.

62 Johns, 'Quranic Exegesis', 264.

63 Johns, *Ibid*, 266.

64 *Ibid*.

65 Al-Sinkīlī, *Mawā'iẓ al-Badī'ah*, MS Jakarta National Library, Ml 341-A; Voorhoeve, *Bayān Tajallī*, 40; Iskandar, *Kesultanan*, 59.

66 For an outline of the *Mawā'iẓ al-Badī'ah*, see Rinkes, *Abdoerraoef*, 33–6.

67 Voorhoeve, *Bayān Tajallī*, 40.

68 Printed in one volume with 'Abd Allāh b. 'Abd al-Raḥīm al-Fatānī, *Muhimmah pada Ḥadīth Nabi*, Penang: Sulaymān Press, 1369/1949. Cf. Mohd Nor bin Ngah, *Kitab Jawi: Islamic Thought of the Malay Muslim Scholars*, Singapore: ISEAS, 1982, esp. 27–8, 35, 46.

69 See M. van Bruinessen, 'Kitab Kuning: Books in Arabic Script used in the Pesantren Milieu', *BKI*, 146 (1990), 255.

70 For a complete list, see Voorhoeve, *Bayān Tajallī*, esp. 39–40, 42–52.

71 A.H. Johns, 'Daḳā'ik al-Ḥurūf by 'Abd al-Ra'ūf of Singkel', *JRAS*, 1, 2 (1955), 55. The same argument is presented by al-Sinkīlī in *Shaṭṭāriyyah*, MS Jakarta National Library, Ml 336D, pp 65–71.

72 *Ibid*, 55.

73 Voorhoeve, *Bayān Tajallī*, 44; Rinkes, *Abdoerraoef*, 39.

74 The verses read: Kunnā ḥurūfan 'āliyātin lam nuqal//Muta'alliqātin fī dhurā a'lā al-qulal//Anā anta fīhi wa naḥnu anta wa anta hū//Wa al-kullu fī hū hū, fas'al 'amman waṣal. (We lofty letters, (yet) unuttered// held latent in the highest peaks of the hills//I am you in Him and we are you, and you are He//and all is He in Him ask those who have attained.) Cited in Johns, 'Daḳā'ik al-Ḥurūf', 61, 69.

75 A. Marie Schimmel similarly praises the way al-Sinkīlī interprets the verses. See Schimmel, 'The Primordial Dot: Some Thoughts about Sufi Letter Mysticism', *Jerusalem Studies in Arabic and Islam (JSAI)*, 9 (1987), 354.

76 Johns, 'Daḳā'ik al-Ḥurūf', 56.

77 *Ibid.*

78 See al-Sinkīlī, *Shaṭṭāriyyah*, MS Jakarta National Library, Ml 336D, p. 74; Johns, 'Daḳā'ik al-Ḥurūf', 154–5.

79 See Ibrāhīm al-Kūrānī, *Itḥāf al-Dhakī bi Sharḥ al Tuḥfat al-Mursalah ilā Rūḥ al-Nabī*, Cairo, MS Dār al-Kutub al-Miṣriyyah, *Taṣawwuf* 2578, fols 14, 20. Cf. al-Sinkīlī, *Shaṭṭāriyyah*, MS Jakarta National Library, Ml 336D, 74.

80 Johns, 'Daḳā'ik al-Ḥurūf', 150, 157. Cf. al-Kūrānī, *Itḥāf al-Dhakī*, fols 6, 9, 11, 15.

81 For a complete description of al-Sinkīlī's method of *dhikr*, see al-Sinkīlī, *'Umdat al-Muḥtājīn*, MS Jakarta National Library, Ml 375, pp. 35–40; *Shaṭṭāriyyah*, MS Jakarta National Library, Ml 336D, p. 74; Rinkes, *Abdoerraoef*, 59–93. Cf. Aḥmad al-Qushāshī, *al-Simṭ al-Majīd fī Sha'n al-Bay'ah wa al-Dhikr wa Talqīnih wa Salāsil Ahl al-Tawḥīd*, Hayderabad: Dā'irat al-Ma'ārif al-Niẓāmiyyah, 1327/1909, esp. 15–21, 30–1; cf. Fathurahman, *Tanbih al-Masyi*, 36–192.

82 See Voorhoeve, *Bayān Tajallī*, 47–8. Cf. al-Qushāshī, *al-Simṭ al-Majīd*, 11–15, 33–6.

83 Johns, 'Daḳā'ik al-Ḥurūf', 143, 153–4. The Arabic text of the *ḥadīth* runs as follows: 'Lā yarmī rajulun rajulan bi al-fusūqi wa lā yarmīhi bi al-kufri illā irtadda alayhi in lam yakun ṣāḥibuhu kadhālik.' The ḥadīth is narrated by al-Bukhārī. See al-Bukhārī, *Ṣaḥīḥ al-Bukhārī*, Cairo: al-Sha'b, n.d., 44.

84 Johns, 'Reflections', 53.

85 See for instance, Snouck Hurgronje, *The Achehnese*, II, 19.

86 See R. LeRoy Archer, 'Muhammadan Mysticism in Sumatra', *JMBRAS*, 15, II (1937), 90, 93.

87 The full title of the work is *Tanbīh al-Māshī al-Mansūb ilā Ṭarīq al-Qushāshī*. See Voorhoeve, *Bayān Tajallī*, 35.

88 See J.S. Trimingham, *The Sufi Orders*, esp. 97–8.

89 See Snouck Hurgronje, *The Achehnese*, II, 10, 18–20, 216; Rinkes, *Abdoerraoef*, 57, 95; S.N. al-Attas, *Some Aspects of Sufism as Understood*

and Practised among the Malays, Singapore: Malaysian Sociological Research Institute, 1963, 28–9.

90 'Tuanku' is one of the highest title of *'ulamā'* in West Sumatra. This title as such cannot be inherited. See Hamka, *Ajahku: Riwajat Hidup Dr. H. Abd Karim Amrullah dan Perdjuangan Kaum Agama di Sumatra*, Jakarta: Djajamurni, 1967, 24 n. 1.

91 See *Silsilah* Abdul Ra'uf, Van Ronkel (ed.), 312–16; J.J. de Hollander (ed.), *Verhaal van den aanvang der Padri-onlusten op Sumatra door Sjech Djilal Eddin*, henceforth, *Ḥikāyat Jalāl al-Dīn*, Leiden: Brill, 1857, 5–6. For a fuller biography of Burhān al-Dīn, see Tamar Djaja, 'Sjech Burhanuddin (1646–1692)', in his *Pusaka Indonesia: Riwajat Hidup Orang-orang Besar Tanah Air*, Djakarta: Bulan Bintang, 1965, 282-90; Hamka, *Antara Fakta dan Khayal Tuanku Rao*, Jakarta: Bulan Bintang, 1974, 110–2, 128–57.

92 *Ḥikāyat Jalāl al-Dīn*, 6; *Silsilah Abdul Ra'uf*, 315. For a complete account of the *surau*, see Azyumardi Azra, 'The Rise and Decline of the Minangkabau Surau: A Traditional Islamic Educational Institution in West Sumatra during the Dutch Colonial Government', unpubl. MA thesis, Columbia University, 1988.

93 *Ḥikāyat Jalāl al-Dīn*, 6–9.

94 See Azyumardi Azra, 'The Surau and the Early Reform Movements in Minangkabau', *Mizan*, 3, II (1990), 64–85.

95 For complete accounts of 'Abd al-Muḥyī's biography and teachings, see Rinkes, *Abdoerraoef*, 96–6; 'De Maqām van Sjech Abdoelmoehji', *TBG*, 52 (1910), 556–89; Mohammad Kosasi, 'Pamidjahan en zijn Heiligdom', *Djawa*, 38 (Oct. 1938), 121–44; A.M. Santrie, 'Martabat (Alam) Tujuh: Suatu Naskah Mistik Islam dari Desa Karang, Pamijahan', in A.R. Hassan (ed.), *Warisan Intelektual Islam Indonesia*, Bandung: Mizan/LSAF, 1987, 105-29; A.W. Mu thi, 'Tarekat Syattariyah, dari Gujarat sampai Caruban', *Pesantren*, 4, III (1987), 7581.

96 H.W.M.S. Abdullah, *Perkembangan Ilmu Fiqh dan Tokoh tokohnya di Asia Tenggara I*, Solo: Ramadhani, 1985, 16, 46–9.

97 See Riddell, *Transferring*, 42–3.

98 A. Hasjmi, 'Pendidikan Islam dalam Sejarah', *Sinar Darussalam*, 63 (1975), 20–1. Cf. Hamka, *Antara Fakta*, 179–80.

99 Snouck Hurgronje, *The Achehnese II*, 17, 20; Riddell, *Transferring*, 43.

5 SEVENTEENTH CENTURY MALAY-INDONESIAN NETWORKS III

1 To mention some of the most recent studies on al-Maqassārī: Abū Hamid, 'Syekh Yusuf Tajul Khalwati: Suatu Kajian Antropologi Agama', unpubl. doctoral diss., Ujung Pandang: Universitas Hasanuddin, 1990; Tudjimah et al., *Syekh Yusuf Makasar: Riwayat Hidup,*

Karya dan Ajarannya, Jakarta: Dep. P&K, 1987; E.P.J. von Kleist, 'Ein indonesischer Muslim des 17. Jahrhunderts in Südafrika: Zwei Sendschreiben des Scheichs Yusuf Makassar', unpubl. MA thesis, Kapstadt: Albert-Ludwigs-Universität, 1986; Suleman Essop Dangor, *Shaykh Yusuf*, Durban: Kat Bros, 1982; H.A. Massiara, *Syekh Yusuf Tuanta Salamaka dari Gowa*, Jakarta: Yayasan Lakipadada, 1983; I.D. du Plessis, *Sjeg Joesoep*, Kaapstad: Nasionale Boekhandel, 1970; Nabilah Lubis, *Syekh Yusuf al-Taj al-Makasari: Menyingkap Intisari Segala Rahasia*, Bandung: Mizan, EFEO & FS UI, 1996; M.R. Feener, 'Syaikh Yusuf and the Appreciation of Muslim Saints in Modern Indonesia', *Journal for Islamic Studies*, 18/19 (1999), 112–31.

2 The work, entitled *Lontara Bilang*, is the oldest historiography of the Kingdoms of Gowa and Tallo in South Sulawesi. It is written in Macassarese according to the hijrah calendar, and has generally been considered reliable by historians of the region. The *Annals* is edited and translated into Dutch by A. Ligtvoet, 'Transcriptie van het dagboek der vorsten van Gowa en Tello', *BKI*, 28 (1880), 1259 (henceforth, *Dagboek*). Reference to al-Maqassārī's date of birth is given on p. 90. For discussion on the *Annals*, see J. Noorduyn, 'Origins of South Celebes Historical Writings', in Soedjatmoko et al. (eds), *An Introduction to Indonesian Historiography*, Ithaca, NY: Cornell University Press, 1965, 13755; A.A. Cense, "Old Buginese and Macassarese Diaries", *BKI*, 122 (1966), 416–28.

3 *Masuknya Islam di Sulawesi Selatan*, Ujung Pandang: Balai Penelitian Lektur, 1985–6, 43. Cf. Hamid, 'Syekh Yusuf', 104–5.

4 For a history of Islamisation of the region, see J. Noorduyn, 'De Islamisering van Makassar', *BKI*, 112 (1956), 247–66; C. Pelras, 'Religion, Tradition and the Dynamics of Islamisation in South Sulawesi', *Archipel*, 29 (1985), 107–35; Mattulada, 'Islam di Sulawesi Selatan', in Taufik Abdullah (ed.), *Agama dan Perubahan Sosial*, Jakarta: Rajawali, 1983, 209–321; *Bugis-Makassar dalam Peta Islamisasi Indonesia*, Ujung Pandang: IAIN Alauddin, 1982.

5 Mattulada, 'Islam', 236, 239–40; Pelras, "Religion", 121–2.

6 *Dagboek*, 105.

7 *Ibid*, 105.

8 See discussion in chapter 3 on al-Rānīrī.

9 Hawash Abdullah, *Perkembangan Ilmu Tasawwuf dan Tokoh-tokohnya di Nusantara*, Surabaya: Al-Ikhlas, 1980, 62–5; Hamka, 'Sjeich Jusuf Tadju'l Chalwati (Tuanta Salamaka), 1626–1699', in *Perbendaharaan Lama*, Medan: Madju, 1963, 40.

10 Al-Maqassārī, *Safīnat al-Najāh*, cited in Hamka, 'Sjech Jusuf', 40–1. Cf. Tudjimah et al., *Syekh Yusuf*, 22–3.

11 Al-Attas, *Rānīrī*, 13. I was unable to substantiate this account, as al-Attas gives no reference to it.

12 Al-Maqassārī, *al-Nafḥat al-Saylāniyyah*, Jakarta National Library, MS A 101, 25.
13 J.O. Voll, 'Linking Groups in the Networks of Eighteenth Century Revivalist Scholars: The Mizjaji Family in Yemen', in N. Levtzion & J.O. Voll (eds), *Eighteenth Century Renewal and Reform in Islam*, Syracuse, NY: Syracuse University Press, 1987, 72.
14 Al-Muḥibbī, *Khulāṣat al-Athar*, II, 283.
15 Al-Maqassārī, *al-Nafḥat al-Saylāniyyah*, MS A 101, 25; *Safīnat al-Najāh*, cited in Tudjimah et al., *Syekh Yusuf*, 23.
16 See al-Maqassārī, *Safīnat al-Najāh*, cited in Tudjimah et al., *Syekh Yusuf*, 23; Hamka, 'Sjech Jusuf', 40.
17 See Al-Muḥibbī, *Khulāṣat al-Athar*, III, 193.
18 *Ibid*, III, 192–3.
19 Al-Maqassārī, *al-Nafḥat al-Saylāniyyah*, MS A 101, 25; *Safīnat al-Najāh*, cited in Tudjimah et al., *Syekh Yusuf*, 23.
20 See MSS Yahuda 2393 and 2395 in R. Mach, *Catalogue of Arabic Manuscripts (Yahuda Section) in the Garrett Collection Princeton University Library*, Princeton, NJ: Princeton University Press, 1977, 205. Al-Kūrānī's commentary is not mentioned in al-Baghdādī's *Hadiyyat al-'Ārifīn*, nor in Brockelmann's *GAL*.
21 See N. Heer, *The Precious Pearl*: *Al-Jāmī's al-Durrah al-Fākhirah together with his Glosses and the Commentary of 'Abd al-Ghafūr al-Lārī*, Albany: State University of New York Press (1979), 13–15.
22 Al-Maqassārī, *al-Nafḥat al-Saylāniyyah*, MS A 101, 25.
23 See al-Kattānī, *Fahras*, II, 829.
24 See al-Maqassārī, *al-Nafḥat al-Saylāniyyah*, MS A 101, 25; Abdullah, *Perkembangan Ilmu Tasawwuf*, 60.
25 For a complete account of Muḥammad Mīrzā, see Al-Muḥibbī, *Khulāṣat al-Athar*, IV, 202–3.
26 For further details of Ayyūb al-Khalwatī's biography and works, see Muṣṭafā Fatḥ Allāh al-Ḥawawī, *Fawā'id al-Irtiḥāl wa Nata'ij al-Safar*, 3 vols, Cairo, MS Dār al-Kutub al-Miṣriyyah, Tārīkh 1093, II, fols 87–8; Al-Muḥibbī, *Khulāṣat al-Athar*, I, 428–33. For his connection in the networks, see al-Kattānī, *Fahras*, I, 133, 252, 497, 505; II, 558.
27 See al-Maqassārī, *al-Nafḥat al-Saylāniyyah*, MS A 101, 25; *Safīnat al-Najāh*, cited in Tudjimah et al., *Syekh Yusuf*, 23; Hamka, 'Sjech Jusuf', 40.
28 Hamka, 'Sjech Jusuf', 41; Tudjimah et al., *Syekh Yusuf*, 19.
29 See Djirong Basang (trans.), *Riwayat Syekh Yusuf dan Kisah Makkutaknang Daeng Mannuntungi*, Jakarta: Dep. P&K, 1981, 149–50; Anonymous, 'Riwajat'na Tuanta Salamaka Rigowa', typescript, Makasar: 1969, 19–20.
30 Hamid, 'Syekh Yusuf', 110; Hamka, 'Sjech Jusuf', 42.
31 Dangor, *Shaykh Yusuf*, 2–3; Hamid, 'Syekh Yusuf', 111.
32 Hamid, 'Syekh Yusuf', 111; Martin van Bruinessen, 'The Origins and

Development of the Naqshbandi Order in Indonesia', *Der Islam*, 67 (1990), 157.
33 'Hamka, 'Sjech Jusuf', 41–2.
34 A.M. Amansyah, 'Tentang Lontara Syekh Yusuf Tajul Halawatiyah', unpubl. typescript, Ujung Pandang: Perpustakaan Universitas Hasanuddin, 1975, 7–8.
35 Mattulada, 'Islam di Sulawesi Selatan', 241.
36 Pelras, 'Religion', 123–5.
37 'Hamid, 'Syekh Yusuf', 111–12.
38 'Hikajat Sjeich Joesoep van H.S.D. Moentoe Labbakang, Pangkadjene', unpubl. typescript, Coll. A.A. Cense, Leiden University, KITLV Or. 545–218, pp 56–7.
39 Dangor, *Shaykh Yusuf*, 3.
40 See Mattulada, 'Islam', 243–4; Hamka, 'Sjech Jusuf', 41–2; Pelras, 'Religion', 123–4.
41 See *Daghregister 1679*, 429; *Daghregister 1680*, 705; cf. A.A. Cense, 'De verering van Sjaich Jusuf in Zuid-Celebes', *in Bingkisan Budi*, Leiden: Sijhoff, 1950, 51.
42 Labbakang, 'Hikajat', 65; *Dagboek*, 154; Massiara, *Syekh Yusuf*, 62; Dangor, Shaykh Yusuf, 4; Hamid, 'Syekh Yusuf', 113.
43 B.H.M. Vlekke, *Nusantara: A History of Indonesia*, The Hague & Bandung: Van Hoeve, 1959, 177; M.C. Ricklefs, *A History of Modern Indonesia*, London: Macmillan, 1990, 175.
44 See *Daghregister 1679*, 429.
45 *Daghregister 1666–1667*, 140, 289, 292; *Daghregister 1670–1671*, 264, 273; *Daghregister 1674*, 12, 127, 157, 196, 271.
46 *Daghregister 1680*, 606.
47 G.W.J. Drewes, 'Sjech Joesoep Makasar', *Djawa*, 6 (1926), 84–5; B.J.O. Schrieke, *Indonesian Sociological Studies*, 2 vols, The Hague & Bandung: Van Hoeve, 1957, II, 242.
48 *Daghregister 1680*, 97, 269, 705.
49 Labbakang, 'Hikajat', 56–7; Basang (trans.), *Riwayat Syekh Yusuf*, 158–60; B.F. Matthes, 'Boegineese en Makassaarsche Legenden', *BKI*, 34 (1885), 449–52.
50 See F. de Haan, *Priangan: De Preanger-regentschappen onder het Nederlandsch bestuur tot 1811*, Batavia & 's-Gravenhage, Kolff & Nijhoff, 1912, III, 282; Drewes, 'Sjech Joesoep', 85.
51 For further accounts of the meeting between al-Maqassārī and 'Abd al-Muḥyī, see an untitled MS in the collection of al-Maqassārī's works, Jakarta National Library, MS A 101, 64.
52 Drewes, 'Sjech Joesoep', 85; Uka Tjandra Sasmita, *Musuh Besar Kompeni Belanda: Sultan Ageng Tirtayasa*, Jakarta: Nusalarang, 1967, 35–6.
53 *Ibid*, 35–6.

54 F.W. Stapel, *Geschiedenis van Nederlandsch-Indië, 5 vols*, Amsterdam: Joost van den Vondel, 1939, II, 414.
55 *Ibid*; Dangor, *Shaykh Yusuf*, 15.
56 For detailed accounts of Sultan Ageng's conduct of the war, see De Haan, *Priangan*, III, 238–78; Sasmita, *Musuh Besar Kompeni*, 38–46.
57 De Haan, *Priangan*, III, 282; Sasmita, *Musuh Besar Kompeni*, 46–7.
58 De Haan, *Priangan*, III, 282–3; *Dagboek*, 154; Drewes, 'Sjech Joesoep', 86. Cf. Sasmita, *Musuh Besar Kompeni*, 48–9.
59 Drewes, 'Sjech Joesoep', 85.
60 De Haan, *Priangan*, III, 283; Drewes, 'Sjech Joesoep', 86.
61 See for instance, A.L. Ab' Bakar (ed.), *Melayu Srilanka*, Kuala Lumpur: Gapena, 1990; B.A. Hussainmiya, *Orang Rejimen: The Malays of the Ceylon Rifle Regiment*, Bangi: Universiti Kebangsaan Malaysia, 1990; 'A Brief Historical Note on the Malay Migration to Sri Lanka', *Jebat*, 14 (1986), 65–92.
62 Of about 29 works attributed to al-Maqassārī, no fewer than eight were written in Srilanka: *al-Barakat al-Saylāniyyah, al-Nafaḥāt al-Saylāniyyah, al-Manhat al-Saylāniyyah fī al-Manhat al-Raḥmāniyyah, Kayfiyāt al-Munghi fī al-Ithbāt bi al-Ḥadīth al-Qudsī, Ḥabl al-Qarīd li Sa'ādat al-Murīd, Safīnat al-Najāh, Maṭālib al-Sālikīn, and Risālat al-Ghayāt al-Ikhtiṣār wa al-Nihāyat al-Intiẓār*. See the collection of al-Maqassārī's works in Jakarta National Library, MS A No. 101 and MS A 108; Tudjimah et al., *Syekh Yusuf*, 20–26; Voorhoeve, *Handlist of Arabic Manuscripts*, 539; Hamid, 'Syekh Yusuf', 155–60.
63 According to Hussainmiya, a number of Malay families in Srilanka at the present time still claim that they are descendants of prominent Malay-Indonesian rulers and princes who live as exiles on the island. Among them is Mas Ghaise Weerabangsa, who possesses a manuscript that states that his family descended from al-Maqassārī. See Hussainmiya, *Orang Rejimen*, 80, 86 n. 15.
64 Hussainmiya, *Orang Rejimen*, 38–8; T.J.P. Ahtmat J.P., 'Kedatangan Orang Melayu ke Srilanka', in Abu Bakar (ed.), *Melayu Srilanka*, 13–15.
65 Al-Maqassārī, *Safīnat al-Najāh*, cited in Hamka, 'Sjech Jusuf', 45.
66 Cf. his introductory notes to his works, written in Srilanka, in Tudjimah et al., *Syekh Yusuf*, 20, 22, 23–5, 26.
67 Hamka, 'Sjech Jusuf', 46–7; Tudjimah et al., *Syekh Yusuf*, 20. I was unable to substantiate this account from Indian and Dutch sources.
68 See al-Maqassārī, *Risalāt al-Ghayāt*, summarised in Tudjimah et al., *Syekh Yusuf*, 26, 107–10.
69 Among them were the *Bustān al-Salāṭīn, Ṣirāṭ al-Mustaqīm* of al-Rānīrī, *Sakarāt al-Mawt* and *Kitāb al-Farā'id* of al-Sinkilī. Rashid Ahmad also mentions that al-Maqassārī's works are found in Srilanka, but he gives no titles. There is also *Hidāyat al-Sālikīn* of 'Abd al-

Ṣamad al-Palimbānī, who is discussed in chapter 6. See Hussainmiya, *Orang Rejimen*, esp. 138–40; Rashid Ahmad, 'Gapena Pelopori Usaha Menjalin Hubungan yang Terputus', 26; A.S. Yahya, 'Budaya Bertulis Melayu Srilanka', 67–72; Arifin Said, 'Manuskrip Melayu di Srilanka', 73–6; Abu Hassan Sham, 'Malay Manuscripts and Srilanka', 153–60. All the last four articles are in Abu Bakar (ed.), *Melayu Srilanka.*

70 The fact that there were attempts among Malay-Indonesian exiles to collaborate with their fellow Muslims in the archipelago in struggles against the Dutch has been shown by Hussainmiya for the period of the eighteenth century. There is reason to believe that such connections also existed in the period of al-Maqassārī. See Hussainmiya, *Orang Rejimen*, 42–3.

71 J.S. Mayson, *The Malays of Capetown*, Manchester: J. Galt & Co, 1861, 11; I.D. du Plessis, *The Cape Malays*, Johannesburg: South African Institute of Race Relations, 1946, 2; F.R. Bradlow, 'The Origins of the Early Cape Muslims', in F.R. Bradlow & Margaret Cairns, *The Early Cape Muslims: A Study of Their Mosques, Genealogy and Origins*, Cape Town: A.A. Balkema, 1978, 81–90; C. Greyling, 'Schech Yusuf, the Founder of Islam in South Africa', *Religion in Southern Africa*, I, 1 (1980), 10–11; M.J. Swart, 'The Karamat of Sheik Yussef', *South African Panorama*, 6 (1961), 18.

72 See for instance, S.M. Zwemer, 'Islam at Cape Town', *MW*, 15, 4 (1925), 328; Du Plessis, The Cape Malays, 2; F.R. Bradlow, 'Islam at the Cape of Good Hope', *Suid-Afrikaanse Historiese Joernaal*, 13 (1981), 9; J.M. Cuoq, *Les Musulmans en Afrique*, Paris: Misoneuve & Larose, 1975, 490.

73 K.M. Jeffreys, 'Sheikh Joseph at the Cape', *Cape Naturalist*, 6 (1939), 195. For the earliest references to al-Maqassārī in South Africa, see François Valentijn, *Oud en Nieuw Oost-Indien*, Dordrecht/Amsterdam: 1724–6, III, 208–9; IV, 109, 123; V, 47; K. Scherzer, *Narrative of the Circumnavigation of the Globe by the Austrian Frigate Novara in the Years 1857, 1858 and 1859*, London: 1861, I, 245–8. For later accounts, see G. McCall Theal, *History and Ethnography of Africa South of the Zambesi*, 3 vols, London: Swan Sonnenschein, 1909, II, 263; A. van Selms, 'Yussuf (Joseph) Sheik', in W.J. de Kock (ed.), *Dictionary of South African Biographies*, 1968, 893; Greyling, 'Schech Yusuf', 15–6; Dangor, *Shaykh Yusuf*, 27–8.

74 Du Plessis, *The Cape Malays*, 4; Greyling, 'Schech Yusuf', 16.

75 Du Plessis, *The Cape Malays*, 4; Dangor, *Syekh Yusuf*, 29. Cf. Bradlow, 'Islam at the Cape', 16.

76 Dangor, *Shaykh Yusuf*, 59; Jeffreys, 'Sheik Joseph', 195.

77 Achmat Davids, 'Politics and the Muslims of Cape Town: A Historical Survey', *Studies in the History of Cape Town*, 4 (1981), 174,

177–9; Dangor, *Shaykh Yusuf*, 29; E.A. Walker, *A History of Southern Africa*, 3rd edn, London: Longmans, 1962, 72.
78 Zwemer, 'Islam at Cape Town', 327.
79 *Ibid*, 330.
80 See C. Thurnberg, *Travels in Europe, Africa and Asia*, 4 vols, London: F. Rivingston, 1795, I, 132–4.
81 Mayson, *The Malays*, 19–20.
82 Cited in I.D. du Plessis & C.A. Luckhoff, *The Malay Quarter and Its People*, Cape Town: A.A. Balkema, 1953, 36.
83 See L.Y. Andaya, *The Heritage of Arung Palakka: A History of South Sulawesi (Celebes) in the Seventeenth Century*, The Hague: Nijhoff, 1981, 273, 276–7.
84 *Ibid*, 273; Jeffrey, 'Sheikh Joseph', 195; Dangor, *Shaykh Yusuf*, 32.
85 *Dagboek*, 169; De Haan, *Priangan*, III, 283.
86 For a detailed description of al-Maqassārī's *karamat* (tomb), see I.D. Du Plessis, *The Cape Malays: History, Religion, Traditions, Folk Tales of the Malay Quarter*, Cape Town: A.A. Balkema, 1972, 4–5; du Plessis & Luckhoff, *The Malay Quarter*, 35–7; Dangor, *Syekh Yusuf*, 51–2; K.M. Jeffreys, 'The Karamat at Zandvlei, Faure. Sheikh Joseph in the East', *The Cape Naturalist*, 5 (1938), 15–17.
87 Van Selm, 'Yussuf (Joseph), Sheik', 893; Drewes, 'Sjech Joesoep', 86–7.
88 De Haan, *Priangan*, III, 284; *Dagboek*, 176; Drewes, 'Sjech Joesoep', 87.
89 For a detailed description of the reverence paid by Muslims in South Sulawesi to Al-Maqassārī, see Cense, 'De verering'; Hamid, 'Syekh Yusuf', 137–9.
90 De Haan, *Priangan*, III, 283–4.
91 Greyling, 'Schech Yusuf', 17.
92 Matthes, 'Boeginese', 451–2.
93 Al-Maqassārī, *al-Nafḥat al-Saylāniyyah*, MS A 101, 2.
94 Al-Maqassārī, *Maṭālib al-Sālikin*, MS A 101, 81–2.
95 Al-Maqassārī, *al-Nafḥat al-Saylāniyyah*, MS A 101, 23; *Maṭālib al-Sālikin*, MS A 101, 81; *Sirr al-Asrār*, MS A 101, 86; *Zubdat al-Asrār*, MS A 101, 31; *Daf' al-Balā*, in Tudjimah et al., *Syekh Yusuf*, esp. 99.
96 Al-Maqassārī, *al-Nafḥat al-Saylāniyyah*, MS A 101, 22; *Zubdat al-Asrār*, MS A 101, 32.
97 Al-Maqassārī, *Zubdat al-Asrār*, MS A 101, 38–9.
98 Al-Maqassārī, Tāj *al-Asrār*, MS A 101, 76–7; *Kayfiyat al-Munghi*, in Tudjimah et.al, 43–4. Cf. Hamid, 'Syekh Yusuf', 197–8.
99 Al-Maqassārī, *al-Nafḥat al-Saylāniyyah*, MS A 101, 2.
100 *Ibid*, 28; *Qurrat al-'Ayn*, MS A 101, 54–5.
101 Al-Maqassārī, *al-Fawā'ih al-Yūsufiyyah*, MS A 108, 80–1; *Tuḥfat al-Abrār*, MS A 101, 78–9; *al-Nafḥat al-Saylāniyyah*, MS A 101, 8–9.

102 Al-Maqassārī, *Zubdat al-Asrār*, MS A 101, 36–7; *Fawā'ih al-Yūsufiyyah*, MS A 108, 80–1.
103 Al-Maqassārī, *Zubdat al-Asrār*, MS A 101, 39.
104 'Abd al-Karīm al-Jīlī, *Universal Man*, extracts trans. with commentary T. Burckhardt, English trans. Angela Culme-Seymor, Paris: Beshara Publication, 1983, 39, 45, 48.
105 Al-Maqassārī, *Sirr al-Asrār*, MS A 101, 95.
106 Al-Maqassārī, *al-Nafḥat al-Saylāniyyah*, MS A 101, 12.
107 Al-Maqassārī, *al-Barakat al-Saylāniyyah*, MS A 108, 71. Cf. *al-Nafḥat al-Saylāniyyah*, MS A 101, 4–5.
108 Al-Maqassārī, *al-Fawā'ih al-Yūsufiyyah*, MS A 108, 83; *Qurrat al-'Ayn*, MS A 101, 52; *Sirr al-Asrār*, MS A 101, 94.
109 Al-Maqassārī, *Zubdat al-Asrār*, MS A 101, 37.
110 *Ibid*, 42.
111 Al-Maqassārī, *al-Fawā'ih al-Yūsufiyyah*, MS A 108, 82; *al-Nafḥat al-Saylāniyyah*, MS A, 101, 4; *Tāj al-Asrār*, MS A 101, 73–4.
112 Al-Maqassārī, *al-Nafḥat al-Saylāniyyah*, MS A 101, 4; Tāj *al-Asrār*, MS A 101, 74.
113 Al-Maqassārī, *Sirr al-Asrār*, MS A 101, 94.
114 Al-Maqassārī, *Maṭālib al-Sālikīn*, MS A 101, 85.
115 al-Maqassārī, *al-Nafḥat al-Saylāniyyah*, MS A 101, 23–4.
116 *Ibid*, 2.
117 *Ibid*, 24–5.
118 Al-Maqassārī, *al-Nafḥat al-Saylāniyyah*, MS A 101, 5, 24–5. I was unable to verify this citation, claimed to have been a statement of Ibn 'Arabī, in the latter's works.
119 Al-Maqassārī, *Tuḥfat al-Asrār*, cited in Tudjimah et.al., *Syekh Yusuf*, 114.
120 For a detailed exposition of devotional services related to *dhikr*, see al-Maqassārī, *Fatḥ al-Kayfiyyat al-Dhikr*, MS A 108, 62-66; *Tuḥfat al-Amr fī Faḍīlat al-Dhikr*, MS A 101, 78–80.
121 Al-Maqassārī, *Tuḥfat al-Amr*, MS A 101, 79.

6 NETWORKS OF THE *'ULAMĀ'* AND ISLAMIC RENEWAL

1 See Hamka, *Ajahku: Riwajat Hidup Dr. H. 'Abd Karim Amrullah dan Perdjuangan Kaum Agama di Sumatera*, Djakarta: Djajamurni, 1963, esp. 26ff; H.M. Federspiel, *Persatuan Islam: Islamic Reform in Twentieth Century Indonesia*, Ithaca, NY: Cornell University, Modern Indonesia Project, 1970, 4.
2 C. Geertz, *Islam Observed: Religious Development in Morocco and Indonesia*, New Haven & London: Yale University Press, 1968, 65–70.
3 See Deliar Noer, *The Modernist Muslim Movement*, Singapore: Oxford University Press, 1973, esp. 10–21, 30–3.

4 Federspiel, *Persatuan Islam*, 3.
5 *Ibid*, 4. Cf. Hamka, *Ajahku*, 26–7.
6 For accounts of the Sultanate Palembang, see M.O. Woelders, *Het Sultanaat Palembang 1811–1825*, Leiden: Nijhoff, 1975; P. de Roo de la Faille, *Dari Zaman Kesultanan Palembang*, trans. S. Poerbakawatja, Djakarta: Bhratara, 1971; Husni Rahim, *Sistem Ororitas dan Masa Kesultanan dan Kolonial cli Palembang*, Jakarta: Logos, 1998.
7 VOC 2934 Palembang to Batavia 10 Sept. 1758, fol. 70; VOC 3733 Resident's reply to Amsterdam's letters of 30 Nov. 1781 and 22 Nov. 1982, fol. 10. I am grateful to Professor Barbara W. Andaya for supplying these sources. She and Professor Leonard Andaya have generously shared some findings of their research concerning Palembang in this period.
8 See 'Palembang Manuscripts and Authors', in G.W.J. Drewes, *Directions for Travellers on the Mystic Path*, The Hague: Nijhoff, 1977, 198–241; T. Iskandar, 'Palembang Kraton Manuscripts', in C.M.S. Hellwig & S.O. Robson (eds), *A Man of Indonesian Letters: Essays in Honour of Professor A. Teeuw*, Dordrecht: Foris Publication, 1986, 67–72; R. Winstedt, *A History of Classical Malay Literature*, Kuala Lumpur: Oxford University Press, 1969, 152–3, 154.
9 Drewes, *Directions*, 220.
10 *Ibid*, esp. 219–21; Winstedt, *A History of Classical Malay*, 153, 154.
11 See 'Abd al-Razāq Al-Bayṭār (1253–1335/1837–1917), *Ḥilyat al-Bashar fī Tārīkh al-Qarn al-Thālith 'Ashar*, 3 vols, Damascus: Maṭbū'āt al-Majma' al-'Ilmī al-'Arabī, 1382/1963, I, 851–2. This is a biographical dictionary which provides us with accounts of al-Palimbānī's career in Arabia. Al-Palimbānī's connections with scholars in the networks are also mentioned in Muḥammad b. Muḥammad b. Yaḥyā Zabārah, *Nayl al-Waṭar min Tarājim Rijāl al-Yaman fī al-Qarn al-Thālith 'Ashar*, 2 vols, Cairo: al-Maṭba'ah al-Salafiyyah, 1350/1931, II, 30, and in 'Abd al-Ḥayy b.'Abd al-Kabīr al-Kattānī, *Fahras al-Fahāris*, 3 vols, Beirut: Dār al-Gharb al-Islāmī, 1402/1982, II, 697; III, 106.
12 See M.H. b. Dato Kerani M. Arshad, *Al-Tārīkh Salāsilah Negeri Kedah*, Kuala Lumpur: Dewan Bahasa & Pustaka, 1968, esp. 123–26. This work should be treated with caution because it contains curious stories which are difficult to accept. For a discussion of *Al-Tārīkh Salāsilah*, see Henri Chambert-Loir, 'Abdussamad al-Palimbani sebagai Ulama Jawi', in al-Palimbānī, *Sayr al-Sālikīn*, [vol. I], Romanised by A. Muin Umar, Banda Aceh: Musium Negeri Aceh, 1985/6, ix–x. An account of the dates of al-Palimbani's birth and death is also given in M. Chatib Quzwain, *Mengenal Allah: Studi mengenai Ajaran Tasawuf Syaikh Abdus-Samad al-Palimbani*, Jakarta: Bulan Bintang, 1984, 12.
13 Al-Bayṭār, *Ḥilyat al-Bashar*, II, 851.
14 See al-Palimbānī's own notes in the colophon of his *Sayr al-Sālikīn ilā 'ibādah Rabb al-'Ālamīn*, 4, Cairo: Muṣṭafā al-Bābī al-Ḥalabī, 1372/1953.

15 See Arshad, *Tārīkh Salāsilah*, 149–50.
16 Al-Bayṭār, *Ḥilyat al-Bashar*, II, 852. Al-Bayṭār accounts cited in this book was disputed by Wan Mohd. Shaghir Abdullah in his *Penyebaran Islam & Silsilah Ulama Sejagat Dunia Melayu Jilid 9*, Kuala Lumpur: Khazanah Fathaniyyah, 1421/2000, 6–14. He asserts that the date of al-Palimbānī's birth had not been originally given by *Tarikh Salasilah Kedah* nor by al-Bayṭār, but by a certain Haji Mahmud bin Muhammad Yusuf Trengganu, whom he claims to be a student of al-Palimbānī. According to Shaghir Abdullah Haji Mahmud wrote many manuscripts, but he fails to mention any.
17 Muhd Shaghir Abdullah, *Syeikh Abdush Shamad al-Palimbani*, Pontianak: al-Fathanah, 1983, 6–8; Quzwain, *Mengenal Allah*, 20.
18 Al-Bayṭār, *Ḥilyat al-Bashar*, II, 851.
19 For Ibrāhīm al-Zamzamī al-Ra'īs' complete biography and works, see 'Abd al-Raḥmān al-Jabartī, *'Ajā'ib al-Athar fī Tarājim wa al-Akhbār*, 3 vols, Beirut: Dār al-Jīl, n.d., I, 560–2; Al-Bayṭār, *Ḥilyat al-Bashar*, I, 33.
20 Al-Kattānī, *Fahras*, I, 539.
21 *Ibid*, II, 903.
22 For Ibrāhīm al-Ra'īs' connections in the networks, see al-Kattānī, *Fahras*, I, 145, 146, 254, 301, 539; II, 620, 697, 755.
23 See al-Jabartī, *'Ajā'ib al-Āthār*, II, 140–2; Al-Bayṭār, *Ḥilyat al-Bashar*, III, 1393–1405; Ismā'īl Bāshā al-Baghdādī, *Hadiyyat al-'Ārifīn*, 2 vols, Istanbul: Milli Egitim Basimevi, 1951, II, 349–50; al-Kattānī, *Fahras*, I, 355, 480; II, 623, 738, 757, 795, 893, 985, 1005, 1006, 1010, 1148, 1166; III, 183; Khayr al-Dīn al-Zarkalī, *al-A'lām: Qāmūs Tarājim*, 12 vols, Beirut: n.p., 3rd edn, VI, 352.
24 For lists of al-Murādi's works, see al-Baghdādī, *Hadiyyat al-'Ārifīn*, II, 349–50; al-Zarkalī, *al-A'lām*, VI, 352; Brockelmann, *GAL*, II, 379; S. II, 404.
25 Al-Jabartī, *'Aja'ib al-Athar*, II, 141. Cf. Al-Bayṭār, *Ḥilyat al-Bashar*, III, 1404.
26 Al-Jabartī, *'Aja'ib al-Athar*, II, 140. Cf. Al-Bayṭār, *Ḥilyat al-Bashar*, III, 1393.
27 Al-Baghdādī, *Hadiyyat al-'Ārifīn*, II, 349.
28 For al-Murādi's further connections in the networks, see al-Kattānī, *Fahras*, III, esp. 623, 738, 795, 985, 1010.
29 It is important to note that Muḥammad al-Jawharī's father (Aḥmad al-Jawharī) studied with 'Abd al-Allāh al-Baṣrī and Aḥmad al-Nakhlī when he visited the Ḥaramayn in 1120/1708, see al-Jabartī, *'Aja'ib al-Athar*, I, 364–6; al-Zarkalī, *al-A'lām*, I, 109; al-Kattānī, *Fahras*, I, 302–3.
30 See Muḥammad al-Jawharī's biography in al-Jabartī, *'Ajā'ib al-Athar*, I, 426–7.

31 Al-Kattānī, *Fahras*, I, 199, 229, 377, 406; II, 785, 796, 844–5, 985, 1128, 1147.
32 For more information on 'Aṭā' Allāh, see al-Jabartī, *'Ajā'ib al-Āthār*, I, 560; al-Kattānī, *Fahras*, I, 94, 121.
33 Al-Kattānī, *Ibid*, I, 200, 201.
34 *Ibid*, I, 535.
35 *Ibid*, I, 149; II, 903, 1128.
36 For 'Aṭā' Allāh's position in *ḥadīth* studies, see *Ibid*, II, 903, 985, 1128.
37 See P. Voorhoeve, 'Abd al-Ṣamad b. 'Abd Allāh al-Palimbānī', *EI*[2], I, 1960; Brockelmann, *GAL*, II, 371; Quzwain, *Mengenal Allah*, 13.
38 Al-Palimbānī, *Sayr al-Sālikīn*, III, 39, 178, 203.
39 Abdullah, *Syeikh Abdush Shamad*, 6, 39.
40 Al-Bayṭār, *Ḥilyat al-Bashar*, II, 851.
41 Abdullah, *Syeikh Abdush Shamad*, 39.
42 I find no MS or printed edition of this work, but al-Kattānī gives a five-page description of it in his *Fahras*, II, 695–700. For a detailed biography and works of Wajīh al-Dīn al-Ahdal, see Zabarah, *Nayl al-Waṭar*, II, 30–1; al-Zarkalī, *al-A'lām*, IV, 79.
43 Al-Kattānī, *Fahras*, II, 697.
44 Zabarah, *Nayl al-Waṭar*, II, 30–1. Cf. Abdullah, *Syeikh Abdush Shamad*, 39–40, who mentioned a Sayyid al-Maqrī, who was very probably Aḥmad b. Ḥasan al-Muqrī Al-Zabīdī, as having been present in al-Palimbānī's teaching sessions in Zabīd.
45 J.J. Ras, *Hikayat Banjar: A Study in Malay Historiography*, The Hague: Nijhoff, 1968, 49, 438–43; A. Basuni, *Nur Islam di Kalimantan Selatan*, Surabaya: Bina Ilmu, 1986, 10–33; A.G. Usman, *Urang Banjar dalam Sejarah*, Banjarmasin: Lambung Mangkurat University Press, 1989, 46–53: 'Kesultanan Banjar', in *Ensiklopedi Islam di Indonesia*, Jakarta: Departemen Agama, 1987/8, II, 487–93. For a concise treatment of the advance of Islam in Kalimantan as a whole, see Mrs Samuel Bryan Scott, 'Mohammedanism in Borneo: Notes for a Study of the Local Modifications of Islam and the Extent of Its Influence on the Native Tribes', *Journal of the American Oriental Society*, 33 (1913), 313–44.
46 Scott, 'Mohammedanism', 319–27.
47 See Basuni, *Nur Islam*, 40–2; Zafry Zamzam, *Syekh Muhammad Arsyad al-Banjari sebagai Ulama Juru Da'wah*, Banjarmasin: Karya, 1974, 3–4; Scott, 'Mohammedanism', 331–5.
48 For a complete biography of Muḥammad Arshad, see Zamzam, *Syekh Muhammad Arsyad*; Jusuf Halidi, *Ulama Besar Kalimantan: Sjech Muhammad Arsjad al-Banjari*, Martapura: Jajasan al-Banjari, 1968; Tamar Djaja, 'Sjeich M. Arsjad Bandjar', in his *Pusaka Indonesia*, Djakarta: Bulan Bintang, 1965, 309–17; Shaghir Abdullah, *Syeikh*

Muhd Arsyad al-Banjari, Matahari Islam, Pontianak: al-Fathanah, 1983; Abu Daudi, *Maulana Syekh Moh. Arsyad al-Banjari*, Martapura: Sullamul ulum, 1980; M.S. Kadir, 'Syekh Muhammad Arsyad al-Banjari Pelopor Da'wah Islam di Kalimantan Selatan', *Mimbar Ulama*, 6 (1976), 69–79.

49 K. Steenbrink, 'Syekh Muhammad Arsyad al-Banjari: 1710–1812, Tokoh *Fiqh* dan Tasawuf', in his *Beberapa Aspek tentang Islam di Indonesia Abad ke-l9*, Jakarta: Bulan Bintang, 1984, 91, 96. Cf. Halidi, *Ulama Besar*, 13; Zamzam, *Syekh Muhammad Arsyad*, 10; Kadir, 'Syekh Muhammad Arsyad', 73.

50 Zamzam, *Syekh Muhammad Arsyad*, 6. Cf. Steenbrink, 'Syekh Muhammad Arsyad', 92.

51 Halidi, *Ulama Besar*, 11–2; Abdullah, *Syeikh Abdush Shamad*, 11–2.

52 Zamzam, *Syekh Muhammad Arsyad*, 67; Steenbrink, 'Syekh Muhammad Arsyad', 92.

53 Halidi, *Ulama Besar*, 14–5; Halidi, *Syekh Muhammad Arsyad*, 7; C. Snouck Hurgronje, *Nasihat-nasihat C. Snouck Hurgronje semasa Kepegawaiannya kepada Pemerintah Hindia Belanda*, trans. Sukarsi, Jakarta: INIS, 1991, V, 898–9. This is an Indonesian edition of E. Gobée & C. Adriaanse (comp.), *Ambtelijke adviezen van C. Snouck Hurgronje, 1889–1936*, 2 vols, 's-Gravenhage: Nijhoff, 1959–65.

54 Snouck Hurgronje, *Nasihat-nasihat*, 900–1.

55 Zamzam, *Syekh Muhammad Arsyad*, 8–9; Halidi, *Ulama Besar*, 16.

56 Halidi, *Ulama Besar*, 18; Zamzam, *Syekh Muhammad Arsyad*, 10–11.

57 See Ph.S. van Ronkel, *Catalogus der maleische handschriften*, Batavia & 's-Gravenhage: Albrecht & Nijhoff, 1909, 403; G.F. Pijper, *Fragmenta Islamica: Studiën over het Islamisme in Nederlandsch-Indië*, Leiden: Brill, 1934, 64; Hawash Abdullah, 'Syekh Muhammad Nafis al-Banjari', in his *Perkembangan Ilmu Tasawwuf*, 121; Anon., 'Muhammad Nafis al-Banjari', in *Ensiklopedi Islam di Indonesia*, Jakarta: Departemen Agama, 1987/8, II, 616; H.M. Laily Mansur, *Kitab Ad-Durun Nafis: Tinjauan atas suatu Ajaran Tasawuf*, Banjarmasin: Hasanu, 1982, 6.

58 For a discussion on Muḥammad Nafīs' life and work, see Mansur, *Kitab ad-Durun Nafis*, esp. 14–59; Abdullah, 'Syekh Muhammad Nafis al-Banjari', 107–22; 'Muhammad Nafis al-Banjari', in *Ensiklopedi Islam*, II, 614–7.

59 Muḥammad Nafīs al-Banjārī, *al-Durr al-Nafīs*, cited in Abdullah, 'Syekh Muhammad Nafis', 108.

60 Abdullah, 'Syekh Muhammad Nafis', 109.

61 See Al-Bayṭār, *Ḥilyat al-Bashar*, II, 852; Abdullah, *Syeikh Abdush Shamad*, 35, 46.

62 For al-Sharqāwī's complete biography, see al-Jabartī, *'Ajā'ib al-Āthār*,

III, 375–80; Al-Bayṭār, *Ḥilyat al-Bashar*, II, 1005–7; al-Kattānī, *Fahras*, II, 1071–3; al-Zarkalī, *al-A'lām*, IV, 206.

63 For an account of al-Sharqāwī's visits to the Ḥaramayn and his other students there, see al-Kattānī, *Fahras*, I, 229.

64 Al-Jabartī, *'Ajā'ib al-Āthār*, III, 375–6; Al-Bayṭār, *Ḥilyat al-Bashar*, II, 1005–6. For further discussion of al-Sharqāwī's reformism, see P. Gran, *Islamic Roots of Capitalism: Egypt, 1760–1840*, Austin: University of Texas Press, 1979, esp. 21–2, 44–6, 56.

65 For al-Sharqāwī's further connection in the networks, see al-Kattānī, *Fahras*, I, 134, 150, 354, 377, 445, 486; II, 578, 713, 754, 776, 777, 778, 826, 890, 1008, 1067, 1143, 1161, 1163.

66 *Ibid*, I, 503–4.

67 'Muhammad Nafis', *Ensiklopedi Islam*, II, 616; Abdullah, 'Syekh Muhammad Nafis', 108.

68 For a further discussion of the contents of the *Durr al-Nafīs*, see Mansur, *Kitab ad-Durun Nafis*; Abdullah, 'Syekh Muhammad Nafis', 109–21.

69 Abdullah, 'Syekh Muhammad Nafis', 110.

70 Usman, *Urang Banjar*, 60; 'Muhammad Nafis', *Ensiklopedi Islam*, 615; Mansur, *Kitab ad-Durun Nafis*, 4.

71 For an excellent treatment of the rise and decline of the Patani Sultanate, see Ibrahim Syukri, *History of the Malay Kingdom of Patani*, trans. C. Bayley & J.N. Miksic, Athens, OH: Center for International Studies, 1985, 13–62.

72 See Syukri, *Ibid*, 21–38; A. Teeuw & D.K. Wyatt, *Hikayat Patani*, The Hague: Nijhoff, 1970, 10–20.

73 *Ibid*, 76–7.

74 *Ibid*, 78–9.

75 *Ibid*, 131.

76 *Ibid*.

77 '*Pondok*' literally means 'hut', but it has also been generally used to refer to a cluster of buildings, used collectively as a centre of Islamic education. The *pondok* is, thus, similar in characteristics to the *surau* and *pesantren*, existing in other parts of the archipelago. For further discussion of all of these terms, see Azyumardi Azra, 'The Rise and Decline of the Minangkabau *Surau*', unpubl. MA thesis, Columbia University, 1988, esp. 19–21; for further discussion of the *pondok* see Hasan Madmarn, *The Pondok and Madrasah in Patani*, Kuala Lumpur: Penerbit Universiti Kebangsaan Malaysia, 1999.

78 Virginia Matheson & M.B. Hooker, 'Jawi Literature in Patani: The Maintenance of an Islamic Tradition', *JMBRAS*, 61, I (1988), 43. Cf. R.L. Winzeler, 'The Social Organisation of Islam in Kelantan', in W.R. Roff (ed.), *Kelantan: Religion, Society and Politics in a Malay State*, Kuala Lumpur: Oxford University Press, 1974, 266, n. 7; cf. A.A.H. Hasan, 'The Development of Islamic Education in Kelantan',

in Khoo Kay Kim (ed.), *Tamaddun Islam di Malaysia*, Kuala Lumpur: Persatuan Sejarah Malaysia, 1980, esp. 190–6. For an account of the Patani *Pondok* in recent years, see W.K. Che Man, 'The Thai Government and Islamic Institutions in the Four Southern Muslim Provinces of Thailand', *Sojourn*, 5, II (1990), esp. 263–70.

79 Matheson & Hooker, 'Jawi Literature in Patani', 43; Hamdan Hassan, 'Pertalian Pemikiran Islam Malaysia-Aceh', in Kim (ed.), *Tamaddun Islam*, esp. 53–5.

80 H.W.M. Shaghir Abdullah, *Syeikh Daud bin Abdullah al-Fatani: Ulama dan Pengarang Terulung Asia Tenggara*, Kuala Lumpur: Hizbi, 1990, 3; Matheson & Hooker, 'Jawi Literature in Patani', 19, 28.

81 This work deals with *ḥadīth* forgeries: see a Beirut reprint of the Cairo(?) edition, 1343.

82 For a biography of Muḥammad Ṭāhir al-Hindī al-Faṭānī, see Abū al-Fallāḥ b. 'Abd al-Ḥayy Ibn al-'Imād, *Shadharāt al-Dhahab fī Akhbār man Dhahab*, 8 vols, Cairo: Maktabat al-Qudsī, 1350–1/1930–1, VIII, 410; Ṣiddīq b. Ḥasan al-Qannūjī, *Abjad al-'Ulūm*, 3 vols, Beirut: Dār al-Kutub al-'Ilmiyyah, n.d., III, 222–3; al-Kattānī, *Fahras*, I, 171; al-Zarkalī, *al-A'lām*, VII, 42–3; Brockelmann, *GAL*, II, 548; S. II, 601.

83 See Dāwūd al-Faṭānī's silsilah of the Sammāniyyah *ṭarīqah* in Abdullah, *Syekh Daud bin Abdullah*, 36–37.

84 *Ibid*, 37–8.

85 *Ibid*, 23–4.

86 P. Voorhoeve, 'Dāwūd b. 'Abd Allāh b. Idrīs al-Faṭānī or Faṭṭānī', *EI*², II, 183.

87 Abdullah, *Syeikh Daud bin Abdullah*, 22.

88 *Ibid*, 10–13. Neither the Hikayat Patani nor Syukri's *History of Patani* mentions Faqīh 'Alī or Datuk Maharajalela. The *Hikayat Patani* makes mention only of Faqīh or Shaykh Ṣafī al-Dīn (pp. 78–9) and Faqīh 'Abd al-Manān (p. 131).

89 Abdullah, *Syeikh Daud bin Abdullah*, 32.

90 *Ibid*, 32.

91 See A. Hasjmi, 'Pendidikan Islam di Aceh dalam Perjalanan Sejarah', *Sinar Darussalam*, 63 (1975), 20; *Sejarah Kebudayaan Islam di Indonesia*, Jakarta: Bulan Bintang, 1990, 230; Abdullah, *Syeikh Daud bin Abdullah*, 32; 'Syekh Muhammad Zain bin Faqih Jalaluddin Aceh', in his *Perkembangan Ilmu Fiqh*, 62–74; Amir Sutarga et al., *Katalogus Koleksi Naskah Melayu Museum Pusat*, Jakarta: Departemen P&K, 1972, 264, 276.

92 Abdullah, *Syeikh Abdush Shamad*, 6; *Syeikh Muhd Arshad*, 8–9; *Syeikh Daud bin Abdullah*, 32–3.

93 Abdullah, *Syekh Abdush Shamad*, 6; *Syeikh Daud bin Abdullah*, 33.

94 Abdullah, *Syeikh Daud bin Abdullah*, 39.

95 For al-Barrāwī's biography and works, see Muḥammad Khalīl

al-Murādī, *Silk al-Durar*, III, 273; al-Jabartī, *'Ajā'ib al-Āthār*, I, 366–7; al-Baghdādī, *Hadiyyat al-'Ārifīn*, I, 811; Brockelmann, *GAL*, S. II, 445; al-Zarkalī, *al-A'lām*, V, 283–4; al-Kattānī, *Fahras*, I, 223.

96 See al-Kattānī, *Fahras*, I, 102, 197, 535, 1078.

97 For Dāwūd al-Faṭānī's complete *isnād* of the *Uṣūl al-Dīn*, see Abdullah, *Syeikh Daud bin Abdullah*, 39.

98 *Ibid*, 38.

99 See Al-Shanwānī's biography in al-Jabartī, *'Ajā'ib al-Āthār*, III, 588; Al-Bayṭār, *Ḥilyat al-Bashar*, III, 1270–1; al-Zarkalī, *al-A'lam*, VII, 190; al-Kattānī, *Fahras*, II, 10789.

100 See al-Kattānī, *Fahras*, I, 229; II, 578, 777, 796.

101 Abdullah, *Syeikh Daud bin Abdullah*, 34, 35, 39.

102 See al-Faṭānī's silsilah of the Shādhiliyyah order in Abdullah, *Ibid*, 41.

103 See al-Kattānī, *Fahras*, I, 198–99.

104 Abdullah, *Syeikh Daud bin Abdullah*, 35.

105 See al-Kattānī, *Fahras*, I, 122–3; II, 1079.

106 See a partial list of his students in Abdullah, *Syekh Daud bin Abdullah*, 42, followed by accounts of the activities and roles of these students in furthering reformism in the archipelago on 43–50. Cf. Matheson & Hooker, 'Jawi Literature in Patani', 26–35, which gives the names of the most important Patani scholars together with their works in the period after Dāwūd al-Faṭānī.

107 Matheson & Hooker, 'Jawi Literature in Patani', 19.

108 For lists of his works and descriptions of their contents, see Abdullah, *Syeikh Daud bin Abdullah*, 55–99; Matheson & Hooker, 'Jawi Literature in Patani', 21–6; Winstedt, *A History of Classical Malay*, 153–4.

7 RENEWAL IN THE NETWORK

1 For a preliminary study of Malay-Indonesian students in the scholarly networks in the nineteenth century, see Azyumardi Azra, 'Ulama Indonesia di Ḥaramayn: Pasang dan Surutnya Sebuah Wacana Intelektual', *Ulumul Qur'an*, 3, III (1992).

2 Drewes, *Directions*, 217. Cf. Iskandar, 'Palembang Kraton Manuscripts', 68–9.

3 Drewes, *Directions*, 219.

4 For descriptive lists of Muḥammad Arshad's works, see Abdullah, *Syeikh Muhammad Arsyad*, 41–58; Zafry Zamzam, 'Karya Ar-Raniry dan al-Bandjari', *Sinar Darussalam*, 25 (1970), 449.

5 Muḥammad Arshad al-Banjārī, *Sabīl al-Muhtadīn li al-Tafaqquh fī al-Dīn*, MS Jakarta National Library, Ml 776, 2–4; Abdullah, *Syeikh Muhammad Arsyad*, 51; 'Syeikh Muhammad Arsyad', in *Perkembangan Ilmu Fiqh*, 81–2; Zamzam, 'Karya ar-Raniry dan al-Bandjari', 49; Mohd Nor bin Ngah, *Kitab Jawi: Islamic Thought of the Malay Muslim Scholars*, Singapore: ISEAS, 1982, 5.

6 Zamzam, 'Karya ar-Raniri dan al-Banjari', 49; Pijper, *Fragmenta*

Islamica, 65; Van Bruinessen, 'Kitab Kuning: Books in Arabic Script used in the Pesantren Milieu', *BKI*, 146 (1990), 250–1; 'Kitab Fiqh di Pesantren Indonesia', *Pesantren*, 6, I (1989), 48.

7 See Geertz, *Islam Observed*, 12–3; Noer, *The Modernist Muslim*, 12.

8 Muḥammad Arshad, *Sabīl al-Muhtadīn*, MS Jakarta National Library, Ml 776, 2–4. Cf. its printed edn, Cairo: 1343/1925, 3–4.

9 See Abdullah, *Syeikh Daud bin Abdullah*, 55–99; Matheson & Hooker, 'Jawi Literature in Patani', Winstedt, *A History of Classical Malay*, 153–4.

10 Abdullah, *Syeikh Daud bin Abdullah*, 99–100; Matheson & Hooker, 'Jawi Literature in Patani', 21; M.B. Hooker, *Islamic Law in South-East Asia*, Singapore: Oxford University Press, 1984, 32; Van Bruinessen, 'Kitab *Fiqh* di Pesantren', 48–9.

11 Dāwūd al-Faṭānī, *Hidāyat al-Muta'allim*, 5, cited in Abdullah, *Syeikh Daud bin Abdulah*, 103–4.

12 Al-Bayṭār, *Ḥilyat al-Bashar*, II, 851. The *Faḍā'il al-Iḥyā' li al-Ghazālī* is not listed in Malay sources among al-Palimbānī's works.

13 Al-Palimbānī, *Hidāyat al-Sālikīn*, Surabaya: 1933, 3.

14 See al-Palimbānī, *Hidāyat al-Sālikīn*, 5. The *Yawāqīt al-Jawāhir* of al-Sha'rānī was printed in Cairo in 1321/1904.

15 Al-Palimbānī, *Hidāyat al-Sālikīn*, 7–8. I was unable to trace the *Durr al-Thamīn*.

16 Al-Palimbānī, *Ibid*, 75. Neither al-Baghdādī nor Brockelmann list the *Bustan al-'Arifin* of al-Qushāshī, but both mention *Bustan al-'Abidin wa Rawdat al-'Arifin*, which is probably the same work. See al-Baghdādī, *Hadiyyat al-'Ārifīn*, I, 161; Brockelmann, *GAL*, II, 515.

17 Al-Palimbānī, *Hidāyat al-Sālikīn*, 273–4. What al-Palimbānī called the *Nafḥat al-Ilahiyyah* were probably al-Sammānī's *al-Futuhat al-Ilahiyyah fī al-Tawajjuhat al-Rūḥiyyah* and *al-Nafḥat al-Qudsiyyah*. See Brockelmann, *GAL*, S. II, 535.

18 Al-Palimbānī, *Sayr al-Sālikīn*, Cairo: Muṣṭafā al-Bābī al-Ḥalabī, 1372/1953, I, 3. Cf. H. Ritter, 'al-Ghazālī, Aḥmad b. Muḥammad', *EI2*, II, 1041.

19 See al-Palimbānī, *Sayr al-Sālikīn*, III, 168–84.

20 Some of al-Palimbānī's teachings are discussed in Quzwain, *Mengenal Allah*, esp. 32–138; M.U. el-Muhammady, 'The Islamic Concept of Education according to Shaykh 'Abdu's-Samad of Palembang and Its Significance in Relation to the Issue of Personality Integration', *Akademika*, 1 (1972), 59–83.

21 Al-Palimbānī, *Sayr al-Sālikīn*, III, 12–3.

22 See al-Palimbānī, *Hidāyat al-Sālikīn*, 270–2.

23 For al-Palimbānī's silsilah of the Khalwatiyyah *ṭarīqah*, see his *Sayr al-Sālikīn*, III, 39–40.

24 *Ibid*, III, 12–13. Cf. al-Sammānī, *al-Nafāḥāt al-Ilāhiyyah*, MS Jakarta National Library, no. DCLII.

25 Al-Palimbānī, *Hidāyat al-Sālikīn*, 285; *Sayr al-Sālikīn*, I, 16.
26 *Ibid*, III, 43–4.
27 See al-Muhammady, 'The Islamic Concept', esp. 75–83.
28 See al-Palimbānī, *Sayr al-Sālikīn*, III, 177–9.
29 *Ibid*, III, 180–1.
30 For a discussion of the *Ḥikam* or *Risālah fī al-Tawḥīd and Fatḥ al-Raḥmān*, see Drewes, *Directions*, 6–38.
31 Al-Palimbānī, *Sayr al-Sālikīn*, III, 180–1.
32 For the complete list of the works, see al-Palimbānī, *Ibid*, III, 182–4.
33 Cf. C.A.O. van Nieuwenhuijze, *Samsu'l-Dīn van Pasai*, Leiden: Brill, 1945, 24.
34 This work is not listed among the known works of al-Sinkīlī. But Voorhoeve, citing al-Palimbānī, mentions it in passing. See P. Voorhoeve, *Bayān Tajallī*, Banda Aceh: PDIA, 1980, 45.
35 The *Zād al-Muttaqīn*, which probably summarises al-Palimbānī's *Taṣawwuf* central doctrines, has not yet been recovered.
36 See al-Palimbānī, *Sayr al-Sālikīn*, III, 183.
37 *Ibid*, III, 171.
38 See al-Palimbānī, *Tuḥfat al-Rāghibīn fī Bayān Ḥaqīqat Imān al-Mu'minīn*, MS Jakarta National Library, Ml. 719, 2, 25–6.
39 *Ibid*, 26.
40 *Ibid*.
41 Al-Rānīrī, *Mā' al-Ḥayyāt li Ahl al-Mamāt*, a full romanised Malay text in A. Daudi, *Syeikh Nuruddin al-Raniri*, Jakarta: Bulan Bintang, 1978, 44–5. Al-Rānīrī's condemnation of the doctrine of *wujūdiyyah mulḥid* can be found in many of his other works. See for instance, in *Hujjat al-Ṣiddīq li Daf' al-Zindīq*, Malay text in Arabic script, 5–6, 9–10, in P. Voorhoeve, *Twee Maleise geschriften van Nūruddīn ar-Rānīrī*, Leiden: Brill, 1955.
42 See al-Palimbānī, *Tuḥfat al-Rāghibīn*, 19–26.
43 Halidi, *Syekh Muhammad Arsyad*, 11–2; Usman, *Urang Banjar*, 60–1; Mansur, *Kitab ad-Durun Nafis*, 4.
44 Halidi, *Syekh Muhammad Arsyad*, 12; Usman, *Urang Banjar*, 61; Mansur, *Kitab ad-Durun Nafis*, 4.
45 See al-Palimbānī, *Tuḥfat al-Rāghibīn*, 26.
46 See al-Palimbānī, *Sayr al-Sālikīn*, IV, 103.
47 See al-Ghazālī, *Iḥyā' 'Ulūm al-Dīn*, Cairo: 1387/1967, 4 vols, IV, 240.
48 Al-Burhānpūrī's work in Arabic and Javanese and their English renderings are given in A.H. Johns, *The Gift Addressed to the Spirit of the Prophet*, Canberra: Australian National University, 196S.
49 See al-Burhānpūrī, *The Gift*, 140.
50 See al-Palimbānī, *Sayr al-Sālikīn*, IV, 36, 123.
51 See al-Ghazālī, *Ihya'*, IV, esp. 85, 240.
52 See Van Ronkel, *Catalogus*, 402; *Ensiklopedi Islam*, II, 616; G.F. Pijper, *Fragmenta Islamica*, 64; Mansur, *Kitab ad-Durun Nafis*, 5–8.

53 For further analysis of the *Durr al-Nafīs*, see Mansur, *Kitab ad-Durun Nafis*, 14–59; Abdullah, 'Syeikh Muhammad Nafis'.
54 Mansur, *Kitab ad-Durun Nafis*, 42, 43, 45–50, 58; Abdullah, 'Sheikh Muhammad Nafis', 112, 116–17.
55 See Matheson & Hooker, 'Jawi Literature', 24; Abdullah, *Syeikh Daud bin Abdullah*, 61, 77.
56 Abdullah, *Ibid*, 109.
57 *Ibid*, 74, 111, 168. The *Kashf al-Ghumma* is listed among al-Sha'rānī's works. See Michael Winter, *Society and Religion in Early Ottoman Egypt: Studies in the Writings of 'Abd al-Wahhāb al-Sha'rānī*, New Brunswick: Transaction Books, 1982, 8.
58 Abdullah, *Ibid*, 62. For a lengthy exposition of the contents of the *Manhal al-Ṣāfī*, see Abdullah, 'Syeikh Daud bin Abdullah al-Fathani', in his *Perkembangan Ilmu Tasawwuf*, 121–46.
59 Al-Faṭānī, *Ward al-Jawāhir*, 55, cited in Abdullah, *Syeikh Daud bin Abdullah*, 107.
60 For further discussion of al-Faṭānī's *taṣawwuf*, see Abdullah, 'Syeikh Daud bin Abdullah al-Fathani', 24–58; *Syeikh Daud bin Abdullah*, 106–11.
61 For further discussion on al-Sha'rānī's defense of Ibn 'Arabī, see Michael Winter, *Society and Religion*, esp. 160–72. Cf. A. Ates, 'Ibn 'Arabī, Muḥyī'l-Dīn Abū 'Abd Allāh b. Muḥammad b. 'Alī b. Muḥammad. Al-'Arabī al-Ḥātimī al-Ṭā'ī', *EI*², III, esp. 710–11. For al-Suyūṭī's defense of Ibn 'Arabī against accusations of heresy and even unbelief, see E.M. Sartain, *Jalāl al-Dīn al-Suyūṭī*, 2 vols, Cambridge: Cambridge University Press, 1975, I, 36–7.
62 For a good summary of the modernists' accusations against Sufism, see Fazlur Rahman, *Islam*, 2nd edn, Chicago: University of Chicago Press, 1966, 212–34, 244–8.
63 See Halidi, *Ulama Besar Kalimantan*, 6–8; Zamzam, *Syekh Muhammad Arsyad*, 17–3; Usman, *Urang Banjar*, 56–9, 66–80.
64 G.W.J. Drewes, 'Further Data Concerning 'Abd al-Ṣamad al-Palimbānī', *BKI*, 132 (1976), 269, 274.
65 For MSS of this work, see Jakarta National Library, MSS no. CCIX and V.d.W. 51; Leiden University, F. Or. A 20c. For an outline of the contents of the *Faḍā'il al-Jihād*, see Ph.S. van Ronkel, *Supplement to the Catalogue of the Arabic Manuscripts preserved in the Museum of the Batavia Society of Arts and Sciences*, Batavia & The Hague: Albrecht & Nijhoff, 1913, 139–40.
66 C. Snouck Hurgronje, *The Achehnese*, 2 vols, trans. A.W.S. Sullivan, Leyden: Brill, 1906, 119–20.
67 See W.R. Roff, 'South-East Asian Islam in the Nineteenth Century', in P.M. Holt et al. (eds), *The Cambridge History of Islam*, Cambridge: University Press, 1970, II, 178–80. Cf. M.C. Ricklefs, *A History of Modern Indonesia*, London: Macmillan, 1981, 136–8.

68 See Drewes, 'Further Data', 267–9; Cf. M.C. Ricklefs, *Jogjakarta under Sultan Mangkubumi 1749–1792*, London: Oxford University Press, 1974, 134, 150–5.
69 The English translation of this letter is taken from Drewes, 'Further Data', 270.
70 Drewes, 'Further Data', 271–3. Most of English translations of this letter are also supplied by Ricklefs, *Jogjakarta under Sultan*, 151–2.
71 *Ibid*, 154.
72 Drewes, 'Further Data', 268–8.
73 Ricklefs, *Jogjakarta under Sultan*, 155.
74 *Ibid*, 154.
75 See Syukri, *History of Patani*, esp. 39–56, on renewed Thai attacks on Patani.
76 Abdullah, *Syeikh Daud bin Abdullah,* 94–5.
77 Matheson & Hooker, 'Jawi Literature in Patani', 25; bin Ngah, *Kitab Jawi*, 29 n. 12, 41 n. 3 and n. 5; 42 n. 8 and 9.
78 Abdullah, *Syeikh Daud bin Abdullah*, 34, 95.
79 Al-Faṭānī, *Hidāyat al-Muta'allim*, 17, cited in Abdullah, *Syeikh Daud bin Abdullah*, 95.
80 Al-Faṭānī, *Furū' al-Masā'il wa Uṣūl al-Wasā'il*, MS Jakarta National Library, Ml 779, 945ff; *Bughyat al-Ṭullāb*, I, 95, cited in Abdullah, *Syeikh Daud bin Abdullah*, 97–8.
81 C. Snouck Hurgronje, 'Een Arabisch bondgenoot der Nederlandsche regering', in *Verspreide Geschriften*, Bonn & 's-Gravenhage: Kurt Schroder & Nijhoff, 1924, VI, 85.
82 See Hamka, *Sejarah Islam di Sumatera*, Medan: Pustaka Nasional, 1950, 24; R. LeRoy Archer, 'Muhammadan Mysticism in Sumatra', *JMBRAS*, 15, II (1931), 103–4.
83 See Abdullah, 'Syeikh Burhanuddin', in his *Perkembangan Ilmu Tasawwuf*, esp. 57–9; Tamar Djaja, 'Sjech Burhanuddin (1646–1692)', in his *Pusaka Indonesia*, Djakarta: Bulan Bintang, 1965, 282–90.
84 For a detailed discussion of Islamic reformism, particularly in its relations to the Minangkabau economy during this period, see Christine Dobbin, *Islamic Revivalism in a Changing Peasant Economy*; Central Sumatra, 1784–1847, London: Curzon, 1983, esp. 117–54. See also, Dobbin, 'Islamic Revivalism in Minangkabau at the Turn of the Nineteenth Century', *Modern Asian Studies*, 8, III (1974), 319–56; Werner Kraus, *Zwischen Reform und Rebellion: über die Entwicklung des Islams in Minangkabau (Westsumatra) zwischen den beiden Reformbewegungen der Padri (1837) und der Modernisten (1908),* Wiesbaden: Franz Steiner, 1984, esp, 13–21, 43–61; Azyumardi Azra, 'The Surau and the Early Reform Movements in Minangkabau', *Mizan*, 3, II (1990), 64–85.
85 See J.J. de Hollander (ed.), *Verhaal van den aanvang der Padri-onlusten op Sumatra door Sjech Djilal Eddin* (henceforth, *Ḥikāyat Jalāl al-Dīn),* Leiden: Brill, 1857, 6.

86 *Ḥikāyat Jalāl al-Dīn*, 6–7.
87 For a further biography of Tuanku Nan Tuo, see Tamar Djaja, 'Tuanku Nan Tuo', in his *Pusaka Indonesia*, 318–27.
88 *Ḥikāyat Jalāl al-Dīn*, 9.
89 *Ibid*, 9–10.
90 *lbid*, 10–13; Dobbin, 'Islamic Revivalism in Minangkabau', 329–30; *Islamic Revivalism in a Changing Peasant Economy*, 127.
91 *Ḥikāyat Jalāl al-Dīn*, 9–11.
92 *Ibid*, 8.
93 *Ibid*, 8–9.
94 For further information on Jamāl al-Dīn, see for instance, Ph.S. van Ronkel, 'Een Maleisch getuigenis over den weg des Islams in Sumatra', *BKI*, 75 (1919), 363–78; A.H. Johns, 'Islam in the Malay World: An Exploratory Survey with Some Reference to Qur'ānic Exegesis', in R. Israeli & A.H. Johns (eds), *Islam in Asia: Volume II, Southeast and East Asia*, Boulder, CO: Westview, 1984, 124–6.
95 See Dobbin, 'Islamic Revivalism in Minangkabau', 3267; *Islamic Revivalism in a Changing Peasant Economy*, 121–4.
96 For complete accounts of the Padri Wars, see *Ḥikāyat Jalāl al-Dīn*, 13–54; Dobbin, *Islamic Revivalism in a Changing Peasant Economy*, 128–87; H.A. Stein Parvé, 'Oorsprong der Padaries: Eene secte op de Westkust van Sumatra', *TNI*, 1, I (1838), 113–31; 'De secte de Padaries (Padries) in de Bovenlanden van Sumatra', *TBG*, 3 (1855), 249–78; Ph.S. van Ronkel, 'Inlandsche Getuigenissen aangaande den Padrioorlog', *IG*, 2 (1915), 1099–1119, 1243–59; M.D. Mansur, *Perang Padri di Sumatera Barat*, Djakarta: 1964; M. Martamin, *Tuanku Imam Bonjol*, 2nd edn, Jakarta: Departemen P&K, 1984.

EPILOGUE

1 See Azyumardi Azra, *Renaisans Islam Asia Tenggara: Sejarah Wacana dan Kekuasaan*, Bandung: Remaja Rosda Karya, 1999, esp. 143–61; For recent research on al-Palimbānī, see Michael Feener, 'Yemeni Sources for the History of Islam in Indonesia: 'Abd al-Samad Palimbani in the Nafs al-Yamani', *La transmission du savoir dans le Monde Musulman pérephérique*, 1999, 19, 128–144. For further accounts of Shaikh Muḥammad Yāsin al-Padanī, who played a prominent role in the education of '*Jāwī*' students after World War II, see Azyumardi Azra, *Menuju Masyarakat Madani*, Bandung: Rosda, 1999: 52–5.
2 The Javanese scholarship has to be treated separately. M.C. Ricklefs has argued convincingly that the religious tendencies discussed in this work were also taking place in Java; see his *The Seen and the Unseen Worlds in Java 1726–1749: History, Literature and Islam in the Court of Pakubuwana II*, Sydney & Hawaii: Allen & Unwin and University of

Hawai'i Press, 1998. I would argue that at the beginning of the nineteenth century, Java as a whole had risen to be one of the important centres of Islamic intellectualism in the archipelago. A number of prominent *'ulamā'* appeared from Java, such as Aḥmad Rifā'ī of Pekalongan (1786–1876), Muḥammad al-Nawawī al-Bantanī (1813–1897), Muḥammad Saleh Darat al-Samaranī (from Semarang, d. 1903) and Muḥammad Maḥfūẓ al-Termasī (from Termas, East Java, d. 1919). For preliminary studies of each of them, see for instance, Peter Riddell, 'Muhammad al-Nawawi al-Jawi 1813–97)', in his *Islam and the Malay-Indonesian World: Transmission and Responses*, London & Singapore: C. Hurst & Horizon Books, 2001, 193–7; Didin Hafiduddin, 'Tinjauan atas Tafsir al-Munir Karya Imam Muhammad Nawawi Tanara', in Ahmad Rifa'i Hasan (ed.), *Warisan Intelektual Islam Indonesia*, Bandung: Mizan, 1987; Abdul Djamil, 'KH Ahmad Rifa'i Kalisalak: Studi tentang Pemikiran dan Gerakan Islam Abad Sembilan Belas (1786–1876)', doctoral dissertation, Program PascaSarjana IAIN Yogyakarta, 1999; HM Muchoyyar HS, 'Tafsīr Faiḍ al-Raḥmān fī Tarjamah Tafsīr Kalām Malik al-Dayyān Karya KHM Saleh al-Samaranī', doctoral dissertation, Program PascaSarjana IAIN Yogyakarta, 2002; Abdurrahman Mas'ud, 'Maḥfūẓ al-Tirmīsī (d. 1338/1919): An Intellectual Biography', *Studia Islamika*, 5, 2 (1998), 27–48.

3 C. Snouck Hurgronje, *Mekka in the Latter Part of the Nineteenth Century*, Leiden: E.J. Brill, 1931, 160.

4 Virginia Matheson & M.B. Hooker, 'Jawi Literature in Patani: The Maintenance of an Islamic Tradition', *JMBRAS*, 61, I (1988), 36.

5 See Peter Riddell, *Islam and the Malay-Indonesian World: Transmission and Responses*, London & Singapore: C. Hurst & Horizon Books, 2001, esp. 192–7; cf. M.F. Laffan, 'The Umma below the Winds: Mecca, Cairo, Reformist Islam and a Conceptualization of Indonesia', doctoral thesis, University of Sydney, 2000, published as *Islamic Nationhood and Colonial Indonesia; The Umma below The Winds*, London & New York: RoutledgeCurzon, 2003; Azyumardi Azra, 'The Transmission of *al-Manar*'s to the Malay-Indonesian World: The Cases of *al-Imam* and *al-Munir*', *Studia Islamika*, 6, 3 (1999), 75–100.

6 See Azyumardi Azra, 'Prof. Dr. Hamka: Pribadi dan Institusi MUI', in Azyumardi Azra & Saiful Umam (eds), *Tokoh dan Pemimpin Agama: Biografi Sosial-Politik*, Jakarta: Litbang Depag RI & PPIM IAIN Jakarta, 1998; cf. Nurwahidin, 'Pemikiran Tasawuf Hamka', MA thesis, Program PascaSarjana IAIN Jakarta, 1995; Karel Steenbrink, 'Hamka (1908–1981) and the Integration of the Islamic *Ummah* of Indonesia', *Studia Islamika*, 1, 3 (1994), 119–47.

7. See Harun Nasution, *Islam Rasional*, Bandung: Mizan, 1995; Saiful Mujani, 'Mu'tazilah Theology and the Modernization of the Indonesian Muslim Community', *Studia Islamika*, 1, 1 (1994), 91–131; Richard C. Martin & Mark R. Woodward with Dwi S. Atmaja, *Defender of Reason in Islam: Mu'tazilism from Medieval School to Modern Symbol*, Oxford: Oneworld, 1997, esp. Part II, 'Harun Nasution and Modern Mu'tazilism'.

BIBLIOGRAPHY

ABBREVIATIONS

BKI	Bijdragen tot de Taal-, Land- en Volkenkunde
BSOAS	Bulletin of School of Oriental and African Studies
EI^2	Encyclopedia of Islam, New Edition
GAL	Geschichte der Arabischen Litteratur
IG	De Indische Gids
JAAS	Journal of Asian and African Studies
JAS	Journal of Asian Studies
JIAEA	Journal of the Indian Archipelago and Eastern Asia
JMBRAS	Journal of Royal Asiatic Society, Malaysian Branch
JRAS	Journal of Royal Asiatic Society of Great Britain and Ireland
JSEAH	Journal of Southeast Asian History
TBG	Tijdschrift voor Indische Taal-, Land- en Volkenkunde
TNI	Tijdschrift voor Nederlandsch-Indie
VBG	Verhandelingen van het Koninklijk Bataviaasch Genootschap van Kunsten en Wetenschappen
VKI	Verhandelingen van het Koninklijk Instituut voor Taal-, Land- en Volkenkunde

PRIMARY SOURCES

Manuscripts

al-Banjarī, Muḥammad Arshad, *Sabīl al-Muhtadīn li al-Tafaqquh fī Amr al-Dīn*, MS Jakarta National Library, Ml 776.

al-Faṭānī, Dāwūd b. ʻAbd Allāh, *Furū' al-Masā'il wa Uṣūl al-Wasā'il*, MS Jakarta National Library, Ml 779.

al-Hamawī, Musṭafā Fatḥ Allāh (d. 1123/1711), *Fawā'id al-Irtiḥāl wa Natā'ij al-Safar fī Akhbār Ahl al-Qarn al-Ḥādī 'Ashar*, 3 vols, Cairo: MS Dār al-Kutub al-Miṣriyyah, Tārikh 1093.

al-Kūranī, Ibrāhīm (1023–1101/1583–1660), *al-Umam li Īqāẓ al-Himam*, Cairo: MS Dār al-Kutub al-Miṣriyyah, Mujami Tal'at 933 & 5040.

al-Kūranī, Ibrāhīm, *Masālik al-Abrār ilā Ḥadīth al-Nabī al-Mukhtār*, Cairo: MS Dār al-Kutub al-Miṣriyyah, Ḥadīth 2293, Microfilm 14904.

al-Kūranī, Ibrāhīm, *Itḥāf al-Dhakī bi Sharḥ al-Tuḥfat al-Mursalah ilā Rūḥ al-Nabī*, Cairo, MSS Dār al-Kutub al-Miṣriyyah, Taṣawwuf 2578, Microfilm 27651; Taṣawwuf 2954, Microfilm 10200.

al-Kūranī, Ibrāhīm, *al-Taḥrīrat al-Bāhirah li Mabāhith al-Durrat al-Fākhirah*, MSS Yahuda Section, the Garrett Collection, Princeton University 2393 and 2395.

al-Kūranī, Ibrāhīm, untitled [answers to questions coming from *min ba'ḍ jazā'ir Jāwah*], MS Leiden University, Cod. Or. 2467 (5660), fols. 12–31.

al-Maqassārī, Muḥammad Yūsuf, *al-Barakat al-Saylāniyyah*, MS A Jakarta National Library, 108.

al-Maqassārī, Muḥammad Yūsuf, *Fatḥ al-Kayfiyyat al-Dhikr*, MS A Jakarta National Library, 108.

al-Maqassārī, Muḥammad Yūsuf, *al-Fawā'ih al-Yūsufiyyah*, MS A Jakarta National Library, 108.

al-Maqassārī, Muḥammad Yūsuf, *Maṭālib al-Sālikīn*, MS A Jakarta National Library, 101.

al-Maqassārī, Muḥammad Yūsuf, *al-Nafhat al-Saylāniyyah*, MS A Jakarta National Library, 101.

al-Maqassārī, Muḥammad Yūsuf, *Sirr al-Asrār*, MS A Jakarta National Library, 101.

al-Maqassārī, Muḥammad Yūsuf, *Tāj al-Asrār*, MS A Jakarta National Library, 101.

al-Maqassārī, Muḥammad Yūsuf, *Tuḥfat al-Abrār*, MS A Jakarta National Library, 101.

al-Maqassārī, Muḥammad Yūsuf, *Tuḥfat al-Amr fī Faḍīlat al-Dhikr*, MS A Jakarta National Library, 101.

al-Maqassārī, Muḥammad Yūsuf, *Zubdat al-Asrār*, MS A Jakarta National Library, 101.

al-Palimbanī, 'Abd al-Ṣamad, *Tuhfat al-Rāghibīn fī Bayān Ḥaqīqat Imān al-Mu'minīn*, MS Jakarta National Library, Ml 719.

al-Palimbanī, 'Abd al-Ṣamad, *Naṣiḥat al-Muslimīn wa Tadhkirat al-Mu'minīn fī Faḍā'il al-Jihād wa Karāmat al-Mujāhidīn fī Sabīl Allāh*, MSS A Jakarta National Library, no. CCIX and V.d.W.51; Leiden University, F. Or. A20C.

al-Rānīrī, Nūr al-Dīn, *Jawāhir al-'Ulūm fī Kashf al-Ma'lūm*, MS Marsden Collection, SOAS, University of London, Text No. 12151; Leiden University, Cod, Or. A41; Jakarta National Library, Ml 795.

al-Rānīrī, Nūr al-Dīn, *Bustān al-Salāṭīn*, MS Leiden University, Cod. Or. 5443; MS. Raffles No. 8, Royal Asiatic Society.
al-Shāmī, 'Abd al-Shukūr, *Ziyādah min 'Ibārat al-Mutaqaddimīn min Ahl al-Jāwī*, Leiden: MS. F. Or. A 13d (17–18).
al-Sinkīlī, 'Abd al-Ra'ūf, *Bayān Tajallī*, MS Jakarta National Library, Ml 107B, and Ml 115A; Leiden University, Cod. Or. 1933.
al-Sinkīlī, 'Abd al-Ra'ūf, *'Umdat al-Muḥtājīn ilā Sulūk Maslak al-Mufradīn*, MS Jakarta National Library, Ml 107B, pp 120–227; Ml 375, pp 20–141.
al-Sinkīlī, 'Abd al-Ra'ūf, *Mir'at al-Ṭullāb*, MS Jakarta National Library, Ml 445.
al-Sinkīlī, 'Abd al-Ra'ūf, *Mawā'iẓ al-Badī'ah*, MS Jakarta National Library, Ml 341A.
al-Sinkīlī, 'Abd al-Ra'ūf, *Shaṭṭāriyyah*, MS Jakarta National Library, Ml 336D, pp 66–82.
al-Sinkīlī, 'Ahd al-Ra'ūf, *Tanbīh al-Māshī*, MS Jakarta National Library, A101.

Printed

al-Abdarī, Ibn al-Ḥajj (d. 738/1336–7), *al-Madkhal*, 4 vols, Cairo: Muṣṭafā al-Bābī al-Ḥalabī, 1380/1960.
Adat Aceh, Arabic text romanised by R. Harun & T.R.M.A. Gani, Jakarta: Departemen P&K, 1985.
Adat Atjeh, ed. G.W.J. Drewes & P. Voorhoeve, VKI, 24, Leiden: KITLV, 1958.
al-'Ajamī, Ḥasan b. 'Alī (d. 1113/1701–2), *Ihdā' al-Laṭā'if min Akhbār al-Ṭā'if*, ed. Yaḥyā Maḥmūd Junayd Sa'atī, Ṭā'if: Dār al-Thaqīf, 1400/1980.
al-Anṣarī, Zakariyyā (d. 925/1519), *Fatḥ al-Wahhāb bi Sharḥ Manhaj al-Ṭullāb*, Beirut: Dār al-Ma'rifah, 1978 [?].
al-Azraqī, Abū al-Walīd Muḥammad b. 'Abd al-Allāh (d. 250/864), 'Kitāb Akhbār Makkah Sharrafahā Allāh Ta'ālā wa mā Jā'a fīhā min an-Āthār', in Wustenfeld (ed.), *Die Chroniken der Stadt Mekka*, Leipzig: Brockhaus, 1858, I.
al-Banjarī, Muḥammad Arshad, *Sabīl al-Muhtadīn li al-Tafaqquh fī Amr al-Dīn*, Cairo: 1343/1925.
al-Barzanjī, Muḥammad b. 'Abd al-Rasūl (1040–1103/1630–92), *Kitāb al-Ishā'ah li Ishārāt al-Sā'ah*, ed. Muḥammad Badr al-Dīn al-Na'sānī, Cairo: Maṭba'at al-Sa'ādah, 1325/1907.
al-Baṣrī, 'Abd Allāh b. Salīm (1048–1134/1638–1722), *Kitāb al-Imdād bi Ma'rifah 'Uluw al-Isnād*, Hayderabad: Dā'irat al-Ma'ārif al-Niẓāmiyyah, 1328/1910.
Bello, Muḥammad (d. 1243/1827), *Infāku'l Maysūrī [Infāq al-Maysūr]*, ed. C.E.J. Whiting, London: Luzac, 1957.

Braddell, T., ed. & trans., 'On the History of Acheen: Translations from the Majellis Ache', *JIAEA*, 5 (1851).

[al-Burhānpūrī, Muḥammad b. Faḍl Allāh, d. 1031/1620], *The Gift Addressed to the Spirit of the Prophet*, ed., trans. from Arabic and Javanese texts with annot. A.H. Johns, Canberra: The Australian National University, 1965.

Daghregister gehouden int Casteel Batavia vant passerende daer ter plaetse als over geheel Nederlandts-India, 31 vols, Batavia & The Hague, 1888–1931.

al-Daybā, 'Abd al-Raḥmān b. 'Alī (866–933/1462–1536), *al-Faḍl al-Māzi' 'alā Bughyat al-Mustafīd fī Akhbār Madīnah Zabīd*, ed. Yūsuf Shulhud, Sanā'a: Markaz al-Dirāsat wa al-Buhūth al-Yamanī, 1983.

al-Dihlāwī, Shāh Walī Allāh (1114–76/1702–62), *Anfās al-'Ārifīn*, Delhi: 1315/1897.

al-Dihlāwī, Shāh Walī Allāh, *Ḥujjat Allāh al-Bālighah*, 2 vols, ed. Sayyid Sābiq, Cairo: Dār al-Kutub al-Ḥadīthah, 1964.

al-Dihlāwī, Shāh Walī Allāh, 'Wahdatul Wujud and Wahdatul Shuhud: Unityism and Apparentism', trans. Fazl Maḥmūd al-Asīrī, in *Studies in Urdu Literature*, Santiniketan: Visbharati, 1954.

al-Dimashqī, 'Abd al-Qādir, b. Muḥammad al-Nu'aymī (d. 927/1527), *al-Dāris fī Tārīkh al-Madāris*, 2 vols, ed. Ja'far al-Husnī, Damascus [?]: Maktabat al-Thaqāfat al-Dīniyyah, 1988.

al-Fāsī, Taqī al-Dīn (775–832/1373–1428), *al-'Iqd al-Thamīn fī Tārīkh al-Balad al-Amīn*, 8 vols, Cairo: Maṭba'at al-Sunnat al-Muḥammadiyah, n.d.

al-Fāsī, Taqī al-Dīn, *Shifā' al-Gharam bi Akhbār al-Balad al-Ḥaram*, 2 vols Makkah: Maktabat al-Nahḍat al-Ḥadīthah, 1965. Also printed in Wustenfeld (ed.), *Die Chroniken der Stadt Mekka*, Leipzig: Brockhaus, 1859, II.

al-Fullānī, Ṣalīḥ (1166–1218/1752–1803), *Qaṭf al-Thamar fī Raf' Asānid al-Muṣannafat fī al-Funūn wa al-Āthār*, Hayderabad: Dā'irat al-Ma'ārif al-Niẓāmiyyah, 1328/1910.

al-Fullānī, Ṣalīḥ, *Iqāẓ Himam Ulī al-Abṣār*, Cairo [?]: Muniriyyah Press, 1355/1937.

al-Ghazālī, *Iḥyā' 'Ulūm al-Dīn*, 4 vols, Cairo: 1347/1967.

Hikayat Atjeh, ed. & annot. T. Iskandar, 's-Gravenhage: H.L. Smith, 1959.

[*Hikayat Jalāl al-Dīn*], in J.J. de Hollander (ed.), *Verhaal van den aanvang der Padri-onlusten op Sumatra door Sjech Djilal Eddin*, Leiden: Brill, 1857.

Hikayat Patani: *The Story of Patani*, eds. A.E. Teeuw & D.K. Wyatt, The Hague: Nijhoff, 1970.

Hikayat Raja-raja Pasai, ed. & trans. A.H. Hill, *JMBRAS*, 33, (1960).

Ibn Baṭṭūtah, *Riḥlah Ibn Baṭṭūtah*, ed. Talāl Ḥarb, Beirut: Dār al-Kutub al-'Ilmiyyah, 1407/1987.

Ibn Baṭṭūtah, *The Travels of Ibn Battutah*, trans. H.A.R. Gibb, Cambridge: University Press, 1958.

Ibn Fahd, 'Umar b. Fahd b. Muḥammad (812–85/1409–80), *Itḥāf al-Wara' bi Akhbār Umm al-Qurrā*, 3 vols, Makkah: Jāmi'ah Umm al-Qurrā, 1404/1893.

Ibn Faraj, 'Abd al-Qādir b. Aḥmad (d. 1010/1602), *al-Ṣilat wa al-'Uddah fī Tārīkh Bandar Juddah—The Bride of the Red Sea: A l0th/16th Century Account of Jeddah*, Arabic text ed., trans. and annot. by G.R. Smith and A. Umar al-Zayla, Durham, Eng.: Centre for Middle Eastern and Islamic Studies, 1984.

Ibn Fūdī, 'Abd Allāh (1180–1245/1766–1829), *'Idā' al-Nusūkh man akhadhtu 'anhu min al-Shuyūkh*, in M. Hiskett, 'Material relating to the State of Learning among the Fullani before Their Jihad', *BSOAS*, 19, I (1957).

[Ibn Fūdī, 'Abd Allāh b. Muḥammad], *Tazyīn al-Waraqāt*, ed. & trans. M. Hiskett, Ibadan: Ibadan University Press, 1963.

[Ibn Fūdī, 'Uthmān], *Shaykh 'Uthmān ibn Fūdī Ḥiṣn al-Afhām min Juyūsh al-Awhām*, ed., trans. with a commentary by F.R. Siddiqy, Kano: Quality Press, 1989.

[Ibn Fūdī, 'Uthmān], 'Unbelief in the Western Sudan: Uthman dan Fodio's 'Ta'līm al-Ikhwān'', ed., trans. and annot. B.G. Martin, Middle Eastern Studies, 4 (1967–8).

Ibn al-'Imād, Abū al-Fallāḥ b. 'Abd al-Ḥayy (d. 1089/1678), *Shadharat al-Akhbār man Dhahab*, Cairo: Maktabat al-Qudsī, 1350–1/1930.

Ibn Jubayr, 'Abd al-Ḥusayn Muḥammad b. Aḥmad, *The Travels of Ibn Jubayr*, trans. from Arabic with an introd. and notes by R.J.C. Broadhurst, London: Jonathan Cape, 1952.

Ibn Khālliqan, *Wafāyāt al-A'yān wa Anbā' al-Zaman*, 8 vols, ed. Ihsan Abbas, Beirut: Dār al-Thaqāfah, 1968–72.

al-Jabartī, 'Abd al-Raḥmān (1169–1239/1754–1822), *Tārīkh Ajā'ib al-Āthār fī al-Tarājim wa al-Akhbār*, 3 vols, Beirut: Dār al-Jil, n.d.

al-Jāhiz, Abī 'Uthmān 'Amr b. Babr (d. 257/868), *Kitāb al-Hayawān*, ed. 'Abd al-Salām Muḥammad Hārūn, Cairo: 1344–58/1925–39, VII.

al-Jīlī, 'Abd al-Karīm, *Universal Man*, extract trans. with commentary by T. Burkhardt, English trans. by Angela Culme-Seymor, Paris: Beshara, 1983.

al-Kūrānī, Ibrāhīm, *al-Umam li Īqāẓ al-Himam*, Hayderabad: Dā'irat al-Ma'ārif al-Niẓāmiyyah, 1328/1910.

[Lontara Bilang—Dagboek or Annals] of Gowa and Tallo, in A. Ligtvoet (ed.), 'Transcriptie van het Dagboek der Vorsten van Gowa en Tello', *BKI*, 4, IV (1880).

al-Muhibbī, Muḥammad Amīn (1061–1111/1651–99), *Khulāṣat al-Āthār fī A'yān al-Qarn al-Ḥādī 'Ashar*, 4 vols, Cairo, 1248/1867–8, repr. Beirut: Dār Ṣadīr, n.d.

al-Murādī, Muḥammad Khalīl (1173–1206/1759–91), *Silk al-Durar fī 'A'yān al-Qarn al-Thānī 'Ashar*, 4 vols, Beirut: Dār Ibn al-Hazm, 1408/1988.

al-Nahrawalī, Muḥammad b. Aḥmad b. Qutb al-Dīn (d. 949/1542), 'Kitāb al-I'lām bi A'lām Bayt al-Ḥaram', in Wustenfeld (ed.), *Die Chroniken der Stadt Mekka*, Leipzig: Brockhaus, 1857, III.

al-Nakhlī, Aḥmad (1044–1130/1639–1718), *Bughyat al-Ṭālibīn li Bayān al-Mashā'ikh al-Mutaḥaqqiqīn al-Mu'tamidīn*, Hayderabad: Dā'irat al-Ma'ārif al-Niẓāmiyyah, 1328/1910.

al-Palimbānī, 'Abd al-Ṣamad, *Sayr al-Sālikīn ilā 'Ibādah Rabb al-'Ālamīn*, 4 vols, Cairo: Muṣṭafā al-Bābī al-Ḥalabī, 1372/1953.

al-Palimbānī, 'Abd al-Ṣamad, *Sayr al-Sālikīn*, [vol. I], romanized by A.M. Umar, Banda Aceh: Museum Negeri Aceh, 1985/6.

al-Palimbānī, 'Abd al-Ṣamad, *Hidāyat al-Sālikīn*, Surabaya: 1933.

[Pires, Tomé], *The Suma Oriental of Tomé Pires*, ed. & trans. Armando Cortesao, London: Hakluyt, 1944.

al-Qushāshī, Aḥmad (991–1071/1583–1660), *al-Simṭ al-Majīd fī Sha'n al-Bay'ah wa al-Dhikr wa al-Talqīnih wa Salāsil Ahl al-Tawḥīd*, Hayderabad: Dāi'rat al-Ma'ārif al-Niẓāmiyyah, 1327/1909.

al-Qutbī, 'Abd al-Karīm b. Muḥibb al-Dīn (d. 1014/1605), *I'lām al-'Ulamā' al-A'lām bi Binā' al-Masjid al-Ḥaram*, ed. Aḥmad Muḥammad Jamāl, 'Abd al-Azīz al-Rifā'i & 'Abd Allah al-Jaburī, Riyāḍ: Dār al-Rifā'ī, 1403/1983.

al-Qutbī, 'Abd al-Karīm, *al-Barq al-Yamānī fī al-Fatḥ al-'Uthmānī*, Riyāḍ: Dār al-Yamāmah li al-Bahth wa al-Nashr wa al-Tarjamah, 1967.

al-Ramhurmuzī, Buzurg b. Shahriyar, *Kitāb 'Ajāyib al-Hind*: Livre les Merveilles de l'Inde, ed. P.A. van der Lith, French trans., L.M. Devic, Leiden: Brill, 1883–6.

al-Ramhurmuzī, Buzurg b. Shahriyar, *'Ajayib al-Hind: Les merveilles de l'Inde*, trans. L.M. Devic, Paris: Imprimerie de Charles Herissey, 1878. Also *The Book of Marvels of India*, trans. P. Quennel, London: Routledge, 1928.

al-Ramlī, Shams al-Dīn (d. 1004/1596), *Nihāyat al-Muḥtāj ilā Sharā al-Manhal fī al-Fiqh 'alā Madhhab al-Imām al-Shāfi'ī*, 8 vols, Miṣr: Muṣṭāfā al-Bābī al-Ḥalabī, 1967.

al-Rānīrī, Nūr al-Dīn, *Bustān al-Salāṭīn Bab II, Fasal 13*, ed. T. Iskandar, Kuala Lumpur: Dewan Bahasa dan Pustaka, 1966.

al-Rānīrī, Nūr al-Dīn, *Khabar Akhirat dalam Hal Kiamat*, Jakarta: Departemen P&K, 1983.

al-Rānīrī, Nūr al-Dīn, *Asrār al-Insān fī Ma'rifa al-Rūḥ wa 'l-Raḥmān*, ed. Tudjimah, Bandung: al-Ma'arif, 1961.

al-Rānīrī, Nūr al-Dīn, *Ṣirāṭ al-Mustaqīm*, ed. Aḥmad b. Muḥammad Zayn Muṣṭafā al-Faṭānī, Singapore: n.d.

al-Rānīrī, Nūr al-Dīn, *Ṣirāṭ al-Mustaqīm*, in the margin of Muḥammad Arshad al-Banjarī, *Sabīl al-Muhtadīn*, Singapore: Sulayman Mar'ie, n.d. [orig. unknown].

al-Sakhawī, Shams al-Dīn (831–902/1428–97), *Tuḥfat al-Laṭīfah fī Tārīkh al-Madīnat al-Sharīfah*, 4 vols, Cairo: Maṭba'at al-Sunnat al-Muḥammadiyah, 1376/1957.

al-Samhudī, Nūr al-Dīn 'Alī b. Aḥmad (911/1505), *Wafā' al-Wafā bi Akhbār Dār al-Muṣṭafā*, 3 vols, ed. Muḥammad Muḥy al-Dīn 'Abd al-Ḥāmid, Beirut: Dār al-Kutub al-'Ilmiyyah, 1373/1955.

al-Sha'rānī, 'Abd al-Wahhāb (899–973/1493–1565), *al-Ṭabaqāt al-Ṣughrā*, ed. 'Abd al-Qādir Aḥmad 'Aṭā, Cairo: Maktabat al-Qāhirah, 1390/1970.

al-Sha'rānī, 'Abd al-Wahhāb, *al-Ṭabaqāt al-Kubrā*, 2 vols, Cairo: Maktabah wa Maṭba'ah Muḥammad 'Alī Sabīh wa Awlāduh, [1965?].

al-Shawkanī, Muḥammad b. 'Alī (d. 1205/1791), *al-Badr al-Tali'*, 2 vols, Cairo: Maṭba'at al-Sa'ādah, 1348/1929.

Sejarah Melayu or Malay Annals, trans. C.C. Brown, Kuala Lumpur: Oxford University Press, 1970.

[Silsilah 'Abd al-Ra'ūf al-Sinkīlī], *Pasal pada Menyatakan Silsilah Tuan Syekh Abdul Ra'uf [sic] tatkala menuntut Ilmu Kepada Syekh Abdul [sic] Qusyasyi*, ed. Ph. S. van Ronkel in, 'Het Heiligdom te Oelakan', *TBG*, 64 (1914).

al-Sinkīlī, 'Abd al-Ra'ūf, *Mir'at al-Ṭullāb*, in S. Keijzer, 'Spiegel voor leergierige wetgeleerden', *BKI*, 11 (1864).

al-Sinkīlī, 'Abd al-Ra'ūf, *Kitāb al-Farā'iḍ*, Singapore & Jeddah: Haramayn, n.d.

al-Sinkīlī, 'Abd al-Ra'ūf, *Kitāb al-Farā'iḍ*, publ. in one vol. with Ismā'īl al-Minangkabawī, *Kifāyat al-Ghulām*, Penang: n.d.

al-Sinkīlī, 'Abd al-Ra'ūf, *Mawā'iẓ al-Badī'ah*, publ. in one vol. with 'Abd Allāh b. 'Abd al-Raḥīm al-Faṭānī, *Muhimmah pada Hadith Nabi*, Penang: Sulayman Press, 1369/1949.

al-Suyūṭī, Jalāl al-Dīn (d. 911/1505), *Ḥusn al-Muḥāḍarah fī Akhbār Miṣr wa al-Qāhirah*, Cairo: al-Mawsū'āt, n.d.

al-Suyūṭī, Jalāl al-Dīn, *al-Hijāj al-Mubayyināt al-Tafḍīl bayn al-Makkah wa al-Madīnah*, ed. 'Abd Allāh Muḥammad al-Darwīsh, Beirut: al-Yamāmah, 1405/1985.

'Tarikh al-Shihri', in R.B. Serjeant, *The Portuguese off the South Arabian Coast: Hadrami Chronicles*, Oxford: Clarendon Press, 1963.

Valentijn, F., *Oud en Nieuw Oost-Indiën*, 5 vols, Dordrecht: J. van Braam, 1724–6.

al-Zābidī, Murtaḍā (d. 1206/1791), *Tarwīh al-Qulūb fī Dhikr al-Muluk Banī Ayyūb*, ed. Ṣalāḥ al-Munajjid, Damascus: Majma al-Lughat al-'Arabiyyah, 1388/1968.

al-Zābidī, Murtaḍā, *Tāj al-'Arūs min Jawāhir al-Qāmūs*, 10 vols, ed. 'Abd al-Sattār Aḥmad Faraj, Kuwait: al-Turāth al-'Arabiyyah, 1385/1985.

al-Zābidī, Murtaḍā, *Kitāb Itḥāf al-Sādat al-Muttaqīn bi Sharh Asrār Iḥyā' 'Ulūm al-Dīn*, 10 vols, Cairo: n.p., 1893.

Unpublished Dissertations and Papers

Abdel Aal, Abdel Hamid, 'God, the Universe, and Man in Islamic Thought: The Contribution of Shah Waliullah of Delhi, (1703–1762)', PhD. diss., University of London, 1971.

Abu Hamid, 'Syekh Yusuf Tajul Khalwati: Suatu Kajian Antropologi Agama', doctoral diss., Universitas Hasanuddin, Ujung Pandang, 1990.

Amansyah, A.M., 'Tentang Lontara Syekh Yusuf Tajul Halawatiyah', typescript, Ujung Pandang: Perpustakaan Universitas Hasanuddin, 1975.

Anonymous, 'Riwajat'na Tuanta Salamaka Rigowa', typescript, Makasar: 1969.

Azra, Azyumardi, 'The Study of the 'Ulama': A Preliminary Research', MA thesis, Columbia University, 1989.

Azra, Azyumardi, 'The Rise and Decline of the Minangkabau Surau: A Traditional Islamic Educational Institution in West Sumatra during the Dutch Colonial Government', MA thesis, Columbia University, 1988.

Djamil, Abdul, 'KH Ahmad Rifa'i Kalisalak: Studi tentang Pemikiran dan Gerakan Islam Abad Sembilan Belas (1786–1876)', doctoral dissertation, Program PascaSarjana IAIN Yogyakarta, 1999.

[Fathurahman, Oman, 'Tarekat Syaṭṭāriyyah di Dunia Melayu-Indonesia; Kajian atas Dinamika Perkembangannya melalui Naskah-naskah di Sumatra Barat', doctoral diss., Program Pasca Sarjana, Universitas Indonesia, 2003.

[Galigo, Syamsul Bahri Andi, 'Syekh Yusuf Makasar dan Pemikiran Tasawufnya dalam al-Nafḥah al-Saylāniyyah', doctoral diss., Universiti Kebangsaan Malaysia, Kuala Lumpur, 1998.

Harun, Salman, 'Hakekat Tafsir Tarjuman al-Mustafid Karya Syekh Abdurrauf Singkel, doctoral diss, Institut Agama Islam Negeri, Jakarta, 1988.

'Hikayat Sjeich Joesoef van H.S.D. Moentoe Labbakang, Pangkadjene', typescript, Collection A.A. Cense, Leiden University, KITLV, Or. 545–218.

von Kleist, E.P.J., 'Ein indonesischer des 17. Jahrhunderts in Südafrika: Zwei Sendschreiben des Scheichs Yusuf Makassar', MA thesis, Albert-Ludwigs-Universitat, Kapstadt, 1986.

Laffan, M.F., 'The Umma below the Winds: Mecca, Cairo, Reformist Islam and a Conceptualization of Indonesia', PhD thesis, University of Sydney, 2000.

Muchoyyar H.S., H.M., 'Tafsir Faidl al-Rahman fi Tarjamah Tafsir Kalam Malik al-Dayyan Karya KHM Saleh al-Samarani', doctoral dissertation, Program PascaSarjana IAIN, Yogyakarta, 2001.

Nurwahidin, 'Pemikiran Tasawuf Hamka', MA thesis, Program Pasca-Sarjana IAIN, Jakarta, 1995.

Reid, A., 'A Religious Revolution', paper delivered at the Conference on the Anthropological and Historical Approaches to the Comparative Study of Islam, Washington University, St. Louis, 1989.

Sangidu, '*Wachdatul-Wujūd* dalam *Mā'ul-Chayāt li Ahlil-Mamāt*', doctoral diss., Universitas Gadjahmada, Yogyakarta, 2002.

Tjokrowinoto, R.S., 'Tindjauan Kitab Sirat 'l-Mustaqim (karangan Nur ad-Din ar-Raniri)', MA thesis, Universitas Gadjah Mada, Yogyakarta, 1964.
Woodward, M.R., 'The Shari'ah and the Doctrine: Muslim Law and Mystical Doctrine in Central Java', PhD diss., University of Illinois, Urbana-Champaign, 1985.

SECONDARY SOURCES

Books

'Abd Allāh, 'Abd al-Raḥmān Ṣāliḥ, *Tārīkh al-Ta'līm fī Makkah al-Mukarramah*, Jeddah: Dār al-Shurūq, 1403/1982.
'Abd al-Jabbār, 'Umar, *Durūs min Māḍī al-Ta'līm wa Ḥāḍirih bi al-Masjid al-Ḥaram*, Cairo: n.p., 1959.
'Abd al-Jabbār, 'Umar, *Siyar wa Tarājim ba'ḍ 'Ulamā'inā fī al-Qarn al-Rābi' 'Ashar li al-Hijrah*, Jeddah: Tihama, 1403/1982.
Abdullah, Hawash, *Perkembangan Ilmu Tasawuf dan Tokoh-tokohnya di Nusantara*, Surabaya: al-Ikhlas, 1980.
Abdullah, H.W.M. Shagir, *Syeikh Daud bin Abdullah al-Fatani: Ulama dan Pengarang Terulung Asia Tenggara*, Kuala Lumpur: Hizbi, 1990.
Abdullah, H.W. Muhd. Shaghir, *Perkembangan Ilmu Fiqh dan Tokoh-tokohnya di Asia Tenggara*, I, Solo: Ramadhani, 1985.
Abdullah, Muhd. Shaghir, *Syeikh Abduh Shamad al-Palimbani*, Pontianak: al-Fathanah, 1983.
Abdullah, Shaghir, *Syeikh Muhd Arsyad al-Banjari, Matahari Islam*, Pontianak: al-Fathanah, 1983.
Abdullah, H.W.M. Shagir, *Penyebaran Islam dan Silsilah Ulama Sejagat Dunia Melayu Jilid 9*, Pengenalan Siri Ke-10, Kuala Lumpur: Persatuan Pengkajian Khazanah Klasik Nusantara & Khazanah Fathaniyah, 2000.
Abu Bakar, Abdul Latiff (ed.), *Melayu Srilanka*, Kuala Lumpur: Gapena, 1990.
Abu-Nasr, Jamil, *The Tijaniyya: A Sufi Order in the Modern World*, London: Oxford University Press, 1965.
Ahmad, Aziz, *Studies in Islamic Culture in the Indian Environment*, Oxford: Oxford University Press, 1966.
Ahmad, Z., *Sekitar Kerajaan Aceh dalam tahun 1520–1675*, Medan: Manora, 1972.
Ahmed, Munir ud-Din, *Muslim Education and the Scholars' Social Status up to the 5th Century Muslim Era (11th Century Christian Era)*, Zurich: Verlag der Islam, 1968.
al-Akwā, Ismā'īl b. 'Alī, *al-Madāris al-Islāmiyyah fī al-Yaman*, Beirut: Mu'assasat al-Risālah, 1406/1986.
Al-'Amrī, Ḥusayn b. 'Abdullāh, *The Yemen in the 18th and 19th Centuries: A Political and Intellectual History*, London: Ithaca Press, 1985.

Andaya, B.W., *To Live as Brothers: Southeast Sumatra in the Seventeenth and Eighteenth Centuries*, Honolulu: University of Hawaii Press, 1993.

Andaya, L.Y., *The Heritage of Arung Palaka: A History of South Sulawesi (Celebes) in the Seventeenth Century*, The Hague: Nijhoff, 1981.

Andaya, L.Y., *The Kingdom of Johor: 1641–1720*, Kuala Lumpur: Oxford University Press, 1975.

Arberry, A.J., *Muslim Saints and Mystics*, London: Routledge & Kegan Paul, 1966.

Arnold, T.W., *The Preaching of Islam: A History of the Propagation of the Muslim Faith*, London: Constable, 1913.

Arshad, M.H. b. Dato Kerani, *Al-Tarikh Salasilah Negeri Kedah*, Kuala Lumpur: Dewan Bahasa dan Pustaka, 1968.

al-Asamī, 'Abd al-Mulk b. Ḥusayn, *Simṭ al-Nujūm al-'Awalī fī Abnā' al-Awātil wa al-Tawālī*, 4 vols, Cairo: al-Maṭba'at al-Salāfiyyah, 1379/1959.

Atjeh, Aboebakar, *Tarekat dalam Tasawuf*, Kota Bharu: Pustaka Aman, 1979.

al-Attas, S.M.N., *The Oldest known Malay Manuscript: A 16th Century Malay Translation of the 'Aqa'id of al-Nasafi*, Kuala Lumpur: University of Malaya Press, 1988.

al-Attas, S.M.N., *A Commentary on the Hujjat al-Siddiq of Nur al-Din al-Raniri*, Kuala Lumpur: Ministry of Culture, 1986.

al-Attas, S.M.N., *Islam dalam Sejarah dan Kebudayaan Melayu*, Kuala Lumpur: Universiti Kebangsaan Malaysia, 1972.

al-Attas, S.M.N., *The Mysticism of Hamzah Fansuri*, Kuala Lumpur: University of Malaya Press, 1970.

al-Attas, S.M.N, *Preliminary Statement on a General Theory of Islamization of the Malay-Indonesian Archipelago*, Kuala Lumpur: Dewan Bahasa dan Pustaka, 1969.

al-Attas, S.M.N., *Raniri and Wujudiyyah of 17th Century Acheh*, Singapore, MBRAS, 1966.

al-Attas, S.N., *Some Aspects of Sufism as Understood and Practised among the Malays*, Singapore: Malaysian Sociological Research Institute, 1963.

Auni, L., *The Decline of the Islamic Empire of Aceh, 1641–1699*, Jakarta: Departemen Agama R.I., 1996/7.

Azami, M.M., *On Schacht's Origins of Muhammadan Jurisprudence*, New York/Riyad: Wiley/King Saud University, 1985.

Azami, M.M., *Studies in Hadith Methodology and Literature*, Indianapolis: American Trust Publication, 1977.

al-'Azimabadī, 'Abī al-Ṭayyib Muḥammad Shams al-Ḥaq, *'Awn al-Ma'būd Sharḥ Sunan Abī Dāwud*, 14 vols, Medina: Maktabat al-Salāfiyyah, 1389/1969.

Azra, Azyumardi, *Islam Nusantara: Jaringan Global dan Lokal*, Bandung: Mizan, 2002.

Azra, Azyumardi, *Menuju Masyarakat Madani*, Bandung: Rosda, 1999.
Azra, Azyumardi, *Renaisans Islam Asia Tenggara: Sejarah Wacana dan Kekuasaan*, Bandung: Remaja Rosda Karya, 1999.
Azra, Azyumardi, *Jarikgan Ulama Timur Tengah dan Kepulanan Nusantara Ahad XVII dan XVIII*, Bandung: Mizan, 3rd edn, 1995.
Badawī, 'Abd al-Raḥmān, *La transmission de la philosophie grecque au monde arabe*, Paris: J. Vrins, 1968.
al-Baghdādī, Ismā'īl Bāshā, *Hadiyyat al-'Ārifīn: Asmā' al-Mu'allifīn 'Athar al-Muṣannifīn*, 2 vols, Istanbul: Milli Egitim Basimevi, 1951.
Baljon, J.M.S., *Religion and Thought of Shāh Walī Allāh Dihlawī, 1703–1762*, Leiden: E.J. Brill, 1986.
al-Bashīr, al-Ṭāhir Muḥammad 'Alī, *al-Adab al-Ṣūfī al-Sūdanī*, Khartoum: al-Dār al-Sūdaniyyah, 1390/1970.
Basuni, A., *Nur Islam di Kalimantan Selatan*, Surabaya: Bina ilmu 1986.
al-Bayṭār, 'Abd al-Razzāq (1253–1335/1837–1917), *Ḥilyat al-Bashar fī Tārīkh al-Qarn al-Thālith 'Ashar*, 3 vols, ed. Muḥammad Baḥjat al-Bayṭār, Damascus: Maṭbū'at Majmā' al-'Ilm al-'Arabī, 1383/1963.
Beg, M.A.J., *Persian and Turkish Loan-Words in Malay*, Kuala Lumpur: University of Malaya, 1982.
van den Berg, L.W.C., *Le Hadhramout et les colonies arabes dans l'archipel indien*, Batavia: Imprimerie de Gouvernement, 1889.
Berkey, J., *The Transmission of Knowledge in Medieval Cairo: A Social History of Islamic Education*, Princeton: Princeton University Press, 1992.
Bowen, J.R., *Sumatran Politics and Poetics: Gayo History, 1900–1989*, New Haven & London: Yale University Press, 1991.
Brockelmann, C., *Geschichte der Arabischen Litteratur*, 2 vols and 2 supplements, Leiden: Brill, 1943–49.
van Bruinessen, M., *Kitab Kuning, Pesantren, dan Tarekat: Tradisi-Tradisi Islam di Indonesia*, Bandung: Mizan, 1995.
van Bruinessen, M., *Tarekat Naqsyabandiyah di Indonesia*, Bandung: Mizan, 1992.
Bugis-Makassar dalam Peta Islamisasi Indonesia, Ujung Pandang: IAIN Alauddin, 1982.
Bulliet, R.W., *Islam: The view from the Edge*, New York: Columbia University Press, 1995.
Bulliet, R.W., *Conversion to Islam in the Medieval Period*, Cambridge, Mass.: Harvard University Press, 1979.
Bulliet, R.W., *The Patricians of Nishapur*, Cambridge, Mass.: Harvard University Press, 1972.
Chatelier, A. le, *Le confréries musulmanes de Hedjaz*, Paris: Ernest Leroux, 1887.
Chaudhuri, K.N., *Trade and Civilization in the Indian Ocean: An Economic History from the Rise of Islam to 1750*, Cambridge: University Press, 1985.

Clifford, H. & F.A. Swettenham, *A Dictionary of the Malay Language*, I, Taiping: 1894.

Coedès, G., *The Indianized States of Southeast Asia*, ed. W.F.Vella, trans. S.B. Cowing, Honolulu: East-West Center.

Cuoq, J.M., *Les musulmans en Afrique*, Paris: Maisonneuve & Larose, 1975.

Dahlān, Aḥmad Zaynī (d. 1305/1886), *Khulāṣat al-Kalām fī Bayān Umarā' al-Bilād al-Ḥaram*, Cairo: n.p., 1305/1888.

Dahlān, Aḥmad Zaynī, *Umarā' Bilād al-Ḥaram mundhu Awwālihim fī 'Aḥd al-Rasūl ḥattā al-Sharīf al-Ḥusayn b. 'Alī*, Beirut: al-Dār al-Muttaḥidah, n.d.

Dangor, Suleman Essop, *Shaykh Yusuf*, Durban: Kat Bros, 1982.

Daud, Ismail Che, *Tokoh-tokoh Ulama' Semenanjung Melayu*, Kota Bharu: Majlis Ugama Islam dan Adat Istiadat Melayu Kelantan, 1992.

Daudi, Abu, *Maulana Syekh Moh. Arsyad al-Banjari*, Martapura: Sullamul Ulum, 1980.

Daudy, Ahmad, *Allah dan Manusia dalam Konsepsi Nuruddin ar-Raniri*, Jakarta: Rajawali, 1983.

Daudy, Ahmad, *Syeikh Nuruddin Ar-Raniry*, Jakarta: Bulan Bintang, 1978.

Deschamps, H., *Histoire de Madagascar*, 3rd ed., Paris, 1965.

van Diffelen, R.W., *De leer der Wahhabieten,* Leiden: E.J. Brill, 1927.

Diradjo, Datuk Sangguno, *Mustiko Adat Alam Minangkabau*, Djakarta: Kementerian PP&K, 1955.

Djajadiningrat, R.H., *Kesultanan Aceh berdasarkan Bahan-bahan yang terdapat dalam Karya Melayu*, trans. T. Hamid, Banda Aceh: Departemen P&K, 1982/83. Dutch original is 'Critisch overzich van de in Maleische vervatte gegevens over de geschiedenis van het Sultanaat van Atjeh', *BKI*, 65 (1911).

Djajadiningrat, R.H., *Critische beschouwing van de Sedjarah Banten*, Haarlem: J. Enschedé, 1913.

Dobbin, C., *Islamic Revivalism in a Changing Peasant Economy: Central Sumatra 1784–1847*, London: Curzon, 1983.

Dodge, B., *Muslim Education in Medieval Times*, Washington, D.C.: The Middle East Institute, 1962.

Dohaish, Abdullatif Abdullah, *History of Education in the Hijaz up to 1925*, Cairo: Dār al-Fikr al-'Arabī, 1398/1978.

Doorenbos, J., *De Geschriften van Hamzah Pansoeri*, Leiden: Batteljee & Terpstra, 1933.

Drewes, G.W.J., *An Early Javanese Code of Muslim Ethics*, Bibliotheca Indonesica, 18, The Hague: KITLV & Nijhoff, 1978.

Drewes, G.W.J., *Directions for Travellers on the Mystic Path*, The Hague, Nijhoff, 1977.

Dunn, R.E., *The Adventures of Ibn Battuta: A Muslim Traveller in the Fourteenth Century*, Berkeley: University of California Press, 1989.

Eaton, R.M., *Sufis of Bijapur 1300–1700: Social Roles of Sufis in Medieval India*, Princeton: Princeton University Press, 1978.
Edmonds, C.J., *Kurds, Turks, and Arabs*, London: Oxford University Press, 1957.
Efendy, Huseyn, *Ottoman Egypt in the Age of the French Revolution*, trans. from the original Arabic with introd. and notes by. S.J. Shaw, Cambridge, Mass.: Harvard University Press, 1964.
Esin, Emel, *Mecca the Blessed, Madinah the Radiant*, London: Elek Books, 1963.
Fang, Liaw Yock, *Undang-undang Melaka*, The Hague: Nijhoff, 1976.
Faroqhi, Suraiya, *Herrscher über Mekka: Die Geschichte der Pilgerfahrt*, Munchen: Artemis Verlag, 1990.
Fathurahman, Oman, *Menyoal Wahdatul Wujud: Kasus Abdurrauf Singkel di Aceh Abad 17*, Bandung: Mizan & EFEO Jakarta, 1999.
Fatimi, S.Q., *Islam Comes to Malaysia*, Singapore: Malaysian Sociological Institute, 1963.
Federspiel, H.M., *Persatuan Islam: Islamic Reform in Twentieth Century Indonesia*, Ithaca, N.Y.: Cornell University, Modern Indonesia Project, 1970.
Fernandes, L., *The Evolution of a Sufi Institution in Mamluk Egypt: The Khangah*, Berlin: Klaus Schwarz, 1988.
Ferrand, G., *Relations de voyages et textes géographiques arabes, persans, et turks relatifs á l'Extrême-Orient*, Paris: Leroux, 1914.
Friedmann, Y., *Shaykh Ahmad Sirhindi: An Outline of His Thought and a Study of His Image in the Eyes of Posterity*, Montreal: Institute of Islamic Studies, McGill University Press, 1971.
de Gaury, G., *Rulers of Mecca, 1951*, repr. ed., New York: New York: Dorset Press, 1991.
Geertz, C., *Islam Observed: Religious Development in Morocco and Indonesia*, New Haven & London, Yale University Press, 1968.
Geertz, C., *The Religion of Java*, New York: Free Press, 1960.
Gibb, H.A.R. & H. Bowen, *Islamic Society and the West*, 2 vols, Oxford: Oxford University Press, 1957.
Gladney, D.C., *Muslim Chinese: Ethnic Nationalism in the People's Republic*, Cambridge, Mass.: Harvard University Press, 1991.
Glazer, N. & D.P. Moynihan, *Beyond the Melting Pot*, Cambridge, Mass.: MIT Press, 1974.
Goldziher, I., *Zur Charakteristik Gelal ud-Din us-Suyuti's und seiner literarischen Tätigkeit*, Vienna: 1872.
de Graaf, H.J., *De Regering van Sultan Agung, vorst van Mataram, 1613–1645, en die van zijn voorganger panembahan Seda-ing-Krapjak, 1601–1613*, VKI, 23, The Hague: Nijhoff, 1958.
de Graaf, H.J. & Th. G. Th. Pigeaud, *Kerajaan-kerajaan Islam di Jawa*, Jakarta: Grafiti, 1984, trans. from *De eerste Moslimse vorstendommen op Java: Studiën over de staatkundige geschiedenis van de 15de en 16de eeuw*, VKI, 69, Leiden: KITLV, 1974.

Gran, P., *Islamic Roots of Capitalism*, Austin: University of Texas Press, 1979.

Gullick, J.M., *Indigenous Political Systems of Western Malaya*, London: Athlone Press, 1965.

de Haan, F., *Priangan: De Preanger-regentschappen onder het Nederlandsch bestuur tot 1811*, Batavia & 's-Gravenhage: Kolff & Nijhoff, 1912, III.

Hāfiẓ, 'Abd al-Salām Hāshim, *Al-Madīnat al-Munawwarah fī Tārīkh*, Cairo: Dār al-Turāth, 1381/1972.

Halidi, Jusuf, *Ulama Besar Kalimantan: Sjech Muhammad Arsjad al-Bandjari*, Martapura: Jajasan al-Bandjari, 1968.

Hall, D.G.E., *A History of South-East Asia*, London: Macmillan, 1964.

Hamid, Abu, *Shaykh Yusuf: Seorang Ulama, Sufi dan Pejuang*, Jakarta: Yayasan Obor Indonesia, 1994.

Hamka, *Ajahku: Riwajat Hidup Dr. H. Abd Karim Amrullah dan Perdjuangan Kaum Agama di Sumatra*, Jakarta: Djajamurni, 1967.

Hamka, *Antara Fakta dan Khayal Tuanku Rao*, Jakarta: Bulan Bintang, 1974.

Hamka, *Dari Perbendaharaan Lama*, Medan: Madju, 1963.

Hamka, *Sejarah Islam di Sumatera*, Medan: Pustaka Nasional, 1950.

Haron, Muhammed, *Muslims in South Africa: an annotated bibliography*, Cape Town: South African Library, 1997.

al-Ḥasanī, 'Abd al-Ḥayy b. Fakhr al-Dīn, *Nuzhat al-Khawaṭīr fī Bahjat al-Masāmi wa al-Nawāzir*, 7 vols, Hayderabad: Dā'irat al-Ma'ārif al-'Uthmāniyyah, 1931–59.

Hashim, Muhammad Yusoff, *Kesultanan Melayu Melaka*, Kuala Lumpur: Dewan Bahasa dan Pustaka, 1989.

Hashim, Muhamad Yusoff, *Persejarahan Melayu Nusantara*, Kuala Lumpur: Teks Publishing Sdn. Bhd., 1988.

Hasjmi, A., *Sejarah Kebudayaan Islam di Indonesia*, Jakarta: Bulan Bintang, 1990.

Hasjmi, A. (ed.), *Sejarah Masuk dan Berkembangnya Islam di Indonesia*, 2nd ed., Bandung: al-Ma'arif, 1989.

Hasjmi, A., *Syiah dan Ahlussunnah saling rebut pengaruh sejak awal Sejarah Islam di Kepulauan Nusantara*, Surabaya: Bina Ilmu, 1983.

Hasjmi, A., *Kebudayaan Aceh dalam Sejarah*, Jakarta: Beuna, 1983.

Hasjmi, A., *Ruba'i Hamzah Fansuri, Karya Sastra Sufi Abad XVII*, Kuala Lumpur: Dewan Bahasa dan Pustaka, 1976.

Heer, N., *The Precious Pearl: Al-Jāmi's al-Durrah al-Fākhirah together with his Glosses and the Commentary of 'Abd al-Ghafūr al-Larī*, Albany: State University of New York Press, 1979.

Hiskett, M., *The Sword of Truth: The Life and Times of the Shehu Usuman dan Fodio*, New York: Oxford University Press, 1973.

Hitti, P.K., N.A. Faris & B. 'Abd-al-Malik, *Descriptive Catalogue of the Garrett Collection of Arabic Manuscripts in the Princeton University Library*, Princeton: Princeton University Press, 1938.

Hodgson, M.G.S., *The Venture of Islam*, 3 vols, Chicago: University of Chicago Press, 1974.

Hooker, M.B., *Islamic Law in South-East Asia*, Singapore: Oxford University 1984.

Hourani, G.F., *Arab Seafaring in the Indian Ocean in Ancient and Early Medieval Times*, Beirut: Khayats, 1963.

Huntington, R., *Gender and Social Structure in Madagascar*, Bloomington & Indianapolis: Indiana University Press, 1988.

Hussainmiya, B.A., *Orang Rejimen: The Malays of the Ceylon Rifle Regiment*, Bangi: University Kebangsaan Malaysia, 1990.

Ibn Bishr, ʻUthmān b. ʻAbd Allāh, *ʻUnwān al-Majd fī Tārīkh Najd*, 2 vols, Riyāḍ: Maktabat al-Riyāḍ al-Ḥadīthah 1971 [?].

Jalbani, G.N., *Life of Shah Wali Allah*, Delhi: Idarah-i adabiyat-i Delli, 1980.

Janson, A., Roger Tol, and Jan Just Witkam (eds), *Mystical Illustrations from the Teachings of Syaikh Ahmad al-Qusyasyi*, Leiden: INIS, 1995.

Jones, A.M., *Africa and Indonesia: The Evidence of the Xylophone and Other Musical and Cultural Factors*, Leiden: Brill, 1971.

de Jong, Frederick & Bernd Radtke (eds), *Islamic Mysticism Contested: Thirteen Centuries of Controversies and Polemics*, Leiden: Brill, 1999. [Azra himself has a contribution to this volume, but there are other pieces relevant to his work in the chapters by Madelung, Peskes, Radtke, and Lipman, among others.]

de Jonge, J.K.J., *De opkomst van het Nederlandsch gezag over Java*, The Hague: Nijhoff, 1870.

Juynboll, G.H.A., *Muslim Tradition: Studies in Chronology, Provenance, and Authorship of Early Hadith*, Cambridge: Cambridge University Press, 1983.

Kartodirdjo, Sartono (ed.), *Profiles of Malay Culture*, Jakarta: Ministry of Education and Culture, 1976.

al-Kattānī, ʻAbd al-Ḥayy b. ʻAbd al-Kabīr, *Fahras al-Fahāris wa al-Athbāt wa Muʻjam al-Maʻājim wa al-Mashyakhat wa al-Musalsalat*, 3 vols, Beirut: Dār al-Gharb al-Islāmī, 1402/1982.

al-Khārijī, ʻAlī, *al-'Uqūd al-Lu'lu'iyyah fī Tārīkh al-Dawlat al-Rasūliyyah*, 2 vols, Cairo: Maṭba'at al-Hilal, 1914.

Kennedy, J., *A History of Malaya*, 2nd ed., London: Macmillan, 1970.

Knysh, A.D., *Ibn ʻArabi in the Later Islamic Tradition: The Making of a Polemical Image in Medieval Islam*, Albany: SUNY Press, 1999.

Kraemer, H., *Een Javaansche Primbon uit de zestiende eeuw*, Leiden: Brill, 1921.

Kraus, W., *Zwischen Reform und Rebellion: über die Entwicklung des Islams in Minangkabau (Westsumatra) zwischen den beiden Reformbewegungen der Padri (1837) und der Modernisten (1908)*, Wiesbaden: Franz Steiner, 1984.

Landon, K.P., *Southeast Asia: Crossroad of Religions*, Chicago: University of Chicago Press, 1949.

van Leur, J.C., *Indonesian Trade and Society*, The Hague: Van Hoeve, 1955.

Levtzion, N. (ed.), *Conversion to Islam*, New York: Holmes & Meyer, 1979.

Levtzion, N. & J.O. Voll (eds), *Eighteenth-Century Renewal and Reform in Islam*, Syracuse: Syracuse University Press, 1987.

Lombard, D., *Le carrefour Javanais* (3 vols.), Paris: EHESS, 1990. Trans. into *Nusa Jawa Silang Budaya* (3 vols.), Jakarta: Gramedia, 1996.

Lombard, D., *Le Sultanat d'Atjéh au Temps d'Iskandar Muda, 1607–1636*, Paris: École Française d'Extrême-Orient, 1967. Trans. into *Kerajaan Aceh Jaman Sultan Iskandar Muda*, Jakarta: Balai Pustaka, 1991.

Lubis, Haji Muhammad Bukhari, *The Ocean of Unity: Waḥdat al-Wujūd in Persian, Turkish and Malay Poetry*, Kuala Lumpur: DBD, 1993.

Lubis, Nabilah, *Syekh Yusuf al-Taj al-Makasari, Menyingkap Intisari Segala Rahasia*, Bandung: Mizan & EFEO Jakarta, 1996.

Madmarn, Hasan, *The Pondok and Madrasah in Patani*, Kuala Lumpur: Penerbit Universiti Kebangsaan Malaysia, 1999.

Majul, C.A., *Muslims in the Philippines*, 2nd ed., Quezon City: University of the Philippines Press, 1979.

Makdisi, G., *The Rise of Humanism in Classical Islam and the Christian West*, Edinburgh: Edinburgh University Press, 1990.

Mansur, H.M. Laily, *Kitab ad-Durun Nafis: Tinjauan atas suatu Ajaran Tasawuf*, Banjarmasin: Hasanu, 1982.

Mansur, M.D., *Perang Padri di Sumatera Barat*, Djakarta: 1964.

Marsden, W., *The History of Sumatra*, first publ., London: 1873, repr. of the 1811 ed., Kuala Lumpur: Oxford University Press, 1975.

Martamin, M., *Tuanku Imam Bonjol*, 2nd ed., Jakarta: Departemen P&K, 1984.

Martin, B.G., *Muslim Brotherhoods in Nineteenth Century Africa*, Cambridge: Cambridge University Press, 1976.

Martin, R.C. & M.R. Woodward with Dwi S. Atmaja, *Defender of Reason in Islam: Mu'tazilism from Medieval School to Modern Symbol*, Oxford: Oneworld, 1997.

Ma'rūf, Nāji, *Madāris Makkah*, Baghdad: Maṭba'at al-Irshād, 1386/1966.

Ma'rūf, Nāji, *'Ulamā' al-Niẓāmiyyah wa al-Madāris al-Mashriq al-Islāmī*, Baghdad: Maṭba'at al-Irshād, 1393/1973.

Ma'rūf, Nājī, *Madāris qabl al-Niẓāmiyyah*, Baghdād [?]: Maṭba'at al-Jam' al-'Ilmī al-'Irāqī, 1393/1973.

Massiara, A.H., *Syekh Yusuf Tuanta Salamaka dari Gowa*, Jakarta: Yayasan Lakipadada, 1983.

Massignon, L., *Essai sur les origines du lexique technique de la mystique musulmane*, Paris: J. Vrin, 1954.

Masuknya Islam di Sulawesi Selatan, Ujung Pandang: Balai Penelitian Lektur, Depag R.I., 1985–6.

Mayson, J.S., *The Malays of Cape Town*, Manchester: J. Galt & Co., 1861.

Meilink-Roelofsz, M.A.P., *Asian Trade and European Influence in the Indonesian Archipelago*, The Hague: Nijhoff, 1962.

Muztar, A.D., *Shah Wali Allah: A Saint Scholar of Muslim India*, Islamabad: National Commission on Historical and Cultural Research, 1979.

al-Naqar, 'Umar, *The Pilgrimage Tradition in West Africa*, Khartoum: Khartoum University Press, 1972.

Nasution, Harun, *Islam Rasional*, Bandung: Mizan, 1995.

Ngah, Mohd Nor Bin, *Kitab Jawi: Islamic Thought of the Malay Muslim Scholars*, Singapore: ISEAS, 1983.

van Nieuwenhuijze, C.A.O., *Samsu'l-Din van Pasai: Bijdrage tot de kennis der Sumatraansche Mystiek*, Leiden: Brill, 1945.

Nock, A.D., *Conversion: The Old and the New-Religion from Alexander the Great to Augustine of Hippo*, Oxford: Clarendon Press, 1933.

Ochsenwald, W., *Religion, Society and the State in Arabia: The Hijaz under Ottoman Control*, Columbus, O.H.: Ohio State University Press, 1984.

Owen, T. (ed.), *Studies in Eighteenth Century Islamic History*, Carbondale: Southern Illinois University Press, 1997.

Pesce, A., *Jiddah: Portrait of an Arabian City*, London: Falcon Press, 1974.

Peters, F.E., *Jerusalem and Mecca: The Typology of the Holy City in the Near East*, New York & London: New York University Press, 1986.

Pigeaud, T.G. Th., *Literature of Java*, 3 vols, Leiden: Bibliotheca Universitatis Leidensis, 1967.

Pigeaud, Th. G. Th. & H.J. de Graaf, *Islamic States in Java 1500–1700*, The Hague: Nijhoff, 1976.

Pijper, G.F., *Fragmenta Islamica: Studiën over het Islamisme in Nederlandsch-Indië*, Leiden: Brill, 1934.

du Plessis, I.D., *The Cape Malays: History, Religion, Traditions, Folk Tales of the Malay Quarter*, Cape Town: A.A. Balkema, 1972.

du Plessis, I.D., *Sjeg Joesoef*, Kaapstad: Nasionale Boekhandel, 1970.

du Plessis, I.D., *The Cape Malays*, Johannesburg: South African Institute of Race Relations, 1946.

al-Qannūjī, Ṣiddīq b. Ḥasan, *Abjad al-'Ulūm*, 3 vols Dār al-Kutub al-'Ilmiyyah, n.d.

al-Qudsī, 'Abd al-Ḥāmid b. Muḥammad 'Alī, *al-Futūḥāt al-Qudsiyyah fī Sharḥ al-Tawassulāt al-Sammāṇiyyah*, Cairo: al-Ḥāmidiyyat al-Miṣriyyah, 1323/1905.

Quzwain, M. Chatib, *Mengenal Allah: Studi mengenai Ajaran Tasawwuf Syaikh 'Abdus Samad al-Palimbani*, Jakarta: Bulan Bintang, 1984.

Raffles, T.S., *The History of Java*, 2 vols, London: Black, Parburg & Allen, 1817, repr. Kuala Lumpur: Oxford Unversity Press, 1965.

Rahim, Husni, *Sistem Otoritas & Administrasi Islam: Studi tentang Pejabat Agama Masa Kesultanan dan Kolonial di Palembang,* Jakarta: Logos, 1998.

Rahman, Fazlur, *Revival and Reform in Islam: A Study of Islamic Fundamentalism*, Oxford: OneWorld, 2000.

Rahman, Fazlur, *Islam* (2nd Edition), Chicago: University of Chicago Press, 1979.

Ras, J.J., *Hikayat Banjar, A Study in Malay Historiography*, The Hague: Nijhoff, 1968.

Rauf, M.A., *A Brief History of Islam with Special Reference to Malaysia*, Kuala Lumpur: Oxford University Press, 1964.

Reid, A., *Southeast Asia in the Age of Commerce, 1450–1680 (Volume Two: Expansion and Crisis)*, New Haven: Yale University Press, 1993.

Ricklefs, M.C., *The Seen and Unseen Worlds in Java, 1726–1749: History, Literature and Islam in the Court of Pakubuwana II*, St Leonard, Australia: Allen & Unwin, 1998.

Ricklefs, M.C., *A History of Modern Indonesia*, London: Macmillan, 1990.

Ricklefs, M.C., *Jogjakarta under Sultan Mangkubumi 1749–1792*, London: Oxford University Press, 1974.

Riddell, P., *Islam and the Malay-Indonesian World: Transmission and Responses*, London & Singapore: C. Hurst & Horizon Books, 2001.

Riddell, P., *Transferring a Tradition: Abd al-Ra'uf al-Singkili's Rendering into Malay of the Jalalayn Commentary*, Berkeley: Monograph No. 31, Centers for South and Southeast Asia Studies, University of California, 1990.

Rinkes, D.A., *Abdoerraoef van Singkel: Bijdrage tot de kennis van de mystiek op, Sumatra en Java*, Heerenveen: Hepkema, 1909.

Riwayat Syekh Yusuf dan Kisah Makkutaknang Daeng Mannuntungi, Trans. Djirong Basang, Jakarta: Departemen P&K, 1981.

Rizvi, S.A.A., *A History of Sufism in India*, 2 vols, New Delhi: Munshiram Manoharlal, 1983.

Rizvi, S.A.A., *Shah Wali Allah and His Times*, Canberra: Ma'rifat Publishing House, 1980.

van Ronkel, Ph. S., *Supplement to the Catalogue of the Arabic Manuscripts . . . in the Batavia Society*, Batavia & The Hague: Albrecht & Nijhoff, 1913.

van Ronkel, Ph. S., *Catalogus der Maleische Handschriften*, Batavia & The Hague: Albrecht & Nijhoff, 1909.

Salam, Solichin, *Shaykh Yusuf 'Singa dari Gowa': Ulama berkaliber Internasional*, Jakarta, 1994.

Saleh, Siti Hawa (ed.), *Hikayat Merong Mahawangsa*, Kuala Lumpur: University of Malaya Press, 1970.

Sandhu, K.S. & P. Wheatley (eds), *Melaka: The Transformation of a Malay Capital c. 1400–1980*, 2 vols, Kuala Lumpur: Oxford University Press, 1983.

Sartain, E.M., *Jalal al-Din al-Suyuti*, 2 vols, Cambridge: Cambridge University Press, 1975.

Sasmita, Uka Tjandra, *Musuh Besar Kompeni Belanda: Sultan Ageng Tirtayasa*, Jakarta: Nusalarang, 1967.

Schacht, *The Origins of Muhammadan Jurisprudence*, Oxford: Clarendon Press, 1979.

Scherzer, K., *Narrative of the Circumnavigation of the Globe by the Austrian Frigate Novara in the Years 1857, 1858 and 1859*, 3 vols, London: 1861–63.

Schimmel, A., *Pain and Grace: A Study of Two Mystical Writers of Eighteenth Century Muslim India*, Leiden: E.J. Brill, 1976.

Schrieke, B.J.O., *Indonesian Sociological Studies*, 2 parts, The Hague & Bandung: Van Hoeve, 1955.

Sell, Rev. C., *Muslims in China*, London [etc.]: Christian Literature for India 1913.

al-Sha'afī, M.S., *The Foreign Trade of Juddah during the Ottoman Period 1840–1916*, Jeddah [?]: n.p., 1405/1985.

al-Shamakh, Muḥammad 'Abd al-Raḥmān, *al-Ta'līm fī Makkah wa al-Madīnah,* Riyāḍ: n.p., 1393/1973.

Shaw, S.J., *The Financial and Administrative Organization and Development of Ottoman Egypt, 1517–1798*, Princeton: Princeton University Press, 1962.

Shaw, S.J., *The Budget of Ottoman Egypt, 1005–1006/1596–1597*, The Hague & Paris: Mouton, 1968.

Sherwani, H.K., *The Bahmanids of the Deccan*, Hyderabad: 1953.

Shushud, Hasan, *Masters of Wisdom of Central Asia*, trans. Muhtar Holland, Moorcote, Eg.: Coombe Springs Press, 1983.

al-Sibā'ī, Aḥmad, *Tārīkh Makkah*, 2 vols, al-Mamlakat al-'Arabiyyat al-Su'ūdiyyah, 1404/1984.

Snouck Hurgronje, C., *Nasihat-nasihat C. Snouck Hurgronje semasa Kepegawaiannya kepada Pemerintahan Hindia Belanda*, Trans. Sukarsi, Jakarta: INIS, 1991, V, from E. Gobée & C. Adriaanse (comp.), *Ambtelijke adviezen van C. Snouck Hurgronje, 1889–1936*, 2 vols, 's-Gravenhage: Nijhoff, 1959–65.

Snouck Hurgronje, C., *Mekka in the Latter Part of the 19th Century*, trans. J.H. Monahan, Leyden & London: Brill & Luzac, 1931.

Snouck Hurgronje, C., *Verspreide geschriften*, Hague: Nijhoff, 1924–27.

Snouck Hurgronje, C., *The Achehnese*, 2 vols, trans. O'Sullivan, Leiden: Brill, 1906.

Soeratno, Siti Chamamah et al., *Memahami Karya-karya Nuruddin Arraniri*, Jakarta: Departemen P&K, 1982.

Stapel, F.W. (ed.), *Geschiedenis van Nederlandsch-Indië*, 5 vols, Amsterdam, Joost van den Vondel, 1938–40, I.

Steenbrink, K., *Kitab Suci atau Kertas Toilet: Nuruddin Ar-Raniri dan Agama Kristen*, Yogyakarta: IAIN Sunan Kalijaga Press, 1988.

Sulaiman, Ibraheem, *A Revolution in History: The Jihad of Usuman dan Fodio*, London: Mansell, 1986.

Sutaarga, Amir et al., *Katalogus Koleksi Naskah Melayu Museum Pusat*, Jakarta: Departemen P&K, 1972.

Syukri, Ibrahim, *History of the Malay Kingdom of Patani*, trans. C. Bailey & J.N. Miksic, Athens, OH: Center for International Studies, 1985.

Talas, Asad, *La Madrasa Nizamiyyah et son Histoire*, Paris: Geuthner, 1939.

Tara, V. & J.C. Woillet, *Madagascar, Mascareignes et Comores*, Paris: Société Continentale, 1969.

Tarling, Nicholas (ed.), *The Cambridge History of Southeast Asia*, Cambridge University Press, 1992—esp. vol. 1, part 2 and vol. 2, part 1.

Temimi, Abdeljelil (ed.), *La vie sociale dans les provinces arabes à l'époque ottomane*, Zoghuan, Centre d'Etudes et de Recherches Ottomanes, Morisques, de Documentation et d'Information, 1988.

Theal, McCall G., *History and Ethnography of Africa South of the Zembesi*, 3 vols, London: Swan Sonnenschein, 1909, II.

Thurnberg, C., *Travels in Europe, Africa and Asia*, 4 vols, London: F. Rivingston, 1795, I.

Tibbett, G.R., *Arab Navigation in the Indian Ocean before the Coming of the Portuguese*, London: Royal Asiatic Society, 1981.

Tibbett, G.R., *A Study of the Arabic Texts containing Material on South-East Asia*, Leiden & London: Brill & Royal Asiatic Society, 1979.

Trimingham, J.S., *The Sufi Orders in Islam*, London: Oxford University Press, 1973.

Trimingham, J.S., *Islam in the Sudan*, New York: Barnes & Noble, 1965.

Tritton, A.S., *Materials on Muslim Education in the Middle Ages*, London: Luzac, 1957.

Tudjimah, *Syekh Yusuf Makasar: Riwayat dan Ajarannya*, Jakarta: Penerbit Universitas Indonesia, 1997.

Tudjimah et al., *Syekh Yusuf Makasar: Riwayat Hidup, Karya dan Ajarannya*, Jakarta: Departemen P&K, 1987.

Usman, A.G., *Urang Banjar dalam Sejarah*, Banjarmasin: Lambung Mangkurat University Press, 1989.

al-Uthaymīn, *al-Shaykh Muḥammad ibn 'Abd al-Wahhāb: Ḥayātuh wa Fikruh*, Riyāḍ: Dār al-'Ulūm, n.d.

Vajda, G., *La transmission du savoir en Islam (VIIe–XVIIIe siècles)*, ed. N. Cottart, London: Variorum Reprints, 1983.

Vansina, J., *Oral Tradition: A Study in Historical Methodology*, Chicago: Aldine, 1965.

Vlekke, B.H.M., *Nusantara: A History of the East Indian Archipelago*, Cambridge, Mass.: Harvard University Press, 1943.

Voorhoeve, P., *Handlist of Arabic Manuscripts in the Library of the University of Leiden and Other Collections in the Netherlands*, Leiden: Leiden University Press, 1980.

Voorhoeve, P., *Twee Maleische geschriften van Nuruddin ar-Raniri*, Leiden: Brill, 1955.

Voorhoeve, P., *Bayan Tajalli: Bahan-bahan untuk Mengadakan Penyelidikan lebih mendalam tentang Abdurra-uf Singkel*, trans. Aboe Bakar, Banda Aceh: PDIA, 1980, from Dutch, 'Bayan Tadjalli: Gegevens voor een nadere studie over Abdurrauf van Singkel', *TBG*, 85, 1952.

Walker, E.A., *A History of Southern Africa*, 3rd ed., London: Longmans, 1962.

Wink, A., *Al-Hind: The Making of the Indo-Islamic World*, Leiden: Brill, 1990.

Winstedt, R.O., *The Malay Magician: Being Shaman, Saiva and Sufi*, London: Routledge & Kegan Paul, 1951.

Winstedt, R.O., *A History of Classical Malay Literature*, Kuala Lumpur: Oxford University Press, 1969.

Winter, M., *Society and Religion in Early Ottoman Egypt: Studies in the Writings of Abd al-Wahhab al-Sha'rani*, New Brunswick: Transaction Books, 1982.

Woelders, M.O., *Het Sultanaat Palembang 1811–1825*, Leiden: Nijhoff, 1975.

Wolters, O.W., *The Fall of Srivijaya in Malay History*, Ithaca, N.Y.: Cornell University Press, 1970.

Wolters, O.W., *Early Indonesian Commerce: A Study of the Origins of Srivijaya*, Ithaca, N.Y.: Cornell University Press, 1967.

Wustenfeld, F., *Geschichte der Stadt Mekka*, in his *Die Chroniken der Stadt Mekka*, Leipzig: Brockhaus, 1861, IV.

Zabarah, Muḥammad b. Muḥammad (b. 1301/1884), *Nubalā' al-Yaman bi al-Qarn al-Thānī 'Ashar li al-Hijrah*, Cairo: al-Maṭba'at al-Salāfiyyah, 1377/1957.

Zabarah, Muḥammad b. Muḥammad, *Nash al-'Arf li Nubalā' al-Yaman ba'ḍ al-'Alf*, Cairo: al-Maṭba'at al-Salāfiyyah, 1359/1940.

Zabarah, Muḥammad b. Muḥammad, *Nayl al-Waṭar min Tarājim Rijāl al-Yaman fī al-Qarn al-Thālith 'Ashar*, 2 vols, Cairo: al-Maṭba'at al-Salāfiyyah, 1348/1929.

Zainuddin, H.M., *Tarich Atjeh dan Nusantara*, Medan: Pustaka Iskandar Muda, 1961.

Zamzam, Zafry, *Syekh Muhammad Arsyad al-Banjari sebagai Ulama Juru Da wah*, Banjarmasin: Karya, 1974.

al-Zarkalī (al-Zerekly), Khayr al-Dīn, *al-A'lām: Qāmūs Tarājim*, 3rd ed., 12 vols, Beirut: n.p., 1389/1969.

Articles

Abdullah, Taufik, 'Modernization in the Minangkabau World: West Sumatra in the Early Decades of the Twentieth Century', in C. Holt (ed.), *Culture and Politics in Indonesia*, Ithaca, N.Y.: Cornell University Press, 1972.

Ahmad, Rashid, 'Gapena Pelopori Usaha Menjalin Hubungan yang Terputus', in Abu Bakar (ed.), *Melayu Srilanka*, Kuala Lumpur, Gapena, 1990.

Ahtmat, J.P., 'Kedatangan Orang Melayu ke Srilanka', in Abu Bakar (ed.), *Melayu Srilanka*, Kuala Lumpur, Gapena, 1990.

al-'Ankawī, Abdullāh, 'The Pilgrimage to Mecca in Mamluk Times', in R.B. Serjeant & R.L. Bidwell (eds), *Arabian Studies*, I, London: C. Hurst, 1974.

al-Anṣarī, Ismā'īl Muḥammad, 'Ḥayāt al-Shaykh Muḥammad ibn 'Abd al-Wahhāb waĀtharuh al-'Ilmiyyah', in *Buhūth Usbū' al-Shaykh Muḥammad bin 'Abd al-Wahhāb*, Riyāḍ [?]: al-Mamlakat al-'Arabiyyat al-Su'ūdiyyah, 1403/1983, I.

Anwar, Khairil, ''Ulamā' Indūnīsiya al-qarni al-thāmin 'ashar: tarjamah Muḥammad Arshad al-Banjarī wa afkāruhu', *Studia Islamika*, III, v (1996): 137–164.

Archer, R.L., 'Muhammadan Mysticism in Sumatra', *JMBRAS*, 15, II (1937).

Asiri, Mahmud, 'Shah Wali Allah's Views on Wahdatul Wujud and Wahdatush Shuhud', *al-Hikmah*, 1 (1964).

Ates, A., 'Ibn al-'Arabi, Muhyi 'l-Din Abu Abd Allah b. Muhammad b. al-Arabi al-Hatimi al-Ta i', *EI*², III.

al-Attas, S.M.N., 'New Light on the Life of Hamzah Fansuri', *JMBRAS*, 40, I (1967).

Azra, Azyumardi, 'The Transmission of *al-Manar* to the Malay-Indonesian World: The Cases of *al-Imam* and *al-Munir*', *Studia Islamika*, 6, 3 (1999).

Azra, Azyumardi, 'Prof. Dr. Hamka: Pribadi dan Institusi MUI', in Azyumardi Azra and Saiful Umam (eds), *Tokoh dan Pemimpin Agama: Biografi Sosial-Politik*, Jakarta: Litbang Depag RI & PPIM IAIN Jakarta, 1998.

Azra, Azyumardi, ''Ulama Indonesia di Haramayn: Pasang dan Surutnya Sebuah Wacana Intelektual', *Ulumul Qur'an*, III, 3 (1992).

Azra, Azyumardi, 'Syi'ah di Indonesia: Tinjauan Ulang', *Pelita*, 11 December, 1990.

Azra, Azyumardi, 'The Surau and the Early Reform Movements in Minangkabau', *Mizan*, 3, II (1990).

Bachtiar, Harsja W., 'The Religion of Java: A Commentary', *Majalah Ilmu-ilmu Sastra Indonesia*, 5 (1973).

Baried, Baroroh, 'Shi'a Elements in Malay Literature', in Kartodirdjo (ed.), *Profiles of Malay Culture*, Jakarta: Ministry of Education and Culture, 1986.

Baried, Baroroh, 'Perkembangan Ilmu Tasawuf di Indonesia', in S. Sutrisno et al. (eds), *Bahasa, Sastra, Budaya*, Yogyakarta: Gadjah Mada University Press, 1985.

Baried, Baroroh, 'Le Shiisme in Indonesie', trans., Ch. Pelras, *Archipel*, 15 (1978).

Bousquet, G.H., 'Introduction à l'étude de l'Islam indonésien', *Revue des Etudes Islamiques*, Cahier 11–111, 1938.

Boxer, C.R., 'A Note on Portuguese Reactions to the Revival of the Red Sea Spice Trade and the Rise of Aceh, 1540–1600', *JSEAH*, 10, III (1969).

Braddell, T., 'Ceremony Observed at the Court of Acheen', *JIAEA*, 4 (1850).

Braddell, T., 'The Ancient Trade of the Indian Archipelago', *JIAEA*, 2, (New Series), III (1857).

Bradlow, F.R., 'The Cape of Good Hope', *Suid-Afrikaanse Historiese Joernaal*, 13 (1981).

Bradlow, F.R., 'The Origins of the Early Cape Muslims', in F.R. Bradlow & M. Cairns, *The Early Cape Muslims: A Study of Their Mosques, Genealogy and Origins*, Cape Town: A.A. Balkema, 1978.

Braginsky, Vladimir I., 'On the Copy of Hamzah Fansuri's Epitaph Published by C. Guillot and L. Kalus', *Archipel* 62, 2001: 21–33.

Brenner, L., 'Sufism in Africa in the Seventeenth and Eighteenth Centuries', in *Islam et Societes au sud du Sahara*, 2 (1988).

Brenner, L., 'Muslim Thought in Eighteenth-Century West Africa: The Case of Shaykh Uthman b. Fudi', in Levtzion & Voll (eds), *Eighteenth Century Renewal and Reform in Islam*, Syracuse: Syracuse University Press, 1987.

van Bruinessen, M., 'Studies of Sufism and the Sufi Orders in Indonesia', *Die Welt des Islams*, 38.2 (1998): 192–219.

van Bruinessen, M., 'The Tariqa Khalwatiyya in South Celebes', *Excursies in Celebes: Een bundel bijdragen bij het afscheid van J. Noorduyn als directeur-secretaris van het Koninklijk Instituut voor Taal-, Land- en Volkenkunde*. Poeze & Schoorl (eds) Leiden: KITLV Uiitgeverij, 1991.

van Bruinessen, M., 'The Origins and Development of the Naqshbandi Order in Indonesia', *Der Islam*, 67 (1990).

van Bruinessen, M., 'Kitab Kuning: Books in Arabic Script used in the Pesantren Milieu', *BKI*, 146 (1990).

van Bruinessen, M., 'Kitab Fiqh di Pesantren Indonesia dan Malaysia', *Pesantren*, 6, I (1989).

Bulliet, R.W., 'Conversion to Islam and the Emergence of a Muslim Society', in Levtzion (ed.), *Conversion to Islam*, N.Y.: Holmes & Meyer, 1979.

Cense, A.A., 'De verering van Sjaich Jusuf in Zuid-Celebes', in *Bingkisan Budi*, Leiden: Sijhoff, 1950.

Chambert-Loir, H., 'Abdussamad al-Palimbani sebagai Ulama Jawi', in al-Palimbani, *Sayr al-Salikin*, [vol. I], Banda Aceh: Musium Negeri Aceh, 1985/6.

Che Man, W.K., 'The Thai Government and Islamic Institutions in the Four Southern Muslim Provinces of Thailand', *Sojourn*, 5, II (1990).

Colless, B.E., 'Persian Merchants and Missionaries in Medieval Malaya', *JMBRAS*, 42, II (1969).

Crecellius, D. & E.A. Beardow, 'A Reputed Sarakata of the Jamal al-Lail Dynasty', *JMBRAS*, 52, II (1979).

Daly, Peunoh, 'Naskah Mirtatut Thullab Karya Abdur-Rauf Singkel', in *Agama, Budaya dan Masyarakat*, Jakarta: Balitbang Depag R.I., 1980.

Dames, M.L., 'The Portuguese and Turks in the Indian Ocean in the Sixteenth Century', *JRAS*, 1921.

Davids, Achmat, 'Politics and the Muslims of Cape Town: A Historical Survey', *Studies in the History of Cape Town*, 4 (1981).

Djajadiningrat, H., 'De ceremonie van het "poela-batee" op het graf van Soeltan Iskandar II van Atjeh (1636–1641)', *TBG*, 69 (1929).

Djaja, Tamar, 'Sjech Burhanuddin (1646–1692)', in his *Pusaka Indonesia: Riwajat Hidup Orang-orang Besar Tanah Air*, Djakarta: Bulan Bintang, 1965.

Djaja, Tamar, 'Sjech Muhammad Arsjad Bandjar', in his *Pusaka Indonesia*, 1965.

Djaja, Tamar, 'Tuanku Nan Tuo', in his *Pusaka Indonesia*, Djakarta: Bulan Bintang, 1965.

Djamaris, Edward, 'Nuruddin ar-Raniri Khabar Akhirat dalam Hal Kiamat', in Sutrisno et al. (eds), *Bahasa, Sastra, Budaya*, Yogyakarta: Gadjah Mada University Press, 1985.

Dobbin, C., 'Islamic Revivalism in Minangkabau at the Turn of the Nineteenth Century', *Modern Asian Studies*, 8, III (1974).

Drakard, J., 'An Indian Ocean Port: Sources for the Earlier History of Barus', *Archipel*, 37 (1989).

Drewes, G.W.J., 'A Note on Muhammad al-Samman, His Writings, and 19th Century Sammaniyya Practices, Chiefly in Batavia, according to Written Data', *Archipel*, 43 (1991): 73–87.

Drewes, G.W.J., 'Nur al-Din al-Raniri's Charge of Heresy against Hamzah and Shamsuddin from an International Point of View', in S.O. Robson & CD Grijns (eds), *Cultural Contact and Textual Interpretation*, Dordrecht: Foris, 1986.

Drewes, G.W.J., 'Further Data concerning Sabd al-Samad al-Palimbanil', *BKI*, 132 (1976).

Drewes, G.W.J., 'New Light on the Coming of Islam to Indonesia?', *BKI*, 124 (1968).

Drewes, G.W.J., 'A.H. Johns Ph.D Malay Sufism', *BKI*, 115, III (1959).

Drewes, G.W.J., 'De herkomst van Nuruddin ar-Raniri', *BKI*, 111 (1955).

Drewes, G.W.J., 'Sjech Joesoep Makasar', *Djawa*, 6 (1926).

Eickelman, D.F., 'The Study of Islam in Local Contexts', *Contribution to Asian Studies*, 17 (1982).

Farooqi, Naim R., 'Moguls, Ottomans, and Pilgrims: Protecting the Routes to Mecca in the Sixteenth and Seventeenth Centuries', *The International History Review*, 10, II (1988).

Faroqhi, Suraiya, 'Ottoman Documents concerning the Hajj during the Sixteenth and Seventeenth Centuries', in Temimi (ed.), *La vie sociale*, 1988, Tôme 3.

Fatimi, S.Q., 'Two Letters from Maharaja to the Khalifah', *Islamic Studies*, (Karachi), 2, I (1963).

Feener, R.M., 'Shaykh Yusuf and the Appreciation of Muslim "Saints" in Modern Indonesia', *Journal for Islamic Studies* (Cape Town), 18–19 (1999): 112–131.

Feener, R.M., 'Yemeni Sources for the History of Islam in Indonesia: 'Abd al-Samad Palimbani in the *Nafs al-Yamānī*'. *La transmission du savoir dans le monde musulman périphérique*, 19 (1999): 128–144.

Feener, R.M., 'A Re-examination of the Place of the al-Hallāj in the Development of Southeast Asian Islam', *BKI*, 54, 4 (1998): 571–592.

Feener, R.M., 'Notes toward a History of Qur'anic Exegesis in Southeast Asia', *Studia Islamika*, 4 (1988).

Ferrand, G., 'Les voyages des Javanais à Madagascar', *Journal Asiatique*, Xe série, 15 (1910).

Fletcher, J., 'The Taylor-Pickens Letters on the Jahri Branch of the Naqshbandiyya in China', *Central and Inner Asian Studies*, 3 (1989).

Fletcher, J., 'Les "voies" (turuq) soufies en Chine', in A. Popovic & G. Veinstein (eds), *Les ordres mystiques dans l'Islam*, Paris: Ecole des Hautes Etudes en Sciences Sociales, 1986.

Fletcher, J., 'Central Asian Sufism and Ma Ming-hsin's New Teaching', *Proceedings of the Fourth East Asian Altaistic Conference*, ed. Ch'en Chieh-hsien, Taipei: National Taiwan University, 1975.

Ford, J.F., 'Some Chinese Muslims of the Seventeenth and Eighteenth Centuries', *Journal of the Royal Central Asian Society*, 61 (New Series 5), 2 (1974).

Gabrieli, F., 'The Transmission of Learning and Literary Influences to Western Europe', in P.M. Holt et al. (eds), *The Cambridge History of Islam*, Cambridge: University Press, 1970, II.

Gellens, S.I., 'The Search for Knowledge in Medieval Muslim Societies: A Comparative Approach', in D.F. Eickelman & J. Piscatory (eds), *Muslim Travellers: Pilgrimage, Migration and the Religious Imagination*, Berkeley: University of California Press, 1990.

Gibb, H.A.R., 'An Interpretation of Islamic History II', *MW*, 45, II (1955).

Gladney, D.C., 'Muslim Tombs and Ethnic Folklore: Charters for Hui Identity', *JAS*, 46, V (1987).

Goldziher, I., 'Materialien zur entwicklungsgeschichte des Sufismus', in *Gesammelte Schriften*, Hildesheim: 1967, IV.

Goyung, Nejat, 'Some Documents concerning the Ka'ba in the 16th Century', *Sources for the History of Arabia*, Riyad: Riyad University Press, 1979, part 2.

de Graaf, H.J., 'South-East Asian Islam to the Eighteenth Century', in

P.M. Holt et al. (eds), *The Cambridge History of Islam*, Cambridge: Cambridge University Press, 1970, II.

Greyling, C., 'Schech Yusuf, the Founder of Islam in South Africa', *Religion in Southern Africa*, 1, I (1980).

Groeneveldt, W.P., 'Notes on the Malay Archipelago and Malacca compiled from Chinese Sources', *VBG*, 39 (1880).

Guillaume, A., 'Al-Lum'at al-Saniya fi Tahqiq al-Ilqa' fi-l-Umniya by Ibrahim al-Kurani', *BSOAS*, XX (1957).

Guillot, Claude & Ludvik Kalus, 'La stéle funéraire de Hamzah Fansuri', *Archipel*, 60 (2000): 3–24.

Guillot, Claude & Ludvik Kalus, 'En réponse â Vladimir I. Braginsky', *Archipel*, 62 (2001): 21–33.

Hafiduddin, Didin, 'Tinjauan atas Tafsir al-Munir Karya Imam Muhammad Nawai Tanara', in Ahmad Rifa'i Hasan (ed.), *Warisan Intelektual Islam Indonesia*, Bandung: Mizan, 1987.

Hafsi, Ibrahim, 'Recherche sur le genre "Tabaqat" dans la littérature arabe', *Arabica*, XXIII (1976): 227–265; & XXIV (1977): 1–41, 150–186.

Hallaq, Wael B., 'On the Origins of the Controversy about the Existence of Mujtahids and the Gate of Ijtihad', *Studia Islamica*, 63 (1986): 129–141.

Hallaq, Wael B., 'Was the Gate of Ijtihad Closed?', *International Journal of Middle Eastern Studies*, 16 (1984): 3–41.

Hamka, 'Sjeich Jusuf Tadju'l Chalwati (Tuanta Salamaka), 1626–1699', in *Perbendaharaan Lama*, Medan: Madju, 1963.

Hasan, A.A.H., 'The Development of Islamic Education in Kelantan', in Khoo Kay Kim (ed.), *Tamaddun Islam di Malaysia*, Kuala Lumpur: Persatuan Sejarah Malaysia, 1980.

Hasjmi, A., 'Syekh Abdurrauf Syiah Kuala, Ulama Negarawan yang Bijaksana', in *Universitas Syiah Kuala Menjelang 20 Tahun*, Medan: Waspada, 1980.

Hasjmi, A., 'Pendidikan Islam di Aceh dalam Perjalanan Sejarah', *Sinar Darussalam*, 63 (1975).

Hassan, Hamdan, 'Pertalian Pemikiran Islam Malaysia-Aceh', in Khoo Kay Kim (ed.), *Tamaddun Islam di Malaysia*, 1980.

Haykal, B., 'Al-Shawkani and the Jurisprudential Unity of Yemen', *Le Yémen, passé et présent de l'unité*, (ed.) Michel Tuchscherer. Aix en Provence: Édisud, 1988, pp 53–65.

Heins, E.L., 'Indonesian Colonization of West and Central Africa?', *BKI*, 72 (1966).

Helfrich, O.L. et al., 'Het Hasan-Hosein of Taboet-feest te Bengkoelen', *Internationales Archiv fur Ethnographie*, 1 (1888).

Hess, A.C., 'The Ottoman Seaborne Empire 1453–1525', *American Historical Review*, 75 (1970).

Heywood, C., 'The Red Sea and Ottoman Wakf Support for the Population of Mecca and Medina in the Latter Seventeenth Century', in Temimi (ed.), *La vie sociale*, 1988, Tôme 3.

Hiskett, M., 'An Islamic Tradition of Reform in the Western Sudan from the Sixteenth to Eighteenth Century', *BSOAS*, 25, III (1962).

Holle, K.F., 'Mededeelingen over de devotie der Naqsjibendijah in den Ned. Indischen Archipelago', *TBG* 31 (1886).

Hooker, M.B., 'Introduction: The Translation of Islam into South-East Asia', in his (ed.), *Islam in South-East Asia*, Leiden: Brill, 1983.

Hornell, J., 'Indonesian Influence on East African Culture', *JRAI*, 64, (1934).

Humphries, S., 'A Cultural Elite: The Role and Status of the 'Ulamā' in Islamic Society', *Islamic History: A Framework for Inquiry*, Princeton University Press, 1991, pp 187–208.

Hunt Esq., J., 'Some Particulars relating to Sulu in the Archipelago of Felicia', in J.H. Moors, *Notices of the Indian Archipelago and Adjacent Countries*, Singapore, 1837.

Hunwick, J.O., 'A Bibliography of the Works of Sh. Uthman b. Muhammad Fudi', *Arabic Literature in Africa*, 1, (1985).

Hunwick, J.O., 'Salih al-Fullani (1752–3–1803): The Career and Teachings of a West African *'ālim* in Medina', in A.H. Green (ed.), *In Quest of an Islamic Humanism: Arabic and Islamic Studies in Memory of Mohamed al-Nowaihi*, Cairo: The American University, 1984.

Hunwick, J.O., 'Salih al-Fullani of Futa Jallon: An Eighteenth Century Scholar and Mujaddid', Bull. *IFAN* (Ser. B), 10 (1978).

Hussainmiya, B.A., 'A Brief Historical Note on Malay Migration to Srilanka', *Jebat*, 14 (1986).

Imamuddin, S.M., 'Navigation and Maritime Trade in Early Medieval Egypt', *Hamdard Islamicus*, 2, IV (1979).

Iskandar, T., 'Abdurrauf Singkel Tokoh Syatariyah (Abad ke17)', in M.D. Mohamad (ed.), *Tokoh-tokoh Sastera Melayu Klasik*, Kuala Lumpur: Dewan Bahasa dan Pustaka, 1987.

Iskandar, T., 'Palembang Kraton Manuscripts', in C.M.S. Hellwig & S.O. Robson (eds), *A Man of Indonesian Letters: Essays in Honour of Professor A. Teeuw*, Dordrecht: Foris, 1986.

Ito, T., 'Why Did Nuruddin ar-Raniri leave Aceh in 1054 A.H.?', *BKI* 134 (1978).

Jeffreys, K.M., 'Sheikh Joseph at the Cape', *Cape Naturalist*, 6 (1939).

Jeffreys, K.M., 'The Karamat at Zandvlei, Faure. Sheikh Joseph in the East', *Cape Naturalist*, 5 (1938).

Johns, A.H., '"She Desired Him and He Desired Her" (Qur'an 12:24): 'Abd al-Ra'uf's Treatment of an Episode of the Joseph story in *Tarjumān al-Mustafīd*', *Archipel*, 57 (1999): 109–134.

Johns, A.H., 'The Qur'an in the Malay World: Reflections on 'Abd al-Ra'uf of Singkel (1615–1693)', *Journal of Islamic Studies*, 9.2 (1998): 120–145.

Johns, A.H., 'Quranic Exegesis in the Malay World: In Search of a Profile', in A. Rippin (ed.), *Approaches to the History of the Interpretation of the Qur'an*, Oxford: Clarendon Press, 1988.

Johns, A.H., 'Islam in the Malay World: An Exploratory Survey with Some Reference to Quranic Exegesis', in R. Israeli & A.H. Johns (eds), *Islam in Asia: Volume II Southeast and East Asia*, Boulder: Westview, 1984.

Johns, A.H., 'From Coastal Settlement to Islamic School and City: Islamization in Sumatra, the Malay Peninsula and Java', *Hamdard Islamicus*, 4, I (1981).

Johns, A.H., 'Friends in Grace: Ibrahim al-Kurani and Abd al-Ra'uf al-Singkeli', in S. Udin (ed.), *Spectrum: Essays Presented to Sutan Takdir Alisjahbana*, Jakarta: Dian Rakyat, 1978.

Johns, A.H., 'Islam in Southeast Asia: Reflections and New Directions', *Indonesia*, 19 (1976).

Johns, A.H., 'al-Kushashi, Safi al-Din Ahmad b. Muhammad b. Yunus, al-Madani al-Dadjani', EI^2, V, 525.

Johns, A.H., 'Al-Kurani, Ibrahim b. al-Shahrazuri al-Hasan Shahrani, al-Madani (1023–1101/1615–90)', EI^2, V, 432–3.

Johns, A.H., 'Muslim Mystics and Historical Writings', in D.G.E. Hall (ed.), *Historians of South East Asia*, London: Oxford University Press, 1961.

Johns, A.H., 'Sufism as a Category in Indonesian Literature and History', *JSEAH*, 2, II (1961).

Johns, A.H., 'Aspects of Sufi Thought in India and Indonesia in the First Half of the 17th Century', *JMBRAS*, 28, I (1955)

Johns, A.H., 'Daka'ik al-Huruf by 'Abd al-Ra'uf of Singkel', *JRAS*, 1, II (1955).

Jones, R., 'Ten Conversion Myths from Indonesia', in Levtzion (ed.), *Conversion to Islam*, New York: Holmes & Meyer, 1979.

de Jong, F., 'Mustafa Kamal al-Din al-Bakri (1688–1749): Revival and Reform of the Khalwatiyyah Tradition', in N. Levtzion & J.O. Voll (eds), *Eighteenth Century Renewal and Reform*, Syracuse: Syracuse University Press, 1987.

Jongejans, J., 'Taboet of Hasan-Hosein-Feesten', *Onze Aarde*, 12 (1939).

Kadir, M.S., 'Syekh Muhammad Arsyad al-Banjari Pelopor Da'wah Islam di Kalimantan Selatan', *Mimbar Ulama*, 6 (1976).

Karni, Awis, 'Al-Taṣawwuf fī Indūnīsiyyā: Dirāsat li Nuskhah Kitāb Maṭālib al-Sālikīn ta'līf Yūsuf al-Maqassārī', *Studia Islamika*, III.2 (1996): 163–189.

Kathirithamby-Wells, J., 'The Islamic City: Melaka to Yogyakarta, c. 1500–1800', *Modern Asian Studies*, 20, II (1986).

Kempe, J.E. & R.O. Winstedt, 'A Malay Legal Digest compiled for Abd al-Ghafur Muhaiyuddin Shah, Sultan of Pahang', *JMBRAS*, 21 (1948).

Kensdale, W.E.N., 'Field-notes on the Arabic Literature of the Western Sudan', *JRAS*, 1955.

Kent, R.K., 'The Possibilities of Indonesian Colonies in Africa with Special Reference to Madagascar', in *Mouvements de populations dans l'océan indien*, Paris: Bibliothèque de l'Ecole des Hautes Etudes, 1979.

'Kesultanan Banjar', in *Ensiklopedi Islam di Indonesia*, Jakarta: Departemen Agama, 1987/8, II.

Kortepeter, C.M., 'A Source for the History of Ottoman-Hijaz Relations: The Seyahatname of Awliya Chalaby and the Rebellion of Sharif Sadb. Zayd in the Years 1671–1672/1081–1082', in *Sources for the History of Arabia*, Riyad: Riyad University Press, 1979, part 2.

Kosasi, Mohammad, 'Pamidjahan en zijn Heiligdom', *Djawa*, 38 (Oct. 1938).

Kunst, J., 'A Musicological Argument for Relationship between Indonesia—probably Java—and Central Africa', *Proceedings of the Musical Association*, Session 62 (1935–6).

Lane, F.C., 'The Mediterranean Spice Trade: Further Evidence of Its Revival in the Sixteenth Century', *The American Historical Review*, 45 (1939/40).

van Langen, K.F.H., 'De inrichting van het Atjehsche staatbestuur onder het Sultanaat', *BKI*, 37 (1888) 236, trans. Aboe Bakar, *Susunan Pemerintahan Aceh semasa Kesultanan*, Banda Aceh: PDIA, 1986.

Lawrence, B. 'Islam in India: The Function of Institutional Sufism in the Islamization of Rajasthan, Gujerat, and Kashmir', *Contributions to Asian Studies*, (ed.) R.C. Martin, Leiden: E.J. Brill, 1982, pp. 27–43.

Lazzerini, E.J., 'The Revival of Islamic Culture in Pre Revolutionary Russia: Or, Why a Prosopography of the Tatar 'Ulema'', in Ch. Lemercier-Quelquljay et al. (eds), *Passé Turco-Tatar: Présent Sovietique*, Paris: Louvain, 1986.

Levtzion, N., 'Eighteenth Century Sufi Brotherhoods', *Islam: Essays on Scripture, Thought and Society – a Festschrift in Honour of Anthony H. Johns* (Peter G. Riddell and Tony Street, eds.), Leiden: E.J. Brill, 1997.

Levtzion, N. & J.O. Voll (eds), 'Introduction', in *Eighteenth-Century Renewal and Reform in Islam*, Syracuse: Syracuse University Press, 1987.

Liaw Yock Fang, 'Undang-undang Melaka', in Sandhu & Wheatley (eds), *Melaka: The Transformation*, Kuala Lumpur: University of Malaya Press, 1983, I.

Lofgren, O., 'Aydarus', *EI*², I.

Lubis, Nabilah, 'Min 'Alāmi 'Indûnīsiya: al-Shaykh Yûsuf al-Maqāsārī (1626–1699)', *Studia Islamika*, I.3 (1994): 149–175.

Majul, C.A., 'Theories on the Introduction of Islam in Malaysia', *Siliman Journal*, 2, IV (1964).

Majul, C.A., 'The Role of Islam in the History of the Filipino People', *AS*, 4, II (1966).

Makdis, 'The Sunni Revival', in D.S. Richards (ed.), *Islamic Civilisation*, London: Bruno Cassirer, 1973.

Makdis, 'Muslim Institutions of Learning in Eleventh Century Baghdad', *BSOAS*, 24 (1961).

Makdisi, G., 'Tabaqat-Biography: Law and Orthodoxy in Classical Islam', *Islamic Studies*, 32,4 (1993): 371–396.

Marrison, G.E., 'Persian Influences in Malay Life (1280–1650)', *JMBRAS*, 28, I (1955).

Marrison, G.E., 'The Coming of Islam to the East Indies', *JMBRAS*, 24, I (1951).

Martin, B.G., 'A Short History of the Khalwati Order of Dervishes', in N. Keddie (ed.), *Scholars, Saints and Sufis*, Berkeley: University of California Press, 1972.

Martin, B.G., 'Notes sur l'origine de la tariqa des Tijaniyya et sur le début d'al-Hajj Umar', *Revue des Etudes Islamiques*, 37 (1969).

Masri, F.H., 'The Life of Shehu Usuman dan Fodio before the Jihad', *Journal of the Historical Society of Nigeria*, 2, IV (1963).

Mas'ud, Abdurraham, 'Mahfuz al-Tirmisi (d.1338/1919): An Intellectual Biography', *Studia Islamika*, 5, 2 (1998).

Matheson, V. & M.B. Hooker, 'Jawi Literature in Patani: The Maintenance of an Islamic Tradition', *JMBRAS*, 61, I (1988).

Matthes, B.F., 'Boegineese en Makassaarsche Legenden', *BKI* , 34 (1885).

Mattulada, 'Islam di Sulawesi Selatan', in Taufik Abdullah (ed.), *Agama dan Perubahan Sosial*, Jakarta: Rajawali, 1983.

Mauny, R., 'The Wakuwak and the Indonesian Invasion in East Africa...', *Studia*, 14 (May 1965).

di Meglio, R.R., 'Arab Trade with Indonesia and the Malay Peninsula from the 8th to the 16th Century', in D.S. Richards (ed.), *Islam and the Trade of Asia*, Philadelphia: Bruno Cassirer & University of Pennsylvania Press.

Mills, J.V., 'Eridia's Descriptions of Malacca, Meridonial India and Cathay', *JMBRAS*, lll, III (1960).

Milner, A.C., 'Islam and the Muslim State', in Hooker (ed.), *Islam in South-East Asia*, Leiden: Brill, 1983.

Millward, W.G., 'Taqi al-Din al-Fasi's Sources for the History of Mecca from the Fourth to Ninth Centuries A.H.', in *Sources for the History of Arabia*, Riyad: Riyad University Press, 1979.

Meier, F., 'Das sauberste über die vorbestimmung. Ein stuck Ibn Taymiyya', *Saeculum*, 32 (1981).

Moquette, J.P.,'De grafsteenen te Pase en Grisse vergeleken met dergelijke monumenten uit Hindoestan', *TBG*, 54 (1912).

'Muhammad Nafis al-Banjari', in *Ensiklopedi Islam di Indonesia*, Jakarta: Departemen Agama, 1987/8, II.

el-Muhammady, M.U., 'The Islamic Concept of Education according to Shaykh Abdu's-Samad of Palembang and Its Significance in Relation to the Issue of Personality Integration', *Akademika*, 1 (1972).

Mujani, Saiful, 'Mu'tazilah Theology and the Modernization of the Indonesian Muslim Community', *Studia Islamika*, 1, 1 (1994).

Mu'thi, A.W., 'Tarekat Syattariyah, dari Gujarat sampai Caruban', *Pesantren*, 4, III (1987).

Nakahara, M., 'Muslim Merchants in Nanhai', in R. Israeli & A.H. Johns (eds), *Islam in Asia: Volume II Southeast and East Asia*, Boulder: Westview, 1984.

van Nieuwenhuijze, C.A.O., 'The Legacy of Islam in Indonesia', *MW*, 59 (1964).

van Nieuwenhuijze, C.A.O., 'Nur al-Din al-Raniri als bestrijder Wugudiya', *BKI*, 104 (1948).

Noorduyn, J., 'Origins of South Celebes Historical Writings', in Soedjatmoko et al (eds), *An Introduction to Indonesian Historiography*, Ithaca, N.Y.: Cornell University Press, 1965.

Noorduyn, J., 'De Islamisering van Makassar', *BKI*, 112 (1956).

Nurhakim, L., 'La ville de Barus: étude de archéologique preliminaire', *Archipel*, 37 (1989).

O'Fahey, R.S. (ed.), *Arabic Literature of Africa I: the writings of Eastern Sudanic Africa to c. 1900*, Leiden: E.J. Brill, 1994, pp.143–144.

O'Fahey, R.S. & Bernd Radtke, 'Neo-Sufism Reconsidered', *Der Islam*, LXX, 1 (1993): 52–87.

O'Fahey, R.S., 'Neo-Sufism and Ibn Idris', in his *Enigmatic Saint: Ahmad ibn Idris and the Idrisi Tradition*, Evanston, Ill.: Nortwestern University Press, 1990.

Othman, Mohammad Redzuan, 'The Role of Makka-Educated Malays in the Development of Early Islamic Scholarship and Education in Malaya', *Journal of Islamic Studies*, 9, 2 (1998): 146–157.

Ozbaran, Salih, 'A Turkish Report on the Red Sea and the Portuguese in the Indian Ocean (1525)', in R.B. Serjeant & R.L. Bidwell (eds), *Arabian Studies*, IV (1978).

Pelras, C., 'Religion, Tradition and the Dynamics of Islamization in South Sulawesi', *Archipel*, 29 (1985).

Peters, Rudolph, 'Reinhard Schulze's Quest for an Islamic Enlightenment', *Die Welt des Islams*, XXX (1990): 160–162.

Peters, Rudolph, 'Idjtihad and Taqlid in 18th and 19th Century Islam', *Die Welt des Islams*, XXX, 3–4 (1980): 131–145.

Radtke, B., 'Sufism in the 18th Century: An Attempt at a Provisional Appraisal', *Die Welt des Islams*, XXXVI, 3 (1996): 326–364.

Radtke, B., 'Wat betekent tariqa muhammadiyya in de islamitische mystiek van de 18e en 19e eeuw?' *Mystiek, het andere gezicht van de Islam*, Marjo Buitelaar & Johan ter Haar, (eds), Bussum, 1999.

Radtke, B., 'Ijtihad and Neo-Sufism', *Asiatische Studien/Etudes Asiatiques*, XLVIII, 3 (1994): 909–921.

Radtke, B., 'Warum ist des Sufi orthodox', *Der Islam*, LXXI (1994): 48–66.

Rahman, Fazlur, 'Revival and Reform', in P.M. Holt et. al (eds), *The Cambridge History of Islam*, Cambridge: Cambridge University Press, 1970, II.

Reid, A., 'Sixteenth Century Turkish Influence in Western Indonesia', in Kartodirdjo (ed.), *Profiles of Malay Culture*, Jakarta: Ministry of Education & Culture, 1986.

Reid, Anthony, 'Islam and the State in Seventeenth Century Southeast Asia', *Proceedings of the International Seminar on Islamic Civilisation in the Malay World,* Istanbul: IRCICA, 1999.

Ricklefs, M.C., 'Six Centuries Islamization in Java', in Levtzion (ed.), *Conversion to Islam*, NY: Holmes & Meyer, 1979.

Riddell, P., 'Earliest Quranic Exegetical Activity in the Malay-Speaking States', *Archipel*, 38 (1989).

Rinkes, D.A., 'De maqam van Sjech Abdoelmoehji', *TBG*, 52 (1910) .

Ritter, H., 'Al-Ghazali, Ahmad b. Muhammad', *EI*², II.

Roff, W.R., 'Islam Obscured?: Some Reflections on Studies of Islam and Society in Southeast Asia', *Archipel*, 29 (1985).

Roff, W.R., 'South-East Asian Islam in the Nineteenth Century', in P.M. Holt et al. (eds), *The Cambridge History of Islam*, II, Cambridge: Cambridge University Press, 1970.

van Ronkel, Ph. S., 'Raniri's Maleische geschrift: Exposé der religies', *BKI*, 102 (1943).

van Ronkel, Ph. S., 'Een Maleisch getuigenis over den weg des Islams in Sumatra', *BKI*, 75 (1919).

van Ronkel, Ph. S., 'Inlandsche getuigenissen aangaande den Padri-oorlog', *IG*, 37 (1915).

de Roo, de la Faille, P., *Dari Zaman Kesultanan Palembang*, trans. S. Poerbakawatja, Djakarta: Bhratara, 1971.

Rosatria, Eri, ''Alāqat Ḥarakat Nashr al-Islām wa al-Tarbiyyah al-Islāmiyyah fī Sultanah Aceh', *Studia Islamika*, III, 1 (1996): 127–155.

Said, Arifin, 'Manuskrip Melayu di Srilanka', in Abu Bakar (ed.), *Melayu Srilanka*, Kuala Lumpur: Gapena, 1990.

Said, Nurman, 'The Significance of al-Ghazali and His Works for Indonesian Muslims: a Preliminary Study', *Studia Islamika*, III, 3 (1996): 21–45.

Santrie, A.M., 'Martabat (Alam) Tujuh: Suatu Naskah Mistik Islam dari Desa Karang, Pamijahan', in Ahmad Rifa'i Hasan (ed.), *Warisan Intelektual Indonesia*, Bandung: Mizan & LSAF, 1987.

al-Sarwajī, Muḥammad Maḥmūd, 'Kitāb Ajā'ib al-Athar fī al-Tarājim wa al-Akhbār li al-Shaykh 'Abd al-Raḥmān al-Jabartī ka-Masdar li Ahdāth al-Jazīrat al-'Arabiyyah fī al-Qarn al-Thālith 'Ashar al-Hijrī (al-Tāsi' 'Ashar al-Mīlādī)', in *Maṣādir Tārīkh al-Jazīrat al-*'Ar*abiyyah*, Riyāḍ: Maṭba'at Jāmi'at al-Riyāḍ, 1279/1979.

Schacht, J., 'Zur Wahhabitischen Literatur', *Zeitschrift für Semitistik und verwandte Gebiete*, 6 (1928): 200-213.

Schimmel, A.M., 'The Primordial Dot: Some Thoughts about Sufi Letter Mysticism', *Jerusalem Studies in Arabic and Islam* (*JSAI*), 9 (1987).

Schulze, R., 'Das Islamische 18 Jahrhundert: versuch einer historiographischen Kritik', *Die Welt des Islams*, XXX (1990): 140–59.

Scott, (Mrs.) S.B., 'Mohammedanism in Borneo: Notes for a Study of the Local Modifications of Islam and the Extent of Its Influence on the Native Tribes', *Journal of the American Oriental Society*, 33 (1913).

van Selms, A., 'Yussuf (Joseph), Sheik', in W.J. de Kock (ed.), *Dictionary of South African Biographies*, 1968.

Sham, Abu Hassan, 'Malay Manuscripts and Srilanka', in Abu Bakar (ed.), *Melayu Srilanka*, 1990.

Shellabear, W.G., 'An Account of Some Oldest Malay MSS now Extant', *JRAS*, 31 (1898).

Snouck Hurgronje, C., 'Een Mekkaansch gezantschap naar Atjeh in 1683', *BKI*, 65 (1911).

Snouck Hurgronje, C., 'Een Arabisch Bondgenoot der Nederlandsch Regering', in *Verspreide Geschriften*, Bonn & 's-Gravenhage: Kurt Schröder & Nijhoff, 1924, VI.

Steenbrink, Karel, 'Hamka (1908–1981) and the integration of the Islamic Ummah of Indonesia', *Studia Islamika*, 1, 3 (1994).

Steenbrink, K., 'Jesus and Holy Spirit in the Writings of Nur al-Din al-Raniri', *ICMR* (Islam and Christian–Muslim Relations), I, 2 (1990).

Steenbrink, K., 'Syekh Muhammad Arsyad al-Banjari: 1710–1812, Tokoh Fiqh dan Tasawuf', in his *Beberapa Aspek tentang Islam di Indonesia Abad ke-l9*, Jakarta: Bulan Bintang, 1984.

Stein Parvé, H.A., 'Oorsprong der Padaries: Eene secte op de Westkust van Sumatra', *TNI*, 1, I (1838).

Stein Parvé, H.A., 'De secte de Padaries (Padries) in de Bovenlanden van Sumatra', *TBG*, 3 (1855).

Swart, M.J., 'The Karamat of Sheik Yussef,' *South African,* Panorama 6 (1961).

Teeuw, A., 'Pertumbuhan Bahasa Melayu menjadi Bahasa Dunia', in Harimurti Kridalaksana (ed.), *Masa Lampau Bahasa Indonesia: Sebuah Bunga Rampai*, Yogyakarta: Kanisius, 1991.

Teeuw, A., 'Some Remarks on the Study of the so-called Historical Texts in Indonesian Language', in Kartodirdjo (ed.), *Profiles of Malay Culture*, Jakarta: Ministry of Education & Malay Culture, 1976.

Tibbett, G.R., 'Pre-Islamic Arabia and Southeast Asia', *JMBRAS*, 29, III (1956).

van der Tuuk, H.N., 'Kort verslag der Maleische handschriften', *BKI*, 13 (1866).

Vakily, Abdollah, 'Sufism, Power Politics, and Reform: al-Rānīrī's Opposition to Hamzah al-Fansūrī's Teachings Reconsidered', *Studia Islamika*, IV, 1 (1997): 113–35.

Valiuddin, Mir, 'Reconciliation between Ibn Arabi's Wahdati-Wujud and the Mujaddid's Wahdat-i-Shuhud', *Islamic Culture*, (Jubilee No.) (1951).

Voll, J.O., 'Scholarly Interrelations between South Asia and the Middle East in the 18th Century', in P. Gaeffke & G.A. Utz (eds), *The Countries of South Asia: Boundaries, Extension, and Interrelations*, Philadelphia: University of Pennsylvania, Dept. of South Asia Regional Studies, 1988.

Voll, J.O., 'Linking Groups in the Networks of Eighteenth Century Revivalist Scholars', in N. Levtzion & J.O. Voll (eds), *Eighteenth Century Renewal and Reform in Islam*, Syracuse: University of Syracuse Press, 1987.

Voll, J.O., 'Hadith Scholars and Tariqahs: an Ulama Group in the 18th Century Haramayn and Their Impact in the Islamic World', *JAAS*, 25, III-IV (1980).

Voll, J.O., 'Muhammad Hayya al-Sindi and Muhammad Ibn 'Abd al-Wahhab: An Analysis of an Intellectual Group in Eighteenth Century Madina'', *BSOAS*, 38 (1975).

Voorhoeve, P., 'Lijst der Geschriften van Raniri', *BKI*, 111 (1955).

Voorhoeve, P., 'Van en over Nuruddin ar-Raniri', *BKI*, 107 (1951).

Voorhoeve, P., ''Abd al-Ra'uf b. 'Ali al-Djawi al-Fansuri al-Sinkili', *EI*^{2}, I.

Voorhoeve, P., 'Abd al-Samad b. 'Abd Allah al-Palimbani', *EI*^{2}, I.

Voorhoeve, P., 'Dawud b. 'Abd Allah b. Idris al-Fatani or al-Fattani', *EI*^{2}, II.

Wake, C.H., 'Melaka in the Fifteenth Century: Malay Historical Traditions and the Politics of Islamization', in Sandhu & Wheatley (eds), *Melaka: The Transformation*, Kuala Lumpur: University of Malaya Press, 1983, I.

Wake, C.H., 'Malacca's Early Kings and the Reception of Islam', *JSEAH*, 5, II (1964).

Wilks, I., 'The Transmission of Islamic Learning in the Western Sudan', in J. Goody (ed.), *Literacy in Traditional Societies*, Cambridge: University Press, 1968.

Winstedt, R.O., 'The Advent of Muhammadanism in the Malay Peninsula and Archipelago', *JMBRAS*, 24, I (1951).

Winstedt, R.O., 'The Chronicle of Pasai', *JMBRAS*, 16, II (1938).

Winstedt, R.O., 'A History of Malaya', *JMBRAS*, 13, I (1935).

Winstedt, R.O., 'The Kedah Laws', *JMBRAS*, 6, I (1928).

Winstedt, R.O., 'Some Malay Mystics, Heretical and Orthodox', *JMBRAS*, 1 (1923).

Winzeler, R.L., 'The Social Organization of Islam in Kelantan', in W.R. Roff (ed.), *Kelantan: Religion, Society and Politics in a Malay State*, Kuala Lumpur: Oxford University 1974.

Woodward, M.R., 'The Slametan: Textual Knowledge and Ritual Performance in Central Javanese Islam', *History of Religion*, 28, I (1988).

Yahya, A.S., 'Budaya Bertulis Melayu Srilanka', in Abu Bakar (ed.), *Melayu Srilanka*, Kuala Lumpur: Gapena, 1990.

Zwemer, S.M., 'Islam at the Cape Town', *MW*, 15, IV (1925).

al-Zulfah, Muḥammad 'Abd Allāh, 'Iṣlāḥat Ḥasīb Bāshā fī Wilāyat al-Ḥijāz (1848–1849) kamā jā'a fī al-Wathā'iq al-'Uthmāniyyah', in 'Abd al-Jalīl al-Tāmīmī (ed.), *al-Ḥayāt al-Ijtimā'iyyah fī al-Wilāyat al-'Arabiyyah 'Athnā' al-'Ahd al-'Uthmāniyyah*, Zaghwan: Markāz al-Dirāsat wa al-Buḥūth al-'Uthmāniyyah wa al-Murisikiyyah wa al-Tawthīq al-Ma'lūmat, 1988.

Index of Personal Names

Subject Index